Gabler Theses

In der Schriftenreihe „Gabler Theses“ erscheinen ausgewählte, englischsprachige Doktorarbeiten, die an renommierten Hochschulen in Deutschland, Österreich und der Schweiz entstanden sind. Die Arbeiten behandeln aktuelle Themen der Wirtschaftswissenschaften und vermitteln innovative Beiträge für Wissenschaft und Praxis. Informationen zum Einreichungsvorgang und eine Übersicht unserer Publikationsangebote finden Sie hier.

Sophie Kunert

The Eight Universal Dimensions of Culture from a Synthesis of Cultural Taxonomies

A Compendium on Cultural Taxonomies and a Tool for the Universal Dimensions of Culture

Springer Gabler

Sophie Kunert
TU Bergakademie Freiberg, Germany

Von der Fakultät für Wirtschaftswissenschaften der Technischen Universität Bergakademie Freiberg genehmigte Dissertation zur Erlangung des akademischen Grades doctor philosophiae, Dr. phil.,
vorgelegt von Sophie Kunert, M.Sc., geboren am 2. Januar 1990 in Rodewisch (Vogtland).
Gutachter: Prof. Dr. Michael B. Hinner (TU Bergakademie Freiberg, Freiberg),
Prof. Dr. Zorica Trajkova Strezovska (Ss. Cyril and Methodius University, Skopje
Tag der Verleihung: 03. Februar 2022

ISSN 2731-3220 ISSN 2731-3239 (electronic)
Gabler Theses
ISBN 978-3-658-38764-8 ISBN 978-3-658-38765-5 (eBook)
https://doi.org/10.1007/978-3-658-38765-5

Responsible Editor: Marija Kojic
This Springer Gabler imprint is published by the registered company Springer Fachmedien Wiesbaden GmbH, part of Springer Nature.
The registered company address is: Abraham-Lincoln-Str. 46, 65189 Wiesbaden, Germany

Preface

"Culture hides much more than it reveals, and strangely enough, what it hides most effectively from its own participants" (Edward T. Hall, 1959, p. 39). Our today's society is fulled by the condition and continuing dynamic, called globalization. Globalization is the catalyst for the so-called "*interdependent global society*", creating not only global economic interdependencies, but also a wide range of circumstances that affect our world (Samovar et al., 2016). Because of these dynamics, there is an urgent need for cooperation, improvement of relations between countries, effective intercultural communication and cooperation, and the creation of a sustainable world in peace through effective intercultural communication (Featherstone, 1990; Hofstede & Hofstede (2005); Samovar et al., 2016; Tayeb, 1994). The overall objective of this dissertation is to provide a valuable and comprehensive understanding and tool for enhancing, international cooperation, improving co-country relationships, and making intercultural communication and collaboration more effective. The crucial element of this dissertation constitutes the synthesis of cultural dimensions from existing cultural taxonomies, extended by the operationalization of the eight identified universal dimensions of culture (UDCs) into a questionnaire. Three research questions guide the research of this dissertation. First, an extensive Systematic Literature Review (SLR) is pursued to identify the current state of research, demonstrating the research gap on a unified approach for classifying national cultures into cultural dimensions. Eight assumptions displaying the eight UDCs are derived from the results of the SLR. Subsequently, an evaluation and selection framework for identifying the research base of comparable existing cultural taxonomies is developed. A research base of 11 cultural taxonomies and 50 cultural dimensions is retrieved. These serve as the basis for developing the eight UDCs, following a synthesis process and protocol. All eight assumptions are demonstrated to form the eight UDCs of

this dissertation. The eight UDCs are operationalized into a questionnaire, which was extensively pre-tested by experts and in the field. An example country study for Germany, Canada, and Brazil is conducted, and the corresponding country profiles for the eight UDCs are displayed.

Keywords: National cultures · National culture classification · Cultural dimensions · Cultural taxonomies · Globalization · Intercultural communication · Synthesis of cultural dimensions · Questionnaire · Universal dimensions of culture

Acknowledgment

THANK YOU to my beloved parents, Sybille & Martin Lothar Danilo Kunert, who support me during every step I have taken. The same thank you goes to my grandparents, Ute & Günther Lochmann, and to my extended family. Thank you!

THANK YOU to my supportive and encouraging doctoral supervisor, Prof. Dr. Michael B. Hinner, who was the best doctoral supervisor I could have ever imagine. Thank you!

THANK YOU to my previous academic supervisor, Prof. Dr. Andreas Horsch, who was a fantastic supervisor to work for! Thank you!

THANK YOU to my second doctoral supervisor Prof. Dr. Zorica Trajkova Strezovska. Thank you for all the valuable feedback and the effort spent on my thesis! Thank you!

THANK YOU. A special thank you goes to David Göttlich. Thank you for all your support! Another great THANK YOU to all my friends who supported me while writing this dissertation. I would like to name a few distinctively Juliane Smola, Jobey Wills, Lena Angerer, Sarah Tautenhahn, Family Laura and Peter Rogalski, and Dr. Marren Zöllner. A special thanks also to Dr. Peter Becker. Thank you!

THANK YOU. Another great thank you to Tina Laubsch, an outstanding secretary who was always able to help and willing to listen. Thank you!

THANK YOU. Another great thank you to the encouraging individuals at the Faculty of Economics at the TU Bergakademie Freiberg. Special thanks go to the three experts, and to name a few, Dr. Benjamin Aust, Dr. Stephan Meschke, Dr. Tobais Nell and Natalie Koppitz, Anne Haufe, Doris Geburek, and Leo Mittelstaedt. Thank you!

Finally, I would also like to say THANK YOU to all my friends and the people who accompanied me at some stages of this dissertation—*sometimes strangers become friends, sometimes friends become strangers, and sometimes friends become family*. Without your encouragement along the stages of this dissertation, I would not have made it. To only name a few, thank you Anja Sopper, Dina Khalifa, Maria Meier, all inspiring people of my lunch group at the co-working space in Hamburg, Family Kundisch, Marcel Böttcher, Kai Burisch, Maik Kötting, Paul Reitemeier, Ralf Bilke and his wife, Sara Schommen, and all other inspiring individuals I met along the way of this dissertation (e.g., that lady in Panama, the man from the Hostel on the Jakobsweg, that one manager at Ramboll Hamburg). Thank you!

"A single arrow is easily broken, but not ten in a bundle"

– Japanese Proverb –

Contents

1 Introduction 1
1.1 Motivation, Problem, and Objective of Research 1
1.2 Research Questions (RQs) 5
1.3 Structure and Classification of Research 6
1.4 Contribution to the Field of Research 8

2 Current State of Research 11
2.1 Methodology and Systematic Literature Review (SLR) 13
2.2 Assumptions 48

3 Evaluation and Selection of Existing Cultural Taxonomies 59
3.1 Evaluation of Cultural Taxonomies 61
3.2 The Resulting Cultural Taxonomies 90

4 Introduction to the Synthesis of the Universal Dimensions of Culture (UDCs) 93
4.1 Premises and Analysis Protocol 93
4.2 Special Report on the Remaining Synthesis Dimension 99
4.3 Overview of the Eight Universal Dimensions of Culture (UDCs) 104

5 The Environment—One Connecting Concept? 111
5.1 Synthesis of the Universal Dimension of Culture (UDC) Distribution of Power and Status 111
5.2 Synthesis of the Universal Dimension of Culture (UDC) Relationship with the Natural Environment 122
5.3 Synthesis of the Universal Dimension of Culture (UDC) Social Organization 131

5.4 Delimitation Between the Concepts of Distribution of Power and Status and Social Organization 145
5.5 Delimitation Between the Concepts of Social Environment and Relationship with the Natural Environment 147
5.6 Results of the Syntheses 149

6 Time—One Connecting Concept? 161
6.1 Synthesis of the Universal Dimension of Culture (UDC) Perception and Use of Time 161
6.2 Synthesis of the Universal Dimension of Culture (UDC) Traditionalism versus Secularism 170
6.3 Synthesis of the Universal Dimension of Culture (UDC) Uncertainty Avoidance and Coping Mechanisms 179
6.4 Delimitation Between the Concepts of Uncertainty Avoidance and Relationship with the (Natural) Environment 189
6.5 Delimitation Between the Concepts of Perception and Use of Time and Traditionalism versus Secularism 193
6.6 Results of the Syntheses 195

7 Human Behavior—One Connecting Concept? 209
7.1 Synthesis of the Universal Dimension of Culture (UDC) Human Orientation 209
7.2 Synthesis of the Universal Dimension of Culture (UDC) Gratification and Expression of Emotions, Feelings, and Desires 215
7.3 Results of the Syntheses 224

8 Questionnaire for the Eight Universal Dimensions of Culture (UDCs) 233
8.1 Process and Methodology of Questionnaire Development 236
8.2 Pre-Test of the UDC Questionnaire 237
8.3 A Country Study for Brazil, Canada, and Germany 297

9 Conclusion 325
9.1 Implications 325
9.2 Limitations of Research 330
9.3 Outlook 332

References 335

List of Figures

Figure 1.1	Process and Research Output	7
Figure 2.1	Thematic Position of Chapter 2	12
Figure 2.2	Methodology of Systematic Literature Review (SLR)	14
Figure 2.3	Search Queries and Search Requirements	18
Figure 2.4	Flow Chart of Search in Electronic Databases	21
Figure 2.5	First Manual Screening	23
Figure 2.6	Second Manual Screening	24
Figure 2.7	Third Manual Screening	25
Figure 2.8	The Framework of the Narrative Synthesis	31
Figure 3.1	Thematic Position of Chapter 3	60
Figure 3.2	Evaluation and Selection Criteria	63
Figure 3.3	Evaluation and Selection Framework	69
Figure 4.1	Thematic Position of Chapter 4	94
Figure 4.2	Approach and Premises of the Synthesis of the Eight Universal Dimensions of Culture (UDCs)	98
Figure 5.1	Assumption 1 (A1): The Universal Dimension of Culture (UDC) Distribution of Power and Status	112
Figure 5.2	Assumption 2 (A2): The Universal Dimension of Culture (UDC) Relationship with the Environment	123
Figure 5.3	Assumption 3 (A3): The Universal Dimension of Culture (UDC) Social Organization	133
Figure 5.4	The Universal Dimension of Culture (UDC) Distribution of Power and Status	150
Figure 5.5	The Universal Dimension of Culture (UDC) Relationship with the Environment	155

Figure 5.6 The Universal Dimension of Culture (UDC) Social Organization 156
Figure 6.1 Assumption 4 (A4): Universal Dimension of Culture (UDC) Perception and Use of Time 162
Figure 6.2 Assumption 8 (A8): The Universal Dimension of Culture (UDC) Traditionalism versus Secularism 171
Figure 6.3 Assumption 5 (A5): The Universal Dimension of Culture (UDC) Uncertainty Avoidance 180
Figure 6.4 The Universal Dimension of Culture (UDC) Perception and Use of Time 197
Figure 6.5 The Universal Dimension of Culture (UDC) Traditionalism versus Secularism 201
Figure 6.6 The Universal Dimension of Culture (UDC) Uncertainty Avoidance and Coping Mechanisms 205
Figure 7.1 Assumption 6 (A6): Universal Dimension of Culture (UDC) Human Orientation 210
Figure 7.2 Assumption 7 (A7): Universal Dimension of Culture (UDC) Indulgence versus Restraint 216
Figure 7.3 The Universal Dimension of Culture (UDC) Human Orientation 225
Figure 7.4 The Universal Dimension of Culture (UDC) Gratification and Expression of Emotions, Feelings, and Desires 228
Figure 8.1 Thematic Position of Chapter 8 234
Figure 8.2 Process of Item Selection 235
Figure 8.3 Results of the First Debriefing Question 271
Figure 8.4 Results of the Second Debriefing Question 273
Figure 8.5 Results of the Third Debriefing Question 274
Figure 8.6 Results of the Fourth Debriefing Question 276

List of Tables

Table 1.1 Classification of Research as Deductive Definition and Measurement ... 8
Table 2.1 Selection of Search Terms ... 17
Table 2.2 Inclusion and Exclusion Criteria ... 19
Table 2.3 Identified Articles from the Search within Electronic Databases ... 22
Table 2.4 Overview of Identified Articles ... 25
Table 2.5 Overview of Evaluation Indicators ... 26
Table 2.6 Evaluation of the Nine Articles from the Systematic Literature Review (SLR) ... 29
Table 2.7 Synthesized Concept of Distribution of Power ... 33
Table 2.8 Synthesized Concept of Relationship with the Environment ... 35
Table 2.9 Synthesized Concept of Social Organization ... 37
Table 2.10 Synthesized Concept of Uncertainty Avoidance ... 41
Table 2.11 Synthesized Concept of Time ... 43
Table 2.12 Synthesized Concept of Human Orientation ... 45
Table 2.13 Summary of Narrative Synthesis and Overview of Concepts ... 47
Table 2.14 Overview of the Eight Assumptions, Details, and Characteristic Features ... 49
Table 3.1 Analyzed Cultural Taxonomies by the Four Synthesis Methodologies ... 60
Table 3.2 The 34 Cultural Taxonomies ... 71
Table 3.3 Overview of Selection Criteria for the 34 Cultural Taxonomies ... 73

Table 3.4 Overview of Evaluation Criteria for the 34 Cultural Taxonomies 85
Table 3.5 Research Base: The 11 Selected Cultural Taxonomies 91
Table 4.1 Overview of the 50 Cultural Dimensions from the 11 Cultural Taxonomies 95
Table 4.2 Analysis Protocol for the Syntheses of the Eight Universal Dimensions of Culture (UDCs) 99
Table 4.3 Higher Gender Egalitarianism Societies vs. Lower Gender Egalitarianism Societies 103
Table 4.4 Overview of the 50 Cultural Dimensions and their Synthesis into the Eight Universal Dimensions of Culture (UDCs) 105
Table 4.5 Overview, Description, and Cultural Components of the Eight Universal Dimensions of Culture (UDCs) 107
Table 5.1 Synthesized Cultural Dimensions of the Universal Dimension of Culture (UDC) Distribution of Power and Status 153
Table 5.2 Synthesized Cultural Dimensions of the Universal Dimension of Culture (UDC) Relationship with the Natural Environment 157
Table 5.3 Synthesized Cultural Dimensions of the Universal Dimension of Culture (UDC) Social Organization 159
Table 6.1 Synthesized Cultural Dimensions of the Universal Dimension of Culture (UDC) Perception and Use of Time 199
Table 6.2 Synthesized Cultural Dimensions of the Universal Dimension of Culture (UDC) Traditionalism versus Secularism 203
Table 6.3 Synthesized Cultural Dimensions of the Universal Dimension of Culture (UDC) Uncertainty Avoidance and Coping Mechanisms 206
Table 7.1 Synthesized Cultural Dimensions of the Universal Dimension of Culture (UDC) Human Orientation 226
Table 7.2 Synthesized Cultural Dimensions of the Universal Dimension of Culture (UDC) Gratification and Expression of Emotions, Feelings, and Desires 230
Table 8.1 Overview of Panel of Experts 238
Table 8.2 Overview of Development of First Revised Set of the 37 Items 241

Table 8.3 General Recommendations from Experts 1–3 250
Table 8.4 Overview of Development of Second Revised Set of the 35 Items 253
Table 8.5 Expert Evaluation of the Second Revised Set of the 35 Items 260
Table 8.6 Background Questions 268
Table 8.7 Background Information on Respondents of the Pre-Test 268
Table 8.8 Overview Respondents Nationality by Category 269
Table 8.9 Comments and Implementation of the First Debriefing Question 271
Table 8.10 Overview of Comments of the Second Debriefing Question 273
Table 8.11 Comments and Implementation of the Third Debriefing Question 275
Table 8.12 Comments and Implementation of the Fourth Debriefing Question 276
Table 8.13 The Universal Dimension of Culture (UDC) Distribution of Power and Status by Items and Implications 279
Table 8.14 The Universal Dimension of Culture (UDC) Relationship with the Natural Environment by Items and Implications 280
Table 8.15 The Universal Dimension of Culture (UDC) Social Organization by Items and Implications 283
Table 8.16 The Universal Dimension of Culture (UDC) Perception and Use of Time by Items and Implications 286
Table 8.17 The Universal Dimension of Culture (UDC) Uncertainty Avoidance and Coping Mechanisms by Items and Implications 287
Table 8.18 The Universal Dimension of Culture (UDC) Human Orientation by Items and Implications 289
Table 8.19 The Universal Dimension of Culture (UDC) Gratification and Expression of Emotions, Desires, and Feelings by Items and Implications 291
Table 8.20 The Universal Dimension of Culture (UDC) Traditionalism versus Secularism by Items and Implications 293
Table 8.21 Overview of Item Adaptation after Field Pre-Test 295

Table 8.22 Overview of Pre-Test Respondents for Brazil, Canada, and Germany 298
Table 8.23 Implications Country Score Calculation per Cultural Taxonomy 300
Table 8.24 Country Study Results for the Universal Dimension of Culture (UDC) Distribution of Power and Status 302
Table 8.25 Country Study Results for the Universal Dimension of Culture (UDC) Relationship with the Natural Environment 304
Table 8.26 Country Study Results for the Universal Dimension of Culture (UDC) Social Organization 307
Table 8.27 Country Study Results for the Universal Dimension of Culture (UDC) Perception and Use of Time 310
Table 8.28 Country Study Results for the Universal Dimension of Culture (UDC) Uncertainty Avoidance and Coping Mechanisms 312
Table 8.29 Country Study Results for the Universal Dimension of Culture (UDC) Human Orientation 314
Table 8.30 Country Study Results for the Universal Dimension of Culture (UDC) Gratification and Expression of Emotions, Desires, and Feelings 316
Table 8.31 Country Study Results for the Universal Dimension of Culture (UDC) Traditionalism versus Secularism 318
Table 8.32 Summary on Country Study per Country and Universal Dimension of Culture (UDC) 323
Table 9.1 Overview of the Eight Universal Dimensions of Culture (UDCs) 328

1 Introduction

> *Culture hides much more than it reveals, and strangely enough, what it hides most effectively from its own participants*
>
> *Edward T. Hall (1959, p. 39)*

1.1 Motivation, Problem, and Objective of Research

More than ever, people are influenced by circumstances in their immediate environment as well as by people and events in other parts of the world (Samovar et al., 2016). In other words, people are confronted more than ever with people who are acting, speaking, and thinking differently. At the same time, people worldwide are exposed to similar problems regarding, for example, political, ecological, economic, or meteorological issues since these issues do not follow human-made borders, neither national nor regional (Hofstede & Hofstede, 2005).

This interdependency of people—*the interdependent global society*—was and is fuelled by the constant increasing mobility of capital, goods, people, and services as well as a fast-paced change in the state-of-the-art and use of technology (Samovar et al., 2016; United Nations Department of Economic and Social Affairs, 2017). The increasing worldwide connectedness is expressed in an existing condition, and a continuing dynamic, known as globalization. Globalization not only causes global economic interdependences, but it also constitutes the cause for a broad spectrum of circumstances that influence and addresses the world in general (Samovar et al., 2016).

With the ongoing dynamic of globalization and thus the ongoing involvement of divergent groups from different parts of the world emerged the need for international cooperations, strengenth of co-country relationships, effective

S. Kunert, *The Eight Universal Dimensions of Culture from a Synthesis of Cultural Taxonomies*, Gabler Theses, https://doi.org/10.1007/978-3-658-38765-5_1

intercultural communication and collaborations, (Featherstone, 1990; Hofstede & Hofstede, 2005; Samovar et al., 2016; Tayeb, 1994). The overall objective of this dissertation is to provide a valuable and comprehensive understanding and tool for enhancing international cooperation, improving co-country relationships, and making intercultural communication and collaboration more effective.

One way to understand globalizing dynamics is to explain the differences in people's thinking, feeling, and acting compared to people from other parts of the world. The concept of culture can serve as one explanation for this. The concept of culture is assumed to give meaning to differences between individuals by explaining their attitudinal, behavioral, and emotional patterns. Although, no simplistic explanation for the behavioral patterns of an individual exists just because the individual can be subsumed to a specific cultural group (Aneas & Sandín, 2009). Even if a cultural pattern is specifically applicable for one cultural group, it is not guaranteed that the pattern is equally distributed among the individuals of that group (Triandis, 1996).

The word culture originates from the Latin word colere meaning to cultivate, its modern anthropological connotation can be traced back to Tylor[1] (1871), and its understanding as an academic subject can be dated back to the 1950s. Mainly Hoggart (1957), Williams (1958, 1976), and Thompson (1963) shaped the transformation from the word culture towards its today's characteristic as the phenomenon it is (Aneas & Sandín, 2009; Kroeber & Kluckhohn, 1952; Sarangi, 1995).

As the introduction quote by Hall (1959) pointed out, the concept of culture cannot easily be understood, applied, nor defined. Over the past decades, many contradictory and incompatible definitions evolved for the concept of culture (Groseschl & Doherty, 2000; Triandis, 2000; Williams, 1976). The challenge is to comprehend the concept to a holistic and accessible concept, especially in Social Sciences (Keesing, 1974). The main reason for the complexity of the concept of culture constitutes its entangled connection to its surrounding context (Sarangi, 1995; Tayeb, 1994).

For the application of the concept of culture in this dissertation, the following two assumptions were made. First, the concept of culture can explain differences in the behavior of humans or a group of humans (Poortinga, 2015). Second, the definition of culture is never detached from the context in which the concept is considered (Chapman, 1996). One basic notion that most researchers agree on

[1] Tylor (1832–1917) is considered as the founder of Cultural Anthropology. His work *Primitve Culture* (1871) is one of the essential works in Cultural Anthropology (Street, 2019).

is that culture consists of "shared elements" that are either explicit or implicit prevalent in a culture (Groseschl & Doherty, 2000; Shweder & Levine, 1984).

The shared elements are displayed in psychological constructs—for example, behaviors, norms, and values (Groseschl & Doherty, 2000)—simplified in a metaphoric illustration as an onion (please refer to Hofstede (1980)). One of the most cited and applied definitions for culture was written by Kroeber and Kluckhohn (1952) (Groseschl & Doherty, 2000; Poortinga, 2015). Their definition served as a "common denominator" for various later definitions (Vijver & Hutschemaekers, 1990). Kroeber and Kluckhohn defined culture as follow:

> Culture consists of pattern, explicit, and implicit, of and for behavior acquired and transmitted by symbols, constituting the distinctive achievement of human groups, including their embodiments in artifacts; the essential core of culture consists of traditional (i.e., historically derived and selected) ideas and especially their attached values; culture systems may, on the one hand, be considered as product of action, on the other as conditioning elements of further action. (Kroeber & Kluckhohn, 1952, p. 181)

This dissertation seizes on the above definition by Kroeber and Kluckhohn (1952) for the concept of culture. However, the concept of culture cannot explain single individual behaviors (Poortinga, 2015). Each individual possesses a unique cultural heritage unique to the individual, and the individual belongs to a group with which it then shares one cultural heritage (Kroeber & Kluckhohn, 1952).

The concept of culture alone is insufficient to provide an easy-to-understand tool for improving co-country relationships, effective intercultural communication, and collaboration. In order to benefit from the implications and assumptions of the concept of culture, it needs to be and is distilled to the more precise form of national culture, inducing the passport approach in this dissertation. Also, the concept of national culture is not free of controversies, mainly when applied in terms of the passport approach (Groseschl & Doherty, 2000; Poortinga, 2015). The main controversy regarding the passport approach originates from implementing the construct nation, applying artificially drawn national boundaries. These artificially drawn national boundaries could cause false conclusions when referring to cultures as one national culture or a nation as one culture. Additionally, due to artificial boundaries, cultural identities could not be homogenously distributed within one nation. In terms of causality, this would lead to biases in the distribution of adequately representative values of a corresponding population (Taras et al., 2016).

The counterarguments against the application of the passport approach and, to a greater extent, against the concept of national culture raise the question of the approach's benefits (Smith, 2004). Hofstede (1980) concluded and justified the application of the passport approach by "cultures are not king-size individuals. They are wholes, and their internal logic cannot be understood in terms used for the personality dynamics of individuals" (Hofstede, 2001, p. 17). Some researchers searched for empirical proof of the application of the concept of national cultures. Inglehart and Baker (2000) analyzed three waves of the World Value Survey (WVS) regarding a link between economic development and the systematic change in individuals' underlying values in a country. The researchers concluded from their statistical analysis that individuals could serve as a study element for national cultures, mainly due to their shared experiences of their surrounding systems (e.g., education, media, institutional system). Similar conclusions were drawn by Taras et al. (2016), Peterson and Smith (2008), and De Mooij (2013).

Researchers distinguish different behavioral aspects of their defined (regional) groupings and form cultural dimensions (Low & Chapman, 2003). As the intangible concept of culture induces, the classification of national cultures into cultural dimensions also induces various biases, bijectivity, and interpretations. At this point, the research of this dissertation sets in. In the search for attempts to classify national cultures in cultural dimensions, one comes across various approaches—*the theory jungle of cultural taxonomies* (Nardon & Steers, 2009). Usually, the following six existing cultural taxonomies are stated for explanations of cross-cultural issues: Hall (1959, 1966, 1976, 1983; Hall & Hall, 1990), Hofstede (1980), House et al. (2004, 2007, 2014), Kluckhohn and Strodtbeck (1961), Schwartz (1992, 1994b), and Trompenaars and Hampden-Turner (2012). These cultural taxonomies provide unique cultural dimensions to classify national cultures, causing a jungle of cultural taxonomies that lacks clarity and conformity (Nardon & Steers, 2009).

This dissertation challenges the inconsistency of cultural dimensions from existing cultural taxonomies, aiming to provide a comprehensive understanding of national culture by identifying the core concepts and cultural components developed over decades to classify national cultures in cultural dimensions. The urgency and currency for such clarification were just before the end of this dissertation demonstrated by Kaasa (2021). Kaasa (2021) focused on the possibility to merge different cultural dimensions from existing cultural taxonomies into one system, applying only the three taxonomies of Hofstede (1980), Schwartz (1994b), and Inglehart (1997).

In this dissertation, various existing cultural taxonomies are analyzed and precisely selected. The focus is placed on taxonomies written in English since English also predominates the research field. All existing cultural taxonomies that significantly influenced the area are written in English (Mangas-Vega et al., 2018). The research of this dissertation does not stay at this point, like Kaasa (2021), only providing synthesized cultural dimensions. It further operationalized the synthesized dimensions into a valid and reliable tool for assessing national cultures.

The focus in this dissertation is distinctively placed on practicability and managerial views. The main aim of this dissertation is to provide a conclusive synthesis of multiple existing cultural taxonomies. The synthesis required the identification of meaningful interlinkages and causal relations among existing cultural taxonomies. This dissertation presents an integrated model of cultural taxonomies, classifying national culture into eight universal dimensions of culture (UDCs)—the eight UDCs of this dissertation. This research demonstrates an in-depth analysis of existing cultural dimensions. Also, this dissertation provides a synthesis of the cultural dimensions and demonstrates their operationalization and thus applicability.

It should be noted that all humans are subjective and every research in Social Sciences implies inevitable subjectivity by the conducting researcher (Hogan & Emler, 1978). As Hofstede pointed out, "one should realize that dimensions [of national culture] do not 'exist'. Like 'culture' itself, they are constructs, products of our imagination, that have been introduced because they subsume complex sets of mental programs into easily remembered packages" (Hofstede, 2001, p. 71).

This dissertation demonstrates an extensive, and thus, unique (as later substantiated by a systematic literature review (SLR)) synthesis of existing cultural taxonomies, guided by the following three research questions.

1.2 Research Questions (RQs)

Research Question 1 (RQ1): Which attempts have been undertaken to synthesize cultural dimensions from existing cultural taxonomies in current literature?

The first research question intends to guide the research of this dissertation to the current state of research on the development of UDCs by a synthesis of existing cultural taxonomies. While identifying the current state of research, the focus is on researches that attempted to clarify and synthesize the heterogenic range of cultural dimensions provided by existing cultural taxonomies. In order to answer RQ1, an SLR is conducted. The results of RQ1 were operationalized into eight assumptions, which were identified in the course of the SLR. The eight assumptions reflect the eight UDCs of this dissertation.

Research Question 2 (RQ2): Which universal dimensions of culture (UDCs) evolve from a synthesis of cultural dimensions from existing cultural taxonomies under the application of a structured and rigorous approach?
RQ2 builds on the results of RQ1 and seeks to verify the eight UDCs of this dissertation, which were isolated in the SLR and displayed in eight assumptions. A structured synthesis following implications is conducted based on a pre-selected range of 11 existing cultural taxonomies. The 11 pre-selected taxonomies constitute the research base of this dissertation. The research base of these taxonomies is filtered out from a range of 34 existing cultural taxonomies, which were identified in the SLR. A selection and evaluation framework is developed to filter the research base out of the 34 existing cultural taxonomies.

Research Question 3 (RQ3): Can the universal dimensions of culture (UDCs) be operationalized, and can a national culture be understood empirically in terms of the eight UDCs?
In RQ3, it is determined whether or not the UDCs can be operationalized with a questionnaire, and how this can be accomplished. A pretest is carried out to determine if the UDCs are suitable to be empirically operationalized and appropriate to describe national cultures empirically.

1.3 Structure and Classification of Research

In order to answer the three research questions—RQ1, RQ2, and RQ3—this dissertation was structured and conducted along the following process. Firstly, the current state of research was identified in an extensive SLR. Eight assumptions were derived from the results of the SLR, demonstrating the eight UDCs of this dissertation.

Secondly, the research base was determined by the evaluation and selection of cultural taxonomies. Thirty-four taxonomies were evaluated by a framework developed for and applied in this dissertation, resulting in 11 existing cultural taxonomies as the research base of this dissertation. Thirdly, 50 cultural dimensions were retrieved from the 11 cultural taxonomies. These 50 cultural dimensions were synthesized following six premises and a rigorous synthesis protocol. Finally, the identified eight UDCs were operationalized by items, and subsequently, a questionnaire was developed to assess the eight UDCs empirically. Four experts reviewed the developed questionnaire, resulting in an improved version of the questionnaire. Then a pre-test was conducted to ensure the validity and reliability of the developed questionnaire. The finalized UDC questionnaire is suitable to be applied in a large-scale cross-cultural study. The research of this dissertation was then concluded with a country study, illustrating the eight UDCs and their cultural components for Brazil, Canada, and Germany based on the pre-test results.

Figure 1.1 demonstrates this dissertation's research process and structure.

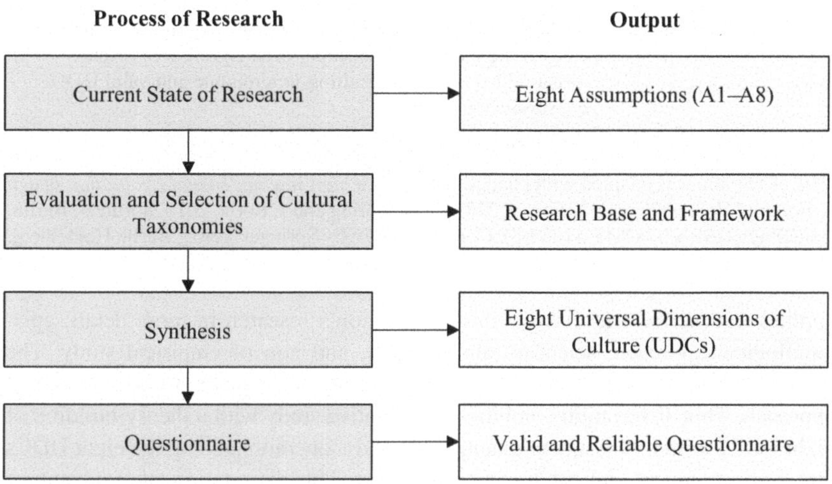

Figure 1.1 Process and Research Output

The research of this dissertation is classified as a deductive definition and measurement of a theoretical concept followed by a subsequent operationalization of the theory to conduct empirical research (Döring & Bortz, 2016). Moreover, the research of this dissertation can be displayed in terms of the guidelines for deductive definition and measurement of theoretical concepts by Döring and Bortz (2016).

Table 1.1 displays the three levels of the guidelines for deductive definition and measurement of theoretical concepts, including their implications for the research of this dissertation, by Döring and Bortz (2016).

Döring and Bortz (2016) provide nine criteria for the classification of research in general[2]. A selection of four out of the nine classification criteria can be

[2] For further information about the nine criteria, please refer to Döring and Bortz (2016, p. 183).

Table 1.1 Classification of Research as Deductive Definition and Measurement

Level	Implication
1. Theoretical Level	**Concept specification** by dimensionalizing national cultures based on a synthesis of selected cultural dimensions from cultural taxonomies, resulting in eight UDCs **Settlement of implications** for the theoretical concept specification as a starting point for a subsequent quantitative study
2. Operationalisation	Selection and development of a **standardized instrument** to convert the theoretical concepts—the eight UDCs—into measurable variables, resulting in a reliable and valid UDC questionnaire
3. Empirical Level	**Development** and **pilot test** of the questionnaire

Note. The table was adapted with changes from *Forschungsmethoden und Evaluation in den Sozial- und Humanwissenschaften* (p. 223), by N. Döring and J. Bortz, 2016, Springer, Berlin, Heidelberg (ISBN 978-642-41088-8). Copyright 2016 by Springer-Verlag Berlin Heidelberg.

applied to describe and classify this dissertation's research in more detail: epistemological approach, scientific aim, subject, and aim of empirical study. The research of this dissertation was pursued with a mixed-method epistemological approach. This dissertation combines a qualitative study with a theory-building of eight UDCs with a subsequent quantitative study, operationalizing the eight UDCs into a questionnaire and conducting a pilot test. This dissertation takes advantage of combining qualitative and quantitative research since both approaches complement each other, enhancing the research and reducing biases and flaws. As the SLR revealed, no previous research attempts at synthesizing cultural dimensions employed the mixed-methods approach discussed here (Döring & Bortz, 2016).

The subject of this dissertation constitutes a theoretical study, merging different existing cultural taxonomies and their concepts argumentatively together into a new theoretical model. Subsequently, the theoretical model was enriched by an empirical assessment of the eight developed UDCs. Finally, the objective of the empirical pilot study is to validate the questionnaire for further applications in large-scale studies.

1.4 Contribution to the Field of Research

This dissertation comprehensively studies cultural dimensions, their underlying concepts, and cultural components from cultural taxonomies. As identified in the

SLR, no existing research demonstrated such a comprehensive study on the topic. Therefore, an objective evaluation and selection framework was developed and applied to identify the research base of this dissertation. As demonstrated in the SLR, the four synthesis methodologies, and the synthesis methodology by Kaasa (2021), published just before submitting the present dissertation, did not apply a structured or objective selection of considered existing cultural taxonomies.

The selected 11 existing cultural taxonomies constitute the base for the next significant advancement and contribution to the area of cross-cultural research of this dissertation by isolating the eight universal dimensions of culture—the eight UDCs of this dissertation. These eight UDCs were synthesized to display the core concepts for distinguishing national cultures in cultural taxonomies. The synthesis in this dissertation, not done by any other synthesis approach, was conducted following a structured, objective, and rigorous procedure.

This dissertation's third advancement and significant contribution to the research area lies in its operationalization of the developed UDCs into a questionnaire, allowing testing and measuring the eight UDCs for further application. No other synthesis approach for cultural dimensions demonstrated such an operationalization of its findings. Finally, the questionnaire was tested to ensure validity and reliability by applying a rigorous pilot test procedure.

2 Current State of Research

This dissertation's current state of research was compiled according to the following first research question (RQ1). Which attempts have been undertaken to synthesize cultural dimensions from existing cultural taxonomies in current literature? The following sub-questions guided the literature review. How did the research of synthesized cultural dimensions evolve over the last years? Which central research lines and results are applicable for synthesizing cultural dimensions from existing cultural taxonomies? What is the extent, quality, and direction of current research attempts in the area? Where would the research of this dissertation be located in the overall landscape for synthesized cultural dimensions?[1].

Figure 2.1 displays the thematic position of the first chapter in the overall structure of this dissertation.

The methodologies of SLRs and narrative literature reviews are most commonly applied in today's research and were more in-depth reviewed for their application (Rother, 2007). Narrative literature reviews are often favored over SLRs. On the one hand, narrative literature reviews provide a general overview of the currently available literature on any topic of interest as well as assessing existing literature in the area of interest reasonably, comprehensively, and critically by applying less explicit inclusion and exclusion barriers (Bryman, 2012). On the other hand, narrative literature reviews are not based on structural approaches, neither applying a review strategy, inclusion and exclusion criteria, or a research protocol, resulting in low informational content. The low informational content is

[1] The sub-questions for the conduction of the current state of research were framed following Döring and Bortz (2016).

S. Kunert, *The Eight Universal Dimensions of Culture from a Synthesis of Cultural Taxonomies*, Gabler Theses, https://doi.org/10.1007/978-3-658-38765-5_2

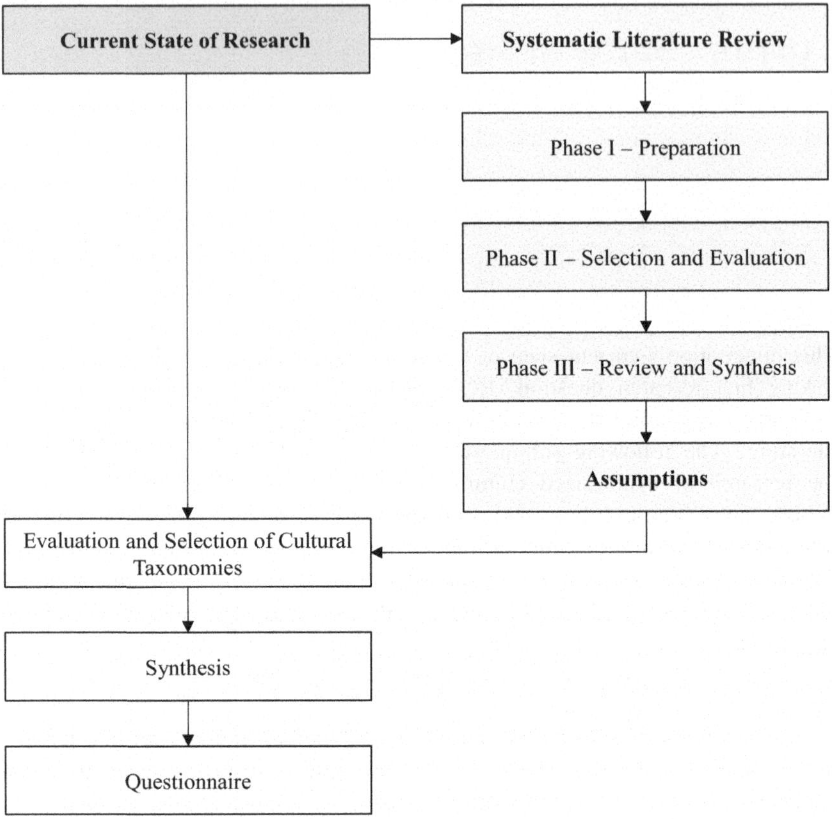

Figure 2.1 Thematic Position of Chapter 2

most likely to cause difficulties reproducing the review itself[2] (Rother, 2007). The lack of transparency and low informational content of a narrative literature review constituted the decisive reasons for this dissertation's rejection of this methodology. Instead, an SLR was conducted to ascertain the current state of research on synthesized cultural dimensions, answering RQ1.

SLRs are acknowledged to enable the conduction of an objective theory foundation on any research question or hypothesis, demonstrating a valuable tool to

[2] For detailed information about the limitations of narrative literature reviews, please refer to Haddaway et al. (2015).

comprehend any range of literature of interest (Rother, 2007; Tranfield et al., 2003). SLRs constitute the most accurate method for conducting scientific literature reviews because SLRs allow for a transparent and practical review of the literature. Their methodology provides guidelines for exploiting any intellectual territory (Mangas-Vega et al., 2018; Needleman, 2002; Tranfield et al., 2003).

The conduction of an SLR consumes considerably more time than the conduction of a standard narrative review, especially since the development of the systematic search strategy can be highly time-consuming. Additionally, the reviewer is advised to keep records of any details during the conduction of the review (Tranfield et al., 2003). The stringent pre-definition of research questions can also be obstructive. Such narrow boundaries can cause constraints to required adaptations during the literature search. Additionally, a stringent methodology can cause "bureaucratization" of the review process. Another common critique on SLRs refers to its evaluation of the quality of an article. The inclusion or exclusion of an identified study depends on the selected evaluation criteria, which could be biased by the reviewer's preferences (Bryman, 2012).

While recognizing these disadvantages, the SLR methodology was selected for the literature review in this dissertation to identify the current state of research on synthesized cultural dimensions from existing cultural taxonomies. For the development of a suitable SLR methodology, the following five approaches were consulted: Centre for Reviews and Dissemination (2009), Mangas-Vega et al. (2018), Massaro et al. (2016), Needleman (2002), and Tranfield et al. (2003)[3].

2.1 Methodology and Systematic Literature Review (SLR)

The SLR of this dissertation, aiming to demonstrate the current state of research on synthesized cultural dimensions from existing cultural taxonomies, was conducted by the author of this dissertation. The conduction of a literature review by one author/the author of a dissertation is common practice for SLR (c.f., Kitchenham, 2004). A specific methodology was developed for the SLR, following the approaches of the five consulted sources. The applied methodology is displayed in Figure 2.2.

[3] The five SLR approaches were identified in a prior literature research. The five listed approaches display a summary on existing approaches; whereas other approaches for SLRs are available and the here given listing is not exhaustible.

Phase I – Preparation

0 Evaluation of Necessity of Review

1 Review Protocol

1.1 Definition of Focus Question

1.2 Definition of Search Strategy

1.3 Keywords and Search Terms

1.4 Definition of Inclusion and Exclusion Criteria

Phase II – Selection and Evaluation

2 Selection of Articles

2.1 Search in Electronic Databases

2.2 Manual Search

3 Evaluation of Articles Against Indicators

Phase III – Review and Synthesis of Data (narrative synthesis)

4 Extraction and Review of Data

5 Synthesis of Data

Figure 2.2 Methodology of Systematic Literature Review (SLR). (*Note.* The titles of the steps were adapted with changes from the five consulted SLR methodologies of Centre for Reviews and Dissemination (2009), Mangas-Vega et al. (2018), Massaro et al. (2016), Needleman (2002), and Tranfield et al. (2003))

2.1.1 Phase I—Preparation (Review Protocol)

Step 0: Evaluation of Necessity of Review

The SLR was conducted to detect the current state of research on the synthesis of cultural dimensions of existing cultural taxonomies, as questioned by RQ1.

Step 1: Review Protocol

Step 1.1: Focus Question

The following focus question was deduced from the necessity and intention of the SLR. What is the current state of research on the synthesis of existing cultural taxonomies and their cultural dimensions, including the assessment of central research lines of the research area, also revealing the corresponding research gap?

Step 1.2: Search Strategy
Following Major et al. (2011), a mixed search strategy for the SLR was applied in this dissertation. The mixed strategy consisted of searching for relevant literature in electronic databases and a subsequent manual search in the reference lists of in the electronic databases identified articles.

Search in Electronic Databases: The two electronic databases *Business Source Complete* (EBSCO) and *Google Scholar,* were selected for this dissertation's SLR. A critical consideration of the advantages and disadvantages of both electronic databases was pursued.

In an overview, Google Scholar constitutes a well-known electronic database, offering a wide range of publications of various sources and types. Nevertheless, its scientific application is often controversially discussed. On the one hand, Google Scholar serves as a valuable starting point for assessing nearly every scientific topic (Massaro et al., 2016). On the other hand, researchers argue that Google Scholar is too imprecise in its output to provide adequate research evidence for scientific research (Voss, 2018). Google Scholar includes peer-reviewed publications primarily. Its range of literature displays almost the complete variety of any written scientific source of information (e.g., papers, theses, abstracts, and books). Moreover, Google Scholar provides access to various authors of scientific literature (e.g., professional societies, academic publishers, universities, and other scholarly organizations) (Bryman, 2012).

In addition, Google Scholar indicates the citation rate for each research result. Overall, it offers a simple electronic search option and broad access to the world of academic literature (Bryman, 2012).

The electronic database EBSCO constitutes one of the world's most prominent journal collections (Pianos & Krüger, 2014; Voss, 2018). EBSCO served as the confirmatory electronic database in the SLR of this dissertation, re-confirming the research results from the electronic database Google Scholar.

Bryman (2012)suggested the electronic database *Web of Science* as the most suitable electronic database for literature reviews in Social Sciences. This electronic database was not consulted in the SLR of this dissertation due to its considerable focus on publications from academic institutions based in the United Kingdom. Another widely used scientific electronic database constitutes *WISO*. WISO encompasses publications from a wide range of research areas but focuses primarily on publications from Germany (Pianos & Krüger, 2014; Voss, 2018). The electronic database WISO was rejected for application in this dissertation's SLR for this reason. A further well-known electronic database constitutes *Science Direct*; likewise, widely applied in literature reviews in Social Sciences. Science Direct is one of the world's most extensive online collections of bibliographic information, covering a wide range of research areas (e.g., technology, science, and medicine) (RMIT University, n.d.). Nevertheless, it was also rejected for application in the SLR of this dissertation because of its resemblance to Google Scholar.

Manual Search: The manual search for articles was carried out in the following two steps: first, the relevant articles' reference lists—articles identified in the search within the two electronic databases—were screened for other relevant articles. Second, Google Scholar offers a search function *related articles* allowing for searching articles with content similar to the original reference.

Step 1.3: Keywords and Search Terms

The SLR of this dissertation encompassed no specific keyword search, nor were keywords defined as inclusion or exclusion criteria. This approach was chosen to avoid potential biases resulting from keyword searches. Keyword searches can be subjective to the author or the publishing institutions (Mangas-Vega et al., 2018; Massaro et al., 2016).

The search terms were divided into two aspects based on the first part of the focus question. The first aspect refers to search terms related to the term *synthesis*. The second aspect refers to search terms related to the term(s) *(cultural) taxonomy(ies)*. Synonyms and related words were identified for each aspect following Pianos and Krüger (2014) and Oehlrich (2019). Table 2.1 illustrates the range of synonyms and related words for the search terms of the SLR in this dissertation.

Every search query was run with a term from aspect one connected with a term from aspect two. The terms from aspect two had to be accompanied by the word *cultural*. A prior pilot search inquiry in both electronic databases—Google Scholar and EBSCO—was conducted under the two following requirements: either using the word *cultural* as a mandatory pre-term for aspect two, or as another aspect connected by the Boolean operator[4] "AND" with the other search aspects.

[4] Boolean operators are "simple words (AND, OR, NOT, or AND NOT) used as conjunctions to combine or exclude keywords in a search, resulting in more focused and productive results" (Libraries, 2013, para. 1).

Table 2.1 Selection of Search Terms

Aspect	Synonyms	Related Words
(1) Synthesis	Amalgamation Unification	Clustering Combination Comparison Integration Overlap
(2) (Cultural) Taxonomy(ies)	Classification Terminology	Categorization Dimension Model Theory Typology

Note. The layout was adapted with changes from *Erfolgreich recherchieren- Wirtschaftswissenschaften*, by T. Pianos and N. Krüger, 2014, De Gruyter Saur. Copyright 2014 by De Gruyter Saur. And from *Wissenschaftliches Arbeiten und Schreiben: Schritt für Schritt zur Bachelor- und Master-Thesis in den Wirtschaftswissenschaften*, by M. Oehlrich, 2019, Springer Gabler. Copyright 2019 by Springer Gabler. The terms are listed in accordance with their relevance and were adapted from Taxonomy and Synthesis, by Dictionary.com, 2020 (https://www.dictionary.com/browse/taxonomy; https://www.dictionary.com/browse/synthesis?s=t). In the public domain.

The search results were far more imprecise when the word cultural was set as a single term connected by the Boolean operator "AND" with the other aspects. Because applying the Boolean operator "And" only ensures that the word *cultural* has to be somewhere included in the search result (e.g., title, abstract, or text). Therefore, the word *cultural* was set as prior-term to the words from aspect two, ensuring that the search results precisely answer the intended focus question of the SLR. Figure 2.3 displays the specification of the search queries applied in the search within the two electronic databases Google Scholar and EBSCO.

The structure of the searches within the two electronic databases was designed differently. In the case of Google Scholar, the aspects were linked with the Boolean operator "AND", indicating that both terms must be found somewhere in the content of the search results. Additionally, each aspect was put in quotation marks, ensuring that the exact term appears in the search queries. The search results were sorted according to their relevance. In the case of EBSCO, the search mode *Smart Text Searching*[5] was applied. The two aspects were not linked with a Boolean operator. A pre-test search was run using the Boolean operator "AND", resulting in almost

[5] Smart Text Searching "leverages a technology that summarizes text entered to the most relevant search term then conducts search" (EBSCO Information Services, 2014, p. 7).

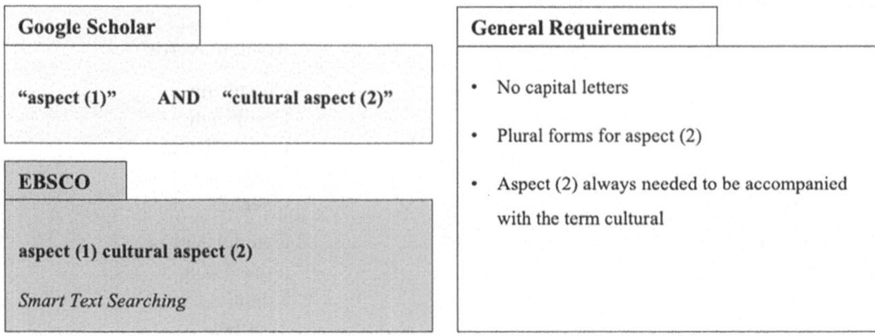

Figure 2.3 Search Queries and Search Requirements

zero search results for each search query. It was assumed that the Boolean operator "AND" in EBSCO implies excessively narrow search boundaries. Therefore, no Boolean operator was applied for the search queries in EBSCO.

It should be pointed out that the search queries were conducted separately and successively. Therefore, the overall number of search results displayed in Figure 2.4 could contain duplicates. The identified and relevant articles were checked for duplicates in a cross-check between the two electronic databases Google Scholar and EBSCO.

Application of the English Language: The SLR of this dissertation, including search terms and aspects, was conducted in English. The conduction of this dissertation's SLR in English was carried out purposefully and under consideration of its influence on the research and the controversial debate around applying the English language in the academic world[6].

The predominance of the English language is acknowledged by several researchers, among others, also by Triandis (1996) and Kroeber and Kluckhohn (1952). Triandis (1996) claimed that most theories and their corresponding data were investigated in or from Western societies in contemporary Social Sciences. Most western researchers claim to design their research from international perspectives, which could aggravate false assumptions. Additionally, most researchers assume the universality of their research and the universal application of their research to other aspects (Triandis, 1996). The vast majority of cross-cultural researchers have backgrounds in Anglo-American societies, educated and trained in the Anglo-American

[6] For example, please refer to Hamel (2007).

system. The cultural background also plays a crucial role in how researchers pursue their research (Kroeber & Kluckhohn, 1952).

Overall, the predominance of the English language in Social Sciences constituted the decisive reason for conducting this dissertation's SLR in English, including search terms and aspects in English.

Step 1.4: Inclusion and Exclusion Criteria

Inclusion and exclusion criteria were applied in this dissertations' SLR to ensure precise results in the search queries, also leading to a precise answer for the intended focus question of the SLR. The criteria were designed following the Centre for Reviews and Dissemination (2009) and Major (2011). Table 2.2 displays the inclusion and exclusion criteria and their corresponding requirements for the SLR of this dissertation in an overview.

Table 2.2 Inclusion and Exclusion Criteria

Criteria	Requirement(s)	Details
Availability	**Full text/data**	Articles were excluded if only their abstract was available, with a prior check of the possibility of interlibrary loans and to pay to borrow the publication.
Language	**English & German**	Articles written in either English or German were included in the SLR. Articles in other languages were not considered. This restriction originates from the language capabilities of the conductor of the SLR—the author of this dissertation. Additionally, as elaborated before, English holds a predominant position in Social Sciences. The inclusion of articles written in English should invoke a comprehensive set of articles.
Publication date	*None*	No restrictions were set on the publication dates.

(continued)

Table 2.2 (continued)

Criteria	Requirement(s)	Details
Publication status / type	*None*	No restrictions were set on the type and status of the articles. All types (e.g., conference papers, reports, books, and book chapters) and status of publications (e.g., grey literature, unpublished literature) were included because there was no need to limit the SLR data in the type and status of articles.
Study design	*None*	No restrictions were set on the study design of the article, allowing qualitative and quantitative, theoretical and empirical study designs
Topic relevance	**Focus question**	Only articles that contain evidence to answer the SLR focus question were considered further.

In Social Sciences, another standard approach clusters articles according to their number of considered cultures (e.g., Schaffer and Riordan (2003)), distinguishing between emic or etic study designs. In the SLR of this dissertation, articles were neither excluded nor included due to their emic or etic study focus.

2.1.2 Phase II—Selection and Evaluation

In the second phase of the SLR of this dissertation, articles were selected following the before demonstrated review protocol. Subsequently, the selected articles were evaluated according to their scientific impact, quality, reliability, and validity.

Step 2: Selection of Articles

The second phase started with searching for relevant articles in electronic databases in Google Scholar first, then in EBSCO. Afterward, a manual search divided into two steps was conducted. At first, the reference lists of the identified relevant articles from the electronic database search were screened for additional suitable articles. Finally, likewise articles correspondingly to the identified articles from the electronic database search were screened for suitability.

Step 2.1: Search in Electronic Databases
Sixty-four search queries were run in Google Scholar and EBSCO, resulting from 64 possible combinations of the search terms and the two aspects (please refer to Table 2.1). Figure 2.4 demonstrates the search process in the two electronic databases of this dissertations' SLR.

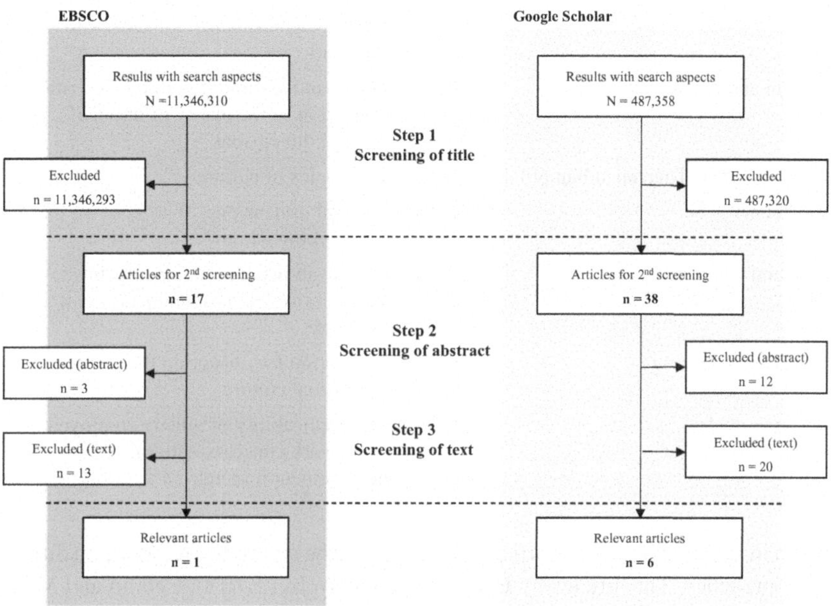

Figure 2.4 Flow Chart of Search in Electronic Databases. (*Note.* "N/n" indicates the (total) number of retrieved articles in each search step)

The articles resulting from the 64 search queries (EBSCO approx. 11.3 million, Google Scholar approx. 0.5 million) were not screened for duplicates. In the first screening step, the titles of the articles were reviewed to identify if the article could answer the intended focus question. In total, 17 articles were retrieved from EBSCO and 38 from Google Scholar, resulting in 55 articles. The 55 articles were then manually screened against the previously defined inclusion and exclusion criteria (please refer to Table 2.2). During the step of manual screening, the main focus was placed on the capability of the articles to answer the first part of the focus question. Overall, seven articles resulted from the first search step—searching in the electronic databases EBSCO and Google Scholar, including manual screening of identified articles. The seven identified articles are displayed in Table 2.3.

Table 2.3 Identified Articles from the Search within Electronic Databases

Author	(year)	Title
Beugelsdijk and Welzel	(2018)	Dimensions and dynamics of national culture: Synthesizing Hofstede with Inglehart
Catalin and Micu	(2013)	The quantification of culture—A critical evaluation of the theory of national cultural dimensions
Chanchani and Theivananthampillai	(2009)	Typologies of culture
Ford et al.	(2005)	Cultural dimensions: Who is stereotyping whom?
Low and Chapman	(2003)	Organizational and national culture: A study of overlap and interaction in the literature
Maleki and de Jong	(2014)	A proposal for clustering the dimensions of national culture
Yeganeh et al.	(2009)	The applicability of widely employed frameworks in cross-cultural management research

An in-depth review of the articles revealed that the researcher focussed on different approaches. The articles by Beugelsdijk and Welzel (2018), Catalin and Micu (2013), Low and Chapman (2003), and Maleki and de Jong (2014) each provide a methodology for the synthesis of cultural dimensions.

The articles by Chanchani and Theivananthampillai (2009), Ford et al. (2005), and Yeganeh et al. (2009) evaluate existing cultural taxonomies and cultural dimensions. The article by Ford et al. (2005) does not provide a detailed evaluation framework. The evaluation frameworks by Chanchani and Theivananthampillai (2009) and Yeganeh et al. (2009) were later utilized for the evaluation and selection of existing cultural taxonomies (please see Chapter 3 Evaluation and Selection of Existing Cultural Taxonomies).

Manual Search: In a second step, as defined in the research protocol (please refer to Section 2.1.1 Phase I—Preparation (Review Protocol)), a manual screening of the reference lists and related articles of the seven identified publications took place. The related articles were identified with the search function "Related articles" provided by Google Scholar. In a first manual search query, the previously identified (please refer to Table 2.3) four articles—Beugelsdijk and Welzel (2018), Catalin and Micu (2013), Low and Chapman (2003), and Maleki and de Jong (2014)—were reviewed in more detail. The first manual screening's search steps and corresponding results are demonstrated in Figure 2.5.

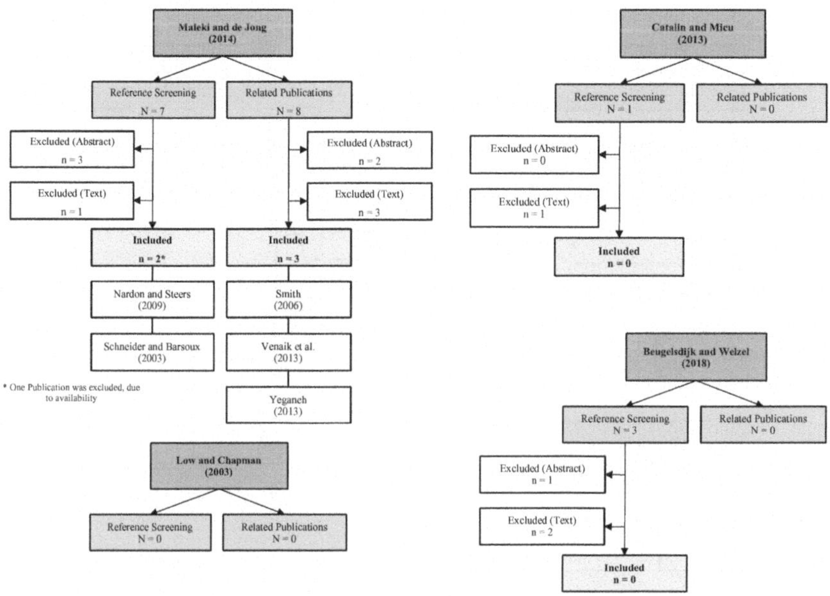

Figure 2.5 First Manual Screening. (*Note.* "N/n" indicates the (total) number of identified publications on each search step)

The in-depth review of the article by Smith (2006) led to its exclusion from further considerations. Smith (2006) focused only on the comparison of the GLOBE study by House et al. (2004) and the cultural taxonomy by Hofstede (1980). Such narrow syntheses are not relevant for this dissertation. The other four identified articles Nardon and Steers (2009)[7], Schneider and Barsoux (2003), Venaik et al. (2013),

[7] Nardon and Steers first published their work as an article, part of the Vlerick Leuven Gent Working Paper Series (2006/38) in 2006 under the title *Navigating the Culture Theory Jungle: Divergence and Convergence in Models of National Culture*. In 2009, the same work was published as one book chapter in *Cambridge Handbook of Culture, Organization, and Work* by Bhagat and Steers. In the later version, they used the title *The Culture Theory Jungle: Divergence and Convergence in Models of National Culture.*

and Yeganeh (2013), were identified to be suitable to answer the intended focus question.

The reference list and related publications of the four identified articles were screened manually in the next step. Figure 2.6 illustrates the second manual screening step results.

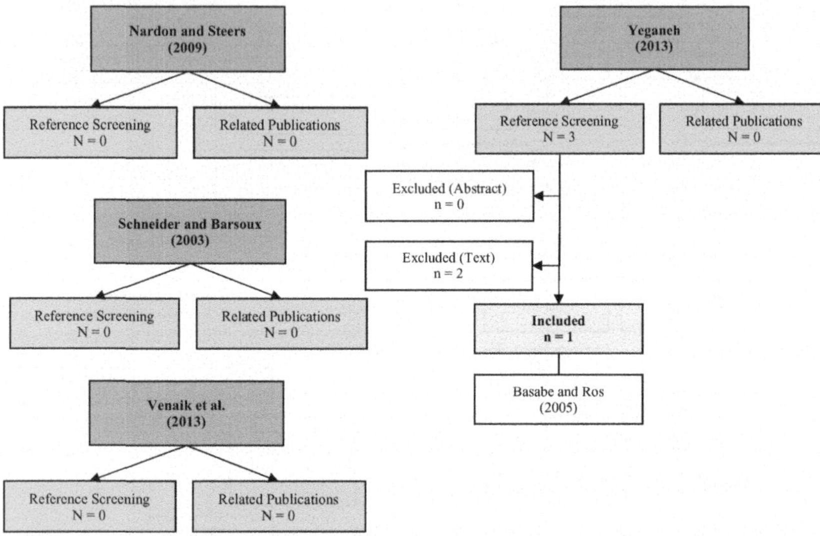

Figure 2.6 Second Manual Screening. (*Note.* "N/n" indicates the (total) number of identified publications on each search step)

In the second manual screening, only the article by Basabe and Ros (2005) was identified to answer the intended focus question of this dissertations' SLR. This article was also screened manually in a third screening process. The result is illustrated in Figure 2.7.

Summary of the Selection of Articles

In total, the five articles Basabe and Ros (2005), Nardon and Steers (2009), Schneider and Barsoux (2003), Venaik et al. (2013), and Yeganeh (2013) were identified in this manual search and added to the four previous articles of Beugelsdijk and Welzel (2018), Catalin and Micu (2013), Low and Chapman (2003), Maleki and de Jong (2014) identified in the previous manual search of the two electronic databases. These nine identified articles are displayed in an overview in Table 2.4.

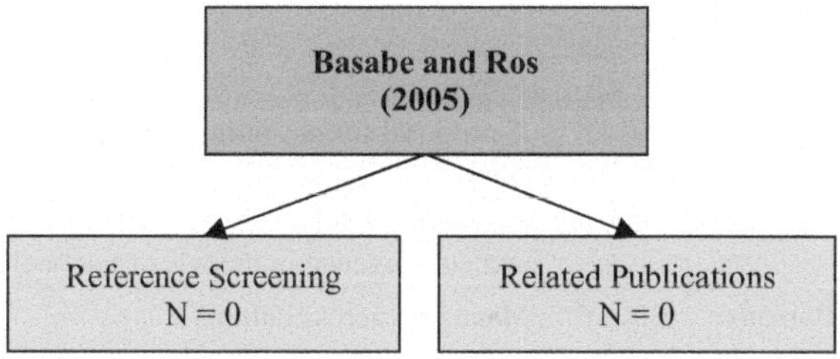

Figure 2.7 Third Manual Screening. (*Note.* "N/n" indicates the (total) number of identified publications on each search step)

In more depth, the majority (78%) of the identified articles were published in scientific journals. The article by Nardon and Steers (2009) was published as an article in 2006 and later as a book chapter in 2009. Most articles were identified in the manual search. Time-wise, the two articles by Low and Chapman (2003) and Schneider and Barsoux (2003) constituted the oldest identified articles. The latest article indicating a research interest in the synthesis of existing cultural taxonomies and cultural dimensions was conducted by Beugelsdijk and Welzel (2018).

Step 3: Evaluation of Articles Against Indicators

Several indicators exist to evaluate the impact, reliability, quality, and validity of an article. A suitable set of indicators was composed for the SLR of this dissertation. The indicators are displayed in an overview in Table 2.5.

Table 2.4 Overview of Identified Articles

Author	(year)	Title
Basabe and Ros	(2005)	Cultural dimensions and social behavior correlates: Individualism-collectivism and power distance
Beugelsdijk and Welzel	(2018)	Dimensions and dynamics of national culture: Synthesizing Hofstede with Inglehart
Catalin and Micu	(2013)	The quantification of culture—A critical evaluation of the theory of national culture dimensions
Low and Chapman	(2003)	Organisational and national culture: A study of overlap and interaction in the literature

(continued)

Table 2.4 (continued)

Author	(year)	Title
Maleki and de Jong	(2014)	A proposal for clustering the dimensions of national culture
Nardon and Steers	(2009)	Navigating the culture theory jungle: Divergence and convergence in models of national culture
Schneider and Barsoux	(2003)[8]	Managing across culture
Venaik et al.	(2013)	Looking into the future: Hofstede long term orientation versus GLOBE future orientation
Yeganeh	(2013)	A compound index of cultural dimensions: Implication and applications

Indicator 1—Impact

The citation rate demonstrates the impact of the articles. The citation rate numbers were retrieved from Google Scholar on June 23, 2021. No further restrictions were set for the evaluation of the impact of each article.

Table 2.5 Overview of Evaluation Indicators

Indicator	Methodology
1—Impact	Rate of Citation Date of Assessment: June 23, 2021 (sorted by relevance, no limitation time-wise) The impact of the reviewed articles was measured by the citation rate retrieved from Google Scholar.
2—Reliability	Use of Relevant Theories The reliability of the reviewed articles was assessed by the number of included existing cultural taxonomies and their proposed synthesis dimensions. The author of this dissertation conducted the reliability test.

(continued)

[8] This article was identified in the reference search in the article by Maleki and de Jong (2014). The first edition of the book *Managing Across Cultures* by Schneider and Barsoux was published in 1997, the second edition in 2003, and the third edition in 2014. Maleki and de Jong (2014) utilized the second edition from 2003. In this research, the second edition of the book was used for the evaluation of the publication itself in order to ensure consistency in the SLR process. The third edition from 2014 was later used for the review and synthesis of the data, ensuring a high currency of the SLR of this dissertation.

Table 2.5 (continued)

Indicator	Methodology
3—Quality	Assessment of Study Design The quality of an article was assessed based on the applied study design—either empirical or theoretical.
4—Validity	Internal Validity The internal validity was assessed by internal study biases. External Validity The following two questions were applied to assess the external validity: Was an own methodology developed? How applicable is the methodology for future research as well as other researchers?

The book chapter by Schneider and Barsoux (2003) indicated the highest impact factor, with a citation rate of 2017 citations in total. Any other author did not cite the journal article by Catalin and Micu (2013). Catalin and Micu (2013) only reproduced and summarized the work by Nardon and Steers (2009). The impact of this work was conceived as the lowest from the nine identified articles. The other articles scored between 14 and 274 citations.

Indicator 2—Reliability

The reliability of an article was evaluated by its included existing cultural taxonomies and the respectively developed synthesized dimensions.

Six of the nine identified articles (please refer to Table 2.4)—Beugelsdijk and Welzel (2018), Catalin and Micu (2013), Low and Chapman (2003), Maleki and de Jong (2014), Nardon and Steers (2009), and Schneider and Barsoux (2003)—carried out a synthesis of existing cultural taxonomies and cultural dimensions. Each publication provided a set of synthesis dimensions for classifying national cultures based on existing cultural taxonomies. The other three publications—Basabe and Ros (2005), Venaik et al. (2013) and, Yeganeh (2013)—focused instead on the comparison of single cultural dimensions.

Overall, only the article by Catalin and Micu (2013) was evaluated as none reliable since Catalin and Micu (2013) utilized the approach by Nardon and Steers (2009), only reproducing the article by Nardon and Steers (2009) without further investigating their synthesis. The other eight articles were considered reliable.

Indicator 3—Quality

The quality of the nine articles was evaluated by their study design. It was distinguished between an empirical quantitative and a theoretical study design. Three of the nine identified articles—Catalin and Micu (2013), Low and Chapman (2003), Schneider and Barsoux (2003)—based their synthesis on theoretical analyses. Nardon and Steers (2009) indicated the investigation of qualitative measures. However, Nardon and Steers (2009) did not reveal further information on their applied qualitative measures, making their approach hardly objective for other researchers.

Maleki and de Jong (2014) analyzed statistical correlations between their proposed synthesis dimensions and conducted an ecological factor analysis. Beugelsdijk and Welzel (2018) applied a similar approach.

Indicator 4—Validity

The validity evaluation was divided into internal and external validity (please refer to Table 2.5). Indicated biases in the articles were applied to evaluate the internal validity of an article. Five articles indicated biases in their study design—Basabe and Ros (2005), Beugelsdijk and Welzel (2018), Nardon and Steers (2009), Venaik et al. (2013), Yeganeh (2013). Maleki and de Jong (2014) specified no biases in their analysis. Schneider and Barsoux (2003) and Low and Chapman (2003) revealed no information about internal biases. Thus, the internal validity of those two articles could not be verified.

The external validity of an article was evaluated by the development of an individual synthesis by the researcher. Additionally, the evaluation took into account if the proposed synthesis dimensions were suitable for future research. The external validity could not be evaluated for the studies of Venaik et al. (2013) and Basabe and Ros (2005) since they did not develop a particular synthesis methodology. Yeganeh's (2013) article does not indicate a separate synthesis of cultural dimensions; hence, it provides an objective measurement for cultural dimensions. The validity was evaluated as given. The other studies by Catalin and Micu (2013), Low and Chapman (2003), Maleki and de Jong (2014), Nardon and Steers (2009), and Schneider and Barsoux (2003) provide a synthesis of existing cultural taxonomies and their syntheses were evaluated as valid.

Summary on the Evaluation of Articles

A summary of the previous evaluation of the impact, reliability, quality, and validity of the nine identified articles of the SLR of this dissertation is displayed in Table 2.6.

The evaluation of the nine articles led to the exclusion of four articles: Basabe and Ros (2005), Beugelsdijk and Welzel (2018), Venaik et al. (2013), and Yeganeh (2013). The work by Beugelsdijk and Welzel (2018) was excluded because of its low-reliability indication. In a more detailed review of the article, it became applicable that the researchers only re-analyzed the cultural taxonomy by Hofstede (1980, 1991, 2001) and provided no particular synthesis methodology. The work by Basabe and Ros (2005) included relevant existing cultural taxonomies, but Basabe and Ros (2005) only underwent a re-exploration of socio-economic, demographic, political, and cultural indicators of their analyzed cultural taxonomies. The resulting low reliability of the article led to its exclusion. Venaik et al. (2013) demonstrated a detailed comparison of three cultural taxonomies focusing on the time concepts in the existing cultural taxonomies. Whereas, Venaik et al. (2013) did not develop a particular synthesis methodology and thus, was excluded from further research. Yeganeh (2013) proposed a "Cultural Compound Indicator". Likewise, this work did not hold the requirements of the defined indicators and was excluded from further research.

Table 2.6 Evaluation of the Nine Articles from the Systematic Literature Review (SLR)

Publication	Impact	Reliability (N studies)	Reliability (N dimensions)	Quality	Validity (internal)	Validity (external)
Basabe and Ros (2005)	275	4	0	Theory	Biases were indicated	No individual synthesis
Beugelsdijk and Welzel (2018)	152	2	3	Theory, Empirical	Biases were indicated	Individual synthesis
Catalin and Micu (2013)	**0**	**6**	**5**	**Empirical**	**Only reproduction of Nardon and Steers (2009)**	**No individual synthesis**
Low and Chapman (2003)	**14**	**6**	**4**	**Empirical**	**No biases were indicated**	**Individual synthesis**
Maleki and de Jong (2014)	**97**	**10**	**9**	**Theory, Empirical**	**No quantitative biases were indicated**	**Individual synthesis**

(continued)

Table 2.6 (continued)

Publication	Impact	Reliability (N studies)	Reliability (N dimensions)	Quality	Validity (internal)	Validity (external)
Nardon and Steers (2009)	**141**	**6**	**5**	**Theory, Empirical**	**Biases were indicated**	**Individual synthesis**
Schneider and Barsoux (2003)	**2022**	**6**	**3**	**Empirical**	**No biases were indicated**	**Individual synthesis**
Venaik et al. (2013)	87	2	0	Theory, Empirical	Biases were indicated	No individual synthesis
Yeganeh (2013)	17	2	0	Theory	Biases were indicated	CCI

Note. Only the articles highlighted in **bold** provide a synthesis of cultural dimensions from existing cultural taxonomies, as comprehended in this dissertation.

2.1.3 Phase III—Review and Synthesis of Data

In the third phase of the SLR, the data of the previously identified four articles were reviewed and synthesized, according to the initially developed framework for narrative data synthesis. The framework of this dissertations' narrative synthesis is displayed in the following figure (please see Figure 2.8). The narrative data synthesis process stemmed from the Cochrane Collaboration recommendations for SLRs (please refer to Centre for Reviews and Dissemination (2009)).

The four synthesis methodologies identified by the SLR—Low and Chapman (2003), Nardon and Steers (2009), Maleki and de Jong (2014), and Schneider et al. (2014)—differ to a great extent in their approaches of synthesizing cultural dimensions. The data from each of the four synthesis methodologies was analyzed and reviewed. The data review also reflects the historical development and the central research lines of synthesizing cultural dimensions in general.

Figure 2.8 The Framework of the Narrative Synthesis. (*Note.* The figure was adapted with changes from Systematic Reviews. CRD's Guidance for undertaking Reviews in Health Care (p. 49), by Centre for Reviews and Dissemination, 2009, CRD, University of York (https://www.york.ac.uk/media/crd/Systematic_Reviews.pdf). Copyright 2008 by Centre for Reviews and Dissemination, University of York)

Step 4: Extraction and Review of Data

In summary[9], Low and Chapman (2003) applied a theoretical synthesis approach without any additional statistic or heuristic reinforcement of the synthesis. In contrast, Maleki and de Jong (2014) pursued a more detailed synthesis, proposing a clustering framework of nine synthesis dimensions. The framework by Maleki

[9] For more detailed information on each synthesis methodology, please refer to the corresponding reference.

and de Jong (2014) aimed to compare and aggregate cultural dimensions, drafting a consistent synthesis. At first, Maleki and de Jong (2014) studied conceptual interrelations between the cultural dimensions of their analyzed existing cultural taxonomies. Subsequently, they analyzed statistical correlations between the cultural dimensions and conducted an ecological factor analysis to verify the credibility of their nine synthesis dimensions. They assembled the country scores from five empirical-based cultural taxonomies and calculated the correlations with their synthesis dimensions.

Nardon and Steers (2009) intended to clarify the confusion about cultural-bound issues in a professional environment by synthesizing cultural dimensions out of the "jungle" of existing cultural taxonomies. The researchers performed a comparative qualitative and quantitative meta-analysis. They assessed the quantitative data provided by Trompenaars and Hampden-Turner (1993), House et al. (2004), and Hofstede (2001) and added additional ethnographic data to their analysis. For each synthesis dimension, they provided a set of questions (items). However, they did not provide any details on their quantitative analysis, no strategic or objective selection, and no evaluation of their included existing cultural taxonomies was demonstrated. Likewise, Schneider et al. (2014) developed six synthesis dimensions by analyzing nine existing cultural taxonomies. The researchers mainly focus on cultural dimensions that can help to understand cultural differences in management practices, centering their assumptions around the cultural taxonomy by Kluckhohn and Strodtbeck (1961). Schneider et al. (2014) also reveal no information about their qualitative synthesis approach or their selection of existing cultural taxonomies.

Step 5: Synthesis of Data

The data of the four synthesis methodologies were analyzed regarding similarities in the conducted synthesis, following the standards for a narrative synthesis (please refer to Figure 2.8) aiming to demonstrate the range of existing synthesis dimensions.

The data synthesis serves as the basis for the development of the eight assumptions of this dissertation. The following six concepts were identified to constitute commonly synthesized cultural dimensions among the four detected synthesis methodologies—Low and Chapman (2003), Maleki and de Jong (2014), Nardon and Steers (2009), and Schneider et al. (2014)—distribution of power, relationship with the environment, social organization, time, uncertainty avoidance, and human orientation.

Concept of Distribution of Power

Each of the four synthesis methodologies identified the concept of distribution of power as a distinguishing tenant for national cultures, running through their analyzed existing cultural taxonomies. Although, the four synthesis methodologies differ considerably in their frameworks. Table 2.7 displays, in summary, the synthesized data for the concept of distribution of power based on the data given by the four synthesis methodologies[10].

Table 2.7 Synthesized Concept of Distribution of Power

	Low and Chapman (2003)	Maleki and de Jong (2014)	Nardon and Steers (2009)	Schneider et al. (2014)
	Relationship	Power Distance	Hierarchy—Equality	–
Adler (1981, 1991)	–	–	–	–
DiStefano and Maznevski (2000a, 2000b, 2003)	–	–	–	–
Douglas (1973)	–	Grid	–	–
Fukuyama (1995a, 1995b, 1999)	–	–	–	–
House et al. (2002, 2004)	–	Power Distance	Power Distance, Gender Egalitarianism	–
Hall (1959, 1966, 1976, 1983; Hall & Hall, 1990)	–	–	Context	–
Hofstede (1980, 2001, 2006, 2010)	Power Distance, Individualism vs. Collectivism	Power Distance	Power Distance	–
Inglehart (2006)	–	Self-Expression vs. Survival	–	–
Kluckhohn and Strodtbeck (1961)	–	Relationship with People	–	–
Lessem and Neubauer (1994)	Pragmatism vs. Wholism	–	–	–

(continued)

[10] For further details, please refer to the corresponding reference.

Table 2.7 (continued)

	Low and Chapman (2003)	Maleki and de Jong (2014)	Nardon and Steers (2009)	Schneider et al. (2014)
Lewis and Finland (1992)	–	–	–	–
Minkov (2007, 2008, 2013)	–	–	–	–
Parsons and Shils (1951)	–	–	–	–
Schein (1985, 1987)	–	–	–	–
Schwartz (1992, 1994b, 1999, 2004, 2006)	–	Hierarchy vs. Egalitarianism	Hierarchy vs. Egalitarianism	–
Triandis (1989, 1996, 2000, 2001, 2002, 2004)	–	Vertical	–	–
Trompenaars and Hampden-Turner (1997)	Individualism vs. Communitarianism, Ascription vs. Achievement, Internal vs. Outer Direction	–	Ascription vs. Achievement	–

Concept of Relationship with the Environment (Mastery versus Harmony) Maleki and de Jong (2014), Nardon and Steers (2009), and Schneider et al. (2014) commonly identified the distinction of national cultures by their individuals' relationship with the environment. The three synthesis methodologies differ in their perception of the concept of environment itself.

Maleki and de Jong (2014) and Schneider et al. (2014) considered the social and natural environment distinct from each other; while Nardon and Steers (2009) considered the social and natural environment under one shared concept. In the methodology by Low and Chapman (2003), no directly related synthesis dimension for the concept of relationship with the environment became applicable. Low and Chapman (2003) referred in their synthesis dimension of Relationship to individual's view of their place in the society. The researchers only indicated that their cultural theme of Relationship correlate with the role of an organization to take over social responsibility.

Table 2.8 illustrates the concept of relationship with the environment in the four in the SLR identified synthesis methodologies.

Table 2.8 Synthesized Concept of Relationship with the Environment

	Low and Chapman (2003)	Maleki and de Jong (2014)	Nardon and Steers (2009)	Schneider et al. (2014)
	–	Mastery vs. Harmony	Mastery vs. Harmony	Relationship with the Environment
Adler (1981, 1991)	–	–	–	Relationship to the World
DiStefano and Maznevski (2000a, 2000b, 2003)	–	–	–	Relationship with Environment
Douglas (1973)	–	–	–	–
Fukuyama (1995a, 1995b, 1999)	–	–	–	–
House et al. (2002, 2004)	–	–	Assertiveness, Performance Orientation, Humane Orientation	Uncertainty Avoidance
Hall (1959, 1966, 1976, 1983; Hall & Hall, 1990)	–	–	–	–
Hofstede (1980, 2001, 2006, 2010)	–	Masculinity vs. Femininity	Masculinity vs. Femininity	Uncertainty Avoidance
Inglehart (2006)	–	–	–	–
Kluckhohn and Strodtbeck (1961)	–	Relationship with Nature	Relationship with Nature, Human Activity	Relationship with Nature
Lessem and Neubauer (1994)	–	–	–	–
Lewis and Finland (1992)	–	–	–	–
Minkov (2007, 2008, 2013)	–	–	–	–

(continued)

Table 2.8 (continued)

	Low and Chapman (2003)	Maleki and de Jong (2014)	Nardon and Steers (2009)	Schneider et al. (2014)
Parsons and Shils (1951)	–	–	–	–
Schein (1985, 1987)	–	–	–	Relationship with Nature
Schwartz (1992, 1994b, 1999, 2004, 2006)	–	Mastery vs. Harmony	Mastery vs. Harmony	Mastery vs. Harmony
Triandis (1989, 1996, 2000, 2001, 2002, 2004)	–	Active	–	–
Trompenaars and Hampden-Turner (1997)	–	Internal vs. Outer Direction	Internal vs. Outer Direction	Internal vs. Outer Direction

Concept of Social Organization (Individualism versus Collectivism)
Reviewing the four synthesis methodologies, the concept of social organization and, more specifically, the concept of individualism versus collectivism became obvious as another general concept among all four synthesis methodologies.

One peculiarity became applicable in Maleki and de Jong (2014), who addressed the concept of social organization in two different synthesis dimensions: Collaborativeness and Individualism versus Collectivism. The two synthesis dimensions originate from the different handling of the two cultural dimensions of Institutional Collectivism and In-Group Collectivism from House et al. (2002, 2004) by Maleki and de Jong (2014). The other three synthesis methodologies of Low and Chapman (2003), Nardon and Steers (2009), and Schneider et al. (2014) either did not consider the two cultural dimensions referring to two different concepts or did not synthesize one or the other of the two cultural dimensions by House et al. (2002, 2004).

Table 2.9 illustrates the execution of the concept of individualism versus collectivism in the four synthesis methodologies identified by the SLR.

Table 2.9 Synthesized Concept of Social Organization

	Low and Chapman (2003)	Maleki and de Jong (2014)		Nardon and Steers (2009)	Schneider et al. (2014)
	Relationship	Collaborativeness	Individualism vs. Collectivism	Individualism vs. Collectivism	Relationship with People
Adler (1981, 1991)	–	–	–	–	Individualism
DiStefano and Maznevski (2000a, 2000b, 2003)	–	–	–	–	Relationship among People
Douglas (1973)	–	–	Group	–	–
Fukuyama (1995a, 1995b, 1999)	–	–	–	–	–
House et al. (2002, 2004)	–	Institutional Collectivism	In-Group Collectivism	Institutional Collectivism, In-Group Collectivism	Assertiveness, Gender Egalitarianism, Human Orientation, Institutional & In-Group Collectivism, Performance Orientation
Hall (1959, 1966, 1976, 1983; Hall & Hall, 1990)	–	–	Context, Time, Space	Context	–

(continued)

Table 2.9 (continued)

	Low and Chapman (2003)	Maleki and de Jong (2014)		Nardon and Steers (2009)	Schneider et al. (2014)
	Relationship	Collaborativeness	Individualism vs. Collectivism	Individualism vs. Collectivism	Relationship with People
Hofstede (1980, 2001, 2006, 2010)	Power Distance, Individualism vs. Collectivism	–	Individualism vs. Collectivism	Individualism vs. Collectivism	Power Distance, Individualism vs. Collectivism
Inglehart (2006)	–	–	Survival Values vs. Self-Expression Values	–	–
Kluckhohn and Strodtbeck (1961)	–	–	Relational Orientation	Relational Orientation	Relationship with People
Lessem and Neubauer (1994)	Pragmatism vs. Wholism	–	–	–	–
Lewis and Finland (1992)	–	–	–	–	–
Minkov (2007, 2008, 2013)	–	–	Universalism vs. Exclusionism	–	–
Parsons and Shils (1951)	–	–	Self-Orientation vs. Universalism, Achievement vs. Specify	–	–
Schein (1985, 1987)	–	–	–	–	Human Relationship

(continued)

Table 2.9 (continued)

	Low and Chapman (2003)	Maleki and de Jong (2014)		Nardon and Steers (2009)	Schneider et al. (2014)
	Relationship	Collaborativeness	Individualism vs. Collectivism	Individualism vs. Collectivism	Relationship with People
Schwartz (1992, 1994b, 1999, 2004, 2006)	–	–	Embeddedness vs. Autonomy	Embeddedness vs. Autonomy	Embeddedness, Affective & Intellectual Autonomy, Hierarchy, Egalitarianism
Triandis (1989, 1996, 2000, 2001, 2002, 2004)	–	–	Individualism vs. Universalistic, Achieved vs. Specific, Instrumental vs. Tightness	–	–
Trompenaars and Hampden-Turner (1997)	Individualism vs. Communitarianism, Achievement vs. Ascription, Internal vs. Outer Direction, Universalism vs. Particularism	–	Individualism vs. Communitarianism, Universalism vs. Particularism, Achievement vs. Ascription, Specific vs. Diffuse, Sequential vs. Synchronous	Individualism vs. Collectivism	Universalism vs. Particularism, Individualism vs. Communitarianism, Neutral vs. Emotional, Specific vs. Diffuse

Concept of Uncertainty Avoidance

The four synthesis methodologies identified the concept of uncertainty avoidance as a distinguishing concept for national cultures among existing cultural taxonomies. Each synthesis methodology differed in its framework for designing a synthesis dimension for the concept of uncertainty avoidance.

The data for the concept of uncertainty avoidance as utilized in the four synthesis methodologies demonstrates the following peculiarities. Nardon and Steers (2009) build the concept of uncertainty avoidance around the establishment and enforcement of rules in national culture, pursuing social control. At the same time, Low and Chapman (2009) referred to the concept of uncertainty avoidance as the willingness of individuals to take on risks. Likewise, although more specifically framed, Schneider et al. (2014) connected the concept of uncertainty avoidance with the desire of national culture to take control over its environment, illustrated by individuals' intention to plan rituals and the extent of importance placed on schedules. Only Maleki and de Jong (2014) considered the concept of uncertainty avoidance as the concept of the extent of individuals feeling uncomfortable in unknown, uncertain, and unstructured situations.

Table 2.10 illustrates the synthesis dimensions identified in the SLR for the concept of uncertainty avoidance as each of the four synthesis methodologies designed them.

Concept of Time

The four synthesis methodologies either directly or indirectly addressed the concept of time, varying in their approaches to synthesize this concept as either one distinct synthesis dimension or as a concept integrated into another synthesis dimension. Distinct from Low and Chapman (2003), Nardon and Steers (2009), and Schneider et al. (2014), Maleki and de Jong (2014) included no distinct dimension for the concept of time. Instead, the concept of time was addressed in different dimensions of their methodology—Traditionalism versus Secularism, Individualism versus Collectivism, and Uncertainty Avoidance. Table 2.11 illustrates the utilization of the concept of time in the four synthesis methodologies.

Table 2.10 Synthesized Concept of Uncertainty Avoidance

	Low and Chapman (2003)	Maleki and de Jong (2014)	Nardon and Steers (2009)	Schneider et al. (2014)
	Confidence	Uncertainty Avoidance	Rule Orientation	*Relationship with the Environment*
Adler (1981, 1991)	–	–	–	*Relationship to the World*
DiStefano and Maznevski (2000a, 2000b, 2003)	–	–	–	*Relationship to the Environment*
Douglas (1973)	–	–	–	–
Fukuyama (1995a, 1995b, 1999)	–	–	–	–
House et al. (2002, 2004)	–	Future Orientation, Performance Orientation	Uncertainty Avoidance	–
Hall (1959, 1966, 1976, 1983; Hall & Hall, 1990)	–	–	–	–
Hofstede (1980, 2001, 2006, 2010)	Uncertainty Avoidance, Masculinity vs. Femininity	Uncertainty Avoidance	Uncertainty Avoidance	*Uncertainty Avoidance*
Inglehart (2006)	–	–	–	–
Kluckhohn and Strodtbeck (1961)	–	Relationship with Time (future)	–[11]	*Relationship with Nature*
Lessem and Neubauer (1994)	–	–	–	–
Lewis and Finland (1992)	–	–	–	–

(continued)

[11] Nardon and Steers (2009) displayed in one of their tables that also one cultural dimension by Kluckhohn and Strodtbeck (1961) was synthesized into their synthesis dimension of Rule Orientation without further reference which cultural dimension by Kluckhohn and Strodtbeck (1961) they synthesized into the dimension. Also, no information was given in regards to the concrete cultural dimension in the description of the synthesis dimension.

Table 2.10 (continued)

	Low and Chapman (2003)	Maleki and de Jong (2014)	Nardon and Steers (2009)	Schneider et al. (2014)
Minkov (2007, 2008, 2013)	–	–	–	–
Parsons and Shils (1951)	–	–	–	–
Schein (1985, 1987)	–	–	–	*Relationship with Nature*
Schwartz (1992, 1994b, 1999, 2004, 2006)	–	–	–	*Mastery vs. Harmony*
Triandis (1989, 1996, 2000, 2001, 2002, 2004)	–	–	–	–
Trompenaars and Hampden-Turner (1997)	Specific vs. Diffuse	Universalism vs. Particularism	–	*Inter vs. Outer direction*

Note. The information of Schneider et al. (2014) is displayed in italics since the conceptual interrelationship to the proposed synthesis dimension for the concept of uncertainty avoidance is not as considerable as for the other three synthesis methodologies.

Concept of Human Orientation

Two of the four synthesis methodologies identified the concept of human orientation as a general concept for distinguishing national cultures among existing cultural taxonomies. Maleki and de Jong (2014) provided a synthesis dimension of Assertiveness versus Tenderness, "which refers to the cultural feature of being assertive and aggressive versus kind and tender in social relationships, also manifested in communication style" (Maleki & de Jong, 2014, pp. 120–121). Schneider et al. (2014) applied the concept of human orientation in two synthesis dimensions—Nature of Human Activity and Human Nature. Table 2.12 displays the synthesis dimensions addressing the concept of human orientation by the four methodologies identified by the SLR.

Additional Synthesis Concepts

The six previously demonstrated concepts—distribution of power, relationship with the environment, social organization, time, uncertainty avoidance, and human orientation—constitute concepts utilized by at least two of the four identified synthesis

Table 2.11 Synthesized Concept of Time

	Low and Chapman (2003)	Maleki and de Jong (2014)	Nardon and Steers (2009)	Schneider et al. (2014)
	Temporal	–	Time Orientation	Time
Adler (1981, 1991)	–	–	–	Time
DiStefano and Maznevski (2000a, 2000b, 2003)	–	–	–	Time
Douglas (1973)	–	–	–	–
Fukuyama (1995a, 1995b, 1999)	–	–	–	–
House et al. (2002, 2004)	–	–	Future Orientation	Future Orientation
Hall (1959, 1966, 1976, 1983; Hall & Hall, 1990)	–	–	Time	Time
Hofstede (1980, 2001, 2006, 2010)	Long-Term vs. Short-Term Orientation	–	Long-Term vs. Short-Term Orientation	Long-Term vs. Short-Term Orientation
Inglehart (2006)	–	–	–	–
Kluckhohn and Strodtbeck (1961)	–	–	Relationship with Time	Relationship with Time
Lessem and Neubauer (1994)	–	–	–	–
Lewis and Finland (1992)	Monochronic vs. Polychronic	–	–	–
Minkov (2007, 2008, 2013)	–	–	–	–
Parsons and Shils (1951)	–	–	–	–
Schein (1985, 1987)	–	–	–	Time
Schwartz (1992, 1994b, 1999, 2004, 2006)	–	–	–	–

(continued)

Table 2.11 (continued)

	Low and Chapman (2003)	Maleki and de Jong (2014)	Nardon and Steers (2009)	Schneider et al. (2014)
Triandis (1989, 1996, 2000, 2001, 2002, 2004)	–	–	–	–
Trompenaars and Hampden-Turner (1997)	Synchronous vs. Sequential	–	Synchronous vs. Sequential	Synchronous vs. Sequential

methodologies. Some concepts were utilized by only one of the synthesis methodologies—communication, indulgence versus restraint, nature of truth and reality, traditionalism versus secularism, gender egalitarianism, space, and language.

Concept of Communication: The concept of communication was only applicable as a distinct synthesis dimension in Low and Chapman (2003), describing the willingness of individuals to listen to the view of others while obtaining decision-making information. Although, Schneider et al. (2014) embedded the concept of communication in a threefold framework of language, space, and time. Additionally, Maleki and de Jong (2014) addressed that the concept of communication is one of their synthesis dimensions, referring to the influence of communication on the concept of assertiveness versus tenderness. It could be assumed that the concept of communication and the concept of language play a role in distinguishing national cultures. Nevertheless, the concept of communication was not applicable enough to constitute a distinct individual concept. Instead, it seems to be prevalent and influenced in and by other cultural concepts. Therefore, the concept of communication and, thus, the concept of language were not considered as concepts for a distinct UDC.

Concept of Indulgence versus Restraint: Maleki and de Jong (2014) were the only researchers to propose the concept of indulgence versus restraint as a distinct synthesis dimension. This concept expresses a national culture's extent for the gratification of desires and feelings. Even only Maleki and de Jong (2014) proposed such a synthesis dimension, the given evidence was considerable. Therefore, a similar investigation is undertaken here regarding a UDC for the concept of indulgence versus restraint.

Table 2.12 Synthesized Concept of Human Orientation

	Low and Chapman (2003)	Maleki and de Jong (2014)	Nardon and Steers (2009)	Schneider et al. (2014)	
	–	Assertiveness vs. Tenderness	–	Human Nature	Nature of Human Activity
Adler (1981, 1991)	–	–	–	Nature of the Individual	Human Activity
DiStefano and Maznevski (2000a, 2000b, 2003)	–	–	–	Nature of Humans	Human Activity
Douglas (1973)	–	–	–	–	–
Fukuyama (1995a, 1995b, 1999)	–	–	–	–	–
House et al. (2002, 2004)	–	Assertiveness	–	–	–
Hall (1959, 1966, 1976, 1983; Hall & Hall, 1990)	–	–	–	–	–
Hofstede (1980, 2001, 2006, 2010)	–	–	–		–
Inglehart (2006)	–	–	–	–	–
Kluckhohn and Strodtbeck (1961)	–	Human Nature Orientation	–	Nature of People	Human Activity
Lessem and Neubauer (1994)	–	–	–	–	–
Lewis and Finland (1992)	–	–	–	–	–
Minkov (2007, 2008, 2013)	–	–	–	–	–
Parsons and Shils (1951)	–	–	–	–	–
Schein (1985, 1987)	–	–	–		Human Activity

(continued)

Table 2.12 (continued)

	Low and Chapman (2003)	Maleki and de Jong (2014)	Nardon and Steers (2009)	Schneider et al. (2014)	
	–	Assertiveness vs. Tenderness	–	Human Nature	Nature of Human Activity
Schwartz (1992, 1994b, 1999, 2004, 2006)	–	–	–		–
Triandis (1989, 1996, 2000, 2001, 2002, 2004)	–	–	–	–	–
Trompenaars and Hampden-Turner (1997)	–	–	–	–	Human Activity

Concept of Nature of Truth and Reality: The concept nature of truth and reality was only ascertained by Schneider et al. (2014) as a distinct synthesis dimension. There was no substantial information given by Schneider et al. (2014) also to pursue such an approach for a UDC in this dissertation. Schneider et al. (2014) only retrieved their approach from conceptual observations and synthesized the cultural dimension of Reality and Truth by Schein (1985, 1987) into their synthesis dimension of Nature of Truth and Reality.

Concept of Traditionalism versus Secularism: The concept of traditionalism versus secularism was only applicable in the synthesis methodology by Maleki and de Jong (2014) as a synthesis dimension, addressing the concepts of religiosity, self-stability, pride, and the consistency between felt and expressed emotions. Maleki and de Jong (2014) also discovered a significant relationship between the concept of traditionalism versus secularism and the concept of (perception and use of) time.

The other three synthesis methodologies of Low and Chapman (2003), Nardon and Steers (2009), and Schneider et al. (2014) did not synthesize a distinct synthesis dimension addressing the concept of traditionalism versus secularism. Nevertheless, the evidence found in the synthesis methodology by Maleki and de Jong (2014) extensively portrayed a synthesis dimension for the concept of traditionalism versus secularism. Therefore, a UDC for the concept of traditionalism versus secularism was assumed for this dissertation.

Concept of Gender Egalitarianism: The concept of gender egalitarianism was only identified as a distinct synthesis dimension by Maleki and de Jong (2014), including only one cultural dimension of one existing cultural taxonomy—the cultural dimension of Gender Egalitarianism by House et al. (2004, 2007, 2014). There was no considerable evidence given by Maleki and de Jong (2014) to justify a synthesis of a distinct dimension of gender egalitarianism by only including one cultural dimension of one existing cultural taxonomy. Therefore, in the synthesis of this dissertation, no distinct UDC for the concept of gender egalitarianism was anticipated. Although, its potential was evaluated and critically considered (please refer to Section 4.2 Special Report on the Remaining Synthesis Dimension).

Concepts of Space and Language: The synthesis methodology by Schneider et al. (2014) provided a threefold framework, including the concepts of time, language, and space. Any other identified synthesis methodologies did not distinctively consider the concepts of language and space. Schneider et al. (2014) seized on the cultural taxonomy by Hall (1959, 1966, 1976, 1983; Hall & Hall, 1990). There was not enough justifiable evidence applicable in the description of the three-fold synthesis dimension by Schneider et al. (2014), which would have substantiated a consideration of the approach in this dissertation.

Summary of the Narrative Synthesis

Table 2.13 displays a summary of the narrative synthesis of the data of the four synthesis methodologies.

Table 2.13 Summary of Narrative Synthesis and Overview of Concepts

	Low and Chapman (2003)	Maleki and de Jong (2014)	Nardon and Steers (2009)	Schneider et al. (2014)
Prevalent Concepts				
Distribution of Power	Relationship	Power Distance	Power Distance	Relationship with People
Relationship with the Environment	–	Mastery vs. Harmony	Mastery vs. Harmony	Relationship with the Environment

(continued)

Table 2.13 (continued)

	Low and Chapman (2003)	Maleki and de Jong (2014)	Nardon and Steers (2009)	Schneider et al. (2014)
Social Organization	Relationship	Individualism vs. Collectivism	Individualism vs. Collectivism	Relationship with People
Time	Temporal	–	Time Orientation	Time
Uncertainty Avoidance	Confidence	Uncertainty Avoidance	Universalism vs. Particularism	*Relationship with Environment*
Human Orientation	–	Assertiveness	–	Human Nature; Nature of Human Activity
Additional synthesis concepts				
Communication	Communication	–	–	Language
Indulgence vs. Restraint	–	Indulgence vs. Restraint	–	–
Nature of Truth and reality	Nature of Truth and Reality	–	–	–
Traditionalism vs. Secularism	–	Traditionalism vs. Secularism	–	–
Gender Egalitarianism	–	Gender Egalitarianism	–	–
Space, Language	–	–	–	Space, Language

Note. The information by Schneider et al. (2014) for the concept of uncertainty avoidance is displayed in italics since the conceptual interrelationship to the proposed synthesis dimension for the concept of uncertainty avoidance is not as straightforward as for the other three synthesis methodologies.

2.2 Assumptions

The eight assumptions (A1–A8) were derived from the data synthesis of the four synthesis methodologies of Low and Chapman (2003), Nardon and Steers (2009), Maleki and de Jong (2014), and Schneider et al. (2014). A summary overview of the eight assumptions is displayed in Table 2.14.

Assumption 1 (A1): The concept of distribution of power is applicable as one main factor for the distinction of national cultures among existing cultural taxonomies. The concept of distribution of power is represented as a cultural dimension in most cultural taxonomies and, therefore, constitutes one UDC in this dissertation.

The data synthesis of the four methodologies revealed that the concept of distribution of power is running as a significant concept through cultural taxonomies. It is projected that a UDC Distribution of Power would encompass the following cultural components: the structure of power relationships, addressing vertical versus horizontal power relationships, and hierarchical versus egalitarian power relationships in national cultures. The cultural component of structure of power relationships was also proposed as a cultural component for the concept of distribution of power by Nardon and Steers (2009) and Maleki and de Jong (2014). Furthermore, the cultural component of allocation of status and reward is proposed to constitute a cultural component of the concept of distribution of power. This assumption was derived from Nardon and Steers (2009) and Low and Chapman (2003). The inclusion of the cultural component of allocation of status and reward into the assumed UDC Distribution of Power requires amending the title of this UDC from *Distribution of Power* to *Distribution of Power and Status*. As a result, A1 proposes the UDC Distribution of Power and Status.

A critical analysis is required for the cultural component of gender egalitarianism. Nardon and Steers (2009) synthesized the cultural component of gender egalitarianism into the same synthesis dimension as the cultural components of structure of power relationships and allocation of status and reward, which was not carried out by any other identified synthesis methodology. Nardon and Steers (2009) proposed that the cultural dimension Gender Egalitarianism by House et al. (2004) reflects the degree to which gender differences are minimized within a national culture.

Table 2.14 Overview of the Eight Assumptions, Details, and Characteristic Features

	Concept	Underlying Concepts / Details	Characteristic Features / Assumptions
A1	**Distribution of Power and Status**	Structure of power relationships, as well as allocation of status and reward	– Inclusion of the concept of gender egalitarianism; – Delimitation to the concept of individualism versus collectivism (A1 vs. A3)

(continued)

Table 2.14 (continued)

	Concept	Underlying Concepts / Details	Characteristic Features / Assumptions
A2	**Relationship with the Environment** (Mastery versus Harmony)	Relationship of individuals with their natural environment, expressed in their desire to either control or to live in harmony with their natural environment	– Inclusion of the cultural component of masculinity versus femininity; – Delimitation to the cultural component of performance orientation; – Delimitation to the concepts of social organization (A2 vs. A3), uncertainty avoidance (A2 vs. A5), human orientation (A2 vs. A6); – Inclusion of the cultural components of assertiveness and gender egalitarianism
A3	**Social Organization** (Individualism versus Collectivism)	Structure of social relationships, regarding the concept of individualism versus collectivism	– Inclusion of the cultural components of diffuse versus specific, universalism versus particularism, context, space, and time; – Delimitation to the concept of distribution of power and status (A1 vs. A3); – Delimitation to the cultural component of ascription versus achievement
A4	**Perception and Use of Time**	Perception (incl. view of) and use of time	– Inclusion of the cultural components of planning ahead (future orientation), number of handled tasks at a time, and time horizon – Delimitation to the concept of traditionalism (past orientation; incl. self-stability, feelings of pride, consistency between expressed versus felt emotions, and religiosity; A4 vs. A8)

(continued)

Table 2.14 (continued)

	Concept	Underlying Concepts / Details	Characteristic Features / Assumptions
A5	**Uncertainty Avoidance**	Coping and dealing with uncertainties and unknown situations	– Inclusion of the cultural components of future orientation, rule and regulation obedience, and innovation orientation as sub-component of performance orientation; – Delimitation to the concept of relationship with the environment (A5 vs. A2); – Delimitation to the concept of confidence level with the sub-components of masculinity versus femininity and power distance
A6	**Human Orientation**	Concepts of human orientation and assertiveness versus tenderness	– Delimitation to the concept of masculinity versus femininity; – Analysis of interference with the concept of communication (style)
A7	**Indulgence versus Restraint**	Extent of gratification of desires and feelings; extent of expression of emotions	–
A8	**Traditionalism versus Secularism**	Feelings of pride, flexibility, consistency between expressed and felt emotions, secular orientation, religiosity, self-stability	– Delimitation to the concept of perception and use of time, particularly in regards to past time orientation (A8 vs. A4)

Maleki and de Jong (2014) proposed that the two concepts of distribution of power and status and individualism versus collectivism should be considered distinct from each other. In contrast, Low and Chapman (2003) conceived no delimitation between the two concepts and synthesized both in one synthesis dimension. In this dissertation, a clear delimitation between the concept of distribution of power and the concept of individualism versus collectivism is proposed per A1 and A3. Both assumptions lead to two distinct UDCs

Assumption 2 (A2): The concept of relationship with the environment is applicable as one universal cultural dimension for distinguishing national cultures in existing cultural taxonomies. The concept of relationship with the environment, referring more precisely to the concept of mastery versus harmony, is represented as a cultural dimension in most cultural taxonomies and constitutes a distinct UDC in this dissertation.
The four synthesis methodologies revealed that the concept of relationship with the environment constitutes a significant concept in existing cultural taxonomies to distinguish national cultures. The concept of relationship with the environment refers specifically to the concept of mastery versus harmony. In this dissertation, a distinction of the two concepts of environment—the social and natural—is assumed, in line with Maleki and de Jong (2014) and Schneider et al. (2014). In contrast, considering the social and natural environment as two distinct concepts is against Nardon and Steers (2009), which perceived the relationship of individuals with the social and natural environment as one unified concept. The relationship of individuals with their social environment is projected in this dissertation as a distinct UDC by A3—the UDC Social Organization. A further delimitation in this context is projected for the concept of uncertainty avoidance and the concept of relationship with the environment (A2 versus A5). Both concepts are projected to constitute two separate UDCs in this dissertation. Schneider et al. (2014) projected a connection between the two concepts, whereas, in this dissertation, a delimitation of the two concepts is assumed.

The following cultural components were reviewed based on the information provided by the four synthesis methodologies for their suitability as cultural components for the A2 projected UDC Relationship with the Environment: Firstly, the two cultural components of performance orientation and human orientation were considered regarding their suitability as cultural components for the UDC.

The inclusion of the two cultural components of performance orientation and human orientation in a synthesis dimension regarding the relationship with the environment was projected by Nardon and Steers (2009). Whereas, in this dissertation, it is assumed that the two cultural components of performance orientation and human orientation do not constitute cultural components of the concept of relationship with the environment. The cultural component of performance orientation is projected to constitute a cultural component of the UDC Social Organization (A3), and the cultural component of human orientation was projected to refer to an individual UDC (A6).

Secondly, the following additional cultural components were considered regarding their suitability as cultural components for the UDC Relationship with the Environment: assertiveness, gender egalitarianism, and masculinity versus femininity. All three cultural components were projected to constitute cultural components of the concept of relationship with the environment by Maleki and de Jong (2014) and Nardon and Steers (2009). In this dissertation, the cultural component of assertiveness was projected to be addressed by A6 projected UDC Human Orientation. The cultural component of gender egalitarianism was projected to be included in the UDC Distribution of Power and Status (A1). Finally, the cultural component of masculinity versus femininity was also considered regarding its suitability as a cultural component of the UDC Relationship with the Environment. Thus, it was projected to constitute a cultural component of the UDC Relationship with the Environment in this dissertation.

Assumption 3 (A3): The concept of social organization is applicable as one universal cultural dimension for distinguishing national cultures in existing cultural taxonomies. The concept of social organization, referring to individualism versus collectivism, is represented as a cultural dimension in most existing cultural taxonomies, constituting one distinct UDC of this dissertation.
The data synthesis of the four synthesis methodologies revealed that the concept of social organization is a significant concept for the distinction of national cultures, and more specifically, distinguishing national cultures by the concept of individualism versus collectivism. Particularly, the projected synthesis of the two cultural dimensions of Institutional Collectivism and In-Group Collectivism by House et al. (2004, 2007, 2014) into one synthesis dimension regarding the concept of social organization was considered critically.

The approach of this dissertation does not follow Maleki and de Jong (2014), who synthesized each cultural dimension of House et al. (2004, 2007, 2014) into a distinct synthesis dimension. The main critical path in the projection of the UDC Social Organization distinguishes it from the A1 projected UDC Distribution of Power and Status. A1 and A3 separately refer to the concepts of individualism versus collectivism and the distribution of power and status. The four synthesis methodologies all differ considerably in their handling of the two concepts. Low and Chapman (2003) and Schneider et al. (2014) synthesized both concepts into one synthesis dimension, whereas Nardon and Steers (2009) and Maleki and de Jong (2014) proposed two distinct synthesis dimensions for the two concepts.

Moreover, each of the four synthesis methodologies proposed different cultural components for their synthesis dimensions for the concepts of social organization and individualism versus collectivism. Firstly, Maleki and de Jong (2014) projected the cultural components of universalism versus collectivism and diffuse versus specific. They assume that individuals' relationships are not restricted to a specific level in diffuse national cultures, and in collectivistic cultures, relationships and loyalty to the in-group are highly important. In this dissertation, both cultural components—diffuse versus specific and universalism versus particularism—are also projected to constitute cultural components of the UDC Social Organization.

Secondly, Maleki and de Jong (2014) and Low and Chapman (2003) projected the cultural component of ascription versus achievement as a cultural component for a synthesis dimension regarding the concept of social organization and the concept of individualism versus collectivism. This dissertation does not follow this approach, and the concept of ascription versus achievement was assumed as one main cultural component for the UDC Distribution of Power and Status by A1.

Finally, a crucial role is projected for the set of cultural dimensions by Hall (1959, 1966, 1976, 1983; Hall & Hall, 1990) since two of the four synthesis methodologies proposed the cultural dimensions Context, Space, and Time by Hall (1959, 1966, 1976, 1983; Hall & Hall, 1990) as cultural components of a synthesis dimension regarding the concept of individualism versus collectivism. Maleki and de Jong (2014) and Nardon and Steers (2009) synthesized the cultural dimension Context by Hall (1976) into their synthesis dimension for the concept of individualism versus collectivism.

Furthermore, Maleki and de Jong (2014) also synthesized the cultural dimensions of Space and Time by Hall (1959, 1966, 1976, 1983; Hall & Hall, 1990) into their synthesis dimension for the concept of individualism versus collectivism, likewise, as the cultural dimension Sequential versus Synchronous Time by Trompenaars and Hampden-Turner (1997). This dissertation follows this approach, and it is projected that the UDC Social Organization includes the cultural dimensions Context, Space, and Time by Hall (1959, 1966, 1976, 1983; Hall & Hall, 1990).

Assumption 4 (A4): The concept of time is applicable as one main factor for distinguishing national cultures in existing cultural taxonomies. The concept of time is represented as a cultural dimension in most cultural taxonomies and, therefore, constitutes one UDC in this dissertation.

The concept of time was applicable in the four synthesis methodologies as one prevalent concept in existing cultural taxonomies for distinguishing national cultures.

Low and Chapman (2003), Nardon and Steers (2009), and Schneider et al. (2014) demonstrated distinct synthesis dimensions for the concept of time, whereas Maleki and de Jong (2014) integrated the concept of time into other synthesis dimensions.

Overall in the four methodologies identified by the SLR, the concept of time was either embedded in a three-fold framework of language, space, and time (e.g., by Schneider et al. (2014)), interpreted as humans' perception and use of time (e.g., deadlines and working hours), or in terms of the number of handled tasks at a time (e.g., by Low and Chapman (2003)). Maleki and de Jong (2014) connected the concept of time with the cultural components of self-stability, feelings of pride, and consistency between expressed and felt emotions, thus, as a sub-component of the concept of past-time orientation as well as connected the concept of time to the concept of uncertainty avoidance referring to the future orientation of individuals.

The UDC Perception and Use of Time was deducted from the information given by the four synthesis methodologies and is projected to refer to the following five cultural components. Firstly, the cultural component of perception of time which relates to the perception of the flow of time as a distinguishing factor for national cultures. This cultural component also addresses the differences of national culture in their time spent working for the same company. The cultural component of perception of time was also identified as a cultural component of a time-related synthesis dimension by Nardon and Steers (2009) and Low and Chapman (2003).

Secondly, the cultural component of the use of time in terms of handling time was also identified as one prevailing cultural component among time-related cultural dimensions. Likewise, Nardon and Steers (2009) and Low and Chapman (2003) considered the concept of the use of time as one dominant cultural component for time-related cultural dimensions among cultural taxonomies.

Thirdly, Low and Chapman (2003), Nardon and Steers (2009), and Schneider et al. (2014) addressed the number of handled tasks at a time as a dominant cultural component for time-related cultural dimensions in existing cultural taxonomies. All three synthesis methodologies seized on the cultural taxonomy of Hall (1959, 1966, 1976, 1983; Hall & Hall, 1990) as a reference for the classification of national cultures by their number of handled tasks.

Fourth, a prevalent cultural component constitutes the time horizon, addressing the planning horizon of national cultures in terms of a short-term versus long-term horizon. The cultural component of the time horizon is assumed to be considerably linked to the cultural component of planning ahead, addressing the future orientation of national cultures. Finally, therefore, the cultural component of planning ahead is projected to constitute a cultural component for a time-related synthesis dimension. This approach differs from Maleki and de Jong (2014), who proposes the cultural component of planning ahead as a component for their synthesis dimension Uncertainty Avoidance. The researchers assumed the cultural component planning ahead as an indicator for the extent of uncertainty avoidance in national culture. Also, Maleki and de Jong (2014) projected that the cultural component of past-time orientation would rather be suitable as a cultural component for a synthesis dimension for the concept of traditionalism versus secularism.

A8 proposes the UDC Traditionalism versus Secularism to address the concept of traditionalism versus secularism, including the cultural components of self-stability, feelings of pride, and the consistency between expressed and felt emotions. Therefore, a critical analysis of the delimitation or relationship of the concept of traditionalism versus secularism and the concept of perception and use of time is pursued in the synthesis analyses of the UDC Perception and Use of Time and the UDC Traditionalism versus Secularism.

Assumption 5 (A5): The concept of uncertainty avoidance, referring to individuals coping and dealing with uncertainties and unknown situations, is applicable as one central concept in distinguishing national cultures among existing cultural taxonomies. The concept of uncertainty avoidance is represented as a cultural dimension in the majority of existing cultural taxonomies, constituting one UDC in this dissertation.

The analysis of the four identified synthesis methodologies revealed that the concept of uncertainty avoidance constitutes a significant concept in existing cultural taxonomies for the distinction of national cultures. In this dissertation, A5 proposes that the UDC Uncertainty Avoidance mainly encompasses cultural dimensions of existing cultural taxonomies that address the classification of national cultures by the concept of coping and dealing with uncertainties and unknown situations.

Additionally, it is assumed that the UDC Uncertainty Avoidance encompasses the cultural component of rule and regulation orientation, distinguishing national cultures following their orientation on relationships versus rules and regulations. Maleki and de Jong (2014) and Nardon and Steers (2009) considered the cultural component of rule and regulation orientation as the main component of their synthesis dimension.

Maleki and de Jong (2014) proposed that the cultural component of future orientation could serve as a prevention and handling mechanism for uncertainties and unknown situations. The cultural component of future orientation is linked to the general concept of time, operationalized previously in A4 as one distinct UDC Perception and Use of Time for this dissertation. The UDC Perception and Use of Time (A4) was projected to encompass a cultural component of planning ahead, inducing the focus on the future as one distinctively prevalent cultural component among existing cultural taxonomies. In this dissertation, an analysis was conducted to display the suitability of the concept of future orientation as a cultural component of the UDC Uncertainty Avoidance as well. Likewise, an analysis was pursued for the cultural component of innovation orientation, relating to the concept of performance orientation. Maleki and de Jong (2014) indicated a conceptual overlap between the cultural component of performance orientation and the concept of uncertainty avoidance since performance orientation could serve as either a prevention mechanism for uncertainties or generation mechanism for certainties or both.

The conceptual overlap between the cultural component of performance orientation and uncertainty avoidance is projected to be present in the UDC Uncertainty Avoidance of this dissertation. As a result, it is projected that the UDC Uncertainty Avoidance would also encompass a cultural component of innovation orientation in terms of performance orientation. Schneider et al. (2014) proposed a conceptual overlap of the concept of relationship with the environment and the concept of uncertainty avoidance. This dissertation projects the two concepts distinct from each other as two distinct UDCs—the UDC Relationship with the Environment (A2) and the UDC Uncertainty Avoidance (A5), rejecting the approach by Schneider et al. (2014). In addition, Nardon and Steers (2009) proposed a conceptual interrelationship between the concept of uncertainty avoidance and the concept of level of confidence, expressed by the extent of masculinity versus femininity within a national culture. This dissertation projected that the UDC Uncertainty Avoidance would not encompass a cultural component of masculinity versus femininity.

Assumption 6 (A6): The concept of human orientation is applicable as one central concept in distinguishing national cultures among existing cultural taxonomies. The concept of human orientation is represented as a cultural dimension in most cultural taxonomies and, therefore, is projected to constitute one UDC in this dissertation.

The analysis of the four synthesis methodologies revealed that the concept of human orientation constitutes one central concept running through cultural taxonomies. Maleki and de Jong (2014) and Schneider et al. (2014) developed three synthesis dimensions, addressing the concept of human orientation—Assertiveness versus Tenderness, Human Nature, and Nature of Human Activity. Based on the data of Maleki and de Jong (2014) and Schneider et al. (2014), it was projected that the UDC Human Orientation would mainly encompass cultural dimensions, addressing, firstly, the cultural concept of human orientation and, secondly, the cultural concept of assertiveness versus tenderness. Following Maleki and de Jong (2014), the UDC Human Orientation would not include the cultural concept of masculinity versus femininity, also inducing a distinction to the cultural concept of mastery versus harmony. Maleki and de Jong (2014) elaborate that the concept of human orientation is applicable in individuals' communication. In this dissertation, the concept of communication was not selected as a distinct UDC concept.

Assumption 7 (A7): The concept of indulgence versus restraint is applicable as one factor for distinguishing national cultures in existing cultural taxonomies. The concept of indulgence versus restraint is represented as a cultural dimension in existing cultural taxonomies and, therefore, is projected to constitute one UDC in this dissertation.
Only Maleki and de Jong (2014) proposed the concept of indulgence versus restraint as a distinct synthesis dimension, providing considerable evidence also to assume a UDC referring to the concept of indulgence versus restraint in this dissertation. A7 projects that the UDC Indulgence versus Restraint encompasses cultural dimensions of existing cultural taxonomies that address the following two cultural components: the extent of gratification of desires and feelings, and the extent of expression of emotions as a distinguishing factor for national cultures.

Assumption 8 (A8): The concept of traditionalism versus secularism is applicable to distinguishing national cultures among existing cultural taxonomies. Therefore, the concept of traditionalism versus secularism is represented as a cultural dimension in existing cultural taxonomies and projected to constitute one UDC in this dissertation.
The concept of traditionalism versus secularism was identified as a synthesis dimension by Maleki and de Jong (2014), including the cultural components of self-stability, feelings of pride, religiosity, consistency between felt and expressed emotions, flexibility, and secular orientation. Additionally, Maleki and de Jong (2014) synthesized the cultural component past-orientation of the cultural dimension of Time by Kluckhohn and Strodtbeck (1961) into their synthesis dimension of Traditionalism versus Secularism. Also, two of the four synthesis methodologies (Nardon and Steers (2009), Low and Chapman (2003)) synthesized the concept of traditionalism versus secularism and the concept of time with particular regards to the past-orientation into one synthesis dimension. Even though the concept of traditionalism versus secularism was only identified as a distinct synthesis dimension by one of the four synthesis methodologies, its existence as a general concept among cultural taxonomies was recognized for this dissertation. The concept of traditionalism versus secularism must constitute a distinct UDC regarding the significant interrelationship between the concept of time and the concept of past orientation. A4 proposed the concept of time as a distinct UDC for this dissertation.

3 Evaluation and Selection of Existing Cultural Taxonomies

In the SLR of this dissertation (please refer to Chapter 2 Current State of Research) the four synthesis methodologies of Low and Chapman (2003), Nardon and Steers (2009), Maleki and de Jong (2014), and Schneider et al. (2014) were identified, synthesizing cultural dimensions from existing cultural taxonomies. None of these four synthesis methodologies demonstrated a structured approach for selecting cultural taxonomies. The four identified synthesis methodologies differ considerably in their applied cultural taxonomies (please see Table 3.1). Some cultural taxonomies (e.g., Hofstede (1980, 2001), Hall (1959, 1966, 1976, 1983; Hall & Hall, 1990)) were applicable in all four synthesis methodologies, and some (e.g., Douglas (1973), Lessem and Neubauer (1994), Schein (1985, 1987)) were only included in one of the four synthesis methodologies. The lack of a structured selection of taxonomies for applying them in synthesizing their cultural dimensions was concerning; therefore, a structured process for selecting cultural taxonomies for the subsequent synthesis of cultural dimensions was implemented in this dissertation. An evaluation and selection framework for analyzing cultural taxonomies was developed, ensuring that the synthesis is pursued on a research base of cultural taxonomies sharing similar characteristics.

Figure 3.1 illustrates the thematic position of Chapter 3 in this dissertation.

Supplementary Information The online version contains supplementary material available at https://doi.org/10.1007/978-3-658-38765-5_3.

S. Kunert, *The Eight Universal Dimensions of Culture from a Synthesis of Cultural Taxonomies*, Gabler Theses, https://doi.org/10.1007/978-3-658-38765-5_3

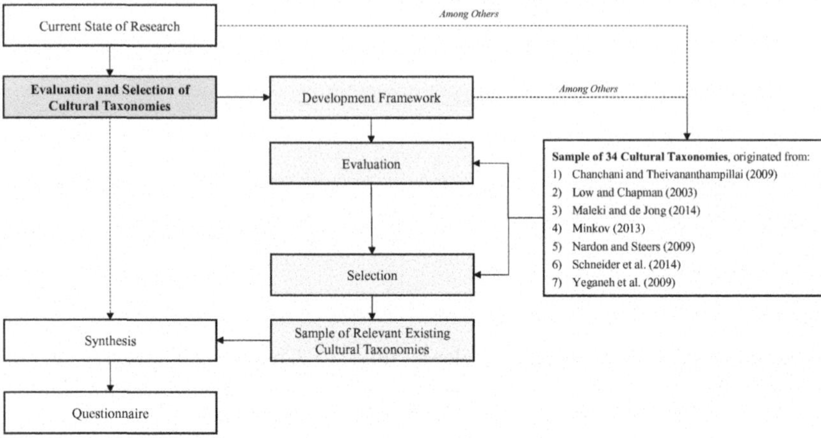

Figure 3.1 Thematic Position of Chapter 3

Table 3.1 Analyzed Cultural Taxonomies by the Four Synthesis Methodologies

	Low and Chapman (2003)	Maleki and de Jong (2014)	Nardon and Steers (2009)	Schneider et al. (2014)
Adler (1981, 1991)				x
DiStefano and Maznevski (2000a, 2000b, 2003)				x
Douglas (1973)		x		
Fukuyama (1995a, 1995b, 1999)	x			
House et al. (2002, 2004)		x	x	x
Hall (1959, 1966, 1976, 1983; Hall & Hall, 1990)	x	x	x	x

(continued)

Table 3.1 (continued)

	Low and Chapman (2003)	Maleki and de Jong (2014)	Nardon and Steers (2009)	Schneider et al. (2014)
Hofstede (1980, 2001, 2006, 2010)	x	x	x	x
Inglehart (2006)		x		
Kluckhohn and Strodtbeck (1961)		x	x	x
Lessem and Neubauer (1994)	x			
Lewis and Finland (1992)	x			
Minkov (2007, 2008, 2013)		x		
Parsons and Shils (1951)		x		
Schein (1985, 1987)				x
Schwartz (1992, 1994b, 1999, 2004, 2006)		x	x	x
Triandis (1989, 1996, 2000, 2001, 2002, 2004)		x		
Trompenaars and Hampden-Turner (1997)	X	x	x	x

3.1 Evaluation of Cultural Taxonomies

The following five sources were consulted for the development of the evaluation and selection framework in this dissertation: Chanchani and Theivananthampillai (2009), Maleki and de Jong (2014), Minkov (2013), Kirkman et al. (2006), and Yeganeh et al. (2009). The five sources were identified in the SLR of this dissertation and selected due to their provided significant criteria[1]. The criteria of

[1] This dissertation does not claim an exhaustible consideration of all current evaluation and selection frameworks for the analysis of existing cultural taxonomies. Rather were the five

the five consulted sources were sorted into two categories—selection and evaluation criteria—to systematically comprehend and conceivable analyze cultural taxonomies. Figure 3.2 displays the selected criteria, their affiliation, and origin.

3.1.1 Introduction to the Selection and Evaluation Criteria

In the following chapter, the depicted selection and evaluation criteria from the five consulted sources of Chanchani and Theivananthampillai (2009), Kirkman et al. (2006), Maleki and de Jong (2014), Minkov (2013), and Yeganeh et al. (2009) are outlined by a brief description and their implications for this dissertation. Some of the criteria were not incorporated into this dissertation's evaluation and selection framework (please see Figure 3.2). Appendix A in the Electronic Supplementary Material outlines information on the causes of the criteria's rejection.

In the first section of the following chapter, the chosen selection criteria—culture as a main distinguishing factor, data collection dates, dichotomy, the discipline of research, the foundation of culture taxonomy, level of analysis, methodology, number of cultural dimensions, number of countries, publication history, respondents (number, class), and response bias-corrected—are illustrated.

Culture as a main distinguishing factor: Kirkman et al. (2006) assessed, among others, if the concept of (national) culture was applied as the primary study object in the cultural taxonomy. The criterion was selected for this dissertation's evaluation and selection framework since the concept of (national) culture also constitutes the primary study object of this dissertation. The criterion ensures that the cultural taxonomies for synthesizing the UDCs in this dissertation homogenously applied the concept of (national) culture as their primary study object.

Data collection dates: The criterion of data collection dates was retrieved from Yeganeh et al. (2009). The criterion reveals information on when the cultural taxonomy was developed or when the empirical data for the cultural taxonomy was collected, presumably also giving insights on potential historical similarities in the development of cultural dimensions in the corresponding cultural taxonomies. Although, most of the theoretical and conceptual-based cultural taxonomies do not specify any data collection dates.

---

sources chosen in regards to their suitability for this dissertation. For further information, please refer to the original reference.

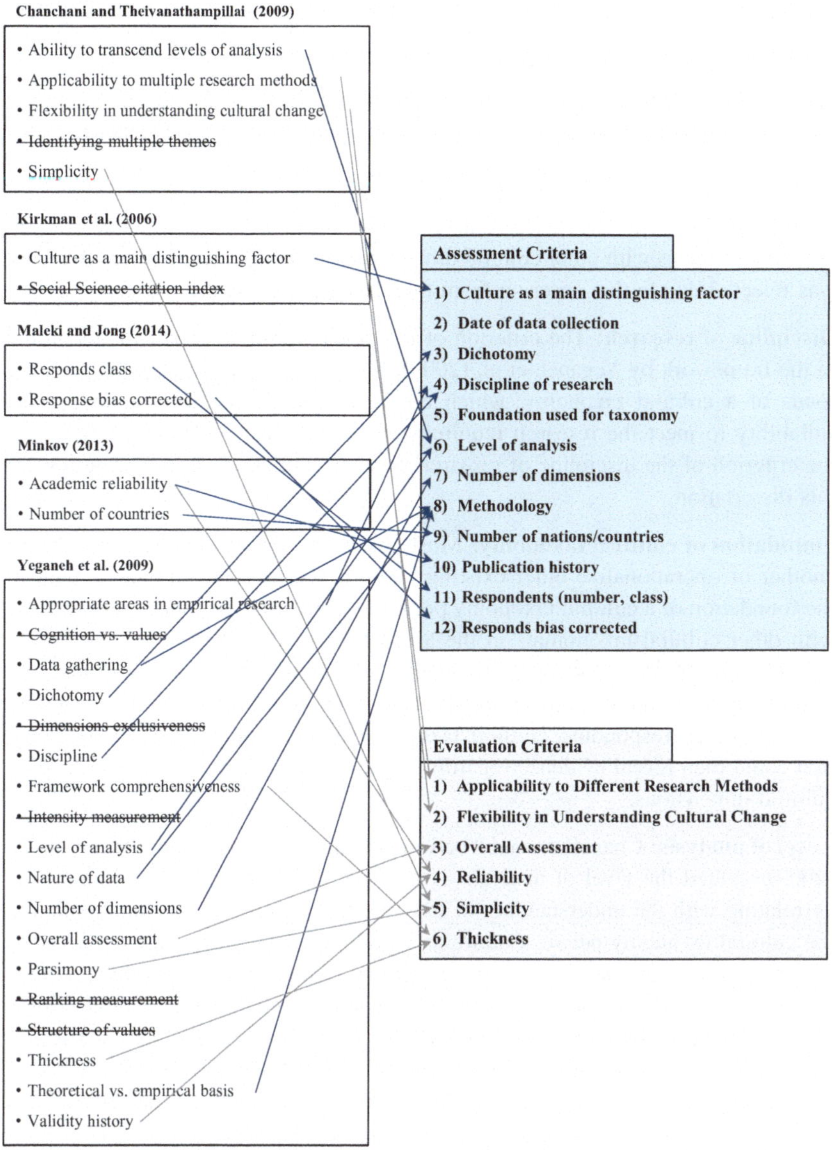

Figure 3.2 Evaluation and Selection Criteria

Dichotomy: The dichotomy of a cultural taxonomy refers to the conceptualization of the cultural dimensions itself and implies "that cultures are static points on dual-axis and one cultural category excluded its opposite" (Yeganeh et al., 2009, p. 4). In contrast, none-dichotomous cultural dimensions are framed in the view of culture as circular, moving from one point to another (Yeganeh et al., 2009).

In this dissertation, the dichotomy of a cultural taxonomy was assessed since the information about the conceptualization of a cultural dimension could point to potential overlaps with other cultural dimensions. Although, no cultural taxonomy was rejected due to this criterion from this dissertation's synthesis.

Discipline of research: The criterion of the discipline of research was identified in the framework by Yeganeh et al. (2009). It reveals information on the research focus of a cultural taxonomy, which could lead to further information on its suitability to meet the research requirements for which it is applied. Therefore, the criterion of the discipline of research was selected as a selection criterion for this dissertation.

Foundation of cultural taxonomy: Most cultural taxonomies either refer to one another or operationalize other existing cultural taxonomies. The assessment of the foundation of a cultural taxonomy point to information on conceptual overlaps with other cultural taxonomies in the area of interest, as Yeganeh et al. (2009) identified. In this dissertation, the foundation of a cultural taxonomy was analyzed to retrieve information on potential other existing cultural taxonomies applied to develop the corresponding cultural taxonomy. It is assumed that this information could then reveal evidence regarding synthesis possibilities of corresponding cultural dimensions.

Level of analysis: Chanchani and Theivananthampillai (2009) and Yeganeh et al. (2009) applied the level of analysis as a selection criterion in their framework, correlating with the understanding of the concept of (national) culture applied in the cultural taxonomy per se. Culture as a multifaceted concept can be described at various levels of analysis—subgroup, group, organization/corporation, as well as local, regional, or national levels (Chanchani & Theivananthampillai, 2009; Yeganeh et al., 2009). The focus was placed on cultural taxonomies that reflect information on a national level. The criterion of level of analysis was applied in this dissertation's evaluation and selection framework to ensure that the cultural dimensions for the synthesis refer to the concept of culture on a similar, thus, national level.

Methodology: Yeganeh et al. (2009) combined multiple criteria for the methodology assessment, describing that cultural taxonomies can be retrieved from empirical data or theoretical assumptions; as well as multiple study items could be applied to assess the concept of (national) culture (e.g., by underlying practices, attitudes, or situational scenarios). In this dissertation, the methodology of an existing cultural taxonomy was assessed to retrieve information on its research base and utilized constructs.

Number of cultural dimensions: Yeganeh et al. (2009) assessed the number of cultural dimensions provided by a cultural taxonomy. This criterion was also included in the evaluation and selection framework for statistical purposes only.

Number of countries: The number of countries was considered a selection criterion by several of the five consulted sources for this dissertation's evaluation and selection framework. Minkov (2013) set the required threshold for the number of countries considered in a cultural taxonomy to a minimum of 20 countries, excluding any cultural taxonomy based on less than 20 countries. Maleki and de Jong (2014) did so as well. In contrast, Kirkman et al. (2006) included monocultural studies in their analysis. This dissertation focuses on existing cultural taxonomies that consider at least two national cultures/countries since the synthesis of this dissertation should result in UDCs suitable to distinguish national cultures from one another.

Publication history: The publication history of each cultural taxonomy was assessed to evaluate the academic reliability of cultural taxonomies. Kirkman et al. (2006) assessed the publication history by the *Social Science Citation Index* offered by the *Web of Science*. Although such citation indices are unsuitable for evaluating a complex cultural taxonomy, they only account for one particular author or publication. Furthermore, citation indices do not offer a cross-search between authors and publications. Therefore, no citation index was applied to evaluate the academic reliability of a cultural taxonomy. Instead, the publication history of the cultural taxonomy (e.g., publishing house) was assessed in this dissertation. The application of this criterion should ensure that the existing cultural taxonomies for synthesizing the UDCs are reliable.

Respondents (number, class, response biases corrected): The class and number of respondents applied in the existing cultural taxonomy, including the correction of response biases[2], were analyzed in this dissertation. This criterion was adopted

---

[2] For further information on the topic of response biases, for example, among others, to Paulhus (1991).

from Maleki and de Jong (2014). The assessment of these criteria enables an in-depth comprehension of the study to develop the respective cultural taxonomies, thus, ensuring a better understanding of the cultural taxonomy per se.

The following section of the chapter describes the evaluation criteria selected from the five consulted sources, including their implications for this dissertation.

Applicability to multiple research methods: The applicability to multiple research methods as an evaluation criterion for cultural taxonomies was suggested by Chanchani and Theivananthampillai (2009). The criterion implies that "the more readily a framework lends itself to adoption and application on a variety of research methods, the more advanced is the classification" (Chanchani & Theivananthampillai, 2009, p. 4). This dissertation evaluated the applicability to multiple research methods on a low, medium, and high scale. In order to evaluate the applicability, the study design (e.g., level of analysis, methodology) of each cultural taxonomy was assessed for its suitability to other than the original applied study design.

The evaluation of a cultural taxonomy with a high level of applicability in this dissertation induces, among others, mainly the following implications: a profound methodology was operationalized, and the methodology of the cultural taxonomy can be applied outside the original study, following the approach by Chanchani and Theivananthampillai (2009). Furthermore, a constant improvement of the study design, proposing consecutive operating modes for the cultural taxonomy, served as an indicator for evaluating the cultural taxonomy in its applicability to multiple research methods. Any deviation from the bevor mentioned implications resulted in a decrease in evaluating the applicability to multiple research methods of a cultural taxonomy in this dissertation.

Flexibility in understanding cultural change: The flexibility in understanding cultural change as a criterion was applicable in Chanchani and Theivananthampillai (2009), requiring a precise understanding of the concept of (national) culture applied in the corresponding analyzed cultural taxonomy. The criterion refers to the ability of a cultural taxonomy to analyze cultural change, leading to explanations, descriptions, and prediction of changes in norms, values, and attitudes. The flexibility of cultural change of a cultural taxonomy is considered an indication of the advancement of a cultural taxonomy (Chanchani & Theivananthampillai, 2009).

In this dissertation, the criterion of flexibility in understanding cultural change of a cultural taxonomy was evaluated as low, medium, or high. A cultural taxonomy was evaluated with high flexibility in understanding cultural change in this dissertation under the following implications: the cultural taxonomy comprehends the concept of (national) culture neither in fixed nor stable terms rather it comprehends (national) cultures as a construct constantly under change.

A high evaluation of a cultural taxonomy in its flexibility in understanding cultural change requires that investigations—empirical- or theoretical-wise—were undertaken to understand the process of change of attitudes, norms, and values of a (national) culture. A deviation from these implications resulted in a lower evaluation of the flexibility in understanding cultural change of a cultural taxonomy in this dissertation. If the cultural taxonomy reveals no information on its understanding in (national) cultures to change over time, its flexibility in understanding cultural change was not assessed in this dissertation.

Reliability (academic): The evaluation criterion of (academic) reliability was detected in the two consulted sources Yeganeh et al. (2009) and Minkov (2013). According to Minkov (2013), a cultural taxonomy should be published in a peer-reviewed journal or published by a renowned international publisher. In this dissertation, the academic reliability of a cultural taxonomy was assessed by the publisher and publication history of the cultural taxonomy. In the case of multiple publishers, an appropriate selection of publishers was reviewed. The academic reliability of a cultural taxonomy was evaluated as given or not given. If a cultural taxonomy's academic reliability was evaluated as given, then it was either published in a peer-reviewed journal or published by an internationally renowned publisher. A deviation from one of those two requirements caused this dissertation's evaluation of "not given."

Simplicity: The simplicity evaluation of this dissertation for a cultural taxonomy was developed based on two evaluation criteria: parsimony by Yeganeh et al. (2009) and simplicity by Chanchani and Theivananthampillai (2009). Yeganeh et al. (2009) stated in their parsimony evaluation of cultural taxonomies that the extent of straightforwardness and simplicity of a cultural taxonomy allows applying the framework of the cultural taxonomy in empirical research.

Following Chanchani and Theivananthampillai (2009), a cultural taxonomy should provide a synthesis of rich and complex constructs into a small number of simple and easily understandable concepts without compromising the analytical rigor and richness of the cultural taxonomy itself. This dissertation's simplicity of an existing cultural taxonomy was evaluated on a low, medium, and high scale. The simplicity of a cultural taxonomy was evaluated as high if the cultural taxonomy demonstrated a balance between parsimoniousness and richness in content.

Furthermore, a high simplicity evaluation of a cultural taxonomy induced an easy comprehension and applicability of the cultural taxonomy without requiring in-depth pre-knowledge, breaking down the complex concept of (national) culture into easily understandable cultural dimensions. Any other implications or lack in the aforementioned implications resulted in a decrease in the evaluation.

Thickness: The thickness of a cultural taxonomy was also evaluated by Yeganeh et al. (2009) and referred to the profoundness and comprehensiveness of understanding the cultural taxonomy's concept of (national) culture. In this dissertation, the thickness of a cultural taxonomy was evaluated on a scale of high, medium, and low under consideration of the following implications (following also Yeganeh et al. (2009)): The thickness of a cultural taxonomy was evaluated as high when the cultural taxonomy displays the utilization of a profound conceptual and empirical analysis as its concept base, providing an overall understanding of the concept of (national) culture and its underlying cultural constructs (e.g., values, attitudes, norms, and behaviors). Also, an evaluation of the thickness as high indicates that the cultural taxonomy provided an individual definition for the concept of (national) culture and corresponding constructs (e.g., attitudes, values, or practices). Any deviation of these implications caused a lower evaluation of the thickness of a cultural taxonomy.

Overall evaluation: In this dissertation, the overall evaluation criterion takes the results of all before demonstrated selection and evaluation criteria into account (please see Figure 3.2), following the approach by Yeganeh et al. (2009). The overall evaluation of a cultural taxonomy was rated on a high, medium, and low scale, constituting the base for selecting or rejecting a cultural taxonomy from synthesizing its cultural dimensions.

This dissertation's evaluation and selection framework is again displayed in an overview in Figure 3.3.

The cultural taxonomies reviewed in this dissertation were gathered from the following sources: Firstly, the four by the SLR identified methodologies considered 16 different cultural taxonomies. Secondly, Minkov (2013) provided an overview of cross-cultural studies in his compendium on cross-cultural research. Finally, two cultural taxonomies were found in the analyzed frameworks of Chanchani and Theivananthampillai (2009) and Yeganeh et al. (2009). In total, a range of 34 cultural taxonomies was compiled and analyzed for and in this dissertation.

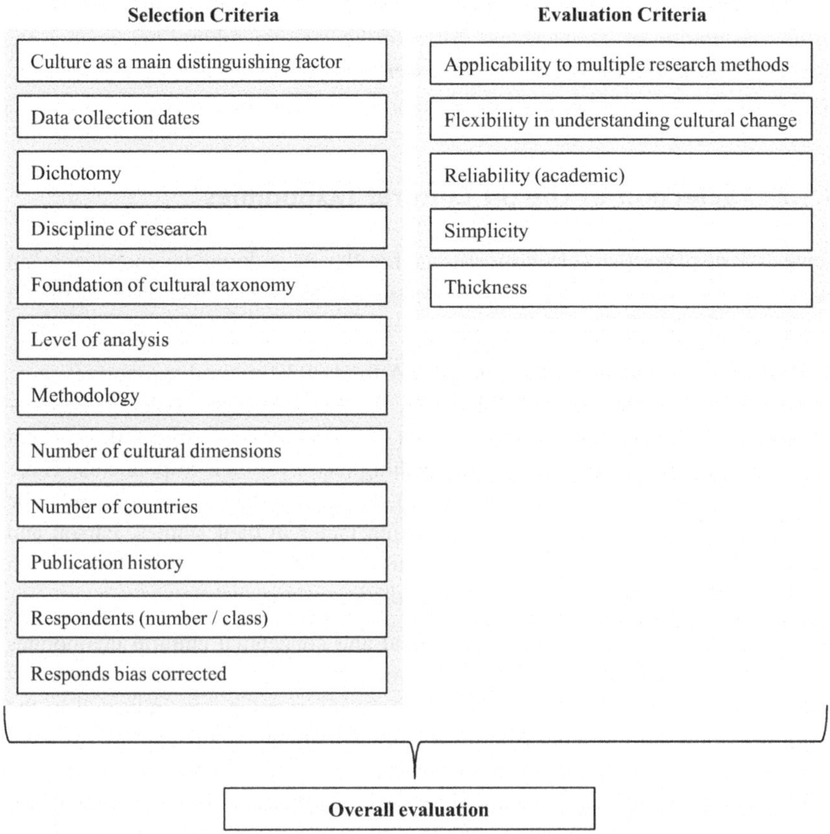

Figure 3.3 Evaluation and Selection Framework

This dissertation does not claim to provide an exhaustive list of all existing cultural taxonomies due to constant developments in Social Sciences. The 34 existing cultural taxonomies are displayed in an overview in Table 3.2. The abbreviations for the sources of origin refer to the following implications: “S” indicates that the cultural taxonomy was identified as one of the four methodologies in the SLR. “M” indicated that the cultural taxonomy was identified in the compendium on cultural studies by Minkov (2013), and “E” indicates that the cultural taxonomy was identified in one of the two evaluation frameworks by Chanchani and Theivananthampillai (2009) or Yeganeh et al. (2009).

The publication dates refer to the primary reference of the cultural taxonomy without aspiration of completeness. Most of the existing cultural taxonomies are linked to multiple publications. In this dissertation, the most current versions were reviewed.

3.1.2 Selection of the 34 Cultural Taxonomies

Table 3.3 displays the selection criteria for the 34 cultural taxonomies in an overview. The author of this dissertation assessed the selection criteria for the 34 cultural taxonomies.

Culture as a main distinguishing factor: A total of 30 cultural taxonomies (e.g., Triandis (1989, 1996, 2000, 2001, 2002, 2004), Trompenaars and Hampden-Turner (2004, 2012)) from the analyzed set of 34 taxonomies utilized the concept of (national) culture as the main distinguishing factor for their respondents. Three cultural taxonomies (e.g., McCrae (2002), Rokeach (1973)) did not apply the concept of culture as the main distinguishing factor in their studies. Parson and Shils (1951) integrated the concept of (national) culture into a three-fold system together with society and individuality as distinguishing factors.

Data collection dates: For some theoretical and conceptual cultural taxonomies (e.g., Alder and Gundersen (2008), Lessem and Neubauer (1994)), no data collection dates were possible to assess since no information was indicated in the cultural taxonomies. It would be an incorrect assumption to refer to the publisher dates of the cultural taxonomy because the dates for the data collection and the dates for publishing do not necessarily correlate. Furthermore, some cultural taxonomies conducted their studies in waves (e.g., GLOBE study by House et al. (2004, 2007, 2014), WVS by Inglehart et al. (2014)), such that their data collection is continuous.

Dichotomy: Most of the analyzed cultural taxonomies (n = 19) revealed no information on whether or not they applied a dichotomic approach for their concept of (national) culture. The majority (n = 9) of the analyzed cultural taxonomies (e.g., House et al. (2004, 2007, 2014)), revealing information on the dichotomy of their concept of (national) culture, do not allow their (national) cultures to move in circular ways. A minority of six cultural taxonomies framed their cultural dimensions in a non-dichotomous way. The most prominent example constitutes the cultural taxonomy by Inglehart et al. (2014) with their WVS,

Table 3.2 The 34 Cultural Taxonomies

Author	Title of Cultural Taxonomy	Sources of Origin		
		E	M	S
Adler and Gundersen[3] (2008)	International Dimensions of Organizational Behavior			x
Chinese Culture Connection (1987)	Confucian Work Dynamism		x	
DiStefano and Maznevski (2000a, 2000b, 2003)	The MBI Model			x
Douglas (1973)	Douglas Grid-Group Theory			x
Fiske (1991, 1992)	The Relational Model Theory	x		
Fukuyama (1995b)	Fukuyama Trust			x
Green et al. (2005)	A Study of Beliefs and Values		x	
Hall (1959, 1966, 1976, 1983; Hall & Hall, 1990)	Halls' Four Cultural Dimensions	x		x
Hofstede (2001; Hofstede et al., 2010)	The 6-D Model of National Culture	x	x	x
House et al. (2004, 2007, 2014)	The GLOBE Study	x	x	x
Inglehart et al. (2014)	The World Value Survey Wave 1—6		x	x
Kluckhohn and Strodtbeck (1961)	The Value Orientation Theory			x
Kuppens et al. (2006)	Positive and Negative Emotions	x		
Lessem and Neubauer (1994)	A European Management System			x
Levine and Norenzayan (1999)	The Pace of Life		x	
Levine et al. (2001)	Cross-Cultural Differences in Helping Strangers		x	

(continued)

[3] An updated version of the work by Adler (1981) was consulted for the evaluation in this dissertation.

Table 3.2 (continued)

Author	Title of Cultural Taxonomy	Sources of Origin		
		E	M	S
Lewis (2018)	When Culture Collide: Leading Across Cultures			x
McCrae (2002)	The Five-Factor Model of Personality		x	
McCrae and Terracciano (2005)	Personality Profile of Cultures		x	
Merritt (2000)	Culture in the Cockpit		x	
Minkov (2007, 2008, 2013)	Minkov's Cultural Dimensions		x	x
Parsons and Shils (1951)	A General Theory of Action			x
Rokeach (1973)	Rokeach Value Survey	x		
Schein and Schein (2016)	Schein's Deeper Cultural Assumptions			x
Schimmack et al. (2002)	Cultural Influence on Emotions		x	
Schmitt (2005)	A study of Sociosexuality		x	
Schmitt et al. (2007)	The Big Five Personality Traits		x	
Schwartz (1992, 1994b, 1999, 2004, 2006)	Schwartz Value Analysis	x	x	x
Smith et al. (1995)	The Rotter Locus of Control		x	
Smith et al. (2002)	Cultural Values and Managerial Behavior		x	
Triandis (1989, 1996, 2000, 2001, 2002, 2004)	Triandis Cultural Syndromes	x		x
Trompenaars and Hampden-Turner (1997)	Trompenaars and Hampden-Tuner's Cultural Dimensions	x		x
Van de Vliert and Janssen (2002)	Performance Motives		x	
Welzel (2010)	Self-Expression Values in the WVS		x	

Note. Each publication can be reviewed in the reference list. The titles of the cultural taxonomies are partly adapted from *Cross-Cultural Analysis: The Science and Art of Comparing the World's Modern Societies and Their Cultures* (pp. 197–397), by M. Minkov, 2013, SAGE Publications, Inc. (ISBN-10: 141299229X).

Table 3.3 Overview of Selection Criteria for the 34 Cultural Taxonomies

	Culture	Date	Dichotomy	Dimensions (N)	Discipline	Foundation	Level of Analysis	Methodology	Countries (n)	Publication History	Respondents	Responds Biases
Adler and Gundersen (2008)	Yes	–	No	6	Organizational Sciences	Kluckhohn and Strodtbeck (1961)	Individual, National	Theory	–	Thomson South-Western	Leaders	–
Chinese Culture Connection (1987)	Yes	1987	–	1	Cultural Study	Hofstede (1980)	National	Empirical, Quantitative (Values)	22	Journal of Cross-Cultural Psychology	Students (220)	Yes
DiStefano and Maznevski (2000a, 2000b,2003)	Yes	–	–	–	Leadership & Management	Kluckhohn and Strodtbeck (1961)	Group, *National*	Theory	–	*e.g., Human Resource Management*	–	–
Douglas (1973)	Yes	–	Yes	2	Anthropology	–	National	Theory	–	*e.g., Psychology Press*	–	–
Fiske (1991,1992)	Yes	–	–	4	Anthropology	–	Individual, Group, National	Ethnographic fieldwork, Experimental Studies	*Africa, 5 cultures*	*e.g., Psychological Review*	–	–
Fukuyama (1995b)	Yes	–	–	1	Political Study	–	National	Theory	–	Free Press Paperback	–	–

(continued)

Table 3.3 (continued)

	Culture	Date	Dichotomy	Dimensions (N)	Discipline	Foundation	Level of Analysis	Methodology	Countries (n)	Publication History	Respondents	Responds Biases
Green et al.(2005)	Yes	2005	Yes	–	Cultural Study	Hofstede (1980)	National	Empirical, Quantitative, (Competitiveness, Interdependence, Self-Reliance)	20	Journal of Cross-Cultural Psychology	Students (2,533)	Yes
Hall (1959,1966, 1976,1983; Hall &Hall, 1990)	Yes	–	No	4	Anthropology	–	National	Observation, Theory	–	Anchor Books	–	–
Hofstede (2001;Hofstede et al.,2010)	Yes	1967–1973	Yes	6	Organizational Sciences	–	National	Empirical, Quantitative (Values)	76	*e.g., Sage Publication Ltd*	IBM workers (171,000)	Yes
House et al.(2004, 2007,2014)	Yes	1995–2013	Yes	9	Cultural Study, Management	e.g., Hofstede (1980)	National, Organisational	Empirical, Quantitative, (Values, Practices)	24–65	Sage Publication Ltd	Managers (6,000–17,370)	Yes
Inglehart et al.(2014)	No	1981–2014	No	2	Cultural Study	–	National	Empirical, Quantitative, (Values)	20–60	Cambridge University Press	All Classes (25,000–96,000)	–

(continued)

Table 3.3 (continued)

	Culture	Date	Dichotomy	Dimensions (N)	Discipline	Foundation	Level of Analysis	Methodology	Countries (n)	Publication History	Respondents	Responds Biases
Kluckhohn and Strodtbeck (1961)	Yes	1951	No	6	Anthropology	Kluckhohn (1949)	National	Theory, Empirical, Qualitative	5[4]	Row Peterson & Co	Residents (approx. 100)	–
Kuppens et al. (2006)	Yes	2001 *(ICS study)*	–	1	Cultural Study	–	Individual, National	Empirical, Quantitative, (Emotions)	48	Journal of Cross-Cultural Psychology	Students (9,300)	Yes
Lessem and Neubauer (1994)	Yes	–	Yes	4	Management	–	Individual, Organisational, National	Theory	*Europe*	–	–	–
Levine and Norenzayan (1999)	Yes	1992–1995	–	–	Cultural Study	Triandis (1995), Hofstede (1980)	National	Empirical, Quantitative (Pace of Life: Walking Speed, Postal Speed, Clock Accuracy)	31	Journal of Cross-Cultural Psychology	*Large cities in each of the 31 countries-*	–

(continued)

[4] Kluckhohn (1951) analyzed in his study five cultural groups of one region in the United States.

Table 3.3 (continued)

	Culture	Date	Dichotomy	Dimensions (N)	Discipline	Foundation	Level of Analysis	Methodology	Countries (n)	Publication History	Respondents	Responds Biases
Levine et al. (2001)	Yes	1992–1997	–	–	Cultural Study	–	National	Empirical, Quantitative (Helping Measures)	23	Journal of Cross-Cultural Psychology	–	–
Lewis (2018)	Yes	–	Yes	3	Management	Hofstede (1980, 1991), Hall (1983), Trompenaars and Hampden-Turner (1993)	National	Theory	84	Nicholas Brealey International	–	–
McCrae (2002)	No	–	–	5	Cultural Study	–	National	Empirical, Quantitative (values)	36	Online Readings in Psychology and Culture	Students, Adults	–
McCrae and Terracciano (2005)	Yes	–	–	–	Cultural Study	–	National	Empirical, quantitative (Values)	51	Journal of Personality and Social Psychology	Students (12,156)	–

(continued)

Table 3.3 (continued)

	Culture	Date	Dichotomy	Dimensions (N)	Discipline	Foundation	Level of Analysis	Methodology	Countries (n)	Publication History	Respondents	Responds Biases
Merritt (2000)	Yes	1993–1997	–	*Replication of Hofstede (1980)*	Cultural Study	Hofstede (1980)	National	Empirical, Quantitative (Values)	19	Journal of Cross-Cultural Psychology	Pilots (9,417)	–
Minkov (2007, 2008, 2013)	Yes	–	Yes	3	Anthropology	e.g., Hofstede (1980)	National	Theory *(Re-Analysis of WVS Wave 4)*	–	*Among others*: Klasika i Stil Publishing House	*WVS 1998–2002*	No
Parsons and Shils (1951)	*Partially*	–	Yes	5	Social Sciences	Weber's and his Four Types of Action	Individual, National	Theory	–	Harvard University Press	–	–
Rokeach (1973)	No	1968	–	18	Psychology	–	Individual	Theory, Empirical, Quantitative (Values)	–	The Free Press	Students	–
Schein and Schein (2016)	Yes	–	–	6	Organizational Science	–	Group, National	Theory	–	Jossey-Bass	Leaders	–
Schimmack et al. (2002)	Yes	–	–	–	Cultural Study	–	National	Empirical, Quantitative (Values)	38	Cognition and Emotions	Students (5,886)	–

(continued)

Table 3.3 (continued)

	Culture	Date	Dichotomy	Dimensions (N)	Discipline	Foundation	Level of Analysis	Methodology	Countries (n)	Publication History	Respondents	Responds Biases
Schmitt (2005)	Yes	2005	–	1	Psychology	–	National	Empirical, Quantitative (Values)	48	Behavioral and Brain Sciences	Students (14,059)	Yes
Schmitt et al. (2007)	Yes	–	–	–	Cultural Study	–	National	Empirical, Quantitative (Values)	56	Journal of Cross-Cultural Psychology	Students (17,408)	–
Schwartz (1992, 1994b, 1999, 2004, 2006)	Yes	*Multiple*	Yes	3	Psychology	e.g., Schwartz and Bilsky (1987, 1990); Kluckhohn (1951), Rokeach (1973), Feather (1995), Allport (1961)	Individual, National	Theory, Empirical, Quantitative (Values)	*Multiple*	*Among Others:* Journal of Cross-Cultural Psychology	*Multiple*	Yes
Smith et al. (1995)	Yes	1983–1993	–	3	Cultural Study	Trompenaars and Hampden-Turner (1997)	National	Theory, Empirical, Quantitative (Values)	43	International Journal of Psychology	Managers, Workers (9,140)	Yes

(continued)

Table 3.3 (continued)

	Culture	Date	Dichotomy	Dimensions (N)	Discipline	Foundation	Level of Analysis	Methodology	Countries (n)	Publication History	Respondents	Responds Biases
Smith et al. (2002)	Yes	–	–	–	Cultural Study	Hofstede (1994), Schwartz (1999), Trompenaars and Hampden-Turner (1997)	National	Empirical, Quantitative (Values)	61	Journal of Cross-Cultural Psychology	Managers (Ø 103 / nation)	–
Triandis (1989, 1996, 2000, 2001, 2002, 2004)	Yes	–	No	10	Psychology	–	National	Theory, Qualitative (Attitudes)	–	Mc-Graw-hill Higher Education	–	–
Trompenaars and Hampden-Turner (1997)	Yes	–	No	7	Organizational Sciences	e.g., Hofstede (1980), Kluckhohn and Strodtbeck (1961), Parsons and Shils (1951)	National, Organizational	Theory, Quantitative, Attitudes (Situations, Values)	43	*Among others:* Nicholas Brealey International	Managers (8,841)	–

(continued)

Table 3.3 (continued)

	Culture	Date	Dichotomy	Dimensions (N)	Discipline	Foundation	Level of Analysis	Methodology	Countries (n)	Publication History	Respondents	Responds Biases
Fiske (199	Yes	–	–	4	Anthropology	–	Individual, Group, National	Ethnographic fieldwork, Experimental Studies	*Africa, 5 cultures*	*e.g., Psychological Review*	–	–
Van de Vliert and Janssen (2002)	Yes	1986–1989	–	–	Cultural Studies	–	National	Empirical, Quantitative (performance, motives, satisfaction)	42	Journal of Cross-Cultural Psychology	Students (240 / nation)	–
Welzel (2010)	Yes	2005–2007	–	–	Cultural Studies	Schwartz Value, WVS (Waves 1981–1984, 1990–1993)	National	Empirical, Quantitative (values)	52	Journal of Cross-Cultural Psychology	Managers (56,000)	–

in which the researchers monitored the movement of national cultures from one side of a dimension to the other.

Discipline of research: The 34 analyzed cultural taxonomies originate from the fields of psychology, anthropology, organizational sciences, and general management.

Foundation of cultural taxonomy: As applicable in Table 3.3, some of the 34 cultural taxonomies include or seize on other cultural existing taxonomies (e.g., Adler and Gundersen (2008), Chinese Culture Connection (1987), Green et al. (2005)). The prominence of the cultural taxonomies of Hofstede (1980), Kluckhohn and Strodtbeck (1961), Parsons and Shils (1951), and Rokeach (1973) was recognizable in multiple of the 34 cultural taxonomies.

Also, other cultural taxonomies were included multiple times in other cultural taxonomies (e.g., Triandis (1989, 1996, 2000, 2001, 2002, 2004), and Trompenaars and Hampden-Turner (2004, 2012)).

Level of analysis: A majority of the 34 analyzed cultural taxonomies (n = 24; e.g., Schimmack et al. (2002), Lewis (2018)) conducted their analyses on national levels. Some other of the 34 analyzed cultural taxonomies performed analyses on the national level along with analyses on an organizational level (n = 2; e.g., House et al. (2004, 2007, 2014)) or an individual level (n = 4; e.g., Kuppens et al. (2006)). The other cultural taxonomies from the analyzed sample performed their analysis on mixed levels of analysis (e.g., individual, organizational, and national).

Methodology: In total, from the 34 analyzed cultural taxonomies, 17 cultural taxonomies were developed from empirical studies (e.g., Merritt (2000)). Another 12 cultural taxonomies were developed from theoretical analyses and assumptions. For example, the cultural taxonomy by Fiske (1991, 1992) is only devised from field observations in Burkina Faso, Africa. Likewise, Hall (1959, 1966, 1976, 1983; Hall & Hall, 1990) derived his cultural taxonomy from theoretical analyses and observations. Four of the 34 analyzed cultural taxonomies mixed theoretical assumptions with empirical analyses. For example, Minkov (2007) performed empirical analyses of the WVS dataset provided by Inglehart et al. (2014). Rokeach (1973) defined her value system by theoretical assumptions and later validated her value system by empirical analyses. Schwartz (2012) began with a theoretical-based cultural classification and later conducted empirical studies to prove his assumptions (*Schwartz Value Survey*).

In analyzing the 34 cultural taxonomies, it became apparent that these varied considerably in their applied measurement instruments. The theory-based cultural taxonomies (e.g., Adler and Gundersen (2008), Douglas (1973), Fukuyama (1995b)) did not apply any empirical measurement instruments. Moreover, 21 of the 34 analyzed cultural taxonomies are based on quantitative analyses (e.g., Welzel (2010)). One cultural taxonomy—Triandis (1989, 1996, 2000, 2001, 2002, 2004)—applied only qualitative measurements for its analyses. Two cultural taxonomies from the sample (Green et al. (2005), Kluckhohn and Strodtbeck (1961)) applied qualitative and quantitative measurements.

The 34 analyzed cultural taxonomies also differ in their utilized data set. Fourteen cultural taxonomies (e.g., Chinese Culture Connection (1987), House et al. (2004, 2007, 2014), Schimmack et al. (2002), Schwartz (2012)) applied values as the study object. Two of the 34 analyzed cultural taxonomies—Triandis (1989, 1996, 2000, 2001, 2002, 2004), Trompenaars and Hampden-Turner (2004, 2012)—utilized attitudes as the study object. The remaining analyzed cultural taxonomies applied various study objects. For example, House et al. (2004, 2007, 2014) analyzed the values and practices of individuals in their GLOBE study. Levine et al. (2001) focused on individuals' behavior as the study object.

Number of cultural dimensions: Not all 34 cultural taxonomies developed individual cultural dimensions (e.g., Van de Vliert and Janssen (2002)). In the analyzed sample, the most cultural dimensions were provided by Rokeach (1973) with two times 18 value dimensions (18 instrumental and 18 terminal value dimensions). In contrast, some cultural taxonomies only replicated cultural dimension sets of other cultural taxonomies (e.g., Merritt (2000)). Besides this, the other analyzed cultural taxonomies developed a set between zero to ten individual cultural dimensions (e.g., Hofstede (2001; Hofstede et al., 2010)).

Number of countries: Most of the theory-based cultural taxonomies from the analyzed sample (e.g., Schein and Schein (2016), Triandis (1989, 1996, 2000, 2001, 2002, 2004)) indicated no further information on their exact numbers of considered nations. Among the 34 analyzed cultural taxonomies, two cultural taxonomies considered one country by several cultural groups or one regional area by several cultural groups. Firstly, Fiske (1991, 1992) deduced his four fundamental cultural dimensions from field observations in Burkina Faso, Africa. Secondly, Lessem and Neubauer (1994) deduced their cultural taxonomies solely from theoretical observations in Europe. Lewis (2018) studied most countries (n = 84) in comparison to the other 33 analyzed cultural taxonomies.

Publication history: The 34 cultural taxonomies display a diverse publication history. Ten of these were published in the Journal of Cross-Cultural Psychology. Most theory-based cultural taxonomies were published as books (e.g., Hall (1959, 1966, 1976, 1983; Hall & Hall, 1990)). Overall, none of the cultural taxonomies were published as grey literature, and thereby, all 34 were assessed as academically reliable.

Respondents (number, class, response biases corrected): In the set of the 34 analyzed cultural taxonomies, Hofstede (2001; Hofstede et al., 2010) studied the most respondents with 171,000 study participants in total. The smallest sample was studied by Chinese Culture Connection (1987), which included 220 respondents. The most precise selection of respondents was undertaken by Merritt (2000), who interviewed approximately 9,500 pilots. Another distinct classification for respondents was done by Hofstede (2001; Hofstede et al., 2010). In the original version, Hofstede (1980) studied respondents belonging to one specific organization—the company IBM. Among the sample of the 34, the primary analyzed class of respondents constitute students, either at school or university level. Nine of the 34 analyzed cultural taxonomies utilized students as their class of respondents. Moreover, five of the 34 (e.g., Trompenaars and Hampden-Turner (2004, 2012), Schein and Schein (2016)) studied leaders or managers with a higher executive level.

Among the 34 taxonomies, not many cultural taxonomies revealed information on correcting response biases in their study. In total, eight of the 34 analyzed cultural taxonomies indicated that they corrected potential response biases for their implication (e.g., Schwartz (2012), Smith et al. (2002)). These eight existing cultural taxonomies did not specify their applied statistical tool for the correction of response biases.

3.1.3 Evaluation of the 34 Cultural Taxonomies

The five chosen evaluation criteria—applicability to multiple research methods, flexibility in understanding cultural change, (academic) reliability, simplicity, and thickness—were collected from Chanchani and Theivananthampillai (2009), Maleki and de Jong (2014), Minkov (2013), Kirkman et al. (2006), and Yeganeh et al. (2009). Following the five selected evaluation criteria, the author of this dissertation pursued evaluating the cultural taxonomies.

Table 3.4 displays the evaluation criteria for the 34 analyzed cultural taxonomies for this dissertation; also, briefly described in the following section of the chapter to stress out the research base for this dissertation's synthesis of cultural dimensions from cultural taxonomies for the eight UDCs.

Applicability to multiple research methods: In summary, seven of the 34 cultural taxonomies were evaluated as medium, four with high, and 23 with low applicability to multiple research methods. For example, the cultural taxonomy by Fiske (1991, 1992) was evaluated as medium applicability to multiple research methods due to its emic and epic study design. In contrast, the taxonomy framework by Hofstede (2001) and later Hofstede et al. (2010) provides only limitedly the opportunity to apply the framework other than the initially intended way. Therefore, the applicability to multiple research methods of the cultural taxonomy by Hofstede (2001; Hofstede et al., 2010) was evaluated as low in this dissertation. The cultural taxonomy by House et al. (2004, 2007, 2014) was evaluated as high in its applicability to different research methods due to its open-source accessible database.

Flexibility in understanding cultural change: Overall, seven cultural taxonomies were rated with a low, three with a medium, and only two with high flexibility in understanding cultural change. Also, the flexibility in understanding cultural change for two analyzed cultural taxonomies was rated between medium and high. For example, the cultural taxonomy by Trompenaars and Hampden-Turner (1997) lacks detailed information on the understanding of cultural change (Chanchani & Theivananthampillai, 2009). In comparison, the cultural taxonomies by Fiske (1991, 1992) as well as by Hofstede (2001; Hofstede et al., 2010) allow (national) cultures to move from one side of a cultural dimension to another. The cultural taxonomy by Schein and Schein (2016) was evaluated with a "medium to high" in its flexibility in understanding cultural change since the cultural taxonomy addressed only the concept of organizational cultural change.

Reliability: The academic reliability of each of the 34 analyzed cultural taxonomies was evaluated by their publication history, seizing on the corresponding original references of the taxonomy. The 34 analyzed cultural taxonomies displayed a broad and diverse publication history. Among others, ten cultural taxonomies were published in the *Journal of Cross-Cultural Psychology*. Most theory-based cultural taxonomies were published as books (e.g., Hall (1959, 1966, 1976, 1983; Hall & Hall, 1990)). Overall, the academic reliability was evaluated as given for each of the 34 cultural taxonomies.

Simplicity: In the overall picture, the cultural taxonomies by Hofstede (2001), Inglehart et al. (2014), and Lewis (2018) constitute in comparison to the other 34 analyzed cultural taxonomies, the most advanced cultural taxonomies, since

Table 3.4 Overview of Evaluation Criteria for the 34 Cultural Taxonomies

	Multiple Research	Flexibility Cultural Change	Reliability	Simplicity	Thickness	**Overall Evaluation** *(Explanation)*
Adler and Gundersen(2008)	Low	–	Given	Medium	Low to Medium	**Low** *(only reflection of Kluckhohn and Strodtbeck (1961))*
Chinese Culture Connection (1987)	Low	–	Given	Medium	Low	**Low** *(no distinctive conception of culture and cultural dimensions)*
DiStefano and Maznevski (2000a, 2000b, 2003)	Low	–	Given	Low	Low	**Low** *(no profound cultural compendium)*
Douglas (1973)	Low	Low	Given	Low	Low to Medium	**Low** *(no profound cultural compendium)*
Fiske (1991, 1992)	Medium	Medium	Given	Low	Medium	**Medium** *(narrow empirical testing of taxonomy)*
Fukuyama (1995b)	Low	Low	Given	Low	Low	**Low** *(focus on trust as a distinctive cultural dimension; no profound compendium for the concept of (national) culture)*
Green et al. (2005)	Low	–	Given	Low	Low	**Low** *(only one cultural dimension; no profound framework)*
Hall (1959, 1966, 1976, 1983; Hall & Hall, 1990)	Medium	Low	Given	Medium	Medium to High	**Medium to High** *(no empirical testing of taxonomy)*
Hofstede (2001; Hofstede et al., 2010)	Low	Medium	Given	High	Medium to High	**High** *(profound cultural framework)*
House et al. (2004, 2007, 2014)	Low	–	Given	Medium to High	Medium to High	**Medium to High** *(profound cultural framework)*

(continued)

Table 3.4 (continued)

	Multiple Research	Flexibility Cultural Change	Reliability	Simplicity	Thickness	**Overall Evaluation** *(Explanation)*
Inglehart et al. (2014)	High	High	Given	High	(*Low*) to Medium	**Medium to High** *(profound cultural framework)*
Kluckhohn and Strodtbeck (1961)	High	Medium to High	Given	Medium to High	Medium *to High*	**Medium to High** *(profound cultural framework)*
Kuppens et al. (2006)	Low	–	Given	Low	Low	**Low** *(no comprehensive framework; no cultural dimensions)*
Lessem and Neubauer (1994)	Low	Low	Given	Low	Low to Medium	**Low** *(only theoretical; strong focus on organizational research)*
Levine and Norenzayan (1999)	Low	–	Given	Low	Low	**Low** *(no comprehensive framework; no cultural dimensions)*
Levine et al. (2001)	Low	–	Given	Low	Low	**Low** *(no comprehensive framework; no cultural dimensions)*
Lewis (2018)	Medium	Low	Given	High	Medium to High	**Medium to High** *(no empirical work)*
McCrae (2002)	Low	–	Given	Low	Low	**Low** *(no comprehensive framework; no cultural dimensions)*
McCrae and Terracciano (2005)	Medium	–	Given	Low	Low	**Low** *(no comprehensive framework; no cultural dimensions)*
Merritt (2000)	Low	–	Given	Low	Low	**Low** *(research focus on specific profession type—pilots)*

(continued)

Table 3.4 (continued)

	Multiple Research	Flexibility Cultural Change	Reliability	Simplicity	Thickness	**Overall Evaluation** *(Explanation)*
Minkov (2007, 2008, 2013)	Medium	–	Given	Medium to High	Medium	**Medium to High** *(re-analysis of WVS)*
Parsons and Shils (1951)	Medium	–	Given	Medium	Medium	**Medium** *(no empirical tests; no qualitative instruments)*
Rokeach (1973)	High	High	Given	Medium	Low	**Medium to High** *(comprehensive work on values)*
Schein and Schein (2016)	Low	Medium to High	Given	Medium	Low	**Low to Medium** *(no empirical tests, only replication of Kluckhohn and Strodtbeck (1961))*
Low	Low	–	Given	Low	Low	**Low** *(no comprehensive dimensional framework)*
Schmitt (2005)	Low	–	Given	Low	Low	**Low** *(no comprehensive dimensional framework)*
Schmitt et al. (2007)	Low	–	Given	Low	Low	**Low** *(focus on Big Five personality traits)*
Schwartz (1992, 1994b, 1999, 2004, 2006)	High	Medium	Given	Medium	Medium to High	**Medium to High** *(comprehensive compendium on culture by values and three dimensions)*
Smith et al. (1995)	Low	–	Given	Low	Low	**Low** *(focus on locus of control)*
Smith et al. (2002)	Low	–	Given	Low	Low	**Low** *(seizes only on other existing cultural taxonomies)*
Triandis (1989, 1996, 2000, 2001, 2002, 2004)	Low	Low	Given	Medium to High	Low to Medium	**Low to Medium** *(traceability of data)*

(continued)

Table 3.4 (continued)

	Multiple Research	Flexibility Cultural Change	Reliability	Simplicity	Thickness	**Overall Evaluation** *(Explanation)*
Trompenaars and Hampden-Turner (1997)	Low	Low	Given	Medium	Medium to High	**Medium** *(profound compendium with dimensions; with a strong research focus on organizations)*
Van de Vliert and Janssen (2002)	Low	–	Given	Low	Low	**Low** *(no comprehensive framework; no dimensional work)*
Welzel (2010)	Medium	–	Given	Low	Low	**Low** *(no comprehensive framework; no dimensional work)*

they are straightforward and rich in meaning in their classification of (national) cultures into cultural dimensions. In comparison, the cultural taxonomy by Fiske (1991, 1992) is considered to provide a rough balance between parsimony and richness of content, and therefore, its simplicity was evaluated as low, following also the approach by Chanchani & Theivananthampillai (2009). The remaining 32 analyzed cultural taxonomies were evaluated between these two extremities.

Thickness: In total, the thickness of the majority of 19 cultural taxonomies was evaluated as low. For example, Schimmack et al. (2002) provided no profound and holistic comprehensive understanding of the concept of (national) culture. Therefore, its thickness was evaluated as low. Three cultural taxonomies were evaluated with a medium thickness, providing a profound and holistic understanding of (national) culture. For example, the thickness of the cultural taxonomy by Rokeach (1973) was evaluated with medium since Rokeach only retrieved assumptions on middle-class Americans (Yeganeh et al., 2009). For none of the 34 analyzed existing cultural taxonomies were the thickness evaluated with high in this dissertation.

Overall evaluation: Only one of the analyzed cultural taxonomies—Hofstede (2001; Hofstede et al., 2010)—resulted in a high overall evaluation, providing an empirically tested profound compendium to classify national cultures. Additionally, the framework can be applied in multiple areas of research and are open to cultural change. Eight of the 34 analyzed cultural taxonomies scored between medium and high in their overall evaluation. For example, the cultural taxonomy by Hall (1959, 1966, 1976, 1983; Hall & Hall, 1990) offered a profound compendium on the understanding and classification of national cultures, including four cultural dimensions; but was only developed from theoretical assumptions. Inglehart et al. (2014) conducted an empirical and quantitative value study, offering two cultural dimensions for classifying national cultures. Kluckhohn and Strodtbeck (1961) revealed a less profound analysis of the concept of (national) cultures but provided a more in-depth classification into cultural dimensions. Likewise, the cultural taxonomy by Minkov (2007).

The cultural taxonomy by Schwartz (1992, 1994a) offers a profound and comprehensive understanding and classification of national cultures; whereas, Schwartz (1992, 1994a) only focused on values without considering other constructs for the classification of national cultures (e.g., attitudes, behavior, practices). Furthermore, Lewis (2018) and Parsons and Shils (1951) each provided an in-depth analysis of the concept of (national) culture and its classification into cultural dimensions without conducting any further empirical studies. In comparison, Trompenaars and Hampden-Turner (1997) provide a quantitative empirical analysis but focus only on organizational sciences. Likewise, the cultural taxonomy by Lessem and Neubauer (1994) only provided a quantitative analysis of their existing cultural taxonomy, solely focussing on the area of Organizational Sciences. Rokeach (1973) emphasized only values without considering any other psychological constructs.

The overall evaluation for three of the 34 analyzed cultural taxonomies was rated with medium. For example, Fiske (1991, 1992) based his four fundamental models of national) cultures on theoretical observations without further empirical analyses. The two cultural taxonomies by Schein and Schein (2016) and Triandis (1989, 1996, 2000, 2001, 2004) were evaluated between low and medium in their overall evaluation. For example, Schein and Schein (2016) operationalized no individual empirical dataset for their (national) cultural classification, and the cultural taxonomy by Triandis (1989, 1996, 2000, 2001, 2004) requires in-depth knowledge of the area of cultural classification. Twenty of the 34 cultural taxonomies scored a low in their overall evaluation, mainly due to their failure to provide a profound understanding and classification framework of national cultures (e.g., Douglas (1973), Lessem and Neubauer (1994), Welzel (2010)).

3.2 The Resulting Cultural Taxonomies

The evaluation of the 34 cultural taxonomies constituted the base for selecting suitable cultural taxonomies to synthesize the UDCs. The provided transparent and objective selection of cultural taxonomies for the synthesis constitutes, among others, one significant advancement of this dissertation. None of the SLR identified synthesis methodologies (please refer to Chapter 2 Current State of Research) demonstrated or based their selection of cultural taxonomies on objective criteria, as it was done in this dissertation.

Table 3.5 displays the selected cultural taxonomies for the synthesis of the UDCs, constituting the research base of this dissertation. In total, 11 cultural taxonomies were selected from a sample of 34 existing cultural taxonomies.

The cultural taxonomies for the synthesis of their cultural dimensions, constituting the research basis of this dissertation, were mainly selected according to their results in the overall evaluation (please refer to Table 3.4).

Table 3.5 Research Base: The 11 Selected Cultural Taxonomies

Cultural taxonomy	Author	Dimensions (N)	Basis	Country scores
The Relational Model Theory	Fiske (1991, 1992)	**4**	Theory	–
Hall's Four Cultural Dimensions	Hall (1959, 1966, 1976, 1983; Hall & Hall, 1990)	**4**	Theory	–
The 6-D Model of National Culture	Hofstede (2001; Hofstede et al., 2010)	**6**	Empirical	**x**
The GLOBE Study	House et al. (2004, 2007, 2014)	**9**	Empirical	**x**
The World Value Survey Waves 1–6	Inglehart et al. (2014)	**2**	Empirical	**x**
The Value Orientation Theory	Kluckhohn and Strodtbeck (1961)	**6**	Theory	–
When Culture Collide: Leading Across Cultures	Lewis (2018)	**3**	Theory	–
Minkov's Cultural Dimensions	Minkov (2007)	**3**	Theory	**x**
A General Theory of Action	Parsons and Shils (1951)	**5**	Theory	–
Schwartz Value Analysis	Schwartz (1992, 1994b)	**3**	Empirical, Theory	–
Trompenaars and Hampden-Turner's Cultural Dimensions	Trompenaars and Hampden-Turner (2004, 2012)	**7**	Theory	–

At first, all cultural taxonomies that scored a high in the overall evaluation were selected for this dissertations UDC synthesis. Only the cultural taxonomy by Hofstede (2001; Hofstede et al., 2010) scored a high overall evaluation. Secondly, the cultural taxonomies, which were evaluated between a medium and a high, were also selected—constituting the cultural taxonomies by Hall (1959, 1966, 1976, 1983; Hall & Hall, 1990), House et al. (2004, 2007, 2014), Kluckhohn and Strodtbeck (1961), Lewis (2018), Minkov (2007), and Schwartz (1992, 1994b). One exception, the cultural taxonomy by Rokeach (1973), was also evaluated in this range but was not selected as a cultural taxonomy for the UDC synthesis in this dissertation. Rokeach (1973) did not develop a distinctive framework for the concept of (national) culture; rather, he described the concept of (national) culture regarding circumstantial factors, e.g., race, sex, and income. Therefore, the cultural taxonomy by Rokeach (1973) was not utilized further in this dissertation. Finally, three cultural taxonomies, rated with medium overall evaluation, were selected for the UDC synthesis too—the cultural taxonomies by Fiske (1991, 1992), Parsons and Shils (1951), and Trompenaars and Hampden-Turner (2004, 2012). The other 23 cultural taxonomies were not selected for the UDC synthesis due to their low overall evaluation.

Introduction to the Synthesis of the Universal Dimensions of Culture (UDCs)

4

The synthesis of the eight UDCs constitutes the central piece of this dissertation, addressed in the following RQ2. Which universal dimensions of culture (UDCs) evolve from a synthesis of cultural dimensions from existing cultural taxonomies under the application of a structured and rigorous approach? The before-selected 11 cultural taxonomies represent a homogenous and solid base on existing cultural taxonomies, serving as the research base for the synthesis of the UDCs in this dissertation. These 11 cultural taxonomies provide 50 cultural dimensions analyzed in the UDC syntheses, resulting in eight UDCs.

Figure 4.1 displays the thematical position of chapter 4 in this dissertation.

Table 4.1 displays the 50 cultural dimensions from the 11 selected cultural taxonomies in an overview.

4.1 Premises and Analysis Protocol

The synthesis of the eight UDCs is mainly build on the eight assumptions (please refer to Table 2.14), derived from the conducted SLR. In addition, the following premises were set for and followed during the synthesis:

1) The synthesis yields a **set of universal dimensions of culture**, for which the cultural components are distinctively applicable. The synthesized set of UDCs is not intended to constitute *just* another cultural taxonomy providing *just* another set of cultural dimensions. Instead, this dissertation's synthesis of cultural dimensions was intended to reveal the core and universal concepts of exiting cultural taxonomies for distinguishing national cultures.

S. Kunert, *The Eight Universal Dimensions of Culture from a Synthesis of Cultural Taxonomies*, Gabler Theses, https://doi.org/10.1007/978-3-658-38765-5_4

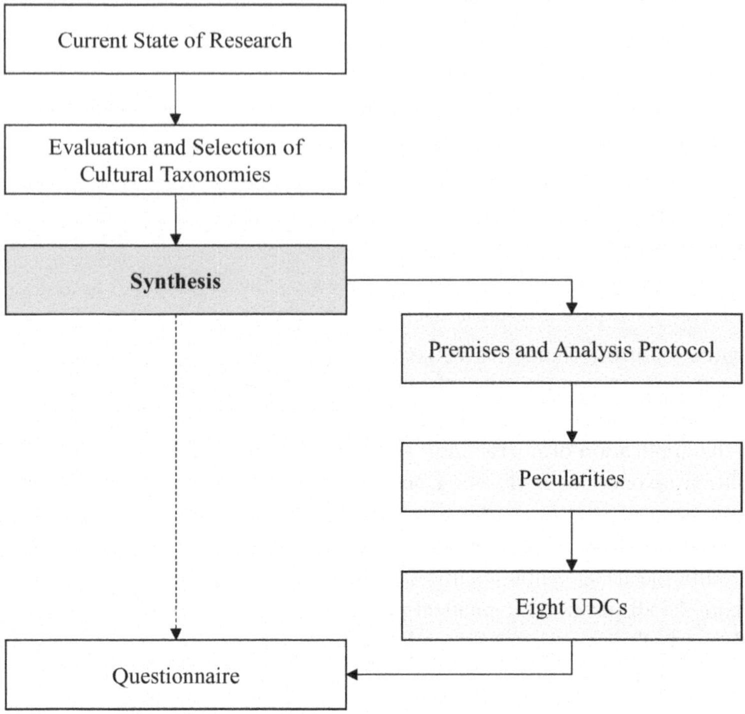

Figure 4.1 Thematic Position of Chapter 4

2) The UDC synthesis was pursued with a **focus on practicability** and **the area of management**. In cases of ambiguities during the synthesis, practicability and a managerial view served as decisive criteria.
3) Some of the 50 selected cultural dimensions demonstrated identical or related titles. These **title doublings** were taken into consideration during the synthesis. Whereas a hasty synthesis of cultural dimensions only based on title doublings would have led to false assumptions. This dissertation's synthesis of UDCs provides a prudent and sufficient consideration of 50 cultural dimensions beyond superficial assumptions. Reviewing the 11 selected cultural taxonomies, it became evident that some researchers themselves investigated potential interrelationships between their cultural dimensions and cultural dimensions from other cultural taxonomies. Such existing analyses (e.g.,

Table 4.1 Overview of the 50 Cultural Dimensions from the 11 Cultural Taxonomies

Fiske (1991, 1992)	**Hall** (1959, 1966, 1976, 1983; Hall & Hall, 1990)	**Hofstede** (2001; Hofstede et al., 2010)	**House et al.** (2004, 2007, 2014)	**Inglehart et al.** (2014)	**Kluckhohn and Strodtbeck** (1961)	**Lewis** (2018)	**Minkov** (2007)	**Parsons and Shils** (1951)	**Schwartz** (1992, 1994b)	**Trompenaars and Hampden-Turner** (2004, 2012)
Authority Ranking	Context	Individualism vs. Collectivism	Assertiveness	Survival Values vs. Self-Expression Values	Activity Orientation	Linear Active	Exclusionism vs. Universalism	Affectivity vs. Affective Neutrality	Autonomy vs. Embeddedness	Achievement vs. Ascription
Communal Sharing	Information Flow	Indulgence vs. Restraint	Future Orientation	Traditional Values vs. Secular-Rational Values	Human Nature Orientation	Multi-Active	Indulgence vs. Restraint	Ascription vs. Achievement	Hierarchy vs. Egalitarianism	Communitarianism vs. Individualism
Equality Matching	Space	Long-Term vs. Short-Term Orientation	Gender Egalitarianism	–	Man-Nature Orientation	Re-Active	Monumentalism vs. Flexhumility	Functional Specificity vs. Functional Diffuseness	Mastery vs. Harmony	Sequential vs. Synchronous Time
Market Pricing	Time	Masculinity vs. Femininity	Humane Orientation	–	Relational Orientation	–	–	Self-Interest vs. Collectivist Interest	–	Diffuse vs. Specific
–	–	Power Distance	In-Group Collectivism	–	Time Orientation	–	–	Universalism vs. Particularism	–	Internal vs. Outer Direction
–	–	Uncertainty Avoidance	Institutional Collectivism		–	–	–	–	–	Neutral vs. Emotional
–	–	–	Performance Orientation	–	–	–	–	–	–	Universalism vs. Particularism
–	–	–	Power Distance	–	–	–	–	–	–	–
–	–	–	Uncertainty Avoidance	–	–	–	–	–	–	–

House et al. (2004, 2007, 2014)) were reviewed and carefully considered for validation and relevance for the UDC syntheses of this dissertation.

4) This dissertation demonstrates an analysis of **interrelationships** between cultural dimensions from existing cultural taxonomies. Maleki and de Jong (2014) pursued an ecological factor analysis of common countries of their set of considered cultural dimensions. A statistical analysis of country scores, as an approach for synthesizing the UDCs in this dissertation, was rejected for the following reasons.

   First, the main problem in quantifying national cultures is to find a model that captures all aspects of the complex phenomenon of culture. There is a strong temptation for simple determinism to conclude cultural components from statistical differences in national averages. Additionally, the quantification of national cultures suffers from a lack of data availability, sample representativeness, cross-sample comparability, and faulty equivalence assumptions across the different levels of measurements (individual, organizational, national). The quantification of national cultures leads to question the foundation of the concept of national culture regarding its measurement by values. Can values serve as a measurement tool for culture? Do current measurement tools for culture reflect values or do they instead measure the personality of individuals? Besides the critical appraisal, the quantitative measurement of national cultures remains useful for comparisons; whereas, the standards to capture all-embracingly the concept of national cultures should be lowered (Taras et al., 2009). Due to the fundamental flaws of the quantification of national culture, no additional analysis of country scores provided by cultural taxonomies was considered during the synthesis of the UDCs. No further enhancement was expected from such a statistical data treatment; instead, it would have extended the scope for controversial flaws in the UDC syntheses.

5) In this dissertation, **values** are seen as the core element for assessing national cultures in general, and the concept of culture was compressed to the concept of national culture. The focus on values in this dissertation originates from the applied definition for national culture, conceiving national cultures as a multi-facet construct with values as the core element. The 11 selected cultural taxonomies, with one exception, all applied values as the study object. The one exception constitutes the cultural taxonomy by House et al. (2004, 2007, 2014), measuring practices (*"the way things are"*) and values (*"the way things should be"*). Several researchers investigated statistical correlations between

the value and practice items of the GLOBE study[1]. For the sake of a solid research base in this dissertation, only the value items of the cultural taxonomy by House et al. (2004, 2007, 2014) were considered during the synthesis analyses of the UDCs. The in-depth analysis of the correlation and relationship of House et al.'s (2004, 2007, 2014) value and practice items constituted no aim of this dissertation.

6) Applying the cultural taxonomy by House et al. (2004, 2007, 2014) induced a further premise regarding the level of analysis for this dissertation's synthesis analyses. House et al. (2004, 2007, 2014) measured their value and practice items on two levels—the societal and organizational level. The researchers postulated that the "absolute differences" measured between values and practices are supposed to be more significant for societies than for organizations; and that the organizational level reflects the societal level of each respective national culture. In the review of the syntax of the GLOBE study of House et al. (2004, 2007, 2014), only items on the **societal level** were considered in the UDC synthesis analyses, ensuring that the focus of the UDCs remains on the societal level.

Figure 4.2 illustrates the approach and the induced premises for synthesizing the UDCs.

The synthesis of each of the eight UDCs was conducted with an individual analysis approach. The general procedure was as follows: First, title doublings or title-related cultural dimensions out of the set of the 50 cultural dimensions were analyzed. Second, the remaining cultural dimensions out of the 50 cultural dimensions were analyzed for potential related cultural components regarding each UDC.

Furthermore, the synthesis analyses of the eight UDCs were pursued in three tranches. First, the UDCs that similarly address the theme of environment were analyzed—the UDC Distribution of Power and Status, the UDC Relationship with the Natural Environment, and the UDC Social Organization. It was demonstrated that the three UDCs relate to the theme of environment, although from different perspectives. Secondly, the UDCs referring to the theme of time were analyzed—the UDC Perception and Use of Time, the UDC Traditionalism versus Secularism, and the UDC Uncertainty Avoidance and Coping Mechanisms. Each of the three UDCs encompasses the theme of time as a cultural component but

[1] For example, please refer to Venaik and Brewer (2010) as well as Maseland and Van Hoorn (2009).

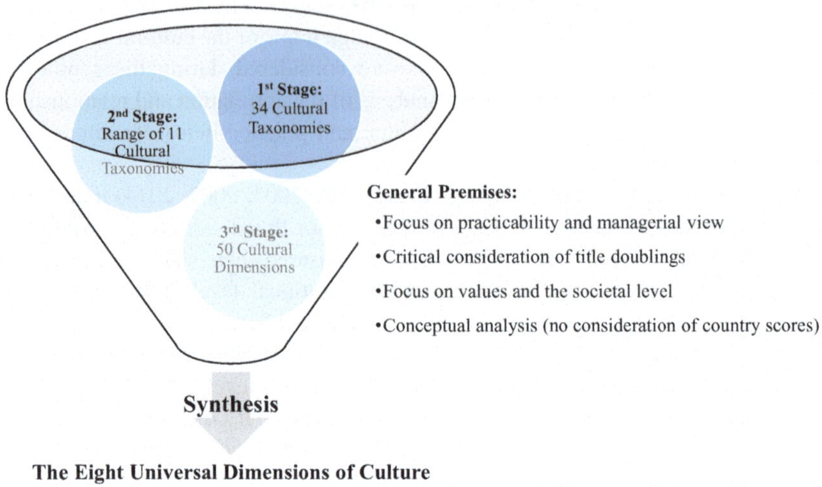

Figure 4.2 Approach and Premises of the Synthesis of the Eight Universal Dimensions of Culture (UDCs)

from a different angle. Finally, the two UDCs Human Orientation and Gratification of Desires, Feelings, and Emotions, were analyzed, referring to the theme of human behavior.

Overall, this resulted in detailed analyses and descriptions for each synthesized UDC. Table 4.2 demonstrates the analysis protocol for conducting the synthesis analyses of the eight UDCs in an overview.

The syntheses of the eight UDCs were not only pursued as conceptual analyses of cultural dimensions. It also encompassed the analysis of the items of the cultural dimensions, later operationalized into a set of items for the UDCs. Out of the analyzed cultural taxonomies, Fiske (1991, 1992), Hofstede (2001; Hofstede et al., 2010), House et al. (2004, 2007, 2014), Inglehart et al. (2014), Minkov (2007), Schwartz (1992, 1994b), and Trompenaars and Hampden-Turner (2004, 2012) developed items for the empirical assessment of their cultural dimensions. The items constitute the basis of the developed tool for operationalizing the eight UDCs by a questionnaire to measure the UDC's extents in national cultures empirically (please refer to Chapter 8 Questionnaire for the Eight Universal Dimensions of Culture (UDCs)).

4.2 Special Report on the Remaining Synthesis Dimension

The four by the SLR identified synthesis methodologies revealed the following six concepts as commonly prevalent among cultural taxonomies: distribution of power, relationship with the environment, social organization, time, uncertainty avoidance, and human orientation (please refer to Table 2.13).

Table 4.2 Analysis Protocol for the Syntheses of the Eight Universal Dimensions of Culture (UDCs)

Concept	UDC	Synthesis Analysis Step	
The Environment	**Distribution of Power and Status**	No. 1	Title-related cultural dimensions for the concept of distribution of power and status
		No. 2	Analysis of the set of 50 cultural dimensions
	Relationship with the Natural Environment	No. 1	Title-related cultural dimensions for the concept of relationship with the environment
		No. 2	Analysis of the set of 50 cultural dimensions
		-	Title reconciliation
	Social Organization	No. 1	Title-related cultural dimensions for the concept of individualism versus collectivism
		No. 2	Analysis of the set of 50 cultural dimensions
	Delimitations	Delimitation between the concepts of distribution of power and status and social organization	
		Delimitation between the concepts of relationship with the social environment and the natural environment	
Time	**Perception and Use of Time**	No. 1	Title-related cultural dimensions for the concept of perception and use of time
		No. 2	Analysis of the set of 50 cultural dimensions

(continued)

Table 4.2 (continued)

Concept	UDC	Synthesis Analysis Step	
	Traditionalism versus Secularism	No. 1	Title-related cultural dimensions for the concept of traditionalism versus secularism
		No. 2	Analysis of the set of 50 cultural dimensions
	Uncertainty Avoidance and Coping Mechanisms	No. 1	Title-related cultural dimensions for the concept of uncertainty avoidance
		No. 2	Analysis of the set of 50 cultural dimensions
		–	Title reconciliation
	Delimitations	Delimitation between the concepts of uncertainty avoidance and relationship with the (natural) environment	
		Delimitation between the concept of perception and use of time and the concept of traditionalism versus secularism	
Human Behavior	**Human Orientation**	No. 1	Title-related cultural dimensions for the concept of human orientation
		No. 2	Analysis of the set of 50 cultural dimensions
	Gratification and Expression of Emotions, Feelings, and Desires	No. 1	Title-related cultural dimensions for the concept of indulgence versus restraint
		No. 2	Analysis of the set of 50 cultural dimensions
		–	Title reconciliation

Besides commonly addressed synthesis concepts, the four synthesis methodologies differ in their projected synthesis dimensions and synthesis frameworks. The eight projected UDCs did not exhaustively cover all synthesis dimensions from the four identified synthesis methodologies. Several synthesis dimensions remained uncovered by the eight UDCs. These remaining synthesis dimensions were discussed as follows regarding their potential for a distinct UDC.

First, Low and Chapman (2003) synthesized a synthesis dimension of **Communication**, including the cultural dimensions of Trust by Fukuyaman (1995b), Context by Hall (1976), Rationalism versus Humanism by Lessem and Neubauer (1994), and Universalism versus Particularism as well as Neutral versus Affective by Trompenaars and Hampden-Turner (1997). Schneider et al. (2014) synthesized a synthesis dimension of Space, Language, and Time, referring to communication and seizing on the understanding of high and low context (national) cultures by Hall (1976). As described by Low and Chapman (2003) and Schneider et al. (2014), the concept of communication in general, and specifically, the concept of language, is somehow embedded and influenced by all other cultural concepts. The concept of communication and the concept of language were elaborated to interfere with other concepts operationalized for the UDCs in this dissertation. Conclusively, the two concepts were not operationalized as a distinct UDC in this dissertation; thus, the concept of communication remains an overarching concept for influencing the distinction of (national) cultures.

Secondly, Schneider et al. (2014) synthesized a synthesis dimension of **Nature of Truth and Reality**, which they based only on observations and one single cultural taxonomy—the cultural taxonomy by Schein (1985, 1987). No evidence was identified in the description of the synthesis dimension of Nature of Truth and Reality of Schneider et al. (2014) that would have pointed to substantial evidence for its existence as a common concept among cultural taxonomies. Therefore, no distinct UDC regarding the concept of nature of truth and reality was projected in this dissertation.

Thirdly, Schneider et al. (2014) synthesized a threefold synthesis dimension, encompassing under one umbrella the concepts of **language, space, and time**; strictly following the approach of Hall (1959, 1966, 1976, 1983; Hall & Hall, 1990). In this dissertation, the concept of time was operationalized in the UDC Perception and Use of Time.

As mentioned before, the concept of language was not considered substantial enough to constitute a distinct UDC. The concept of space was included in some of the UDCs as a cultural component (e.g., UDC Social Organization, UDC Human Orientation). Schneider et al. (2014) elaborated that the concept of space as a distinguishing factor for national cultures influences the dealing of individuals with the environment and the interaction of individuals with each other. Furthermore, Schneider et al. (2014) elaborated that the concept of space is applicable by artifacts and behavior (e.g., informal versus formal communication) and in the degree of information. Overall, the description of the cultural concept of space by Schneider et al. (2014) as a distinct synthesis dimension did not reveal enough evidence to apply the approach in this dissertation.

Lastly, Maleki and de Jong (2014) projected a synthesis dimension of **Gender Egalitarianism**, encompassing only one cultural dimension—the cultural dimension of Gender Egalitarianism by House et al. (2004, 2007, 2014). In this dissertation, the UDC Distribution of Power and Status was projected by A1 to encompass a cultural component of gender egalitarianism. Furthermore, Maleki and de Jong (2014) elaborated that the cultural dimension of Masculinity versus Femininity by Hofstede (2001; Hofstede et al., 2010) includes items that refer to the discriminatory role of genders in a national culture and argue for a delimitation of the three concepts assertiveness, mastery versus harmony, and gender egalitarianism. Although, they only identified the concept of gender egalitarianism as distinct in the cultural dimension of Gender Egalitarianism by House et al. (2004, 2007, 2014).

In this dissertation, the cultural dimension of Gender Egalitarianism by House et al. (2004, 2007, 2014) was synthesized into the UDC Distribution of Power and Status, constituting one cultural component of the concept distribution of power and status. The cultural component of gender egalitarianism describes the allocation of power, status, and reward per gender of individuals as a distinguishing factor for national cultures. Individuals of national cultures with a high score of gender egalitarianism tend to accord higher status to female individuals (House et al., 2004).

The in-depth review of the cultural dimension of Gender Egalitarianism by House et al. (2004, 2007, 2014) revealed the following insights.

House et al. (2004) described gender egalitarianism as the concept of division of roles between women and men. In more detail, House et al. (2004) identified in their study that national cultures that rank higher on gender egalitarianism tend to believe that women and men are suitable for similar roles. In contrast, individuals of less gender-egalitarian national cultures tend to assume different roles for men and women (House et al., 2004). House et al. (2004) argued that the most fundamental issue for differentiating national cultures lies in the prescription of different roles for different sexes. Following this approach, the core of the concept of gender egalitarianism as a cultural dimension lies in a national culture's belief about the determination of roles per biological sex of individuals. Specifically, national cultures with a greater gender egalitarianism extent are projected to rely less on biological sexes to allocate roles in contrast to national cultures with a lower extent of gender egalitarianism (House et al., 2004). House et al. (2004) assigned national cultures the in Table 4.3. displayed behavior traits.

The conceptual analysis of the cultural dimension of Gender Egalitarianism by House et al. (2004, 2007, 2014) led to the conclusion that the central concept of the cultural dimension constitutes the idea to distinguish national cultures by their division of roles by sexes, and thus, the allocation of status, power, and reward by the gender of individuals. To further substantiate the approach, the empirical items of the cultural dimension were reviewed.

There was no doubt that the items of the cultural dimension of Gender Egalitarianism by House et al. (2004, 2007, 2014) also address the distinction of

Table 4.3 Higher Gender Egalitarianism Societies vs. Lower Gender Egalitarianism Societies

Societies that score **higher on gender egalitarianism** tend to:	Societies that score **lower on gender egalitarianism** tend to:
Have more women in positions of authority	Have fewer women in positions of authority
Accord women a higher status in society	Accord women a lower status in society
Afford women a greater role in community decision making	Afford women no or a smaller role in community decision making
Have a higher percentage of women participating in the labor force	Have a lower percentage of women participating in labor forces
Have less occupational sex segregation	Have more occupational sex segregation
Have higher female literacy rates	Have lower female literacy rates
Have similar levels of education of females and males	Have a lower level of education of females relative to males

Note. The table was adapted with changes from *Culture, Leadership, and Organization: The GLOBE Study of 62 Societies* (p. 359), by R. J. House, P. J. Hanges, M. Javidan, P. W. Dorfman, and V. Gupta, 2004, Sage Publication. Copyright 2004 by Sage Publication, Inc.

national cultures by allocating roles according to genders. Maleki and de Jong (2014) elaborated further on the interferences of the cultural dimension with the cultural dimension of Masculinity versus Femininity by Hofstede (2001; Hofstede et al., 2010). Even though Hofstede (2001) also mentioned the domination of gender role patterns as a distinguishing factor for national cultures, from the definition of the cultural dimension of Masculinity versus Femininity by Hofstede (2001; Hofstede et al., 2010), it was concluded that the two cultural dimensions differ strongly. Also, the items of the cultural dimension of Masculinity versus Femininity by Hofstede and Minkov (2013) were reviewed.

With particular regards to the statistical correlation between the two cultural dimensions, the following evidence was identified. House et al. (2004) identified a correlation of the cultural dimension of Masculinity versus Femininity by Hofstede (2001; Hofstede et al., 2010) with other than the gender egalitarianism items applied in the GLOBE study. These items constitute the items that were labeled with assertiveness. In more detail, House et al. (2004) identified a positive correlation of the cultural dimension of Masculinity versus Femininity by Hofstede (2001; Hofstede et al., 2010) with items of mastery and self-assertation of Schwartz (1992, 1994b). Nevertheless, House et al. (2004) identified no correlation between the cultural dimension of Masculinity versus Femininity by Hofstede

(2001; Hofstede et al., 2010) and the value and practice items from their cultural dimension of Gender Egalitarianism by House et al. (2004, 2007, 2014). In conclusion, there was not enough evidence to substantiate a synthesis of a distinct UDC Gender Egalitarianism in this dissertation; thus, the concept of gender egalitarianism was incorporated into the UDC Distribution of Power and Status.

4.3 Overview of the Eight Universal Dimensions of Culture (UDCs)

The synthesis of the eight UDCs was conducted, seizing on the results of RQ1, answering RQ2 of this dissertation. All eight UDCs, and thus, all eight assumptions, were confirmed during the synthesis analyses. Each of the 50 cultural dimensions from the 11 selected cultural taxonomies was affiliated with one of the eight UDCs. Whereas, it should be pointed out that some of the cultural dimensions were only synthesized in conceptual terms, which could be explained by that some of the cultural taxonomies did not develop items for the empirical assessment of their cultural dimensions and thus, a synthesis of the cultural dimensions was only possible in conceptual terms (without items). Some other cultural dimensions were synthesized into several UDCs. Table 4.4 displays the affiliation of the 50 cultural dimensions to the UDCs in an overview and Table 4.5 displays each resulting UDC by its concept and synthesized cultural components in an overview.

Table 4.4 Overview of the 50 Cultural Dimensions and their Synthesis into the Eight Universal Dimensions of Culture (UDCs)

Fiske (1991, 1992)	**Hall** (1959, 1966, 1976, 1983; Hall & Hall, 1990)	**Hofstede** (2001; Hofstede et al., 2010)	**House et al.** (2004, 2007, 2014)	**Inglehart et al.** (2014)	**Kluckhohn and Strodtbeck** (1961)	**Lewis** (2018)	**Minkov** (2007)	**Parsons and Shils** (1951)	**Schwartz** (1992, 1994b)	**Trompenaars and Hampden-Turner** (2004, 2012)
Authority Ranking	Context	Individualism vs. Collectivism	Assertiveness	Survival Values vs. Self-Expression Values	Activity Orientation	Linear Active	Exclusionism vs. Universalism	Affectivity vs. Affective Neutrality	Autonomy vs. Embeddedness	Achievement vs. Ascription
A1	**A3**	**A3**	**A6**	**A3**	A7	A4 / A7	A2 / **A3** / A5	**A7**	**A3 / A7**	**A1**
Communal Sharing	Information Flow	Indulgence vs. Restraint	Future Orientation	Traditional Values vs. Secular-Rational Values	Human Nature Orientation	Multi-Active	Indulgence vs. Restraint	Ascription vs. Achievement	Hierarchy vs. Egalitarianism	Communitarianism vs. Individualism
A3	A3	**A7**	**A4** / A5	**A8**	**A6**	A4 / A7	**A7**	**A1**	A1	**A3**
Equality Matching	Space	Long-Term vs. Short-Term Orientation	Gender Egalitarianism	–	Man-Nature Orientation	Re-Active	Monumentalism vs. Flexhumility	Functional Specificity vs. Functional Diffuseness	Mastery vs. Harmony	Sequential vs. Synchronous Time
A1	**A3** / A6	**A8**	**A1**	–	**A2**	A4 / A7	**A8**	A7	A2 / A3	**A4** / A5
Market Pricing	Time	Masculinity vs. Femininity	Humane Orientation	–	Relational Orientation	–	–	Self-Interest vs. Collectivist Interest	–	Diffuse vs. Specific
A3	**A4**	A2 / **A6**	**A6**	–	**A1** / A3	–	–	**A3**	–	A7
–	–	Power Distance	In-Group Collectivism	–	Time Orientation	–	–	Universalism vs. Particularism	–	Internal vs. Outer Direction

(continued)

Table 4.4 (continued)

Fiske (1991, 1992)	**Hall** (1959, 1966, 1976, 1983; Hall & Hall, 1990)	**Hofstede** (2001; Hofstede et al., 2010)	**House et al.** (2004, 2007, 2014)	**Inglehart et al.** (2014)	**Kluckhohn and Strodtbeck** (1961)	**Lewis** (2018)	**Minkov** (2007)	**Parsons and Shils** (1951)	**Schwartz** (1992, 1994b)	**Trompenaars and Hampden-Turner** (2004, 2012)
–	–	**A1**	**A3**	–	**A4** / A5 / A8	–	–	**A3** / A5	–	**A2**
–	–	Uncertainty Avoidance	Institutional Collectivism	–	–	–	–	–	–	Neutral vs. Emotional
–	–	**A5**	**A3**	–	–	–	–	–	–	**A7**
–	–	–	Performance Orientation	–	–	–	–	–	–	Universalism vs. Particularism
–	–	–	**A1**	–	–	–	–	–	–	A5
–	–	–	Power Distance	–	–	–	–	–	–	–
–	–	–	**A1**	–	–	–	–	–	–	–
–	–	–	Uncertainty Avoidance	–	–	–	–	–	–	–
–	–	–	A5	–	–	–	–	–	–	–

Note. A1 (UDC Distribution of Power and Status), A2 (UDC Relationship with the Natural Environment), A3 (UDC Social Organization), A4 (UDC Perception and Use of Time), A5 (UDC Uncertainty Avoidance and Coping Mechanisms), A6 (UDC Human Orientation), A7 (UDC Gratification and Expression of Emotions, Desires, and Feelings), A8 (UDC Traditionalism versus Secularism). The boldly indicated affiliations display the cultural dimensions that have a more substantial influence in the UDC.

Table 4.5 Overview, Description, and Cultural Components of the Eight Universal Dimensions of Culture (UDCs)

No.	UDC	Description	Cultural Components
1	**Distribution of Power and Status**	**Acknowledgment of the extent of inequalities among individuals and extent of dependency of individuals on higher-ranked individuals in national cultures**	– Structure of power relationships: individuals, indicating to value power relationships, are also projected to value the cultural components of hierarchy versus egalitarianism, distribution of power, and obeying of supervisor – Employee fear – Allocation of status and reward: individuals, indicating to value allocation of status and reward are also projected to value the cultural components of performances, achieved versus ascribed roles, and gender egalitarianism
2	**Relationship with the Natural Environment**	**Relationship of individuals with their natural environment in national cultures expressed in their desire to control or to live in harmony with their natural environment**	– Mastery versus harmony

(continued)

Table 4.5 (continued)

No.	UDC	Description	Cultural Components
3	**Social Organization**	**Structure of social relationships regarding the concept of individualism versus collectivism in national cultures**	– Individualism versus collectivism: Individuals who tend to value either individualism or collectivism are projected to value group decision making, group affiliation, pride, and loyalty – Universalism versus particularism
4	**Perception and Use of Time**	**Extent of perception (incl., view of) and use of time in national cultures**	– Time horizon (long-term versus short-term orientation) – Planning ahead (focus on the future) – Flow of time (perception and view of time) – Number of handled tasks at a time
5	**Uncertainty Avoidance and Coping Mechanisms**	**Extent of uncertainty avoidance and the mechanisms for coping and dealing with uncertain and unknown situations in national cultures**	– Stress – Rule and regulation obedience – Time in terms of future perspective and planning ahead
6	**Human Orientation**	**Extent of assertiveness versus tenderness and the nature of individuals national cultures**	– Assertiveness versus tenderness – Human orientation

(continued)

Table 4.5 (continued)

No.	UDC	Description	Cultural Components
7	**Gratification and Expression of Emotions, Feelings, and Desires**	**Extent of gratification and expression of desires, feelings, and emotions, referring especially to the concept of indulgence versus restraint in national cultures**	– Extent of gratification of desires and feelings: Individuals, indicting to value the gratification of desires and feelings are also projected to value the cultural components of the importance of leisure, moderation, level of happiness, and perception of life control – Extent of expression of emotions
8	**Traditionalism versus Secularism**	**Extent of feelings of pride, flexibility, consistency between expressed and felt emotions, secular orientation, religiosity, self-stability in national cultures**	– Self-stability – Secular orientation – Religiosity – Feelings of pride: individuals indicating to value feelings of pride are also projected to value the cultural components of national pride and self-enhancement – Thrift – Past-time orientation

The Environment—One Connecting Concept? 5

Low and Chapman (2003), Nardon and Steers (2009), Maleki and de Jong (2014), as well as Schneider et al. (2014) commonly assigned the concepts of distribution of power and status, social organization, and relationship with the (social and natural) environment dominant roles among cultural taxonomies for distinguishing national cultures. Based on the information provided by the four synthesis methodologies, the three assumptions A1, A2, and A3 were developed for this dissertation, correspondingly representing the three UDCs Distribution of Power and Status, Social Organization, and Relationship with the Natural Environment. Each of these concepts addresses the extent of individuals' handling of either the social environment, natural environment, or the hierarchical order of their environment. In a broader sense, each of the three concepts relates to individuals handling of or relationship with their environment as a main distinguishing factor for national cultures. In this dissertation, to demonstrate the three concepts in terms of the three assumed UDCs—Distribution of Power and Status, Social Organization, and Relationship with the Natural Environment—their syntheses are displayed in one chapter, including their delimitations and commonalities.

5.1 Synthesis of the Universal Dimension of Culture (UDC) Distribution of Power and Status

A1 proposed the UDC Distribution of Power and Status, illustrating the concept of distribution of power and status as one central concept among cultural taxonomies for distinguishing national cultures. The UDC Distribution of Power and Status is assumed to distinguish national cultures by the following three cultural components: firstly, the cultural component of structure of power relationships (vertical versus horizontal, hierarchy versus egalitarianism), secondly, the cultural

S. Kunert, *The Eight Universal Dimensions of Culture from a Synthesis of Cultural Taxonomies*, Gabler Theses, https://doi.org/10.1007/978-3-658-38765-5_5

component of allocation of status and reward, and thirdly, the cultural component of gender egalitarianism. Each of these three cultural components is built on the assumption of existing inequalities among individuals and the dependency of individuals on higher-ranked individuals (c.f., Hofstede (2001)). A critical aspect in the synthesis of the UDC Distribution of Power and Status constituted the delimitation of the three proposed cultural components to the concept of individualism versus collectivism, operationalized in this dissertation per A3 as the UDC Social Organization.

It is assumed that the concept of individualism versus collectivism refers to group affiliation and power relationships, in accordance with Hofstede (2001).

Figure 5.1 displays, in summary, the assumed UDC Distribution of Power and Status and its embedded cultural components.

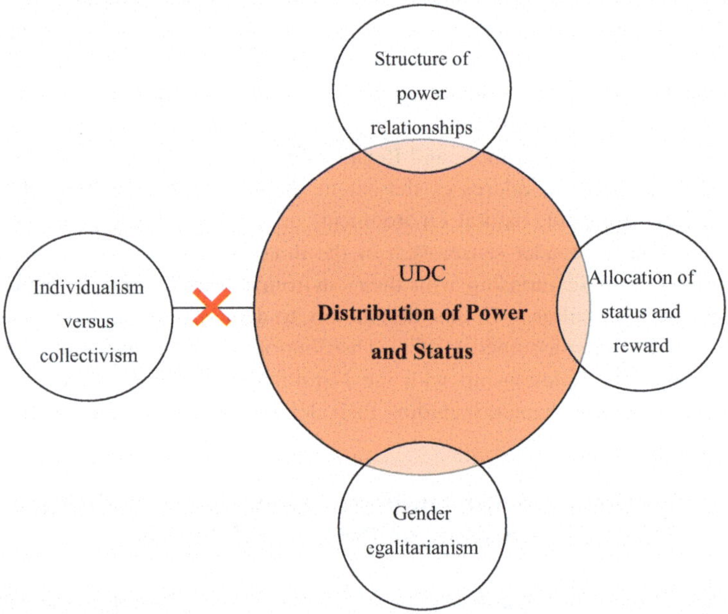

Figure 5.1 Assumption 1 (A1): The Universal Dimension of Culture (UDC) Distribution of Power and Status

Synthesis Analysis Step 1: Title-Related Cultural Dimensions
Among the 50 cultural dimensions of the selected 11 cultural taxonomies, the following five cultural dimensions were identified per their title, assumingly addressing the concept of distribution of power and status: Power Distance by Hofstede (2001; Hofstede et al., 2010), Power Distance by House et al. (2004, 2007, 2014), Authority Ranking and Equality Matching by Fiske (1991, 1992), as well as Hierarchy versus Egalitarianism by Schwartz (1992, 1994b).

At first, the cultural dimension of **Power Distance** by **Hofstede (2001; Hofstede et al., 2010)** was extensively analyzed, including its definition, description, and the two versions of its items from 1980 and 2013. The cultural dimensions' conceptual analysis revealed that it addresses at its core the (equal or unequal) distribution of power in a national culture without further specifying the cause of the equal or unequal power distribution. In this dissertation, the cultural concept of distribution of power, expressed in the extent of (in-) equalities among individuals, is assumed to belong to the cultural component of structure of power relationships, projected for the UDC Distribution of Power and Status by A1.

The four items of the cultural dimension Power Distance by Hofstede and Minkov (2013) seem to address various cultural components, referring to the concept of power distribution. Two items (item no. 02 and no. 07 from the VSM 2013) were assumed to reflect the cultural concept of hierarchy versus egalitarianism by asking respondents to rate their importance for a superior, whom they can respect, and who consults them in decisions involving their work. Another item (item no. 20 of the VSM 2013) addressed the concept of employee fear, asking if subordinates in the respective national culture are afraid to contradict their superiors. The concept of hierarchy versus egalitarianism was subsumed already by A1 to constitute a sub-cultural component of the cultural component of structure of power relationships of the UDC Distribution of Power and Status. In contrast, A1 did not assume the concept of employee fear to constitute a cultural component of the UDC Distribution of Power and Status. In the original version of the items of the cultural dimension of Power Distance by Hofstede (2001), the cultural component of employee fear was assigned a dominant role in terms of the concept of distribution of power. One other item (item no. 23 of the VSM 2013) questioned respondents' preferences regarding the existence of two superiors simultaneously. This item was not considered further since the relation to the initially assumed UDC Distribution of Power and Status was not evident in the analysis.

Overall, it was decided to synthesize the cultural dimension of Power Distance by Hofstede (2001; Hofstede et al., 2010) into the UDC Distribution of Power and Status. This synthesis was in line with Maleki and de Jong (2014) as well as Nardon and Steers (2009). The synthesis of the cultural dimension of Power

Distance by Hofstede (2001; Hofstede et al., 2010) induced the inclusion of the cultural component of employee fear due to considerable evidence of its relation to the general concept of distribution of power and status. Also, the items (item no. 02, no. 07, and no. 20 from the VSM 2013) were included in the set of potential items for the UDC Distribution of Power and Status.

The second analyzed by title-related cultural dimension constituted the cultural dimension of **Power Distance** by **House et al. (2004, 2007, 2014)**, also addressing the concept of distribution of power and status at its core. House et al. (2004, 2007, 2014) pointed out that they designed their cultural dimension of Power Distance following the cultural dimension of Power Distance by Hofstede (1980). Likewise, House et al. (2004, 2007, 2014) borrowed the concept of power distance and its basic principles from Mulder (1977)[1]. Thus, a certain commonality between the two cultural dimensions was expected and confirmed in this dissertation's synthesis analysis.

The analysis of the societal value items of the cultural dimensions revealed evidence, which substantiated the synthesis of the cultural dimension of Power Distance by House et al. (2004, 2007, 2014) into the UDC Distribution of Power and Status. One of the items (item no. V3_13) referred to the concept of obeying supervisors by asking respondents if leaders should be followed without scrutinizing them in disagreement. Just, House et al. (2004, 2007, 2014) did not ask in the same precise sense as Hofstede (2001; Hofstede et al., 2010) for employee fear.

In this dissertation, the cultural component of obeying supervisors was affiliated to the cultural component of structure of power relationships since it demonstrates the extent of acknowledgment of inequalities among individuals in national cultures. Another two items (items no. V3_28 and no. V3_35), asking respondents if social distance should be increased or decreased and if power should be concentrated at the top or shared throughout the society, are assumed to address the concept of distribution of power as a distinguishing factor for national cultures.

The two remaining societal value items (items no. V3_5 and no. V3_33) were interpreted to empirically assess the cultural component of allocation of status and reward by addressing the distribution of power based on abilities and contribution to the society, position, or age.

---

[1] Mulder (1976, 1977) retrieved his concept of power distance from field laboratory experiments and developed the *Power Distance Reduction Tendency* theory (Hofstede, 2001). Mulder (1977) defines power as "the potential to determine or direct (to a certain extent) the behaviour of another person/other persons more so than the other way around" (p. 90) and the concept of power distance as "the degree of inequality in power between a less powerful Individual (I) and a more power Other (O), in which I and O belong to the same (loosely or tightly knit) social system" (p. 90).

In summary, the cultural dimension of Power Distance by House et al. (2004, 2007, 2014) was synthesized into the UDC Distribution of Power and Status. Also, its five societal value items (items no. V3_5, no. V3_13, no. V3_28, no. V3_33, and no. V3_35) were incorporated as potential items for the empirical measurement of the UDC Distribution of Power and Status.

An additional assessment of conceptual interrelationships between the two cultural dimensions of Power Distance by Hofstede (2001; Hofstede et al., 2010) and Power Distance by House et al. (2004, 2007, 2014) justified the synthesis of both cultural dimensions into one UDC regarding the concept of distribution of power and status. The two cultural dimensions are assumed to be conceptually similar in thus, both address the concept of distribution of power due to inequalities among individuals within national cultures. A1 assumed the concept of distribution of power and status to constitute one of the main concepts of the UDC Distribution of Power and Status. Nevertheless, the two cultural dimensions of Power Distance differ in their supplementary included cultural components. The cultural dimension of Power Distance by Hofstede (2001; Hofstede et al., 2010) encompasses the cultural component of employee fear. The cultural dimension of Power Distance by House et al. (2004, 2007, 2014) encompasses the cultural component of allocation of status and reward, power distribution, obeying supervisors, and hierarchy versus egalitarianism.

House et al. (2004, 2007, 2014) themselves investigated statistical similarities between their cultural dimension of Power Distance and the cultural dimension of Power Distance by Hofstede (2001; Hofstede et al., 2010). They concluded that the practices items of the cultural dimension of Power Distance by House et al. (2004, 2007, 2014) correlate significantly positively with the items for the cultural dimension of Power Distance by Hofstede (2001; Hofstede et al., 2010). Furthermore, House et al. (2004) identified that the Power Distance value items by House et al. (2004) do not at all correlate with the Power Distance index by Hofstede (2001). This empirical assessment substantiates the assumption that Hofstede et al. (2010) also proposed that their Power Distance index assesses employees' perceptions, likewise to the practice items applied by House et al. (2004, 2007, 2014). In summary, this information affirms the synthesis analysis and the synthesis of both cultural dimensions into the UDC Distribution of Power and Status in this dissertation.

The third reviewed title-related cultural dimensions constituted the cultural dimension of **Authority Ranking** by **Fiske (1991, 1992)**. Reviewing Fiske's (1991, 1992) definition of the cultural dimension of Authority Ranking, which refers to the structuring of relationships along with hierarchical orders and in asymmetrical ways, led to its synthesis in the UDC Distribution of Power and Status. From the analysis of the items of the cultural dimension of Authority Ranking by Haslam and Fiske

(1999), it was derived that the following cultural components are addressed in the cultural dimension: obeying superiors (evidence found in items no. 3, no. 5, and no. 6), structure of power relationships in terms of hierarchy versus egalitarianism (evidence found in item no. 8), and the distribution of power (evidence found in items no. 2, no. 4, and no. 7). The seven items—items no. 2, no. 3, no. 4, no. 5, no. 6, no. 7, and no. 8—were considered potential items for the UDC Distribution of Power's empirical measurement Only item no. 1 was not considered further in the synthesis analysis since it did not display any evidence to be related to one of the by A1 assumed cultural components of the UDC Distribution of Power and Status. Overall, the cultural dimension of Authority Ranking by Fiske (1991, 1992) was synthesized into the UDC Distribution of Power and Status.

The second title-related cultural dimension by **Fiske (1991, 1992)**, which was analyzed for synthesis into the UDC Distribution of Power and Status, constituted the cultural dimension of **Equality Matching**. The evidence of an affiliation of the cultural dimension to the concept of distribution of power and status was not explicit as it was, for example, for the two cultural dimensions of Power Distance by Hofstede (2001; Hofstede et al., 2010) and Power Distance by House et al. (2004, 2007, 2014). Three items (items no. 1, no. 4, and no. 7) of the cultural dimension could be assumed, to a certain extent, to address the concept of (in-) equalities among individuals. In this dissertation, the concept of (in-) equal treatment of individuals was assumed to belong to the cultural component of structure of power relationships. The evidence given in the items was evaluated as too weak to incorporate the items into the item set of the UDC Distribution of Power and Status. Furthermore, the other applied items (items no. 2, no. 3, no. 5, no. 6, and no. 8) of the cultural dimension of Equality Matching by Fiske (1991, 1992) displayed no indication for a conceptual interrelationship with the concept of distribution of power and status.

In summary, the cultural dimension of Equality Matching by Fiske (1991, 1992) revealed minor evidence (please refer to the three items no. 1, no. 4, and no. 7; and the definition) for a conceptual interrelationship with the by A1 assumed cultural components (structure of power relationships, allocation of status and reward, and gender egalitarianism) of the UDC Distribution of Power and Status. By definition, the cultural dimension "organizes relationships with references to their degree of balance or imbalance, it is manifested most distinctly in turn-taking reciprocity, distributions of equal shares, democratic voting, and tit-for-tat-relations" (Haslam & Fiske, 1999, p. 242). The minor evidence was not neglected in this dissertation. The cultural dimension of Equality Matching by Fiske (1991, 1992) was synthesized into the UDC Distribution of Power and Status under acknowledging its less significant contribution to the UDC.

In the cultural taxonomy by **Schwartz (1992, 1994b)**, the cultural dimension of **Hierarchy versus Egalitarianism** displayed a potential affiliation to the concept of distribution of power and status by its title. The analysis of the dimension side of egalitarianism revealed no evidence for a synthesis of the cultural dimension into the UDC Distribution of Power and Status. In contrast, the dimension side of hierarchy revealed by its definition conceptual information regarding the concept of distribution of power and status. Two—Nardon and Steers (2009) and Maleki and de Jong (2014)—of the four synthesis methodologies, synthesized the cultural dimension of Egalitarianism versus Hierarchy by Schwartz (1992, 1994b) into their synthesis dimension for the concept of distribution of power and status. The items applied by Schwartz (1992, 1994b) for the empirical assessment of the cultural dimension side of hierarchy were also analyzed. Two of the four items (items no. 3 and no. 27) were peculiarly related to the concept of distribution of power and status, asking respondents for their importance placed on social power and authority; whereas the other two items (items no. 12 and no. 36) did not directly address the concept of distribution of power and status. Schwartz (2004) analyzed conceptual and empirical overlaps of his cultural dimension of Hierarchy versus Egalitarianism and the cultural dimension of Power Distance by Hofstede (1980, 2001). Schwartz (2004) elaborated that both cultural dimensions address the legitimization of social inequalities within national cultures, whereas individuals tend to fear individuals in higher positions.

In the analysis, no substantial indication was found that the dimension side of hierarchy also encompasses the cultural component of fear for superiors. In conclusion, the cultural dimension analysis demonstrated substantial evidence to synthesize its dimension side of hierarchy into the UDC Distribution of Power and Status. Additionally, the two items (items no. 3 and no. 27) were incorporated into the UDC Distribution of Power and Status potential item set.

Synthesis Analysis Step 2: Analysis of the Remaining Cultural Dimensions
First, the cultural taxonomy by **Fiske (1991, 1992)** was analyzed. In the first synthesis analysis step of the UDC Distribution of Power and Status, the cultural dimensions of Authority Ranking and partially also Equality Matching by Fiske (1991, 1992) were already synthesized into the UDC. The cultural dimensions of Communal Sharing and Market Pricing by Fiske (1991, 1992) were rejected from the synthesis. The cultural dimension of Communal Sharing refers to the concept of individualism versus collectivism; the cultural dimension of Market Pricing refers to the assignment of values as a distinguishing factor for national cultures.

Next, the cultural taxonomy by **Hall (1959, 1966, 1976, 1983; Hall & Hall, 1990)** was in-depth reviewed. No conceptual interrelationship was identified in the analysis of the four cultural dimensions—Context, Information Flow, Space, and Time of Hall (1959, 1966, 1976, 1983; Hall & Hall, 1990)—with the A1 projected UDC Distribution of Power and Status. Therefore, none of the four cultural dimensions Hall (1959, 1966, 1976, 1983; Hall & Hall, 1990) was synthesized into the UDC Distribution of Power and Status.

The third analyzed cultural taxonomy constituted **Hofstede (2001; Hofstede et al., 2010)**. The cultural dimension of Power Distance by Hofstede (2001; Hofstede et al., 2010) was already synthesized into the UDC Distribution of Power and Status in the first synthesis analysis step of the UDC. No evidence for synthesis into the UDC Distribution of Power and Status was identified for the cultural dimensions of Indulgence versus Restraint, Individualism versus Collectivism, Long-Term versus Short-Term Orientation, and Uncertainty Avoidance. The definition of the cultural dimension of Masculinity versus Femininity of Hofstede (2001; Hofstede et al., 2010) pointed to evidence for a conceptual interrelationship to the cultural component of gender egalitarianism, which was projected to constitute a cultural component of the UDC Distribution of Power and Status.

Mainly, the affiliation of the cultural dimension of Masculinity versus Femininity by Hofstede (2001; Hofstede et al., 2010) to the concept of distribution of power and status was assumed in the family context. The role of parents displays the concept of power within a family (Hofstede, 2001). No further correlations between the concept of masculinity versus femininity and the concept of distribution of power and status were indicated by Hofstede (2001; Hofstede et al., 2010).

Hofstede et al. (2010) did not detect any statistical correlation between their cultural dimension of Masculinity versus Femininity and the cultural dimension of Gender Egalitarianism by House et al. (2004, 2007, 2014). In comparison, House et al. (2004) described in more detail their assumed conceptual affiliation of the cultural dimension of Masculinity versus Femininity by Hofstede (2001) to the concept of distribution of power and status. House et al. (2004) elaborated that Hofstede (2001) displays with his cultural dimension of Masculinity versus Femininity the concepts of striving for personal success, valuing challenging work, and material wealth. The three cultural components of striving for personal success, valuing challenging work, and material wealth could be assumed to be related to the concept of distribution of power and status. Due to this evidence, it was decided to review the items of the cultural dimension of Masculinity versus Femininity by Hofstede and Minkov (2013) in more detail. None of the displayed items could be conceptually affiliated to the concept of distribution of power and status. The at first glance assumed affiliation of the cultural dimension of Masculinity versus Femininity of Hofstede (2001; Hofstede et al., 2010) to the cultural component of gender equalitarianism was not confirmed; the in-depth review did not substantiate its synthesis into the UDC Distribution of Power and Status.

The fourth cultural taxonomy, which was analyzed regarding its suitability for synthesis into the UDC Distribution of Power and Status, constituted the cultural taxonomy by **House et al. (2004, 2007, 2014)**. The cultural dimension of Power Distance by House et al. (2004, 2007, 2014) was already synthesized into the UDC Distribution of Power and Status during the first synthesis analysis step of the UDC. For the cultural dimensions of Assertiveness, Future Orientation, In-Group Collectivism, Institutional Collectivism, and Uncertainty Avoidance by House et al. (2004, 2007, 2014), no evidence justifying a synthesis into the UDC Distribution of Power and Status was identified.

The cultural dimension of Performance Orientation by House et al. (2004, 2007, 2014), referring to the classification of national cultures by their extent of rewarding innovations and continuous improvement, displayed at a first sign no conceptual interrelationship to the concept of distribution of power and status. The operationalized items for the cultural dimension of Performance Orientation by House et al. (n.d.) allowed the conclusion that the cultural dimension addresses the concept of allocation of status in a broader sense. The three societal value items no. V3_18, no. V3_20, and no. V3_32 asks for allocating major rewards by performance effectiveness or other factors, rewarding innovation for improving performance, and setting challenging goals. One item (item no. V3_15) was rejected since it focuses on children-parents ties, which were not considered further in this dissertation. In summary, the cultural dimension of Performance Orientation by House et al. (2004, 2007, 2014) and three of its societal value items were synthesized and included in the UDC Distribution of Power and Status.

From the definition of the cultural dimension of Humane Orientation by House et al. (2004, 2007, 2014), it was not explicitly detectable if the cultural dimension is suitable to be synthesized into the UDC Distribution of Power and Status. The cultural dimension could be interpreted as referring to the allocation of status and reward by individuals' behavior of being fair, generous, altruistic, caring, and kind to others. The analysis of the items operationalized for the empirical measurement of the cultural dimension revealed no factual information that the cultural dimension of Humane Orientation addresses the cultural component of allocation of status and reward in this dissertation's sense. House et al. (2004) identified a statistical correlation of their cultural dimension of Humane Orientation and the practice items of their cultural dimension of Power Distance. Also, the value items of their cultural dimension of Power Distance correlated significantly negatively with the value items of the cultural dimension of Humane Orientation (House et al., 2004). The evidence of the statistical correlation between the concept of humane orientation and the concept of distribution of power and status, as indicated by House et al. (2004), was evaluated as not substantial enough to justify a synthesis of the cultural dimension of Humane Orientation by House et al. (2004, 2007, 2014) into the UDC Distribution of Power and Status.

Nardon and Steers (2009) synthesized the cultural dimension of Gender Egalitarianism by House et al. (2004, 2007, 2014) into their synthesis dimension addressing the concept of distribution of power and status. Low and Chapman (2003) and Maleki and de Jong (2014) considered the cultural dimension of Gender Egalitarianism by House et al. (2004, 2007, 2014) distinct from the concept of distribution of power and status.

It was concluded that the cultural dimension of Gender Egalitarianism of House et al. (2004, 2007, 2014) displays evidence to be synthesized into the UDC Distribution of Power and Status since it refers to the structures of relationships by gender roles and the allocation of status and reward. A1 assumed the concept of gender egalitarianism as one cultural component for this dissertation's UDC Distribution of Power and Status. Evidence for the synthesis of the cultural dimension of Gender Egalitarianism by House et al. (2004, 2007, 2014) into the UDC Distribution of Power and Status constituted that House et al. (2004) identified that national cultures with a high score of gender egalitarianism also tend to accord females a higher status in the society, and females possess positions of authority and more significant roles in the community. Vice versa accounts for national cultures which score lower in gender egalitarianism. Overall, it was decided to synthesize the cultural dimension of Gender Egalitarianism by House et al. (2004, 2007, 2014) into the UDC Distribution of Power and Status, in line with Nardon and Steers (2009), but in contrast to Low and Chapman (2003) and Maleki and de Jong (2014). Additionally, five societal value items (items no. V3_17, no. V3_22, no. V3_26, no. V3_38, and no. V3_39) of the cultural dimension of Gender Egalitarianism were incorporated into the potential item set of the UDC Distribution of Power and Status.

In the synthesis analysis, the next analyzed cultural taxonomy constituted the cultural taxonomy by **Inglehart et al. (2014)**. The two cultural dimensions of Survival Values versus Self-Expression Values and Traditional Values vs. Secular-Rational Values by Inglehart et al. (2014) indicated no evidence for affiliation to the concept of distribution of power and status. Thus, both cultural dimensions were rejected for synthesis into the UDC Distribution of Power and Status.

Afterward, the five cultural dimensions of the cultural taxonomy by **Kluckhohn and Strodtbeck (1961)** were analyzed regarding their suitability for synthesis into the UDC Distribution of Power and Status.

The cultural dimension of Relational Orientation displayed the peculiarity that it demonstrates the concept of distribution of power and status and the concept of individualism versus collectivism at once. Also, Maleki and de Jong (2014) critically considered the connection between both concepts in the cultural dimension. The cultural dimension distinguishes national cultures according to their individual, collective, or hierarchical relationship system (Kluckhohn & Strodtbeck, 1961). It was decided to synthesize the dimension side of hierarchy into the UDC Distribution of Power and Status. None of the other four cultural dimensions of Activity Orientation, Time Orientation, Man-Nature Orientation, and Human-Nature Orientation by Kluckhohn and Strodtbeck (1961) indicated evidence for synthesis into the UDC Distribution of Power and Status.

The seventh analyzed cultural taxonomy constitutes the cultural taxonomy by **Lewis (2018)**, offering the cultural dimensions of Linear Active, Multi-Active, and Re-Active to distinguish national cultures. Overall, there was no information applicable, which would have justified a synthesis of the three cultural dimensions by Lewis (2018) into the UDC Distribution of Power and Status.

Another analyzed cultural taxonomy constitutes **Minkov (2007)**, distinguishing national cultures by the three cultural dimensions of Exclusionism versus Universalism, Indulgence versus Restraint, and Monumentalism versus Flexhumility. The in-depth review of the cultural dimensions revealed no evidence which would have justified a synthesis of the cultural dimensions into the UDC Distribution of Power and Status.

The next analyzed cultural taxonomy constituted the cultural taxonomy by **Parsons and Shils (1951)**. Four of the five cultural dimensions of Affectivity versus Affective Neutrality, Functional Specificity versus Functional Diffuseness, Self-Interest versus Collectivist Interest, and Universalism versus Particularism revealed no evidence to be suitable for synthesized into the UDC Distribution of Power and Status. Only, the cultural dimension of Ascription versus Achievement by Parsons and Shils (1951) pointed to evidence for affiliation to the concept of distribution of power and status, referring to the option of individuals to perceive objects regarding either their quality or their performance.

In more detail, the ascription dimension side refers to the judgment of individuals regarding the prioritization of specific attributes instead of the prescribed performance of an object. In contrast, the dimension side of achievement refers to individuals prioritizing specific performances over attributes of an object. The focus in achievement-driven national cultures is on the direct condition of the performance of an object (Parsons & Shils, 1951). The cultural dimension of Ascription versus Achievement by Parsons and Shils (1951) was synthesized into the UDC Distribution of Power and Status.

Regarding the cultural taxonomy by **Schwartz** (1992, 1994b), its cultural dimension of Hierarchy versus Egalitarianism was already partially synthesized into the

UDC Distribution of Power and Status in the first analysis step of the UDC. The two cultural dimensions of Autonomy versus Embeddedness and Mastery versus Harmony indicated no affiliation to the underlying concepts of the UDC Distribution of Power and Status.

The last reviewed cultural taxonomy constituted **Trompenaars and Hampden-Turner (2004, 2012)**. The six cultural dimensions of Communitarianism versus Individualism, Sequential versus Synchronous Time, Diffuseness versus Specific, Internal versus Outer Direction, Neutral versus Emotional, and Universalism versus Particularism pointed to no evidence for a relation to the concept of distribution of power and status. Only the cultural dimension of Achievement versus Ascription by Trompenaars and Hampden-Turner (2004, 2012) showed evidence to address the UDC Distribution of Power and Status concept and cultural components. Deductible from the definition and the items applied by Trompenaars and Hampden-Turner (2012), it was retrieved that the cultural dimension of Ascription versus Achievement addresses the concept of allocation of status and reward, which was also projected as a cultural component for the UDC Distribution of Power and Status by A1. Conclusively, the cultural dimension of Ascription versus Achievement by Trompenaars and Hampden-Turner (2004, 2012) was synthesized into the UDC. Likewise, the two items applied by Trompenaars and Hampden-Turner (2004, 2012)—item no. 1 under the umbrella of the concept of allocation of power and status based on performances, and item no. 2 under the umbrella of the concept of allocation of status and reward in general.

5.2 Synthesis of the Universal Dimension of Culture (UDC) Relationship with the Natural Environment

A2 of this dissertation proposed the UDC Relationship with the Environment, referring to the concept of relationship with the natural environment in a national culture as one general concept in existing cultural taxonomies. In more detail, the UDC Relationship with the Environment was projected to address the distinction of national cultures by the concept of mastery versus harmony and the cultural components of masculinity versus femininity, assertiveness, and gender egalitarianism, addressing the relationship of individuals with the natural environment.

Among the four synthesis methodologies, evidence was detected that the concept of relationship with the natural environment could interfere with the concepts of social organization, uncertainty avoidance, and human orientation.

The three stated concepts were operationalized in this dissertation into the three UDCs Human Orientation, Social Organization, and Uncertainty Avoidance and Coping Mechanisms. Specifically, the interferences between the concepts of relationship with the social environment and relationship with the natural environment required a more in-depth analysis (please refer to Section 5.5 Delimitation Between the Concepts of Social Environment and Relationship with the Natural Environment). Figure 5.2 displays, in summary, the projected UDC Relationship with the Environment and its embedded cultural components for this dissertation.

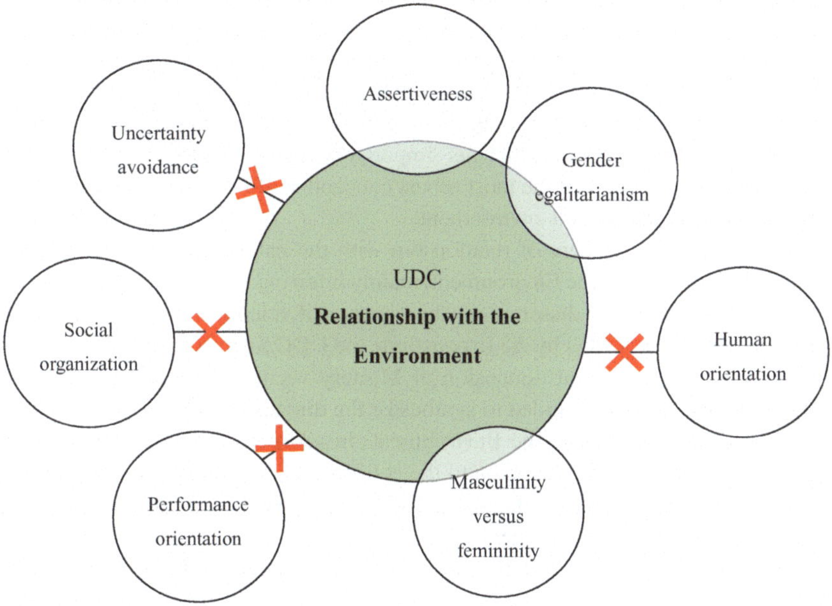

Figure 5.2 Assumption 2 (A2): The Universal Dimension of Culture (UDC) Relationship with the Environment

Synthesis Analysis Step 1: Title-Related Cultural Dimensions

The following cultural dimensions were identified as title-related cultural dimensions for the UDC Relationship with the Environment in the set of 50 cultural dimensions from 11 selected existing cultural taxonomies: Space by Hall (1966), Human-Nature Orientation by Kluckhohn and Strodtbeck (1961), Man-Nature Orientation by Kluckhohn and Strodtbeck (1961), Mastery versus Harmony by

Schwartz (1992, 1994b), and Internal versus Outer Direction by Trompenaars and Hampden-Turner (2004, 2012).

At first, the cultural dimension of **Mastery versus Harmony** by **Schwartz** (1992, 1994b) was analyzed. The conceptual analysis of the cultural dimension revealed that it addresses the two concepts of relationship with the natural environment and the relationship with the social environment simultaneously. It was identified that the dimension side of harmony refers to the relationship of individuals with the natural environment, and the mastery dimension side refers to the relationship of individuals to the social environment. Schwartz (1992, 1994b) also operationalized items specifically for each dimension side. In summary, the four items no. 17, no. 24, no. 29, and no. 38 of the dimension side of harmony by Schwartz (1992, 1994b) indicated an affiliation to the concept of relationship with the natural environment. The items refer to respondent's importance regarding a world at peace, unity with nature, a world of beauty, and protecting the natural environment. Item no. 38, respondents' importance regarding protecting the (natural) environment, displayed the most robust conceptual affiliation to the concept of relationship with the natural environment.

A2 assumed the concept of relationship with the natural environment for the UDC Relationship with the Environment, mainly referring to the concept of mastery versus harmony. In this dissertation, the concept of relationship with the social environment was projected by A3 to constitute the UDC Social Organization. From the analysis of the cultural dimension of Mastery versus Harmony by Schwartz (1992, 1994b), it was concluded to synthesize the dimension side of harmony into the UDC Relationship with the Environment. In addition, the two items, no. 24 and item no. 38, primarily referring to the concept of relationship with the natural environment, were incorporated into this dissertation's potential item set of the UDC Relationship with the Environment.

The synthesis of the cultural dimension of Mastery versus Harmony by Schwartz (1992, 1994b) into a synthesis dimension for the concept of relationship with the environment was in line with Maleki and de Jong (2014), Nardon and Steers (2009), and Schneider et al. (2014).

The second analyzed title-related cultural dimension constituted the cultural dimension of **Man-Nature Orientation** by **Kluckhohn and Strodtbeck (1961)**, classifying national cultures by the three concepts of subjugation-to-nature, mastery-over-nature, and harmony-with-nature. The conceptual analysis of the cultural dimension of Man-Nature Orientation by Kluckhohn and Strodtbeck (1961) revealed enough evidence for its synthesis into the UDC Relationship with the Environment in this dissertation. The definition of the cultural dimension addressed the cultural concept of relationship with the natural environment, and more specifically, the cultural concept of mastery versus harmony per se. The synthesis follows at this point Maleki and de Jong (2014), Nardon and Steers (2009), and Schneider et al. (2014). Also, the synthesis of Man-Nature Orientation by Kluckhohn and Strodtbeck (1961) into the UDC Relationship with the Environment substantiated the affiliation between the concepts of relationship with the natural environment and mastery versus harmony.

Next, the cultural dimension of **Human-Nature Orientation** by **Kluckhohn and Strodtbeck (1961)**, classifying national cultures into evil, evil and good, and good, was analyzed. The in-depth analysis of the cultural dimension revealed no evidence of its affiliation to the concept of relationship with the natural environment as understood in the UDC Relationship with the Environment in this dissertation. Thus, the cultural dimension was not synthesized into the UDC Relationship with the Environment.

Afterward, the cultural dimension of **Internal versus Outer Direction** by **Trompenaars and Hampden-Turner (2004, 2012)** was analyzed. Three of the four in the SLR identified synthesis methodologies (Maleki and de Jong (2014), Nardon and Steers (2009), and Schneider et al. (2014)) synthesized the cultural dimension into their synthesis dimension regarding the concept of relationship with the (natural) environment. The description and definition of the cultural dimension of Internal versus Outer Direction by Trompenaars and Hampden-Turner (2004, 2012) pointed to affiliation to the concept of relationship with the natural environment.

For the empirical measurement of the cultural dimension, Trompenaars and Hampden-Turner (2004, 2012) asked their respondents to choose from the following two sets of alternatives: Firstly, "Is it worthwhile trying to control important national forces, such as the weather" or "Nature should take its curse, and we just have to accept it the way it comes and do the best we can" (Trompenaars & Hampden-Turner, 1997, p. 142). Secondly, "What happens to me is my own doing" or "Sometimes I feel that I do not have enough control over the directions my life is taking" (Trompenaars & Hampden-Turner, 1997, p. 142).

Summarizing the analysis of the cultural dimension of Internal versus Outer Direction of Trompenaars and Hampden-Turner (2004, 2012), the cultural dimension was synthesized into the UDC Relationship with the Environment of this dissertation. Additionally, the two proposed sets of alternatives for the empirical assessment of the cultural dimension were also incorporated into this dissertation's potential item set of the UDC Relationship with the Environment.

The last considered title-related cultural dimension constituted the cultural dimension of **Space** by **Hall (1966)**. The description and definition of the cultural dimension did not indicate any conceptual overlap to the concept of relationship with the natural environment. As Hall (1966) studied it, the concept of space was not possible to collate to the relationship of individuals with their natural environment as assumed by A2 for the UDC Relationship with the Environment. Conclusively, the cultural dimension of Space by Hall (1966) was not synthesized into the UDC Relationship with the Environment in this dissertation.

Synthesis Analysis Step 2: Analysis of the Remaining Cultural Dimensions
At first, the cultural taxonomy by **Fiske (1991, 1992)** was reviewed. None of the four cultural dimensions demonstrated a strong relationship with the concept of relationship with the natural environment as it was operationalized for the UDC Relationship with the Environment in this dissertation. The cultural dimension of Communal Sharing by Fiske (1991, 1992) pointed to evidence for addressing both concepts—the concept of relationship with the social environment and the concept of relationship with the natural environment—at once. Therefore, the cultural dimension was analyzed regarding the delimitation of both concepts again (please refer to Section 5.5 Delimitation Between the Concepts of Social Environment and Relationship with the Natural Environment).

Secondly, **Hall (1959, 1966, 1976, 1983; Hall & Hall, 1990)** was in-depth analyzed. The cultural dimensions of Space by Hall (1959, 1966, 1976, 1983; Hall & Hall, 1990) was already rejected for synthesis into the UDC Relationship with the Environment of this dissertation during the first analysis steps. Moreover, the cultural dimension of Context was reviewed due to the delimitation between the concept of relationship with the social environment and the relationship with the natural environment (please refer to Section 5.5 Delimitation Between the Concepts of Social Environment and Relationship with the Natural Environment). The remaining two cultural dimensions of Time and Information Flow by Hall (1983; Hall & Hall, 1990) indicated no conceptual interference with the concept of relationship with the natural environment. As a result, no cultural dimension by Hall (1959, 1966, 1976, 1983; Hall & Hall, 1990) was synthesized into the UDC Relationship with the Environment.

The third analyzed cultural taxonomy constituted **Hofstede (2001; Hofstede et al., 2010)**. The three cultural dimensions of Indulgence versus Restraint, Long-Term versus Short-Term Orientation, and Power Distance by Hofstede (2001; Hofstede et al., 2010) revealed no evidence in their in-depth analysis for affiliation to the concept of relationship with the natural environment; thus, were rejected for synthesis into the UDC Relationship with the Environment in this dissertation. The two cultural dimensions of Individualism versus Collectivism and Uncertainty Avoidance by Hofstede (2001; Hofstede et al., 2010) displayed information that addresses the concept of relationship with the natural environment in terms of the concept of uncertainty avoidance and the concept of relationship with the social environment. In the in-depth analysis of both cultural dimensions, no evidence was identified which would have substantiated their synthesis into the UDC Relationship with the Environment.

Maleki and de Jong (2014) and Nardon and Steers (2009) synthesized the cultural dimension of Masculinity versus Femininity by Hofstede (2001; Hofstede et al., 2010) into their synthesis dimension addressing the concept of relationship with the natural environment. In addition, A2 also assumed a cultural component of masculinity versus femininity for the UDC Relationship with the Environment. A first review of the definition of the cultural dimension pointed to no indication of a conceptual overlap of the cultural dimension of Masculinity versus Femininity by Hofstede (2001; Hofstede et al., 2010) with the cultural concept of relationship with the natural environment.

The review of the description of the cultural dimension revealed that Hofstede (2001; Hofstede et al., 2010) designed the dimension side of femininity regarding the cultural concept of female caring, inducing more significant concerns for the living environment. Hofstede and Minkov (2013) applied four items to empirically assess the cultural dimension of Masculinity versus Femininity. None of the four items addressed the concept of relationship with the natural environment as understood in this dissertation.

Summarizing the analysis of the cultural dimension of Masculinity versus Femininity by Hofstede (2001; Hofstede et al., 2010), it was given credit to its synthesis into the UDC Relationship with the Environment since its affiliation to the concept of relationship with the natural environment became applicable in the description of the cultural dimension. The synthesis was pursued by acknowledging the limited influence of the cultural dimension in the UDC Relationship with the Environment.

The fourth cultural taxonomy analyzed regarding the suitability of its cultural dimensions for a synthesis in the UDC Relationship with the Environment constituted the cultural taxonomy by **House et al. (2004, 2007, 2014)**. The cultural dimensions of In-Group Collectivism, Institutional Collectivism, and Uncertainty Avoidance were rejected for synthesis into the UDC Relationship with the Environment during the analysis of the affiliation of the concepts of relationship with the social environment and relationship with the natural environment as well as the concepts of relationship with the natural environment and uncertainty avoidance. The two cultural dimensions of Future Orientation and Power Distance by House et al. (2004, 2007, 2014) indicated no further evidence for their synthesis in the UDC Relationship with the Environment.

A2 proposed for the UDC Relationship with the Environment a cultural component of assertiveness, which was also assumed to be mirrored in the cultural dimension of Assertiveness by House et al. (2004, 2007, 2014). The in-depth analysis of the cultural dimension revealed that House et al. (2004, 2007, 2014) understand the concept of assertiveness in terms of individual's beliefs to be encouraged for assertive, aggressive, and though behavior or non-aggressive, tender, and non-assertive behavior in social relationship.

Furthermore, House et al. (2004, 2007, 2014) indicated conceptual overlaps between their cultural dimension and the cultural dimension of Masculinity versus Femininity by Hofstede (2001; Hofstede et al., 2010). Nevertheless, neither the in-depth analysis of the description and definition of the cultural dimension of Assertiveness by House et al. (2004) nor the analysis of the applied items of the cultural dimension revealed any indication for a conceptual overlap to the concept of relationship with the natural environment as understood in the UDC Relationship with the Environment in this dissertation. As a result, the cultural dimension of Assertiveness by House et al. (2004, 2007, 2014) was rejected from the synthesis into the UDC Relationship with the Environment. Conclusively, the concept of assertiveness as a cultural component for the UDC was not confirmed in this dissertation's analysis.

The cultural dimension of Gender Egalitarianism by House et al. (2004, 2007, 2014) was also in-depth analyzed since the concept of gender egalitarianism was projected by A2 as a cultural component for the UDC Relationship with the Environment. Maleki and de Jong (2014) demonstrated in their analysis conceptual overlaps between the concepts of masculinity versus femininity, gender egalitarianism, and relationship with the natural environment. The cultural dimension of Gender Egalitarianism demonstrated the assessment of the basis for individuals' roles in their homes, business organizations, and communities regarding their biological sexes. Among others, the degree of gender egalitarianism is applicable in parental investments, religion, economic development, mode of production, and the political system of and within a national culture (House et al., 2004). None of the identified information pointed to any substantial evidence for the projected conceptual overlaps. Likewise, the analysis of the items for the cultural dimension revealed no evidence for affiliation to the UDC Relationship with the Environment. As a result, the cultural dimension of Gender Egalitarianism by House et al. (2004, 2007, 2014) was not synthesized into the UDC Relationship with the Environment.

Next, the cultural dimension of Humane Orientation by House et al. (2004, 2007, 2014) was analyzed in more detail since Nardon and Steers (2009) synthesized the cultural dimension into their synthesis dimension for the concept of relationship with the (natural and social) environment. In this dissertation, A2 assumed that the cultural concept of human orientation does not constitute a cultural component of the UDC Relationship with the Environment.

The description and definition of the cultural dimension did not reveal any further information nor evidence for a relation of the cultural dimension with the concept of relationship with the natural environment nor the concept of mastery versus harmony. Also, the analysis of the empirically applied items for the cultural dimension demonstrated no further information that would have substantiated a synthesis of the cultural dimension of Humane Orientation by House et al. (2004, 2007, 2014) into the UDC Relationship with the Environment, also inducing a rejection of the concept of human orientation as a cultural component for the UDC Relationship with the Environment in this dissertation.

Finally, the cultural dimension of Performance Orientation by House et al. (2004, 2007, 2014) was reviewed since Nardon and Steers (2009) connected the concept of performance orientation to the concept of relationship with the environment. A2 did not project a cultural component of performance orientation for this dissertation's UDC Relationship with the Environment. The cultural dimension of Performance Orientation by House et al. (2004, 2007, 2014) classifies national cultures according to their individual's definition of success by adapting to external challenges and internal management of relationships. The analysis of the description and definition of the cultural dimension did not demonstrate any information that would substantiate Nardon and Steers (2009). The review of the items applied by House et al. (n.d.) for the empirical assessment of the cultural dimension of Performance Orientation did not point to any evidence that would have substantiated a synthesis of the items nor of the cultural dimension into the UDC Relationship with the Environment. Therefore, the cultural dimension of Performance Orientation by House et al. (2004, 2007, 2014) was not synthesized into the UDC Relationship with the Environment in this dissertation and the by A2 assumed rejection of a cultural component of performance orientation for the UDC was confirmed.

The fifth analyzed existing cultural taxonomy constituted the cultural taxonomy by **Inglehart et al. (2014)**. The cultural dimension of Traditional Values versus Secular-Rational Values revealed no evidence for affiliation to the concept of relationship with the natural environment; thus, it was not synthesized into the UDC. The cultural dimension of Self-Expression Values versus Survival Values by Inglehart et al. (2014) indicated in its definition minor evidence for a conceptual overlap to the cultural concept of relationship with the natural environment.

The dimension side of self-expression encompassed evidence for addressing the concept of environmental protection. Therefore, the items of the cultural dimension of Survival Values versus Self-Expression Values were analyzed. No item was applicable that indicated an affiliation to the concept of relationship with the natural environment, as the evidence in the definition of the cultural dimension indicated. Also, none of the four in the SLR identified synthesis methodology synthesized the cultural dimension of Survival Values versus Self-Expression Values by Inglehart et al. (2014) into their synthesis dimension regarding the concept of relationship with the natural environment. Conclusively, the cultural dimension of Survival Values versus Self-Expression Values by Inglehart et al. (2014) was not synthesized into the UDC.

Next, the cultural taxonomy by **Kluckhohn and Strodtbeck (1961)** was reviewed, from which already the cultural dimension of Man-Nature Orientation by Kluckhohn and Strodtbeck (1961) was synthesized in the first UDC analysis step into the UDC Relationship with the Environment in this dissertation. The two cultural dimensions of Relational Orientation and Human Nature Orientation of Kluckhohn and Strodtbeck (1961) were rejected for synthesis into the UDC Relationship with the Environment due to missing evidence. Also, the cultural dimension of Time Orientation by Kluckhohn and Strodtbeck (1961) revealed no evidence for affiliation to the cultural concept of relationship with the natural environment. Nardon and Steers (2009) synthesized the cultural dimension of Activity Orientation by Kluckhohn and Strodtbeck (1961) into their synthesis dimension for the concept of mastery versus harmony. Nardon and Steers (2009) assumed that the cultural dimension reflects the importance of striving for goals as a cultural component for the concept of relationship with the natural environment. Especially, doing national cultures is assumed to stress environmental activities (Nardon & Steers, 2009). The cultural dimension analysis revealed no evidence that substantiated the approach by Nardon and Steers (2009). No information was identified that pointed to a synthesis of the cultural dimension of Activity Orientation by Kluckhohn and Strodtbeck (1961) into the UDC Relationship with the Environment.

Afterward, the three cultural dimensions of the cultural taxonomy by **Lewis (2018)** were reviewed. None of the three cultural dimensions of Linear Active, Multi-Active, and Re-Active by Lewis (2018) demonstrated any substantial evidence for synthesis in this dissertation's UDC Relationship with the Environment.

The eighth analyzed cultural taxonomy constituted the cultural taxonomy by **Minkov (2007)**. The cultural dimension of Exclusionism versus Universalism was already partially synthesized into the UDC during the first analysis steps. The other two cultural dimensions of Indulgence versus Restraint and Monumentalism versus Flexhumility by Minkov (2007) revealed no further evidence that would have substantiated their synthesis into the UDC Relationship with the Environment.

Next, the cultural taxonomy by **Parsons and Shils (1951)** and their cultural dimensions were analyzed. The cultural dimension of Self-Interest versus Collectivist Interest by Parsons and Shils (1951) was already analyzed in the first analysis steps of the UDC Relationship with the Environment and rejected for synthesis into the UDC. The in-depth review of the cultural dimensions of Affectivity versus Affective Neutrality, Ascription versus Achievements, Functional Specificity versus Functional Diffuseness, and Universalism versus Particularism revealed no evidence for an affiliation to the relationship with the natural environment. In result, none of the cultural dimensions was synthesized into the UDC Relationship with the Environment.

The tenth analyzed cultural taxonomy constituted the cultural taxonomy by **Schwartz** (1992, 1994b), from which the cultural dimension of Mastery versus Harmony was already partly synthesized into the UDC Relationship with the Environment. The analysis of the other two cultural dimensions, including their items, revealed no further information to substantiate their synthesis into the UDC.

Last, the cultural taxonomy by **Trompenaars and Hampden-Turner (2004, 2012)** was reviewed. The cultural dimension of Internal versus Outer Direction by Trompenaars and Hampden-Turner (2004, 2012) was already synthesized into the UDC Relationship with the Environment during the first UDC analysis step. None of the other cultural dimensions of the cultural taxonomy—Achievement versus Ascription, Sequential versus Synchronous Time, Diffuse versus Specific, Neutral versus Emotional, Communitarianism versus Individualism, and Universalism versus Particularism—revealed any evidence for synthesis into the UDC.

5.3 Synthesis of the Universal Dimension of Culture (UDC) Social Organization

A3 proposed the UDC Social Organization, illustrating the concept of individualism versus collectivism as a general concept among existing cultural taxonomies to distinguish national cultures. A3 assumed that the UDC Social Organization distinguishes national cultures by the cultural components of universalism versus particularism and diffuse versus specific. In addition, according to A3, the UDC Social Organization encompasses in conceptual terms, the cultural components of context, space, and time, originating from the existing cultural taxonomy by Hall (1959, 1966, 1976, 1983; Hall & Hall, 1990), as one conglomerative cultural component. The term *social organization* as heading for the UDC was identified and borrowed from Nardon and Steers (2009), demonstrating a synthesis dimension regarding the concept of individualism versus collectivism. A critical aspect in the synthesis of the UDC constituted the delimitation of its three assumed cultural components—universalism versus collectivism, diffuse versus specific, and context, space, and time—to the concepts of distribution of power and status as well as ascription versus achievement.

In this dissertation, the concept of ascription versus achievement was subsumed to the UDC Distribution of Power and Status. Following the approach by Hofstede (2001; Hofstede et al., 2010), the concept of individualism versus collectivism refers to the characteristics of individuals' group memberships as distinguishing factor for national cultures; in contrast, the concept of distribution of power and status refers to the individuals' emotional dependency to others, mainly higher-ranked individuals in the national culture. In this dissertation, both concepts—the concept of individualism versus collectivism and the concept of distribution of power and status—were operationalized into two different UDCs Distribution of Power and Status and Social Organization.

Figure 5.3 displays the by A3 assumed UDC Social Organization and its embedded cultural components.

Synthesis Analysis Step 1: Title-Related Cultural Dimensions

Among the 50 cultural dimensions, the following seven cultural dimensions were identified, indicating by their title an affiliation to the concepts of social organization: Communal Sharing by Fiske (1991, 1992), Individualism versus Collectivism by Hofstede (2001; Hofstede et al., 2010), In-Group Collectivism and Institutional Collectivism by House et al. (2004, 2007, 2014), Relational Orientation by Kluckhohn and Strodtbeck (1961), Self-Interest versus Collectivist Interest by Parsons and Shils (1951), and Communitarianism versus Individualism by Trompenaars and Hampden-Turner (2004, 2012).

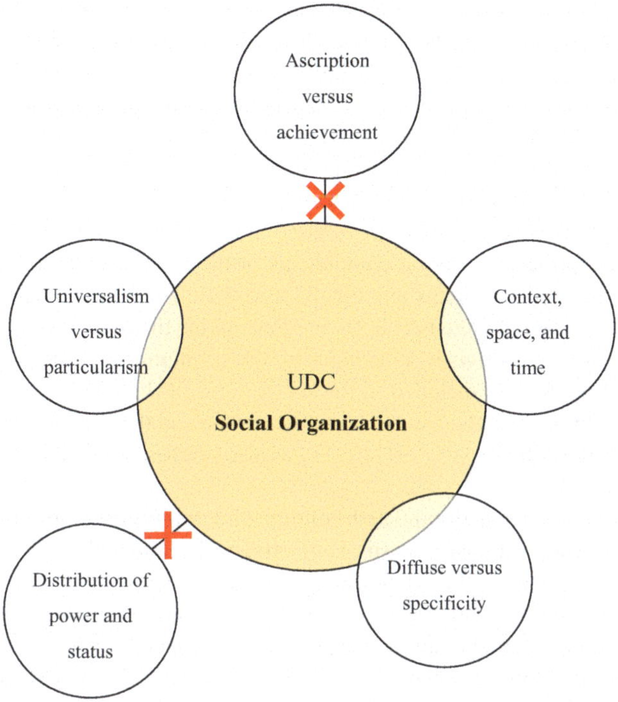

Figure 5.3 Assumption 3 (A3): The Universal Dimension of Culture (UDC) Social Organization

The cultural dimension of **Communal Sharing** by **Fiske (1991, 1992)** is assumed to address the concept of individualism versus collectivism, thus, the emotional dependence of individuals on collectives, by addressing the favor of individuals for group memberships and the alignment with a common identity. Fiske (1991, 1992) also operationalized eight items for the empirical measurement of his cultural dimension of Communal Sharing. Two items (items no. 1 and no. 2) were considered unsuitable to be incorporated into the UDC Social Organization potential item set. The remaining six items (items no. 3, no. 4, no. 5, no. 6, no. 7, and no. 8) indicated evidence for affiliation to the concepts of social organization and individualism versus collectivism. Item no. 4 referred to respondents' moral obligation to feel compassionate and kind about other individuals. Item no. 5 was considered to display the decision-making process based on group consensus. By

A3, the UDC Social Organization was not assumed to include the concept of group decision-making. Based on the evidence found in the cultural dimension of Communal Sharing by Fiske (1991, 1992), item no. 5 was assumed to relate in a broader sense to the concept of individualism versus collectivism. The remaining items no. 3, no. 6, no. 7, and no. 8 were interpreted to address the concept of group affiliation by asking respondents to evaluate the preference for joint responsibilities, similar attitudes and values, and unity in their national culture.

Likewise, to item no. 5, items no. 3, no. 6, no.7, and no. 8 reflected not explicitly one of the projected cultural components of the UDC Social Organization of this dissertation. All four items empirically assessed the emotional dependency of individuals on other individuals/collectives, constituting the cultural concept of individualism versus collectivism. Conclusively, the six items no. 3, no. 4, no. 5, no. 6, no. 7, and no. 8 were included in the set of items of the UDC, referring to the general concept of individualism versus collectivism and the cultural dimension of Communal Sharing by Fiske (1991, 1992) was also synthesized into the UDC Social Organization.

The second analyzed title-related cultural dimension constituted the cultural dimension of **Individualism versus Collectivism** by **Hofstede** (2001; Hofstede et al., 2010)[2], displaying the relationships between individual and collectives as a distinguishing factor for national cultures, reflecting on how individuals live together in corresponding national cultures. For the empirical operationalization of his cultural dimension of Individualism versus Collectivism, Hofstede and Minkov (2013) developed four items and a formula for calculating national country scores.

Summarizing the evidence from the analysis of the cultural dimension of Individualism versus Collectivism by Hofstede (2001; Hofstede et al., 2010), it can be stated that by definition, the cultural dimension addresses the concept of individualism versus collectivism, reflecting the emotional dependency of individuals on collectives. This affiliation did not become applicable explicitly for the items operationalized for the cultural dimension by Hofstede and Minkov (2013). As elaborated in Hofstede (2001), the basis for the cultural dimension served the concept of 14 work goals. The applied items in the VSM 2013 by Hofstede and Minkov (2013) seized on these 14 work goals. None of the four items by Hofstede and Minkov (2013) was applicable to address one of the three assumed cultural components of the UDC Social Organization of this dissertation. Conclusively, the cultural dimension of Individualism versus Collectivism was synthesized into the UDC Social

[2] In the analysis the cultural dimension by Hofstede (2001; Hofstede et al., 2010) and the initial conducted factor analysis of 14 different work goals (e.g., freedom, training, physical condition) by Hofstede (1980) were reviewed.

Organization. Moreover, none of the four items was included in the potential item set for the UDC Social Organization of this dissertation due to their strong focus on work-related goals.

Next, the two cultural dimensions of **Institutional Collectivism** and **In-Group Collectivism** by **House et al. (2004, 2007, 2014)** were analyzed. Maleki and de Jong (2014) demonstrated two distinct synthesis dimensions for the two cultural dimensions. In this dissertation, both cultural dimensions were assumed to be synthesized into one UDC, according to Nardon and Steers (2009).

The cultural dimension of In-Group Collectivism is defined by House et al. (2004) as: "the degree to which individuals express pride, loyalty, and cohesiveness in their organizations or families" (p. 30). By its definition and description, the cultural dimension of In-Group Collectivism by House et al. (2004) indicates evidence for its synthesis into the UDC Social Organization. Reviewing the societal value items of the cultural dimension, two items (items no. V3_11 and no. V3_23) were excluded from the incorporation into the item set of the UDC Social Organization due to their considerable focus on children-parents ties, constituting no focus of this dissertation. Furthermore, item no. V3_34 relates to the cultural component of pride in general. A3 initially assumed no cultural component of pride for the UDC Social Organization, although the evidence for its incorporation into the UDC Social Organization was given credit in this dissertation. Thus, the item (item no. V3_34) was included in the potential item set of the UDC Social Organization regarding indicating the cultural component of pride for the UDC. The affiliation of the societal value item no. V3_29 of the cultural dimension of In-Group Collectivism by House et al. (2004), referring to individuals' importance regarding a positive picture of their own national culture by other individuals, to the concept of social organization cannot be clearly defined. Conclusively, item no. V3_29 was not incorporated in the UDC Social Organization item set. Overall, the cultural dimension of In-Group Collectivism of House et al. (2004, 2007, 2014) was synthesized into the UDC Social Organization of this dissertation.

By definition, the cultural dimension of Institutional Collectivism by House et al. (2004) describes "the degree to which organizational and societal institutional practices encourage and reward collective distribution of resources and collective action" (p. 30), also displaying the balance between the emphasis on group loyalty in contrast to the emphasis on individual's goals. The societal value items of the cultural dimension of Institutional Collectivism by House et al. (n.d.) indicated the following evidence regarding the concepts of social organization and/or individualism versus collectivism.

None of the four societal value items (items no. V3_7, no. V3_12, no. V3_36, and no. V3_37) directly addressed one of the three cultural components of universalism versus collectivism, diffuse versus specific, and context, space, and time of the UDC Social Organization. In summary, the four items referred to individuals' importance for group loyalty, maximization of individual interests versus collective interests, preferences for individual or team sports, and the evaluation between group cohesion versus individualism. This dissertation concluded that all four of the societal value items of the cultural dimension of Institutional Collectivism by House et al. (2004, 2007, 2014) assess the concept of individualism versus collectivism from a rather general but concrete angle. All four items were incorporated into the potential item set of the UDC Social Organization. Likewise, the cultural dimension of Institutional Collectivism by House et al. (2004, 2007, 2014) was synthesized into the UDC Social Organization.

The next analyzed title-related cultural dimension constituted the cultural dimension of **Relational Orientation** by **Kluckhohn and Strodtbeck (1961)**, synthesized by two of the four in the SLR identified synthesis methodologies—Maleki and de Jong (2014) and Nardon and Steers (2009)—into their synthesis dimensions regarding the concept of individualism versus collectivism. The dimension side of hierarchy was already synthesized into the UDC Distribution of Power and Status. The analysis of the dimension sides of collectivism and individualism of the cultural dimension Relational Orientation by Kluckhohn and Strodtbeck (1961) substantiated the segregated synthesis of the cultural dimension, and the two dimension sides of collectivism and individualism were synthesized into the UDC Social Organization.

Another title-related cultural dimension constituted the cultural dimension of **Self-Interest versus Collectivist Interest** by **Parsons and Shils (1951)**. The cultural dimension of Self-Interest versus Collectivist Interest by Parsons and Shils (1951) was synthesized by Maleki and de Jong (2014) into their synthesis dimension for the concept of individualism versus collectivism. The conceptual review of the cultural dimension revealed enough evidence to substantiate its affiliation to the concept of social organization and the concept of individualism versus collectivism as understood in this dissertation. Conclusively, in line with Maleki and de Jong (2014), the cultural dimension of Self-Interest versus Collectivist Interest was synthesized into the UDC Social Organization.

The last title-related analyzed cultural dimension constituted **Communitarianism versus Individualism** by **Trompenaars and Hampden-Turner (2004, 2012)**. Low and Chapman (2003), Nardon and Steers (2009), and Maleki and de Jong (2014) synthesized the cultural dimension into their synthesis dimension for the concept of individualism versus collectivism. From the analysis of the definition and description of the cultural dimension, its affiliation to the concept of social organization and the concept of individualism versus collectivism became applicable. Trompenaars and Hampden-Turner (2004, 2012) operationalized three items for the empirical assessment of their cultural dimension. All three items were considered suitable for incorporating into the potential item set of the UDC Social Organization in this dissertation, substantiating the synthesis of the cultural dimension of Communitarianism versus Collectivism by Trompenaars and Hampden-Turner (2004, 2012) into the UDC Social Organization.

Synthesis Analysis Step 2: Analysis of the Remaining Cultural Dimensions
At first, the cultural taxonomy by **Fiske (1991, 1992)** was reviewed, from which the cultural dimension of Communal Sharing was synthesized into the UDC Social Organization during the first analysis step of the UDC. The in-depth analysis of the cultural dimensions of Authority Ranking and Equality Matching pointed to no evidence for the affiliation to the cultural concept of social organization nor the concept of individualism versus collectivism. Regarding the cultural dimension of Market Pricing, Fiske (1991, 1992) himself indicated a correlation to the cultural concept of individualism versus collectivism since individuals of market pricing national cultures base their social relationships on proportionality. In order to identify additional evidence for an affiliation of the cultural dimension to the concept of social organization and individualism versus collectivism, the items for the cultural dimension were analyzed. Among the eight items, three items (items no. 1, no. 5, and no. 8) were applicable to refer to the underlying concepts of the UDC Social Organization of this dissertation, asking for respondents' calculation of payoffs in terms of rational interactions, respondents' decisions according to the ratio of the receiving benefits, and the proportionality between how much they give and how much they expect to receive. The three items were incorporated into the potential item set, as well as the cultural dimension of Market Pricing by Fiske (1991, 1992) was synthesized into the UDC Social Organization.

The second analyzed existing cultural taxonomy constituted the cultural taxonomy by **Hall (1959, 1966, 1976, 1983; Hall & Hall, 1990)**. In the UDC Social Organization projection by A3 in this dissertation, the cultural dimensions of Context, Space, and Time were assumed to constitute one conglomerative cultural component of the UDC. Reviewing the four in the SLR identified synthesis methodologies, two of them synthesized various cultural dimensions of Hall (1959, 1966, 1976, 1983; Hall & Hall, 1990) into their synthesis dimension regarding the concept of individualism versus collectivism. In the analysis of the cultural dimension of Time by Hall (1983) in this dissertation, no further evidence was identified beside the by Maleki and de Jong (2014) mentioned relationship of the concept of time to the concept of individualism versus collectivism. Therefore, the cultural dimension of Time by Hall (1983) was not synthesized into the UDC Social Organization in this dissertation. Conclusively, the by A3 assumed three-fold conglomerative cultural component of context, space, and time for the UDC Social Organization was rejected regarding the time component.

Hofstede (2001) indicates in his description of the cultural dimension of Individualism versus Collectivism, which was synthesized into the UDC Social Organization in the first UDC synthesis analysis step, an interference of the cultural dimension with the cultural dimension of Context by Hall (1976), elaborating that high context (national) cultures tend to be collectivistic (national) cultures. Vice versa accounts for low context (national) cultures, tending to be individualistic (national) cultures (Hofstede, 2001). Hofstede (2001) seized for his elaborations on Gudykunst et al. (1988). Overall, this dissertation concluded synthesizing the cultural dimension of Context by Hall (1976) into the UDC Social Organization. However, solely in conceptual terms since Hall (1976) developed no measurement for his cultural dimension of Context.

Next, the cultural dimension of Information Flow by Hall and Hall (1990), distinguishing national cultures by the time it takes for a message to travel within a group and to produce the desired response, was reviewed. Hall and Hall (1990) indicated a strong connection between the cultural dimension of Context by Hall (1976) and the cultural dimension of Information Flow. Regarding the strong connection of the two cultural dimensions of Information Flow and Context, the cultural dimension of Information Flow by Hall and Hall (1990) was also synthesized into the UDC Social Organization under the acknowledgment of its low influence.

The last considered cultural dimension from the cultural taxonomy by Hall (1959, 1966, 1976, 1983; Hall & Hall, 1990) constituted the cultural dimension of Space, proposed to be related to the concept of individualism versus collectivism by Maleki and de Jong (2014). Overall, taken the evidence found in the cultural dimension and the synthesis methodology by Maleki and de Jong (2014) into account, it was concluded that the cultural dimension is suitable for synthesis into the UDC Social Organization.

Afterward, the cultural taxonomy by **Hofstede (2001; Hofstede et al., 2010)** was reviewed, from which the cultural dimension of Individualism versus Collectivism was already synthesized into the UDC Social Organization during the first synthesis analysis step of the UDC. The four cultural dimensions of Indulgence versus Restraint, Long-Term versus Short-Term Orientation, Masculinity versus Femininity, and Power Distance pointed to no further evidence for their affiliation to the underlying concepts of the UDC Social Organization.

Regarding the cultural dimension of Uncertainty Avoidance by Hofstede (2001; Hofstede et al., 2010), Hofstede (2001) identified that the index of his cultural dimension of Individualism versus Collectivism tends to correlate with the index of his cultural dimension of Uncertainty Avoidance. Thus, in wealthier countries, individualism leads to a weaker extent of uncertainty avoidance (Hofstede, 2001). Besides this information, no further evidence for an affiliation of the cultural dimension of Uncertainty Avoidance by Hofstede (2001; Hofstede et al., 2010) to the underlying concepts of the UDC Social Organization was found. Conclusively, the cultural dimension of Uncertainty Avoidance was not synthesized into the UDC.

The fourth analyzed existing cultural taxonomy constituted the cultural taxonomy by **House et al. (2004, 2007, 2014)**. Two of its cultural dimensions—the cultural dimensions of In-Group Collectivism and Institutional Collectivism—were already synthesized into the UDC Social Organization during the first synthesis analysis step of the UDC. The six cultural dimensions of Assertiveness, Future Orientation, Gender Egalitarianism, Performance Orientation, Power Distance, and Uncertainty Avoidance of the cultural taxonomy revealed no further evidence in their in-depth analysis to be affiliated to the concept of social organization or the concept of individualism versus collectivism. Thus, these cultural dimensions were not synthesized into the UDC Social Organization in this dissertation.

The analysis of the cultural dimension of Humane Orientation by House et al. (2004, 2007, 2014) revealed evidence by its description and items that the cultural dimension could be synthesized into the UDC Social Organization. The four societal value items (items no. V3_9, no. V3_21, no. V3_27, and no. V3_31) of the cultural dimension of Humane Orientation by House et al. (2004, 2007, 2014) indicated in the juxtaposition with the items of the already synthesized cultural dimension of Communal Sharing by Haslam and Fiske (1999) similarities. Both item sets applied similar phrases addressing the behavior of individuals to other individuals. In more detail, Fiske (1991, 1992) focussed on the moral obligation of individuals to feel compassionate to each other, and House et al. (2004) focused in his cultural dimension of Humane Orientation on the behavior of individuals regarding each other in more general terms. However, a synthesis of the cultural dimension of Humane Orientation by House et al. (2004, 2007, 2014) into the UDC Social Organization based on similarities between the applied items of the synthesized cultural dimension of Communal Sharing by Fiske (1991, 1992) and the cultural dimension was not considered as proof enough for this dissertation. Therefore, the cultural dimension of Humane Orientation by House et al. (2004, 2007, 2014) was not synthesized into the UDC Social Organization.

Next, the cultural taxonomy by **Inglehart et al. (2014)** and its two cultural dimensions were analyzed. The cultural dimension of Traditional Values versus Secular-Rational by Inglehart et al. (2014) was considered unsuitable for synthesis into the UDC. The cultural dimension of Survival Values versus Self-Expression Values by Inglehart et al. (2014) was synthesized by Maleki and de Jong (2014) into their synthesis dimension of Individualism versus Collectivism. Hofstede (2001) indicated a correlation of the cultural dimension with his cultural dimension of Individualism versus Collectivism, which was already synthesized into the UDC Social Organization during the first UDC synthesis analysis step. Hofstede (2001) elaborated that the cultural dimension of Survival Values versus Self-Expression Values by Inglehart et al. (2014) displays the idea of in- and out-groups. The definition of the cultural dimension of Survival Values versus Self-Expression Values by Inglehart et al. (2014) considers the concerns for in-group feelings in the self-expression value side and out-group feelings in the survival value side. Survival value national cultures are proposed to have an ethnocentric outlook, and self-expression values national cultures instead possess a low level of ethnocentric outlook (Inglehart et al., 2014).

The review of the items applied for the empirical assessment of the cultural dimension of Survival Values versus Self-Expression Values by Haerpfer et al. (2020) did not reveal any factual information for their affiliation to the assumed UDC Social Organization of this dissertation. Conclusively, it was decided to synthesize the cultural dimension of Survival Values versus Self-Expression Values by Inglehart et al. (2014) into the UDC Social Organization without incorporating its items into the potential UDC item set.

Afterward, the cultural taxonomy by **Kluckhohn and Strodtbeck (1961)** was analyzed; one of its cultural dimensions was already synthesized into the UDC Social Organization of this dissertation in the first UDC synthesis analysis step. Its other cultural dimensions of Activity Orientation, Human Nature Orientation, Man-Nature Orientation, and Time Orientation pointed to no substantial evidence for affiliation to the concepts of social organization or individualism versus collectivism. Therefore, none of these cultural dimensions were synthesized into the UDC Social Organization.

The seventh analyzed existing cultural taxonomy constituted cultural taxonomy by **Lewis (2018)**. In summary, none of the cultural dimensions of Linear Active, Multi-Active, or Re-Active by Lewis (2018) revealed any evidence which would have substantiated their synthesis into the UDC Social Organization.

The next analyzed cultural taxonomy constituted the existing cultural taxonomy by **Minkov (2007)**. The review of the two cultural dimensions of Indulgence versus Restraint and Monumentalism versus Flexhumility revealed no information to synthesize these two cultural dimensions into the UDC Social Organization. The cultural dimension of Exclusionism versus Universalism by Minkov (2007) required an in-depth analysis since A3 assumed the cultural component of universalism versus particularism as a cultural component for the UDC Social Organization. Additionally, Maleki and de Jong (2014) synthesized the cultural dimension into their synthesis dimension regarding the concept of individualism versus collectivism. Hofstede (2001) elaborated that his cultural dimension of Individualism versus Collectivism is negatively correlated, hence, not perfect, with the cultural dimension of Universalism versus Exclusionism by Minkov (2007). Conceptually, the cultural dimension of Exclusionism versus Universalism by Minkov (2007) was assumed to refer to the concept of in-groups versus out-groups.

The concept of in-group versus out-group was projected to be mirrored in the concept of individualism versus collectivism. Thus, A3 suggested that the UDC Social Organization of this dissertation encompasses the concept of universalism versus particularism as a cultural component. The items of the cultural dimension of Exclusionism versus Universalism by Minkov (2007) were reviewed in more detail: A025 (one must always love one's parents), D028 (a child needs both a father and a mother), D019 (a woman needs children to be fulfilled), A125 (people from another race undesirable as neighbors), and A035 (a child should learn tolerance and respect for other people). The following evidence was concluded from the analysis of the six items: Firstly, item A025 was interpreted regarding the cultural component of children-parent ties, which was not considered further in this dissertation. Likewise accounted for item D028, indicating a conceptual correlation in terms of the bondage of children with their parents. Thirdly, item A125 was assumed to display the concept of in- versus out-group, which was subsumed as a cultural component for the UDC Social Organization in this dissertation. Fourthly, also item A035 was excluded due to its strong focus on the cultural concept of children-parent ties. Finally, item D019 did not reveal any conceptual interrelationship to this dissertation's projected UDC Social Organization. Based on this evidence, only item A125 of the cultural dimension of Exclusionism versus Collectivism by Minkov (2007) was incorporated in the item set of UDC, and the cultural dimension was synthesized in the UDC Social Organization.

Next, the **cultural taxonomy** by **Parsons and Shils (1951)** was in-depth analyzed for evidence for a synthesis of its cultural dimensions into the UDC Social Organization. The cultural dimension of Self-Interest versus Collectivist Interest was already synthesized into the UDC Social Organization during the first UDC synthesis step. No evidence for affiliation to the concepts of social organization and individualism versus collectivism was applicable in the cultural dimensions of Affectivity versus Affective Neutrality and Ascription versus Achievement. Maleki and de Jong (2014) synthesized the cultural dimension of Functional Specificity versus Functional Diffuseness by Parsons and Shils (1951) into their synthesis dimension of Individualism versus Collectivism. The proposed evidence was not substantiated by the conducted in-depth review of the cultural dimension. Conclusively, the cultural dimension of Functional Specificity versus Functional Diffuseness by Parsons and Shils (1951) was not synthesized into the UDC Social Organization.

Maleki and de Jong also synthesized the cultural dimension of Universalism versus Particularism by Parsons and Shils (1951) into their synthesis dimension of Individualism versus Collectivism, justified by the approach that "in a collectivist culture the relationship and the loyalty to the in-group is a matter of importance, while in individualistic cultures, no such strong commitment exists and the universal rules should be ideally applied" (Maleki & de Jong, 2014, p. 116). Additional evidence for this approach was found in Hofstede (2001), who postulated a statistical relationship between the concept of individualism versus collectivism and the concept of universalism versus particularism. Hofstede (2001) claimed that both concepts address if an individual's value system should also consider relationship systems, assuming that individualistic cultures are also universalistic cultures. In the first synthesis analysis step of the UDC Social Organization, the cultural dimension of Exclusionism versus Universalism by Minkov (2007) was synthesized into the UDC. The identified evidence in the analysis of the cultural dimension of Universalism versus Particularism by Parsons and Shils (1951) substantiated the synthesis of the cultural dimension into the UDC Social Organization of this dissertation.

The tenth analyzed existing cultural taxonomy constituted the cultural taxonomy by **Schwartz** (1992, 1994b). The cultural dimension of Autonomy versus Embeddedness by Schwartz (1992, 1994b) was also synthesized into a synthesis dimension regarding the concept of individualism versus collectivism by Maleki and de Jong (2014) and Nardon and Steers (2009). The analysis of the definition and description of the cultural dimension pointed to evidence for its affiliation to the concepts of social organization and individualism versus collectivism. Additionally, the items of the cultural dimension were also reviewed for evidence. The following assumptions were concluded from the analysis of the items applied to empirically measure the cultural dimension of Autonomy versus Embeddedness by Schwartz (1992, 1994b). Firstly, the items of the dimension side of affective autonomy (items no. 4, no. 9, no. 25, no. 50, and no. 57) did not indicate any conceptual interrelationship to the concept of social organization nor with the concept of individualism versus collectivism. None of these items seemed suitable for the potential item set of UDC Social Organization in this dissertation. Conclusively, the dimension side of affective autonomy was rejected for synthesis into UDC Social Organization.

Secondly, the items of the dimension side of intellectual autonomy (items no. 5, no. 16, no. 35, and no. 53) displayed evidence for their inclusion in the UDC Social Organization item set. Three items no. 5, no. 16, and no. 35 are assumed to reflect the concept of individualism versus collectivism since each item addressed individuals' emotional dependency on collectives in the broader sense. Item no. 53 did not indicate any conceptual relationship to the concept of individualism versus collectivism or the concept of social organization. As a result of the analysis, the dimension side of intellectual autonomy of the cultural dimension of Autonomy versus Embeddedness by Schwartz (1992, 1994b) was synthesized into the UDC Social Organization, including its three items.

Regarding the items of the cultural dimension side of embeddedness, the following was concluded: 11 items (item no. 11, no. 13, no. 18, no. 20, no. 26, no. 32, no. 40, no. 46, no. 51, no. 54, and no. 56) were considered as not related to the concept of individualism versus collectivism. Only three of the items (items no. 8, no. 15, and no. 47) of the dimension side of embeddedness by Schwartz (1992, 1994b) were considered to relate to the concept of individualism versus collectivism by asking respondence for their importance placed on social order (including the stability of the society), reciprocation of favors, and obedience. These items were also incorporate into the UDC since, by definition, in embedded (national) cultures, individuals are seen as entities embedded in collectives, finding their meaning of life in social relationships. The dimension side of embeddedness was synthesized into the UDC Social Organization.

From the cultural dimension of Hierarchy versus Egalitarianism by Schwartz (1992, 1994b), the cultural dimension side of hierarchy was synthesized into the UDC Distribution of Power and Status; but, the cultural dimension side of egalitarianism indicated evidence in its definition for affiliation to the concepts of social organization and individualism versus collectivism. The review of the items of the dimension side of egalitarianism revealed that only one item—item no. 33—indicates a conceptual relationship to the assumed UDC Social Organization since it refers to if the individuals of a national culture either value loyalty to friends and the group or not. Neither the definition nor the items indicated further considerable evidence for a relation to the concept of individualism versus collectivism. Conclusively, the cultural dimension of Hierarchy versus Egalitarianism by Schwartz (1992, 1994b) was not synthesized into the UDC Social Organization.

The third cultural dimension of Mastery versus Harmony by Schwartz (1992, 1994b) reflects on the relationship of individuals to their natural and social environment, classifying national cultures by their individuals' emphasis to fit into the surrounding social and natural world by trying to appreciate and to accept the surrounding social and natural environment. From the items operationalized for the cultural dimension of Mastery versus Harmony, the dimension side of harmony does not display any conceptual relationship to the concept of individualism versus collectivism. Four items—items no. 23, no. 31, no. 39, and no. 41—were identified in the mastery dimension side, related to the concept of individualism versus collectivism. The other items of the dimension side of mastery—items no. 34, no. 37, no. 43, and no. 55—were not applicable to relate to the concept of individualism versus collectivism after all. As a result of the analysis, the dimension side of mastery of the cultural dimension of Harmony versus Mastery by Schwartz (1992, 1994b) was synthesized into the UDC Social Organization in this dissertation. The four items no. 23, no. 31, no. 39, and no. 41 were integrated into the potential item set of the UDC. It should be pointed out that the influence of the cultural dimension side of mastery was acknowledged to be less than for the previously synthesized cultural dimensions for the UDC Social Organization.

At last, the existing cultural taxonomy by **Trompenaars and Hampden-Turner (2004, 2012)** was analyzed, from which the cultural dimension of Communitarianism versus Individualism was already synthesized into the UDC Social Organization. No evidence for affiliation to the concepts of individualism versus collectivism and social organization was identified in analyzing the cultural dimension of Neutral versus Emotional of Trompenaars and Hampden-Turner (2004, 2012).

The cultural dimension of Ascription versus Achievement by Trompenaars and Hampden-Turner (2004, 2012) was synthesized by Low and Chapman (2003) and Maleki and de Jong (2014) into their synthesis dimensions for the concept of individualism versus collectivism. The in-depth analysis of the cultural dimension revealed no information that substantiated or justified the synthesis of the cultural dimension into the UDC Social Organization of this dissertation, also inducing the overall rejection of the by A3 assumed cultural component of ascription versus achievement for the UDC Social Organization of this dissertation.

Likewise, accounted for the cultural dimension of Sequential versus Synchronous Time, which was also synthesized by Maleki and de Jong (2014) into their synthesis dimension for the concept of individualism versus collectivism, due to their assumed affiliation of the cultural dimension to the cultural dimension of Time by Hall (1983). The cultural dimension of Time by Hall (1983) was rejected for synthesis into the UDC Social Organisation previously. Also, for the cultural dimension of Sequential versus Synchronous Time of Trompenaars and Hampden-Turner (2004, 2012), not enough substantial evidence for its affiliation to the concepts of individualism versus collectivism and social organization was identified. Thus, the cultural dimension was not synthesized into the UDC Social Organization in this dissertation. Moreover, Maleki and de Jong (2014) identified evidence for synthesizing the cultural dimensions of Diffuse versus Specific and Universalism versus Particularism into a synthesis dimension regarding the concept of individualism versus collectivism. However, this approach was in-depth analyzed too; but no substantial evidence was identified which would have justified a synthesis of the two cultural dimensions into the UDC Social Organization. Conclusively, none of the two cultural dimensions was synthesized in the UDC Social Organization.

Lastly, Low and Chapman (2003) assumed an affiliation of the cultural dimension of Internal versus Outer Direction by Trompenaars and Hampden-Turner (2004, 2012) to the concepts of social organization and individualism versus collectivism. Likewise, here, the analysis for the synthesis of the UDC Social Organization revealed no further evidence which would have substantiated the approach.

5.4 Delimitation Between the Concepts of Distribution of Power and Status and Social Organization

The four in the SLR identified synthesis methodologies differ considerably in integrating or separating the two concepts of distribution of power and status and social organization in a synthesis dimension. Therefore, it was assumed that existing cultural taxonomies also handle both concepts—the concept of distribution of power and status and the concept of individualism versus collectivism—differently, either as one concept in one cultural dimension or as two concepts in two cultural dimensions. The concepts were assumed to differ in this dissertation, representing the two UDCs Distribution of Power and Status and Social Organization.

To justify the delimitation of the two concepts—the concept of distribution of power and status and the concept of individualism versus collectivism—Hofstede (2001) plotted the statistical and empirical correlation of his Power Distance and his Individualism versus Collectivism cultural dimension. The scores of both cultural dimensions indicated a negative correlation. Nevertheless, Hofstede (2001) identified countries of exceptions (e.g., Latin Europe (France, Belgium), and Costa Rica) among his country set. Only considering the statistical evidence, the two concepts can be integrated into one cultural dimension since both concepts lead to similar classifications of national cultures.

Hofstede (2001) argues against the unilateral consideration of the statistical evidence for the two concepts because it would induce an obfuscation of the unique value pattern of (national) cultures. In conceptual terms, the concept of distribution of power displays in its core the emotional dependence of individuals on more powerful individuals in the group. In contrast, the concept of individualism versus collectivism displays the emotional dependency of individuals on collectives (e.g., groups and organizations) (Hofstede, 2001).

Furthermore, House et al. (2004, 2007, 2014) considered the two concepts of distribution of power and status and individualism versus collectivism distinct from each other by providing a cultural dimension of Power Distance, a cultural dimension of Institutional Collectivism, and a cultural dimension of In-Group Collectivism. House et al. (2004, 2007, 2014) replicated the assumptions of Hofstede (2001) for the delimitation between the concepts of distribution of power and status and individualism versus collectivism. Maleki and de Jong (2014) critically considered the connection between both concepts and analyzed their operationalization as two cultural dimensions in the existing cultural taxonomies by Kluckhohn and Strodtbeck (1961) and Inglehart et al. (2014). The two cultural taxonomies were also among the 11 selected cultural taxonomies for this dissertation's UDC synthesis. Maleki and de Jong (2014) subsumed that the cultural dimension of Self-Expression Values versus Survival Values by Inglehart et al. (2014) addresses both concepts at once. The analysis of the cultural dimension revealed that only the definition of the self-expression value dimension side displayed a minor conceptual overlap to the by A1 proposed cultural component of gender egalitarianism of the UDC Distribution of Power and Status by describing those cultures with high self-expression values tend to give priority to gender equality.

Nevertheless, the review of the items of the cultural dimension of Self-Expression Values versus Survival Values of Haerpfer et al. (2020) revealed no further substantial evidence. The evidence was evaluated as too weak to substantiate an affiliation of the concept of distribution of power and status and the concept of individualism versus secularism in this dissertation.

The second cultural dimension, which was introduced by Maleki and de Jong (2014), reflecting the consideration of both concepts—the concept of distribution of power and status and the concept of individualism versus collectivism—as one concept constituted the cultural dimension of Relational Orientation by Kluckhohn and Strodtbeck (1961), distinguishing national cultures per their either individual, collectivistic, or hierarchical relationship system. From the review of the definition and the item, developed by Hills (1977, 1998) and Lane (1976) for the cultural dimension of Relational Orientation by Kluckhohn and Strodtbeck (1961), it was concluded that the cultural dimension indeed addresses both concepts. By definition, the hierarchical dimension pool emphasizes "hierarchical principles and deferring to higher authority or authorities within the group" (Hills, 2002, p. 5), the collectivistic dimension pool describes the "emphasis on consensus within the extended group of equals" (Hills, 2002, p. 5), and the individualistic dimension pool considers (national) cultures that place their "emphasis on the individual or individual families within the group who make decisions independently from others" (Hills, 2002, p. 5).

Maleki and de Jong (2014) tried to assess the interrelationships of the two concepts distribution of power and status and individualism versus collectivism also empirically, demonstrating a statistical analysis of both concepts. The researchers identified a heavy weighting of both concepts on one similar factor[3]. Their statistical evidence would also substantiate a combination of both concepts—the concept of distribution of power and the concept of status and individualism versus collectivism—in one UDC for this dissertation. Nevertheless, Maleki and de Jong (2014) rejected their identified empirical evidence due to the contrasting conceptual evidence, which distinguishes the two concepts. The researchers argued that most existing cultural taxonomies consider both concepts distinct from each other (Maleki & de Jong, 2014).

In this dissertation, under careful consideration of the identified evidence for the combination and distinction of the two concepts—the concept of distribution of power and status and the concept of individualism versus collectivism—it was decided to treat the concepts as two separate concepts, following the approach by Low and Chapman (2003), Maleki and de Jong (2014), Hofstede (2001; Hofstede et al., 2010), and House et al. (2004, 2007, 2014). In detail, following Hofstede (2001), in this dissertation, the concept of distribution of power and status is comprehended as a dependency of individuals on higher-ranked individuals, and the concept of social organization in terms of individualism versus collectivism is understood as the dependency of individuals on other individuals in national cultures.

5.5 Delimitation Between the Concepts of Social Environment and Relationship with the Natural Environment

The UDC Relationship with the Natural Environment[4] encompasses cultural dimensions that address the relationship of individuals with their natural environment as a distinguishing factor for (national) cultures. The critical point in the synthesis of the UDC Relationship with the Natural Environment constituted its

[3] Maleki and de Jong (2014) gave no detailed information on the factor. Therefore, the information cannot be specified further.

[4] Please be aware, that in Section 4.5 already the revised title for the UDC Relationship with the Natural Environment is applied. The revision is described in the results for the synthesis of the UDC.

delimitation to the cultural concept of social environment. In this dissertation, A3 proposed a separate UDC for the concept of an individual's relationship with the social environment—the UDC Social Organization.

The four in the SLR identified synthesis methodologies followed no unified approach in handling the cultural concepts of social environment and natural environment as either two separate concepts or as one unified concept. The delimitation analysis between the concepts of relationship with the natural environment and relationship with the social environment was pursued by analyzing the cultural dimension of Exclusionism versus Universalism by Minkov (2007). The cultural dimension was selected since it was revealed in the synthesis analysis of the UDC Social Organization and UDC Relationship with the Natural Environment evidence for addressing the critical issue of a delimitation of both underlying concepts. Minkov (2007) assigned exclusionist national cultures the feature of a lower concern for the environment and universalistic national cultures the feature of greater concern for the environment.

Additionally, Minkov (2007) elaborated in a sub-chapter on the overlaps between the concept of relationship with the natural environment and his cultural dimension of Exclusionism versus Universalism. In a correlation test of his cultural dimensions and the IMD Report on International Competitiveness, he identified a correlation of -0.58 between environmental protection behavior and exclusionism. Minkov (2007) deducted a connection between the concept of cleanliness[5] and the concept of exclusionism versus universalism, concluding that individuals are not taught to adhere to standards regarding public property in exclusionist national cultures. Vice versa accounts for universalistic national cultures (Minkov, 2007).

Minkov (2007) compiled his cultural dimension with the following items from the World Value Survey Wave 4: A025 (one must always love own parents), D028 (a child needs both a father and a mother), D019 (a woman needs children to be fulfilled), A125 (people from another race are undesirable as neighbors), A035 (a child should learn tolerance and respect for other people). These items showed no indication of the concept of relationship with the natural environment. In summary, the before elaborated conceptual evidence gave cause to synthesized the cultural dimension in the UDC Relationship with the Natural Environment, under the acknowledgment of its minor influence in the UDC.

Furthermore, the cultural dimension of Exclusionism versus Universalism by Minkov (2007) substantiated the projected distinction between the two concepts

---

[5] Minkov (2007) referred to the term cleanness without further elaborations.

of relationship with the natural environment and relationship with the social environment since no evidence was detected to subsume the two concepts as one concept.

In summary, there was not enough information identified in the analyzed cultural dimension that would have substantiated a combination of the concept of relationship with the natural environment and the concept of relationship with the social environment. Conclusively, the analysis confirmed the by A2 assumed delimitation of the two concepts relationship with the natural environment and relationship with the social environment, which is in line with Maleki and de Jong (2014) and Schneider et al. (2014). The delimitation of the two concepts is against the synthesis approach by Nardon and Steers (2009).

5.6 Results of the Syntheses

Overall, in the synthesis analysis of the three UDCs Distribution of Power and Status, Relationship with the Natural Environment, and Social Organization, it became evident that each of the UDC addresses the extent of individuals handling of either the social environment, the natural environment, or the environment in a hierarchical order. Although, as the delimitation analysis expressed, the three concepts, even though subsumed under the umbrella of the concept of the environment, have their justification to constitute three distinct UDCs in this dissertation.

5.6.1 The Universal Dimension of Culture (UDC) Distribution of Power and Status

A1 projected that the concept of distribution of power and status is applicable as one main factor in classifying and distinguishing national cultures in existing cultural taxonomies, addressing the following three cultural components: structure of power relationships, allocation of status and reward, and gender egalitarianism. Additionally, A1 projected the distinction between the concept of distribution of power and status and the concept of individualism versus collectivism. The UDC Distribution of Power and Status's synthesis analysis revealed the following evidence, which partly rejected and confirmed A1, as displayed in Figure 5.4.

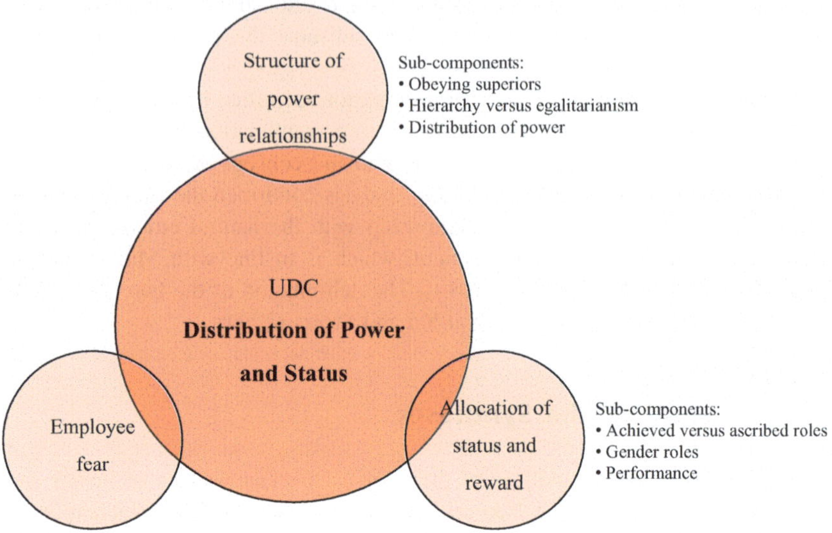

Figure 5.4 The Universal Dimension of Culture (UDC) Distribution of Power and Status

Firstly, the synthesis analysis confirmed that the concepts of distribution of power and status and individualism versus collectivism should be seen as distinct.

Secondly, the projected cultural component of structure of power relationships was confirmed as one cultural component for the UDC Distribution of Power and Status, as it was addressed by five cultural dimensions of five existing cultural taxonomies—Power Distance by Hofstede (2001; Hofstede et al., 2010), Power Distance by House et al. (2004, 2007, 2014), Authority Ranking by Fiske (1991, 1992), Relational Orientation by Kluckhohn and Strodtbeck (1961), and Hierarchy versus Egalitarianism by Schwartz (1992, 1994b). Each of the five cultural dimensions demonstrated different sub-components to address the concept of distribution of power and status. In summary, these sub-components are as follows: obeying superiors, hierarchy versus egalitarianism, and distribution of power.

Thirdly, the projected cultural component of gender egalitarianism was not confirmed as a distinct cultural component. None of the synthesized cultural dimensions addressed the concept of gender egalitarianism in particular. Although, the cultural dimension of Gender Egalitarianism by House et al. (2004, 2007, 2014) was synthesized into the UDC Distribution of Power and Status.

Instead, the cultural dimension of Gender Egalitarianism by House et al. (2004, 2007, 2014) described the allocation of status and higher positions based on biological sexes, serving as evidence to merge the bevor distinct cultural component of gender egalitarianism into the cultural component of allocation of status and reward.

Fourthly, the projected cultural component of allocation of status and reward was confirmed as a cultural component for the UDC, since it was applicable in the five synthesized cultural dimensions of Power Distance by House et al. (2004, 2007, 2014), Ascription versus Achievement by Parsons and Shils (1951), Ascription versus Achievement by Trompenaars and Hampden-Turner (2004, 2012), Performance Orientation by House et al. (2004, 2007, 2014), and Gender Egalitarianism by House et al., (2004, 2007, 2014). Each cultural dimension referred to the distribution of status and reward based on performances, achieved or ascribed roles, or gender roles.

Fifthly, the synthesis analysis revealed the cultural component of employee fear as a potential cultural component for the UDC Distribution of Power and Status of this dissertation. The cultural component of employee fear was addressed by Hofstede (2001; Hofstede et al., 2010) in his cultural dimension of Power Distance.

None of the other synthesized cultural dimensions demonstrated the cultural component of employee fear too. Hofstede (2001; Hofstede et al., 2010) demonstrated the considerable correlation between the concept of distribution of power and status and the cultural component of employee fear.

Table 5.1 displays the synthesized cultural dimensions of the UDC Distribution of Power and Status.

5.6.2 The Universal Dimension of Culture (UDC) Relationship with the Natural Environment

A2 projected that the concept of relationship with the natural environment is applicable as one main factor in classifying and distinguishing national cultures among existing cultural taxonomies. Furthermore, it was assumed that the concept of relationship with the natural environment would be represented as a cultural dimension in most existing cultural taxonomies. Furthermore, it was projected that most existing cultural taxonomies that classify national cultures by the concept of relationship with the natural environment also classifies national cultures by the more specific concept of mastery versus harmony. Also, the UDC Relationship with the Environment was projected to encompass the following three cultural components: assertiveness, gender egalitarianism, and masculinity versus femininity. In addition, A2 projected a delimitation of the cultural concept of relationship with the natural environment to the cultural concepts of social organization, uncertainty avoidance, humane orientation, and performance orientation. The synthesis analysis of the UDC Relationship with the Environment resulted in the following evidence (please see Figure 5.5), which partly rejected and partly confirmed A2.

Firstly, the first analysis step of title-related cultural dimensions confirmed the synthesis of three cultural dimensions. The two cultural dimensions of Man-Nature Orientation by Kluckhohn and Strodtbeck (1961) and Internal versus Outer Direction by Trompenaars and Hampden-Turner (2004, 2012) demonstrated the most robust affiliation to the concept of relationship with the natural environment.

Secondly, the initial projected cultural components of assertiveness and gender egalitarianism as cultural components for the UDC Relationship with the Environment were not confirmed during the analysis.

Only the projected cultural component of masculinity versus femininity was confirmed as a cultural component by synthesizing the cultural dimension of Masculinity versus Femininity by Hofstede (2001; Hofstede et al., 2010).

Thirdly, the by A2 assumed distinction of the cultural concept of relationship with the natural environment and the cultural concepts of uncertainty avoidance, human orientation, performance orientation, and social organization could be confirmed during the analysis. Five cultural dimensions out of the 50 cultural dimensions from the 11 selected existing cultural taxonomies were synthesized into the UDC Relationship with the Environment in this dissertation. Only two cultural dimensions directly addressed the concept of relationship with the natural environment—Man-Nature Orientation by Kluckhohn and Strodtbeck (1961) and Internal versus Outer Direction by Trompenaars and Hampden-Turner (2004, 2012).

Title Revision for the UDC Relationship with the Environment

A2 projected that the UDC Relationship with the Environment, addressing the concept of relationship with the natural environment, is headed by the term *relationship with the environment*. The term *relationship with the environment* seemed insufficient since the term of *relationship with the environment* addresses the environment not explicitly in its delimitation of the natural and social environment. The headings of the eight UDCs should be determined regarding the separation of the by A3 projected UDC Social Organization and the by A2 projected UDC Relationship with the Environment.

Table 5.1 Synthesized Cultural Dimensions of the Universal Dimension of Culture (UDC) Distribution of Power and Status

Fiske (1991, 1992)	Hall (1959, 1966, 1976, 1983; Hall & Hall, 1990)	Hofstede (2001; Hofstede et al., 2010)	House et al. (2004, 2007, 2014)	Inglehart et al. (2014)	Kluckhohn and Strodtbeck (1961)	Lewis (2018)	Minkov (2007)	Parsons and Shils (1951)	Schwartz (1992, 1994b)	Trompenaars and Hampden-Turner (2004, 2012)
Authority Ranking	~~Context~~	~~Individualism vs. Collectivism~~	~~Assertiveness~~	~~Survival Values vs. Self-Expression Values~~	~~Activity Orientation~~	~~Linear Active~~	~~Exclusionism vs. Universalism~~	~~Affectivity vs. Affective Neutrality~~	~~Autonomy vs. Embeddedness~~	**Achievement vs. Ascription**
~~Communal Sharing~~	~~Information Flow~~	~~Indulgence vs. Restraint~~	~~Future Orientation~~	~~Traditional Values vs. Secular-Rational Values~~	~~Human Nature Orientation~~	~~Multi-Active~~	~~Indulgence vs. Restraint~~	**Ascription vs. Achievement**	Hierarchy vs. Egalitarianism[6]	~~Communitarianism vs. Individualism~~
Equality Matching	~~Space~~	~~Long vs. Short-Term Orientation~~	**Gender Egalitarianism**	–	~~Man-Nature Orientation~~	~~Re-Active~~	~~Monumentalism vs. Flexhumility~~	~~Functional Specificity vs. Functional Diffuseness~~	~~Mastery vs. Harmony~~	~~Sequential vs. Synchronous Time~~
~~Market Pricing~~	~~Time~~	~~Masculinity vs. Femininity~~	~~Humane Orientation~~	–	Relational Orientation[7]	–	–	~~Self-Interest vs. Collectivist Interest~~	–	~~Diffuse vs. Specific~~
–	–	**Power Distance**	~~In-Group Collectivism~~	–	~~Time Orientation~~	–	–	~~Universalism vs. Particularism~~	–	~~Internal vs. Outer Direction~~

(continued)

[6] Only the dimension side of hierarchy was synthesized into the UDC Distribution of Power and Status.

[7] Only the dimension side of hierarchy was synthesized into the UDC Distribution of Power and Status.

Table 5.1 (continued)

Fiske (1991, 1992)	Hall (1959, 1966, 1976, 1983; Hall & Hall, 1990)	Hofstede (2001; Hofstede et al., 2010)	House et al. (2004, 2007, 2014)	Inglehart et al. (2014)	Kluckhohn and Strodtbeck (1961)	Lewis (2018)	Minkov (2007)	Parsons and Shils (1951)	Schwartz (1992, 1994b)	Trompenaars and Hampden-Turner (2004, 2012)
–	–	~~Uncertainty Avoidance~~	~~Institutional Collectivism~~		–		–	–	–	~~Neutral vs. Emotional~~
–	–	–	**Performance Orientation**	–	–	–	–	–	–	~~Universalism vs. Particularism~~
–	–	–	**Power Distance**	–	–	–	–	–	–	–
–	–	–	~~Uncertainty Avoidance~~	–	–	–	–	–	–	–

Note. The in bold written cultural dimensions indicated a stronger affiliation to the concept of distribution of power and status; the non-bold cultural dimensions were only partially synthesized into the UDC.

Figure 5.5 The Universal Dimension of Culture (UDC) Relationship with the Environment

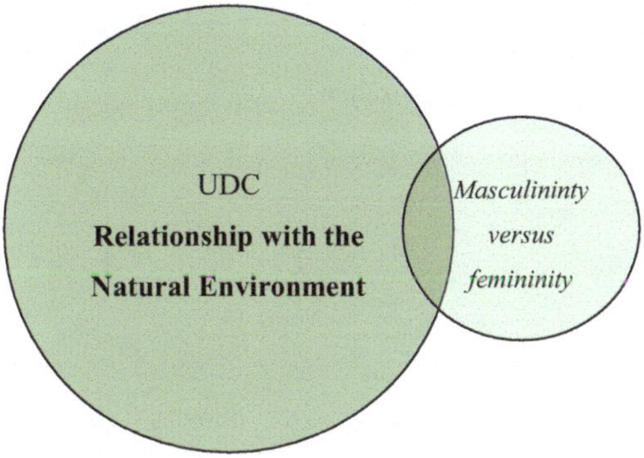

Conclusively, it was decided to reconcile the heading of the by A2 assumed UDC to the more precise heading "Relationship with the Natural Environment" for further application in this dissertation. A summary of the synthesized cultural dimension for the UDC Relationship with the Natural Environment is demonstrated in Table 5.2.

5.6.3 The Universal Dimension of Culture (UDC) Social Organization

A3 projected that the concept of individualism versus collectivism is applicable as one main factor in classifying and distinguishing national cultures among a majority of existing cultural taxonomies. More specifically, it was projected that the majority of the existing cultural taxonomies that classify national cultures by the concept of individualism versus collectivism refer to the following three cultural components: diffuseness versus specificity, universalism versus particularism, and context, space, and time. Additionally, A3 assumed a strict delimitation of the concept of individualism versus collectivism and the concept of distribution of power and status. The delimitation of the two concepts was demonstrated in Section 5.4 Delimitation Between the Concepts of Distribution of Power and Status and Social Organization. The synthesis analysis of the UDC Social Organization revealed the following evidence, which partly rejected and partly confirmed A3, as displayed in summary in Figure 5.6.

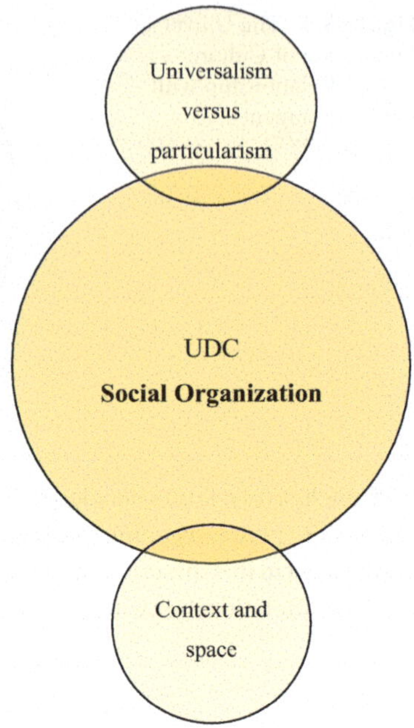

Figure 5.6 The Universal Dimension of Culture (UDC) Social Organization

First, it became applicable that most synthesized cultural dimensions mainly refer to the concept of individualism versus collectivism in general but address the concepts of, among others, group affiliation, pride, loyalty, and group decision making. Second, the two cultural components of diffuseness versus specify and ascription versus achievement were not confirmed as cultural components for the UDC Social Organization in this dissertation. Third, for the three-fold cultural component of context, space, and time only evidence for the cultural component of context and space to the UDC Social Organization was identified during the analysis. Last, the concept of universalism versus particularism was confirmed as a cultural component for the UDC under the assumption of its relationship to the concept of feelings of in-group versus out-group.

The final set of synthesized cultural dimensions of the UDC Social Organization can be reviewed in Table 5.3.

Table 5.2 Synthesized Cultural Dimensions of the Universal Dimension of Culture (UDC) Relationship with the Natural Environment

Fiske (1991, 1992)	Hall (1959, 1966, 1976, 1983; Hall & Hall, 1990)	Hofstede (2001; Hofstede et al., 2010)	House et al. (2004, 2007, 2014)	Inglehart et al. (2014)	Kluckhohn and Strodtbeck (1961)	Lewis (2018)	Minkov (2007)	Parsons and Shils (1951)	Schwartz (1992, 1994b)	Trompenaars and Hampden-Turner (2004, 2012)
~~Authority Ranking~~	~~Context~~	~~Individualism vs. Collectivism~~	~~Assertiveness~~	~~Survival Values vs. Self-Expression Values~~	~~Activity Orientation~~	~~Linear-Active~~	Exclusionism vs. Universalism	~~Affectivity vs. Affective Neutrality~~	~~Autonomy vs. Embeddedness~~	~~Achievement vs. Ascription~~
~~Communal Sharing~~	~~Information Flow~~	~~Indulgence vs. Restraint~~	~~Future Orientation~~	~~Traditional Values vs. Secular-Rational Values~~	~~Human Nature Orientation~~	~~Multi-Active~~	~~Indulgence vs. Restraint~~	~~Ascription vs. Achievement~~	~~Hierarchy vs. Egalitarianism~~	~~Communitarianism vs. Individualism~~
~~Equality Matching~~	~~Space~~	~~Long vs. Short-Term Orientation~~	~~Gender Egalitarianism~~	–	**Man-Nature Orientation**	~~Re-Active~~	~~Monumentalism vs. Flexhumility~~	~~Functional Specificity vs. Functional Diffuseness~~	Mastery vs. Harmony[8]	~~Sequential vs. Synchronous Time~~
~~Market Pricing~~	~~Time~~	Masculinity vs. Femininity	~~Humane Orientation~~	–	~~Relational Orientation~~	–	–	~~Self-Interest vs. Collectivist Interest~~	–	~~Diffuse vs. Specific~~
–	–	~~Power Distance~~	~~In-Group Collectivism~~	–	~~Time Orientation~~	–	–	~~Universalism vs. Particularism~~	–	**Internal vs. Outer Direction**

(continued)

[8] Only the dimension side of harmony was synthesized into the UDC Relationship with the Natural Environment.

Table 5.2 (continued)

Fiske (1991, 1992)	Hall (1959, 1966, 1976, 1983; Hall & Hall, 1990)	Hofstede (2001; Hofstede et al., 2010)	House et al. (2004, 2007, 2014)	Inglehart et al. (2014)	Kluckhohn and Strodtbeck (1961)	Lewis (2018)	Minkov (2007)	Parsons and Shils (1951)	Schwartz (1992, 1994b)	Trompenaars and Hampden-Turner (2004, 2012)
–	–	~~Uncertainty Avoidance~~	~~Institutional Collectivism~~		–		–	–	–	~~Neutral vs. Emotional~~
–	–	–	~~Performance Orientation~~	–	–	–	–	–	–	~~Universalism vs. Particularism~~
–	–	–	~~Power Distance~~	–	–	–	–	–	–	–
–	–	–	~~Uncertainty Avoidance~~	–	–	–	–	–	–	–

Note. The in bold written cultural dimensions indicated a stronger affiliation to the concept of relationship with the natural environment; the non-bold cultural dimensions were only partially synthesized into the UDC Relationship with the Natural Environment.

Table 5.3 Synthesized Cultural Dimensions of the Universal Dimension of Culture (UDC) Social Organization

Fiske (1991, 1992)	Hall (1959, 1966, 1976, 1983; Hall & Hall, 1990)	Hofstede (2001; Hofstede et al., 2010)	House et al. (2004, 2007, 2014)	Inglehart et al. (2014)	Kluckhohn and Strodtbeck (1961)	Lewis (2018)	Minkov (2007)	Parsons and Shils (1951)	Schwartz (1992, 1994b)	Trompenaars and Hampden-Turner (2004, 2012)
~~Authority Ranking~~	**Context**	**Individualism vs. Collectivism**	~~Assertiveness~~	**Survival Values vs. Self-Expression Values**	~~Activity Orientation~~	~~Linear Active~~	**Exclusionism vs. Universalism**	~~Affectivity vs. Affective Neutrality~~	**Autonomy vs. Embeddedness**[9]	~~Achievement vs. Ascription~~
Communal Sharing	Information Flow	~~Indulgence vs. Restraint~~	~~Future Orientation~~	~~Traditional Values vs. Secular-Rational Values~~	~~Human Nature Orientation~~	~~Multi-Active~~	~~Indulgence vs. Restraint~~	~~Ascription vs. Achievement~~	~~Hierarchy vs. Egalitarianism~~	**Communitarianism vs. Individualism**
~~Equality Matching~~	**Space**	~~Long vs. Short-Term Orientation~~	~~Gender Egalitarianism~~	–	~~Man-Nature Orientation~~	~~Re-Active~~	~~Monumentalism vs. Flexhumility~~	~~Functional Specificity vs. Functional Diffuseness~~	Mastery vs. Harmony[10]	~~Sequential vs. Synchronous Time~~
Market Pricing	~~Time~~	~~Masculinity vs. Femininity~~	~~Humane Orientation~~	–	Relational Orientation	–	–	**Self-Interest vs. Collectivist Interest**	–	~~Diffuse vs. Specific~~
–	–	~~Power Distance~~	**In-Group Collectivism**	–	~~Time Orientation~~	–	–	**Universalism vs. Particularism**	–	~~Internal vs. Outer Direction~~

(continued)

[9] Only the dimension sides of intellectual autonomy and embeddedness were synthesized into the UDC Social Organization.

[10] Only the dimension side of mastery way synthesized into the UDC Social Organization.

Table 5.3 (continued)

Fiske (1991, 1992)	Hall (1959, 1966, 1976, 1983; Hall & Hall, 1990)	Hofstede (2001; Hofstede et al., 2010)	House et al. (2004, 2007, 2014)	Inglehart et al. (2014)	Kluckhohn and Strodtbeck (1961)	Lewis (2018)	Minkov (2007)	Parsons and Shils (1951)	Schwartz (1992, 1994b)	Trompenaars and Hampden-Turner (2004, 2012)
–	–	~~Uncertainty Avoidance~~	**Institutional Collectivism**		–		–	–	–	~~Neutral vs. Emotional~~
–	–	–	~~Performance Orientation~~	–	–	–	–	–	–	~~Universalism vs. Particularism~~
–	–	–	~~Power Distance~~	–	–	–	–	–	–	–
–	–	–	~~Uncertainty Avoidance~~	–	–	–	–	–	–	–

Note. The in bold written cultural dimensions indicated a stronger affiliation to the concept of social organization; the non-bold cultural dimensions were only partially synthesized into the UDC Social Organization.

6 Time—One Connecting Concept?

The analysis of the data provided by the four synthesis methodologies showed that the concepts of uncertainty avoidance, perception and use of time, and traditionalism versus secularism constitute three distinct concepts for classifying national cultures in cultural taxonomies. Also, applicable in the three corresponding assumptions A4, A5, and A8, the concept of perception and use of time constitutes a distinct UDC in this dissertation and, the overall theme of time serves as the connecting factor between the three corresponding UDCs Perception and Use of Time, Uncertainty Avoidance, and Traditionalism versus Secularism.

Therefore, the three UDCs Perception and Use of Time, Uncertainty Avoidance, and Traditionalism versus Secularism are displayed in one chapter, including their delimitation towards each other, justifying the existence of the three UDCs for the underlying theme of time.

6.1 Synthesis of the Universal Dimension of Culture (UDC) Perception and Use of Time

A4 proposed the UDC Perception and Use of Time, illustrating the concept of time as one prevailing concept for the classification of national cultures in cultural taxonomies. The UDC Perception and Use of Time was projected to distinguish national cultures per four cultural components. Firstly, the cultural component of perception of time, demonstrating, among others, the time individuals spend working for one company and the view on the flow of time. Secondly, the cultural component of the use of time, addressing, for example, the handling of deadlines. The first two cultural components were projected to constitute the main cultural components of the UDC Perception and Use of Time. Thirdly, the cultural components of the number of handled tasks at a time. Fourthly, the cultural component

S. Kunert, *The Eight Universal Dimensions of Culture from a Synthesis of Cultural Taxonomies*, Gabler Theses, https://doi.org/10.1007/978-3-658-38765-5_6

of the time horizon, referring mainly to the planning horizon (short-term versus long-term orientation) as a distinguishing factor for national cultures. Also, A4 assumed that the cultural component of planning ahead, addressing the extent of future orientation of national cultures, constitutes a distinct cultural component of the UDC Perception and Use of Time in this dissertation.

A critical analysis in the synthesis of the UDC Perception and Use of Time was required for the concept of traditionalism versus secularism, including the sub-components of self-stability, feelings of (national) pride, consistency between expressed and felt emotion, and religiosity. In line with Maleki and de Jong (2014) and against Low and Chapman (2003) and Nardon and Steers (2009), A8 projected a distinct UDC Traditionalism versus Secularism, addressing the cultural components of self-stability, feelings of pride, consistency between expressed and felt emotions, and religiosity.

Figure 6.1 displays, in summary, the by A4 projected UDC Perception and Use of Time and its respectively embedded cultural components.

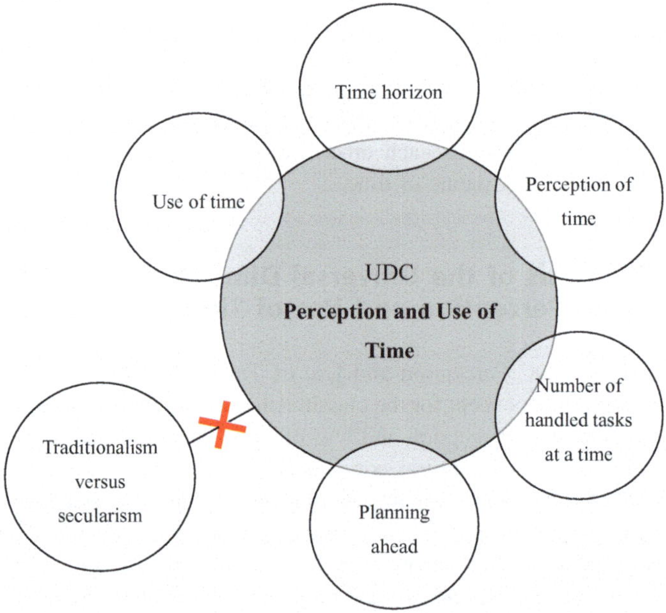

Figure 6.1 Assumption 4 (A4): Universal Dimension of Culture (UDC) Perception and Use of Time

Synthesis Analysis Step 1: Title-Related Cultural Dimensions
In the set of the 50 cultural dimensions, the following five cultural dimensions were identified to relate by their title to the concept of perception and use of time: Time by Hall (1983), Long-Term versus Short-Term Orientation by Hofstede (2001; Hofstede et al., 2010), Future Orientation by House et al. (2004, 2007, 2014), Time Orientation by Kluckhohn and Strodtbeck (1961), and Sequential versus Synchronous Time by Trompenaars and Hampden-Turner (2004, 2012).

The cultural dimension of **Time** by **Hall (1983)** plays a predominant role among the time-related cultural dimensions, applying the concept of numbers of handled at a time as a distinguishing factor for national cultures. Also, Low and Chapman (2003) and Nardon and Steers (2009) synthesized the cultural component of the number of handled tasks at a time into their temporal synthesis dimension. From the in-depth analysis of the cultural dimension of Time by Hall (1983), it was concluded that the cultural dimension refers at its core to the cultural components of perception and view of time, distinguishing national cultures by their circular or linear view of time, and the number of handled tasks at a time. These two cultural components were projected as cultural components for the UDC Perception and Use of Time by A4. Conclusively, the cultural dimension of Time by Hall (1983) was synthesized into the UDC Perception and Use of Time. Hall and Hall (1990) proposed a functional interrelationship of their cultural dimension of Time with their cultural dimensions of Space and Information Flow. No further evidence was identified in the synthesis analysis, which would have substantiated a synthesis of the two cultural dimensions of Information Flow and Space into the UDC Perception and Use of Time due to the proposed functional interrelationship.

The second considered title-related cultural dimension constituted the cultural dimension of **Sequential versus Synchronous Time** by **Trompenaars and Hampden-Turner (2004, 2012)**. Trompenaars and Hampden-Turner (2004, 2012) developed their cultural dimension of Sequential versus Synchronous Time following the concept of the cultural dimension of Time by Hall (1983). For the cultural dimension of Sequential versus Synchronous Time, Trompenaars and Hampden-Turner (2004, 2012) used the Circle Test by Cottle (1967) to mark differences in national culture's assignment in the meaning of time. Trompenaars and Hampden-Turner (2004, 2012) applied the following question in order to assess the extent of the meaning of time in national cultures:

> Think of the past, present and future as being in the shape of circles. Please draw three circles on the space available, representing past, present and future. Arrange these circles in any way you want that best shows how you feel about the relationship of the past, present and future. You may use different sized circles. When you have finished,

> label each circle to show which one is the past, which on the present and which one the future. (Trompenaars & Hampden-Turner, 1997, p. 126)

In addition, Trompenaars and Hampden-Turner (2004, 2012) assessed the differences in the perception of the time horizon among national cultures, which refers to differences in the preferences of individuals regarding either a short-term or a long-term time horizon. The following question was demonstrated by Trompenaars and Hampden-Turner (2004, 2012) to analyze the preference for a short-time or a long-term time horizon among national cultures:

> Consider the relative significance of the past, present and future. You will be asked to indicate your relative time horizons for the past, present and future by giving a number: (7 = years, 6 = months, 5 = weeks, 4 = days, 3 = hours, 2 = minutes, 1 = seconds) My past started…ago, and ended…ago. My present started…ago, and ended…from now. My future started…from now, and ended…from now. (Trompenaars & Hampden-Turner, 1997, pp. 126–127)

Overall, it was concluded that the cultural dimension of Sequential versus Synchronous Time by Trompenaars and Hampden-Turner (2004, 2012) refers to the following four cultural components. In the first addressed cultural component of flow of time, Trompenaars and Hampden-Turner (2004, 2012) illustrated the distinction of national cultures by their perception of time as either a series of linear passing events or a series of parallel events.

In the UDC Perception and Use of Time as A4 projected, the cultural component of the flow of time was proposed as a sub-component of the cultural component of perception of time. The second conceptually addressed cultural component of the number of handled tasks at a time was projected as a distinct cultural component for the UDC Perception and Use of Time. The cultural component of relationship of past, present, and future, for what Trompenaars and Hampden-Turner (2004, 2012) applied the Cottle Test, reveals not only information on the relationship of the three-time sequences it also demonstrates information on the significance of individuals for one of the time sequences. Therefore, the significance and relationship of past, present, and future were interpreted as sub-components of the cultural component of perception of time for the UDC Perception and Use of Time. The last identified empirically addressed cultural component for the cultural dimension of Sequential versus Synchronous Time by Trompenaars and Hampden-Turner (2004, 2012) constituted the cultural component of time horizon. The concept of time horizon was projected as one cultural component for the UDC Perception and Use of Time.

In summary of the analysis of the cultural dimension of Synchronous versus Sequential Time by Trompenaars and Hampden-Turner (2004, 2012), it was concluded that the cultural dimension was suitable for synthesis into the UDC Perception and Use of Time. The cultural dimension of Synchronous versus Sequential Time by Trompenaars and Hampden-Turner (2004, 2012) confirmed the three projected cultural components of perception of time, the number of handled tasks at a time, and time horizon as cultural components for the UDC. In addition, the two applied items were incorporated into the potential item set of the UDC Perception and Use of Time.

Next, the cultural dimension of **Long-Term versus Short-Term Orientation** by **Hofstede (2001; Hofstede et al., 2010)** was analyzed. Hofstede (2001) seized on the information identified in the Chinese Value Survey. Besides the title relation, neither the description nor the definition of the cultural dimension showed any substantial evidence to synthesize the cultural dimension into the UDC Perception and Use of Time. In order to confirm the synthesis rejection of the cultural dimension, the applied items for the empirical operationalization of the cultural dimension were analyzed. At first glance, none of the items indicated any conceptual interrelationship to the concept of perception and use of time, and none of the four items referred to any of the by A4 projected cultural components of perception and view of time, use of time, number of handled tasks at a time, time horizon, or planning ahead.

The review of the four synthesis methodology did not add any substantial evidence which would have justified or substantiated the synthesis of the cultural dimension of Long-Term versus Short-Term Orientation by Hofstede (2001; Hofstede et al., 2010) in a time-related synthesis dimension. Although, it was critically assessed that one item, asking how important is thrift in terms of spending more than needed (item no. 14 of the VSM 2013), could constitute a sub-component of the cultural component of tradition, which could be considered as a cultural component of the concept of past-time orientation. During the analysis, no further evidence was identified that substantiated such a broader understanding of the thrift item. In conclusion, the cultural dimension of Long-Term versus Short-Term Orientation by Hofstede (2001; Hofstede et al., 2010) was not synthesized into the UDC Perception and Use of Time, which was in line with Maleki and de Jong (2014) and contrasting to Low and Chapman (2003) and Nardon and Steers (2009).

This approach constituted a piece of evidence for the rejection of the cultural component of traditionalism for the UDC Perception and Use of Time, substantiating the distinction between the UDC Traditionalism versus Secularism and the UDC Perception and Use of Time. At this analysis stage, the concept of traditionalism versus secularism remained distinct from the general concept of perception and use of time.

Next, the cultural dimension of **Future Orientation** by **House et al. (2004, 2007, 2014)** was in-depth analyzed. The analysis of the description and definition of the cultural dimensions pointed to substantial evidence for its synthesis into the UDC Perception and Use of Time since the cultural dimension is based on the understanding of time as a process of different personal and societal experiences. The experiences give meaning and order to other experiences, objects, and events (House et al., 2004). Additionally, the items for the empirical measurement of the cultural dimension were reviewed.

In this dissertation, the items of the cultural dimension of Future Orientation by House et al. (2004) were conceptually affiliated to the following cultural components: planning ahead in order to be successful, planning ahead as an accepted norm, planning ahead has a higher value as solving current problems, and living in the moment. Specifically, the two societal value items no. V3_4 and no. V3_30 were subsumed to the overall concept of time horizon, asking respondents if the accepted norms should be to plan for the future or accept the status quo and if people should live for the present or the future. At this stage of the analysis, it was concluded that the cultural dimension of Future Orientation by House et al. (2004, 2007, 2014) places a strong emphasis on future-orientated behavior and addresses the concept of time horizon only to a certain extent. These concepts were proposed as cultural components for the UDC Perception and Use of Time by A4. No contradiction was identified to reject the cultural component of planning ahead as one cultural component for the UDC. As a result, the cultural dimension of Future Orientation by House et al. (2004, 2007, 2014) was synthesized into the UDC Perception and Use of Time. In addition, the four societal value items no. V3_3, no. V3_4, no. V3_8, and no. V3_30 were also incorporated into the potential item set of the UDC Perception and Use of Time.

House et al. (2004) juxtaposed their cultural dimension of Future Orientation to other cultural dimensions, e.g., the cultural dimension of Sequential versus Synchronous Time by Trompenaars and Hampden-Turner (2004, 2012). House et al. (2004) analyzed the correlation between the long-term horizon measurement by Trompenaars and Hampden-Turner (2004, 2012) and their cultural dimension of Future Orientation. On the one hand, House et al. (2004) identified a significant negative correlation between the two cultural dimensions regarding their value items. On the other hand, House et al. (2004) identified no significant correlation between the two cultural dimensions regarding practices items, which is reasonable since Trompenaars and Hampden-Turner (2004, 2012) did not intend to measure practices in their cultural dimension. The identified correlations substantiated the proposed synthesis of the cultural dimension of Sequential versus Synchronous Time by Trompenaars and Hampden-Turner (2004, 2012) together with the cultural dimension of Future Orientation by House et al. (2004, 2007, 2014) in one UDC. House et al. (2004) also analyzed the correlation between their cultural dimension of Future Orientation and the cultural dimension of Long-Term versus Short-Term Orientation by Hofstede (2001; Hofstede et al., 2010). No significant correlation was identified between the two cultural dimensions, which confirms the previous analysis of the cultural dimension of Long-Term versus Short-Term Orientation by Hofstede (2001) and its rejection for synthesis into the UDC Perception and Use of Time .

The last considered title-related cultural dimension constituted **Time Orientation** by **Kluckhohn and Strodtbeck (1961)**. In conceptual terms, the cultural dimension can be narrowed down to separating national cultures by their meaning for the three-time sequences of past, present, and future. Hills (1977, 1998) and Lane (1976) operationalized the following item for the assessment of the cultural dimension: "When I send money for use overseas I think it should be spent to: a) make a better life for the future b) make a better life now and c) keep the old ways and customs alive" (Hills, 2002, p. 8). As a result of the analysis, the cultural dimension of Time Orientation by Kluckhohn and Strodtbeck (1961) was synthesized into the UDC Perception and Use of Time. Whereas, it should be pointed out that the past-time-oriented pool of the cultural dimension refers instead to the distinction of national cultures by their decision-making following traditions and their actions to preserve traditions. Synthesizing the cultural dimension into the UDC Perception and Use of Time would also induce the cultural component of traditionalism versus secularism for the UDC Perception and Use of Time. This approach was rejected in this dissertation. At this point of the analysis, no further resistance against the synthesis of the cultural dimension of Time Orientation by Kluckhohn and Strodtbeck (1961) was identified; thereby, the cultural dimension was synthesized into the UDC Perception and Use of Time. Likewise, the item proposed by Hills (2002) for Time Orientation by Kluckhohn and Strodtbeck (1961) was incorporated in the potential item set of the UDC Perception and Use of Time.

Synthesis Analysis Step 2: Analysis of the Remaining Cultural Dimensions

The analysis started with the cultural taxonomy by **Fiske (1991, 1992)**. None of its four cultural dimensions pointed to any evidence for affiliation to the concept of perception and use of time, nor to one of the four for the UDC Perception and Use of Time projected cultural components. Therefore, none of the cultural dimensions was synthesized into the UDC Perception and Use of Time.

Secondly, the cultural taxonomy by **Hall (1959, 1966, 1976, 1983; Hall & Hall, 1990)** was analyzed, from which the cultural dimension of Time was already synthesized into the UDC Perception and Use of Time, and its two cultural dimensions of

Context and Information Flow were rejected for a synthesis in the UDC during the first UDC analysis steps. Likewise, the cultural dimension of Space by Hall (1976) also revealed no evidence for synthesis into the UDC Perception and Use of Time.

In the following, the cultural taxonomy by **Hofstede (2001; Hofstede et al., 2010)** was reviewed. The cultural dimension of Long-Term versus Short-Term Orientation by Hofstede (2001; Hofstede et al., 2010) was already rejected for synthesis into the UDC Perception and Use of Time during the first analysis step. Also, the remaining five cultural dimensions—Power Distance, Individualism versus Collectivism, Masculinity versus Femininity, Uncertainty Avoidance, and Indulgence versus Restraint—indicated no evidence for their affiliation to the concept of perception and use of time as understood by A4. Conclusively, none of the six cultural dimensions by Hofstede (2001; Hofstede et al., 2010) were synthesized into the UDC Perception and Use of Time.

At fourth, the cultural taxonomy by **House et al. (2004, 2007, 2014)** was reviewed, from which the cultural dimension of Future Orientation was already synthesized into the UDC Perception and Use of Time during a first analysis step. The remaining eight cultural dimensions—Assertiveness, Gender Egalitarianism, Humane Orientation, In-Group Collectivism, Institutional Collectivism, Performance Orientation, Power Distance, and Uncertainty Avoidance—of the cultural taxonomy revealed in their in-depth analysis no substantial evidence for potential suitability of synthesis in the UDC Perception and Use of Time.

Likewise, the two cultural dimensions of the cultural taxonomy by **Inglehart et al. (2014)**—Survival Values versus Self-Expression Values and Traditional Values versus Secular-Rational Values, also indicated no evidence for affiliation to the concept of perception and use of time as projected for a UDC by A4.

Afterward, the cultural taxonomy by **Kluckhohn and Strodtbeck (1961)** was reviewed, from which the cultural dimension of Time Orientation was already synthesized into the UDC Perception and Use of Time during the first analysis step. None of the other four cultural dimensions pointed in their analysis to substantial evidence for affiliation to the concept of perception and use of time. Therefore, none of the cultural dimensions were synthesized into the UDC.

Another considered cultural taxonomy constitutes **Lewis (2018)**. Several facets describe its three cultural dimensions of Linear-Active, Re-Active, and Multiple Active. Lewis (2018) indicated that he seized on the cultural taxonomy by Hall (1959, 1966, 1976, 1983; Hall & Hall, 1990). It was concluded that the cultural taxonomy by Lewis (2018) and each of its three cultural dimensions address the cultural components of perception and view of time and the number of handled tasks at a time. The cultural dimension of Linear-Active by Lewis (2018) refers to national cultures in which individuals tend to be highly organized planners and pursue only one thing at a time.

In contrast, Lewis (2018) describes that the cultural dimension of Multi-Active encompasses national cultures where individuals tend to pursue several things at once and rarely rely on agendas. For the third cultural dimension of Re-Active by Lewis (2018), the evidence of a time relation is not as distinctively applicable as for the cultural dimensions of Multi-Active and Linear-Active by Lewis (2018). For the cultural dimension of Re-Active, Lewis (2018) only mentioned that individuals of these cultures tend to have a punctual attitude and slow planning behavior. Overall, each of the three cultural dimensions of Lewis (2018), was synthesized into the UDC Perception and Use of Time. However, it should be acknowledged that the synthesis of the cultural dimensions was assumed to be not as profound as for the other previously into the UDC Perception and Use of Time synthesized cultural dimensions since only conceptual evidence for the synthesis was identified.

Next, the cultural taxonomy by **Minkov (2007)** was in-depth screened. The two cultural dimensions of Exclusionism versus Universalism and Monumentalism versus Flexhumility by Minkov (2007) did not indicate any evidence for conceptual interferences to the concept of perception and use of time. The cultural dimension of Indulgence versus Restraint by Minkov (2007) revealed in its definition some evidence for a potential affiliation to the concept of perception and use of time. Minkov (2007) analyzed the WVS Wave 4 (1999–2004) items in regards to developing the cultural dimension of Indulgence versus Restraint. Likewise, to the cultural dimension of Long-Term versus Short-Term Orientation by Hofstede (2001; Hofstede et al., 2010), Minkov (2007) referred to the cultural facet of thrift, which could have been interpreted as an orientation to past-time, as a time-correlated cultural component. In this dissertation, this approach was not seen as substantial enough for a synthesis, resulting in the rejection of the assumed conceptual interference of the cultural dimension of Indulgence versus Restraint by Minkov (2007) and the concept of perception and use of time. Conclusively, the cultural dimension of Indulgence versus Restraint by Minkov (2007) was also not synthesized into the UDC Perception and Use of Time.

The cultural taxonomy by **Parsons and Shils (1951)** constituted the ninth analyzed cultural taxonomy. In summary, none of the five cultural dimensions of the cultural taxonomy pointed to any affiliation to the concept of perception and use of time, nor to one of the by A4 assumed cultural components of the UDC Perception and Use of Time. Thus, none of the cultural dimensions were synthesized into the UDC.

Next, the cultural taxonomy by **Schwartz (1992, 1994b)** and its three cultural dimensions was in-depth reviewed and analyzed. Likewise, to the previous cultural taxonomies, none of the cultural dimensions indicated any evidence for an interrelationship to the concept of perception and use of time as understood in A4.

Lastly, the cultural taxonomy by **Trompenaars and Hampden-Turner (2004, 2012)** was reviewed, from which the cultural dimension of Sequential versus Synchronous Time was already synthesized into the UDC during the first analysis steps.

The other six cultural dimensions—Achievement versus Ascription, Communitarianism versus Individualism, Diffuse versus Specific, Internal versus Outer Direction, Neutral versus Emotional, and Universalism versus Particularism—of Trompenaars and Hampden-Turner (2004, 2012) of the cultural taxonomy revealed no indication for affiliation to the concept and cultural components of the UDC Perception and Use of Time. In conclusion, none of the cultural dimensions was synthesized into the UDC Perception and Use of Time in this dissertation.

6.2 Synthesis of the Universal Dimension of Culture (UDC) Traditionalism versus Secularism

A8 proposed the UDC Traditionalism versus Secularism, illustrating the concept of traditionalism versus secularism as one prevailing concept among cultural taxonomies for classifying national cultures. The UDC Traditionalism versus Secularism was projected to distinguish national cultures by the following cultural components: consistency between felt versus expressed emotions, flexibility, feelings of pride, secular orientation, religiosity, and self-stability. Maleki and de Jong (2014) also synthesized a distinct synthesis dimension for the concept of traditionalism versus secularism; Low and Chapman (2003) and Nardon and Steers (2009) synthesized the concept of traditionalism versus secularism under the umbrella of the concept of perception and use of time.

For the UDC Traditionalism versus Secularism, a critical aspect in the synthesis of the UDC Traditionalism versus Secularism constituted the delimitation of the six proposed cultural components to the concept of (perception and use of) time with particular regards to the cultural component of past-time orientation. In the projection of the UDC Traditionalism versus Secularism, the concept of time regarding past orientation was rejected as a cultural component for the UDC. The concept of time was captured by the assumed UDC Perception and Use of Time as a distinct prevailing concept among cultural taxonomies, inducing that most cultural taxonomies encompass a distinct cultural dimension for the concept of (perception and use of) time and a distinct cultural dimension for the concept of traditionalism versus secularism.

Figure 6.2 displays, in summary, the assumed UDC Traditionalism versus Secularism (A8) and its respectively embedded cultural components.

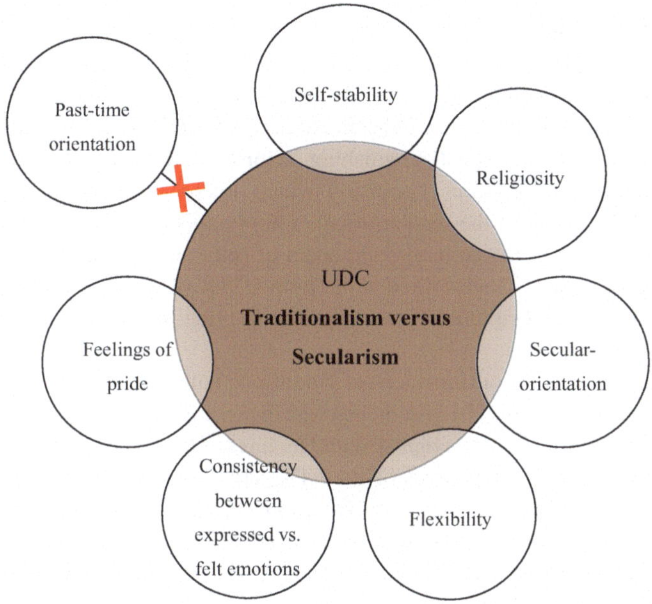

Figure 6.2 Assumption 8 (A8): The Universal Dimension of Culture (UDC) Traditionalism versus Secularism

Synthesis Analysis Step 1: Title-Related Cultural Dimensions

In the review of the 50 cultural dimensions, only the cultural dimension **Traditional Values versus Secular-Rational Values** by **Inglehart et al. (2014)** became applicable as a title-related cultural dimension for the UDC Traditionalism versus Secularism this dissertation.

The review of the definition and description of the cultural dimension revealed evidence that substantiated its synthesis into the UDC Traditionalism versus Secularism. The cultural dimension is defined as follows:

> Traditional values emphasize the importance of religion, parent-child ties, defense to authority and traditional family values. These societies have high levels of national pride and a nationalistic outlook. Secular-rational values have the opposite preferences to the traditional values. These societies place less emphasis on religion, traditional family values and authority. Divorce, abortion, euthanasia and suicide are seen as relatively acceptable (World Value Survey Association, 2020, para. 3).

Also, the items applied to empirically measure the cultural dimension pointed to evidence for its synthesis into the UDC Traditionalism versus Secularism. The six items Q8, Q14, Q15, Q146, Q184, and Q254, were identified to relate to the concept of the UDC Traditionalism versus Secularism.

In more detail, it was concluded that the items Q146 and Q15 address the cultural component of religiosity as a distinguishing factor for national cultures. Item Q184 refers explicitly to the concept of abortion, which was seen in a broader sense as an indicator of the extent of the secular orientation of national culture. Item Q14 was interpreted to refer to the cultural component of self-stability, and item Q8 to the cultural component of secular orientation. Item Q254 was deducted to address the distinction of national cultures by their feelings of pride, specifically regarding the feeling of national pride.

In summary, the cultural dimension of Traditional Values versus Secular-Rational Values by Inglehart et al. (2014) demonstrated the four cultural components of self-stability, secular orientation, religiosity, and feelings of (national) pride constituting all projected cultural components of the UDC Traditionalism versus Secularism. Therefore, the cultural dimension of Traditional Values versus Secular-Rational Values by Inglehart et al. (2014) was synthesized into the UDC, and the items Q8, Q14, Q15, Q146, Q184, and Q254 were also incorporated in the potential item set of the UDC Traditionalism versus Secularism.

Synthesis Analysis Step 2: Analysis of the Remaining Cultural Dimensions

The first analyzed existing cultural taxonomy constituted the cultural taxonomy by **Fiske (1991, 1992)**. The in-depth analysis of its four cultural dimensions of Authority Ranking, Communal Sharing, Equality Matching, and Market Pricing pointed to no evidence for a conceptual relationship between the cultural dimensions and the concept and cultural components of the UDC Traditionalism versus Secularism. Conclusively, none of the four cultural dimensions by Fiske (1991, 1992) was synthesized into the UDC Traditionalism versus Secularism.

Next, the cultural dimensions of the cultural taxonomy by **Hall (1959, 1966, 1976, 1983; Hall & Hall, 1990)** were analyzed. The three cultural dimensions of Context, Information Flow, and Space revealed no evidence for affiliation to the concept of traditionalism versus secularism. A more in-depth analysis of the cultural dimension of Time by Hall (1983) was pursued regarding the delimitation of the concepts of past orientation and traditionalism versus secularism. As a result, none of the four cultural dimensions of Context, Information Flow, Space, and Time by Hall (1959, 1966, 1976, 1983; Hall & Hall, 1990) was suitable for synthesis into the UDC Traditionalism versus Secularism.

Thirdly, the cultural taxonomy by **Hofstede (2001; Hofstede et al., 2010)** was analyzed, from which the five cultural dimensions of Individualism versus Collectivism, Indulgence versus Restraint, Masculinity versus Femininity, Power Distance, and Uncertainty Avoidance did not indicate any affiliation to the projected concept and cultural components of the UDC Traditionalism versus Secularism. Conclusively, these five cultural dimensions were not synthesized into the UDC Traditionalism versus Secularism.

The cultural dimension of Long-Term versus Short-Term Orientation[1] by Hofstede (2001; Hofstede et al., 2010) indicated a conceptual interrelationship to the UDC Traditionalism versus Secularism as assumed by A8. On the one hand, the cultural dimension refers to the cultural values of "persistence, thrift, ordering relationships by status, and having a sense of shame (Hofstede, 2001, pp. 209–210); on the other hand, the cultural dimension relates to cultural values of "reciprocation of greetings, favors and gifts, respect for tradition, protecting one's face, personal steadiness and stability" (Hofstede, 2001, pp. 209–210).

At first glance, from the analysis of the items for the cultural dimension of Long-Term versus Short-Term Orientation, only one item (item no. 19) was deductible to relate to the projected UDC Traditionalism versus Secularism by referring to respondents' feeling of pride, explicitly national pride. Additionally, Hofstede (2001; Hofstede et al., 2010) indicated that item no. 13 could be interpreted as a form of self-enhancement of individuals by asking respondents for their importance in doing a service to a friend. The cultural component of self-enhancement was not distinctively assumed to constitute a cultural component of the UDC Traditionalism versus Secularism. Minkov (2007) summarized two well-known definitions[2] for the cultural component of self-enhancement as follows: "a central element of

[1] The cultural dimension of Long-Term versus Short-Term Orientation was initially (in the version of Hofstede (2001) deducted on the basis of the database of the Chinese Value Survey. Hofstede et al. (2010) changed in his version of Hofstede et al. (2010) the empirical basis and used instead the database of the WVS. Both versions are considered as conceptually and statistically close to each other (Minkov & Hofstede, 2011).

[2] One definition by Heine describes self-enhancement as "the tendency to overly dwell on, elaborate, and exaggerate positive aspects of the self, relative to one's weakness" (Heine, 2003, p. 101), and one definition by Brown defines self-enhancement as "a tendency to process information in ways that cast the self in a positive light" (Brown, 2003, p. 604).

self-enhancement is a maintenance of positive self-opinion, be it exaggerated or not, as well as discounting information that could lead to a negative self-opinion" (Minkov, 2007, p. 173).

Also, Minkov (2007) subsumed that self-enhancement constitutes a subcomponent of the cultural component of pride. This assumption was followed here. Although, it should be acknowledged that there exists a difference between feelings of national pride, applied as an item in the cultural dimension of Traditional Values versus Secular-Rational Values by Inglehart et al. (2014), and the cultural dimension of Long-Term versus Short-Term Orientation by Hofstede (2001; Hofstede et al., 2010), and feelings of self-enhancement as cultural components in terms of pride.

Summarizing the in-depth analysis of the cultural dimension of Long-Term versus Short-Term Orientation by Hofstede (2001; Hofstede et al., 2010), the following was concluded regarding its synthesis into the UDC Traditionalism versus Secularism. The two items, no. 13 and no. 19 were incorporated into the UDC's potential item set since they refer to the cultural component of pride. Additionally, item no. 22 addresses the cultural component of self-stability, which was subsumed to the cultural component of persistency, and thus, included in the potential item set of the UDC Traditionalism versus Secularism.

In regards to item no. 14, the analysis revealed that Hofstede (2001) deducted the concept of thrift as a cultural component from the Ph.D. thesis by Read (1993) and analyses by de Mooij (1998a, 1998b, 2001). Maleki and de Jong (2014) also questioned the indicator of thrift for long-term orientation. The evidence for thrift as a concept for long-term versus short-term orientation was evaluated as low and was not substantial enough for this dissertation. Therefore, the cultural component of thrift was not synthesized into the UDC Traditionalism versus Secularism, and thus item no. 14 by Hofstede and Minkov (2013) was not included into the potential item set of the UDC Traditionalism versus Secularism. Overall, the cultural dimension of Long-Term versus Short-Term Orientation by Hofstede (2001; Hofstede et al., 2010) was synthesized into the UDC Traditionalism versus Secularism.

The following analyzed existing cultural taxonomy constituted the cultural taxonomy by **House et al. (2004, 2007, 2014)**, revealing no evidence for seven of its nine cultural dimensions—the cultural dimensions of Power Distance, Uncertainty Avoidance, Institutional Collectivism, Assertiveness, Gender Egalitarianism, Future Orientation, and Performance Orientation—to be conceptually related to the concept and cultural components of the UDC Traditionalism versus Secularism. Thus, these seven cultural dimensions were not synthesized into the UDC Traditionalism versus Secularism.

The cultural dimension of Humane Orientation by House et al. (2004, 2007, 2014) refers to "the degree to which a collective encourages and rewards individuals for being fair, altruistic, generous, caring, and kind to others" (House et al., 2004, p. 30), which could be interpreted as referring to the concept of service to others. The concept of service to others was previously related to the concept of self-enhancement, and thus, to the cultural component of pride. House et al. (2004) indicated that they intended to operationalize five different cultural components—the cultural components of being sensitive towards others, being concerned, generous, friendly, and tolerant to mistakes in their cultural dimension of Humane Orientation. Overall, it was concluded not to synthesize the cultural dimension of Humane Orientation by House et al. (2004, 2007, 2014) into the UDC Traditionalism versus Secularism due to its primary focus on being concerned and sensitive to other individuals (or not on the contrasting side).

The second cultural dimension from the cultural taxonomy by House et al. (2004, 2007, 2014), which required a more in-depth analysis, constituted the cultural dimension of In-Group Collectivism. The indication of the cultural component of pride in the definition of the cultural dimension, by being defined as "the degree to which individuals express pride, loyalty, and cohesiveness in their organizations or families" (House et al., 2004, p. 30), gave cause for the in-depth analysis in regards to the cultural dimensions' synthesis into the UDC Traditionalism versus Secularism.

Juxtaposing the items of the cultural dimension of In-Group Collectivism by House et al. (n.d.) with the items of the already synthesized cultural dimension of Traditional Values versus Secular-Rational Values by Haerpfer et al. (2020) and the cultural dimension of Long-Term versus Short-Term Orientation by Hofstede and Minkov (2013) the following was concluded. Both cultural dimensions, the cultural dimension of Traditional Values versus Secular-Rational Values by Inglehart et al. (2014) and the cultural dimension Long-Term versus Short-Term Orientation by Hofstede (2001; Hofstede et al., 2010), considered in their items the cultural component of national pride, which was subsumed to belong to the more general cultural component of pride, projected as a cultural component for the UDC Traditionalism versus Secularism.

Additionally, the cultural dimension of Long-Term versus Short-Term Orientation by Hofstede (2001; Hofstede et al., 2010) considered the cultural component of doing a service to a friend. Comparing the items of the cultural dimensions with the cultural dimension of In-Group Collectivism by House et al. (2004, 2007, 2014), none of its items seemed to be conceptually related to the cultural component of pride, as A8 assumed it for the UDC Traditionalism versus Secularism. However, the items of the cultural dimension of In-Group Collectivism by House et al. (2004, 2007, 2014) seem to connect the concept of pride with the concept of parent-child ties, which was not further considered in this dissertation. In conclusion, the cultural dimension of In-Group Collectivism by House et al. (2004, 2007, 2014) was rejected from a synthesis into the UDC Traditionalism versus Secularism.

The fifth considered cultural taxonomy constituted **Inglehart et al. (2014)**, encompassing the cultural dimensions of Traditional Values versus Secular-Rational Values and Survival Values versus Self-Expression Values. The cultural dimension of Traditional Values versus Secular-Rational Values was synthesized into the UDC Traditionalism versus Secularism during the first synthesis analysis step. No indication was identified, which pointed to any conceptual relationship of the other cultural dimension of Survival Values versus Self-Expression Values by Inglehart et al. (2014) with the concept of the UDC Traditionalism versus Secularism.

Afterward, the cultural taxonomy by **Kluckhohn and Strodtbeck (1961)** was analyzed. In the analysis, none of its cultural dimensions indicated any relation to the projected cultural components of the UDC Traditionalism versus Secularism. Thus, at this point of the analysis, the four cultural dimensions of Activity Orientation, Relational Orientation, Man-Nature Orientation, and Human-Nature Orientation were rejected for synthesis into the UDC Traditionalism versus Secularism. The cultural dimension of Time Orientation by Kluckhohn and Strodtbeck (1961) was synthesized by Maleki and de Jong (2014) with particular regards to the past-time dimension side into their synthesis dimension of Traditionalism versus Secularism. The interrelationship between the concept of time, focussing on past orientation, and the concept of traditionalism versus secularism was analyzed in a separate analysis step. As a result of the analysis, the dimension side of past orientation from the cultural dimension was integrated as a cultural component into the UDC Traditionalism versus Secularism.

Next, the cultural taxonomy by **Lewis (2018)** was analyzed. As already demonstrated in the UDC Perception and Use of Time synthesis analysis, the three cultural dimensions indicated conceptual interrelationships to the concept of perception and use of time. A deeper analysis of the three cultural dimensions is demonstrated in the delimitation analysis of the UDC Perception and Use of Time and the UDC Traditionalism versus Secularism. As a result, Lewis's (2018) three cultural dimensions were suitable for being conceptually synthesized into the UDC Traditionalism versus Secularism.

The cultural taxonomy by **Minkov (2007)** was subsequently analyzed. The analysis of the cultural dimension of Exclusionism versus Universalism by Minkov (2007) revealed no conceptual interrelationship of the cultural dimension to the concept or cultural components of the UDC Traditionalism versus Secularism. Therefore, the cultural dimension of Exclusionism versus Universalism by Minkov (2007) was not synthesized into the UDC Traditionalism versus Secularism.

The cultural dimension of Monumentalism versus Flexhumility by Minkov (2007) pointed to evidence in its description and definition for affiliation to the concept of traditionalism versus secularism, since the general prevalent theme of the cultural dimension is self-enhancement, which Minkov (2007) describes as "a tendency to have a positive self-regard and seek and value positive information about oneself" (p. 165). Minkov (2007) deduced the cultural dimension from four items of the WVS wave 4, displaying the four distinct cultural components of national pride, religiosity, service to others, and making your parents proud. Three of Minkov's (2007) items for the cultural dimension of Monumentalism versus Flexhumility are subsumed to display the cultural component of pride. These three items are "how proud are you to be country's nationality", "the importance of doing service to others", and "one of my main goals in life has been to make my parents proud". More specifically, the item of "one of my main goals in life has been to make my parents proud" was addressed by Minkov (2007) himself to measure the cultural component of pride in general. By the item of "importance of religion" the cultural component of religiosity was addressed. Regarding the given evidence, the cultural dimension of Monumentalism versus Secularism by Minkov (2007) was synthesized into the UDC Traditionalism versus Secularism since it addresses two of the projected cultural components religiosity and feelings of pride of the UDC Traditionalism versus Secularism.

Minkov and Hofstede (2011) admitted in one of their joint papers that their conceptions of the two cultural dimensions of Monumentalism versus Flexhumility by Minkov (2007) and Long-Term versus Short-Term Orientation by Hofstede (2001; Hofstede et al., 2010) only partly overlap. The cultural dimension of Monumentalism versus Flexhumility by Minkov (2007) refers not to the cultural traits of thrift and persistence. The cultural dimension of Long-Term versus Short-Term Orientation by Hofstede (2001; Hofstede et al., 2010) misses out on the consideration of religiosity. Furthermore, Minkov and Hofstede (2011) analyzed the relationship of their two cultural dimensions based on commonly considered countries ($N = 22$). The researchers deduced a significant negative correlation of -0.62 between the two cultural dimensions. The three items G006, A007, and A006 were incorporated into the potential item set of the UDC Traditionalism versus Secularism, referring to the concept of religiosity and pride. Item D054 was omitted since it was assumed to display the concept of parent-child ties, which was not considered further in this dissertation.

The cultural dimension of Indulgence versus Restraint by Minkov (2007) also required in-depth analysis to clarify its potential for synthesis in UDC Traditionalism versus Secularism. In a deeper conceptual analysis, the cultural dimension refers on the indulgence side to a low value of savings and thrift; in contrast, restraint cultures highly value thrift and savings. In a previous synthesis analysis, the thrift concept was considered unsuitable for a cultural component for the UDC Traditionalism versus Secularism. Deductible from the definition, the main focus of the cultural dimension of Indulgence versus Restraint by Minkov (2007) was placed on the happiness level of society as a distinguishing factor for national cultures. The cultural concept was also operationalized in this dissertation's UDC Gratification and Expression of Emotions, Feelings, and Desires.

Minkov (2007) deducted the cultural dimension of Indulgence versus Restraint from items regarding "the feeling that one can act as one pleases, spend money, and indulgence in leisurely activities and other sorts of fun" (Minkov, 2007, p. 115). Item A173 considering life control, was not possible to be subsumed to any by A8 projected cultural components of the UDC Traditionalism versus Secularism. Similar was conducted for item A003 referring to the importance of leisure within a national culture.

Furthermore, item A038 refers to the cultural component of thrift. Also, Hofstede (2001; Hofstede et al., 2010), in his cultural dimension of Long-Term versus Short-Term Orientation, considered the cultural component of thrift. The cultural dimension Long-Term versus Short-Term Orientation by Hofstede (2001; Hofstede et al., 2010) was already synthesized into the UDC Traditionalism versus Secularism.

Hofstede also elaborated that high long-term oriented national cultures connotate "children should learn thrift" (Hofstede, 2001, p. 360). It was subsumed that both cultural dimensions measure two different cultural components in regards to importance. The item by Hofstede et al. (2010) measures the general importance, and the item by Minkov (2007) measures the importance placed on the transmission of the value of thrift and saving money. The happiness item A008 related not to the by A8 projected cultural components of the UDC Traditionalism versus Secularism. In conclusion, the analysis of the cultural dimension of Indulgence versus Restraint by Minkov (2007) did not substantiate the synthesis of the cultural dimension into the UDC Traditionalism versus Secularism.

Afterward, the cultural taxonomy by **Parsons and Shils (1951)** was analyzed. The analysis of its five cultural dimensions of Affectivity versus Affective Neutrality, Ascription versus Achievement, Functional Specificity versus Functional Diffuseness, Self-Interest versus Collectivist Interest, and Universalism versus Particularism revealed no evidence for affiliation to the concept nor the cultural components of the UDC Traditionalism versus Secularism. Conclusively, none of the cultural dimensions by Parsons and Shils (1951) was synthesized into the UDC Traditionalism versus Secularism.

The tenth analyzed cultural taxonomy constituted **Schwartz (1992, 1994b)**. The two cultural dimensions of Hierarchy versus Egalitarianism and Mastery versus Harmony of the cultural taxonomy pointed to no evidence for synthesis into the UDC Traditionalism versus Secularism. Maleki and de Jong (2014) proposed in their synthesis methodology a slight conceptual overlap of the dimension side of embeddedness of the cultural dimension of Autonomy versus Embeddedness by Schwartz (1992, 1994b) to their concept of traditionalism versus secularism; whereby, in their final version of their synthesis methodology, the cultural dimension was not synthesized into their synthesis dimension Traditionalism versus Secularism.

The items operationalized for the cultural dimension of Autonomy versus Embeddedness by Schwartz (1992, 1994b) were also reviewed. Item no. 18 addressed the concept of traditionalism versus secularism. Additionally, item no. 51 could have also been related to the cultural component of religiosity. The remaining items of the cultural dimension did not indicate any relationship to the concept of traditionalism versus secularism. Overall, there was insufficient evidence to synthesize the cultural dimension of Embeddedness versus Autonomy by Schwartz (1992, 1994b) into the UDC Traditionalism versus Secularism.

The last reviewed cultural existing taxonomy constituted the cultural taxonomy by **Trompenaars and Hampden-Turner (2004, 2012)**. The cultural dimension of Sequential versus Synchronous Time was analyzed in more depth in the delimitation demonstration between the concept of past orientation and the concept of traditionalism versus secularism. The other six cultural dimensions of Achievement versus Ascription, Communitarianism versus Individualism, Diffuse versus Specific, Internal versus Outer Direction, Neutral versus Emotional, and Universalism versus Particularism by Trompenaars and Hampden-Turner (2004, 2012) revealed no further evidence for affiliation to the concept of the UDC Traditionalism versus Secularism. Therefore, none of these cultural dimensions were synthesized into the UDC.

6.3 Synthesis of the Universal Dimension of Culture (UDC) Uncertainty Avoidance and Coping Mechanisms

A5 assumed the UDC Uncertainty Avoidance, illustrating the concept of coping and dealing with uncertainties and unknown situations as a distinguishing concept for national cultures, and thus, as a prevalent concept among existing cultural taxonomies. The UDC Uncertainty Avoidance was mainly assumed to distinguish national cultures by the underlying concept of coping and dealing with uncertainties and unknown situations, addressing the cultural component of rule and regulation obedience. A5 assumed further that the UDC Uncertainty Avoidance also distinguishes national cultures by the cultural component of innovation orientation, expressed in terms of performance orientation, and the cultural component of future orientation. A critical aspect in the synthesis of the UDC Uncertainty Avoidance constituted the delimitation of its cultural components to the concept of masculinity versus femininity, expressed as confidence level.

Also, a delimitation of the concept of relationship with the (natural) environment and the concept of coping and dealing with uncertainties and unknown situations was assumed (A2 versus A5).

Figure 6.3 displays, in summary, the projected UDC Uncertainty Avoidance for this dissertation.

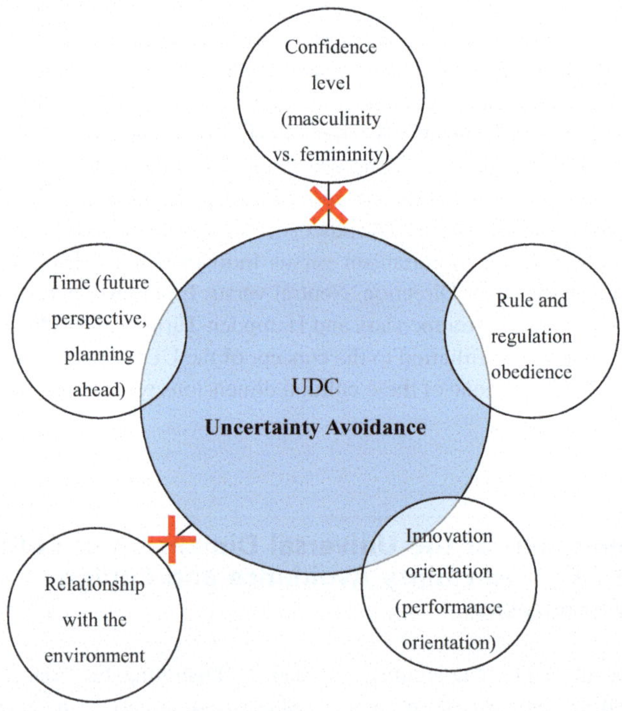

Figure 6.3 Assumption 5 (A5): The Universal Dimension of Culture (UDC) Uncertainty Avoidance

Synthesis Analysis Step 1: Title-Related Cultural Dimensions

The two cultural dimensions of Uncertainty Avoidance by Hofstede (2001; Hofstede et al., 2010) and Uncertainty Avoidance by House et al. (2004, 2007, 2014) were applicable as title-related cultural dimensions for the UDC Uncertainty Avoidance.

At first, the cultural dimension of **Uncertainty Avoidance** by **Hofstede (2001; Hofstede et al., 2010)**[3], pointing to the essential assumption that the need for predictability of individuals comes into action by unwritten and written rules.

In summary, it was concluded that the cultural dimension of Uncertainty Avoidance by Hofstede (2001; Hofstede et al., 2010) relates mainly to the concept of stress and the concept of rule obedience, explicitly emphasizing the concept of stress by placing a higher weighting factor on it in the uncertainty avoidance index formula. Overall, the cultural dimension was applicable to be suitable for synthesis into the UDC Uncertainty Avoidance. Its synthesis also confirmed the projected cultural component of rule and regulation obedience for the UDC Uncertainty Avoidance. Although, the initially assumed UDC Uncertainty Avoidance did not encompass a cultural component of stress. The synthesis of the cultural dimension of Uncertainty Avoidance by Hofstede (2001; Hofstede et al., 2010) expanded the cultural components of the UDC to the cultural component of stress. Likewise, all four items (items no. 18, no. 15, no. 21, and no. 24 of the VSM 2013) were incorporated into the potential item set of the UDC Uncertainty Avoidance.

The second title-related analyzed cultural dimension constituted the cultural dimension of **Uncertainty Avoidance** by **House et al. (2004, 2007, 2014)**. The conceptual analysis of the definition and description of the cultural dimension revealed enough evidence that substantiated its synthesis into the UDC Uncertainty Avoidance. The cultural dimension of Uncertainty Avoidance by House et al. (2004) illustrates "the extent to which ambiguous situations are threatening to individuals, to which rules and order are preferred and to which uncertainty is tolerated in a society" (p. 602).

For the empirical measurement of the cultural dimension, House et al. (n.d.) operationalized five societal value items. Reviewing the operationalized items by House et al. (2004), it became apparent that they can be classified and broken down into the following concepts: orderliness, consistency, structure, requirements, instructions, rules, laws, and planning in order to achieve goals. Overall, these concepts were assumed to appear as conceptual sub-components of the cultural component of rule and regulation obedience. The four societal value items no. V3_16, no. V3_19,

[3] Hofstede (2001) distinguished the concept of uncertainty from the concept of risk, in that sense that risk refers to a specific and often in percentage of probability expressed measure for the likelihood of an event.

no. V3_24, and no. V3_25 of the cultural dimension of Uncertainty Avoidance by House et al. (2004, 2007, 2014) were incorporated into the potential item set of the UDC Uncertainty Avoidance. The societal value item V3_16 precisely depicts the concept of coping and dealing with uncertainties.

And the three societal value items no. V3_19, no. V3_25, and no. V3_24 were considered to address the concept of rule and regulation obedience, which was projected to constitute a cultural component of the UDC Uncertainty Avoidance. Only, the societal value item no. V3_1 was not incorporated into the item set of the UDC, even if orderliness and consistency could have been seen conceptually related to the concept of coping and dealing with uncertainties. A5 assumed no cultural component regarding the concept consistency and orderliness for the UDC Uncertainty Avoidance and there was not enough evidence applicable which would have justified an integration of the concepts of consistency and orderliness in the UDC[4]. Conclusively, the cultural dimension of Uncertainty Avoidance by House et al. (2004, 2007, 2014) was also synthesized into the UDC Uncertainty Avoidance.

In summary, the two by title-related cultural dimensions of Uncertainty Avoidance by Hofstede (2001; Hofstede et al., 2010) and Uncertainty Avoidance by House et al. (2004, 2007, 2014) measures specific but distinct aspects of the concept of coping and dealing with uncertainties and unknown situations, as a distinguishing factor for national cultures. The definitions of both cultural dimensions of Uncertainty Avoidance are conceptually similar, whereas not identical. The cultural dimension of Uncertainty Avoidance by Hofstede (2001; Hofstede et al., 2010) focuses on the cultural component of stress (as it was weighted more significantly than the rule and regulation obedience items in the demonstrated formula). The cultural dimension of Uncertainty Avoidance by House et al. (2004) stressed mainly the cultural facet of rule and regulation obedience as a distinguishing factor for national cultures.

Synthesis Analysis Step: Analysis of the Set of 50 Cultural Dimensions

At first, the cultural dimensions of **Fiske (1991, 1992)** were analyzed. None of the four reviewed cultural dimensions indicated any evidence for affiliation to the concept of uncertainty avoidance. Therefore, none of its cultural dimensions was synthesized into the UDC Uncertainty Avoidance.

Likewise, it accounted for the four cultural dimensions of the cultural taxonomy by **Hall (1959, 1966, 1976, 1983; Hall & Hall, 1990)**. There was no evidence identified which would have justified the synthesis of the cultural dimensions of Hall

[4] Several researchers compared the cultural dimensions of Uncertainty Avoidance by Hofstede (2001; Hofstede et al., 2010) and House et al. (2004, 2007, 2014). For an example, please refer to Venaik and Brewer (2010).

(1959, 1966, 1976, 1983; Hall & Hall, 1990) into the assumed UDC Uncertainty Avoidance.

However, for the cultural dimension of Time by Hall (1983), Hall described national cultural differences regarding relying on schedules. It was assumed that the reliance on schedules constitutes a coping and/or prevention mechanism for uncertain situations. This approach was demonstrated by Nardon and Steers (2009). Also, the initially assumed UDC Uncertainty Avoidance encompassed a cultural component of time, including the sub-components of future perspective and planning ahead. However, there was not enough evidence detectable in the cultural dimension of Time by Hall (1983), which would have substantiated the synthesis of the cultural dimension into the UDC Uncertainty Avoidance in regards to the by Nardon and Steers (2009) projected conceptual interference.

The third analyzed existing cultural taxonomy constituted the cultural taxonomy by **Hofstede (2001; Hofstede et al., 2010)**. The cultural dimension of Uncertainty Avoidance by Hofstede (2001; Hofstede et al., 2010) was already synthesized during the first analysis step into the UDC Uncertainty Avoidance. The four cultural dimensions of Individualism versus Collectivism, Indulgence versus Restraint, Long-Term versus Short-Term Orientation, and Power Distance demonstrated no further evidence for synthesis into the UDC Uncertainty Avoidance; thus, these cultural dimensions were not synthesized into the UDC Uncertainty Avoidance.

Low and Chapman (2003) assumed a link between the concept of confidence level, also expressed in the concept of masculinity versus femininity, and the concept of uncertainty avoidance. A5 assumed the two concepts as distinct from each other for the UDC Uncertainty Avoidance of this dissertation. In this regard, the cultural dimension of Masculinity versus Femininity by Hofstede (2001; Hofstede et al., 2010) was in-depth-reviewed, including its operationalized items. By definition, the cultural dimension is described as follows:

> A society is called masculine when emotional gender roles are clearly distinct: men are supposed to be assertive, tough, and focused on material success, whereas women are supposed to be more modest, tender, and concerned with the quality of life. A society is called feminine when emotional gender roles overlap: both men and women are supposed to be modest, tender, and concerned with the quality of life. (Hofstede et al., 2010, p. 140)

Overall, none of the reviewed items nor the description within the work by Hofstede (2001) and Hofstede et al. (2010) pointed to any evidence which would confirm or strengthen the approach by Low and Chapman (2003). Also, no information was identified which would have explicitly or implicitly linked the cultural dimension of

Masculinity versus Femininity by Hofstede (2001; Hofstede et al., 2010) to the concept of dealing and coping with uncertainty and unknown situation. Conclusively, the cultural dimension was not synthesized into the UDC Uncertainty Avoidance.

Afterward, the cultural taxonomy by **House et al. (2004, 2007, 2014)** was reviewed in more detail. The cultural dimension of Uncertainty Avoidance by House et al. (2004, 2007, 2014) was already synthesized into the UDC Uncertainty Avoidance during the first UDC synthesis analysis step. The cultural dimensions of Assertiveness, Gender Egalitarianism, Humane Orientation, In-Group Collectivism, and Institutional Collectivism by House et al. (2004, 2007, 2014) indicated no affiliation to the concept of uncertainty avoidance.

Maleki and de Jong (2014) proposed the synthesis of the cultural dimension of Performance Orientation by House et al. (2004, 2007, 2014) in a synthesis dimension related to the concept of uncertainty avoidance. The two researchers assumed that individuals pursue continuous improvements in performance in order to improve future perspectives continuously. The steady improvement for future prospective was considered as a prevention mechanism of uncertain and unknown situations in the future (Maleki & de Jong, 2014). The in-depth review of the cultural dimension of Performance Orientation by House et al. (2004, 2007, 2014) revealed no information or evidence that substantiated the approach by Maleki and de Jong (2014). The operationalized items only addressed the concept of continuous performance improvement. Conclusively, the cultural dimension of Performance Orientation by House et al. (2004, 2007, 2014) was not synthesized into the UDC Uncertainty Avoidance.

House et al. (2004, 2007, 2014) investigated the correlation of their cultural dimension of Power Distance and the concept of uncertainty avoidance; thus, their cultural dimension of Uncertainty Avoidance. The in-depth analysis of the cultural dimension of Power Distance by House et al. (2004, 2007, 2014) yields no further evidence which would have substantiated an affiliation between the two concepts for this dissertation. The cultural dimension was not synthesized into the UDC Uncertainty Avoidance.

Furthermore, the cultural dimension of Future Orientation by House et al. (2004, 2007, 2014) was reviewed more deeply since the initial UDC Uncertainty Avoidance was projected to encompass a cultural component of time regarding the sub-components of future perspective and planning ahead. In the in-depth review, including the operationalized items of the cultural dimension of Future Orientation by House et al. (n.d.), it became applicable that high future-oriented national cultures tend to be free of past worries as well as future anxiety. In practical terms, House et al. (2004) identified a positive correlation between the value items of the cultural dimensions of Uncertainty Avoidance by House et al. (2004, 2007, 2014) and Future Orientation by House et al. (2004, 2007, 2014). The researchers postulated that aspiration for higher future orientation causes an understanding that most uncertainties can be prevented and managed. In this dissertation, A5 followed the approaches by Nardon and Steers (2009) and Maleki and de Jong (2014) and assigned the concept of planning ahead to generate certainties to prevent and cope with future anxieties.

Overall, the cultural dimension of Future Orientation by House et al. (2004, 2007, 2014) was synthesized into the UDC Uncertainty Avoidance under the assumption of its function as prevention and coping mechanism for uncertainties and unknown situations. The four societal value items of the cultural dimension of Future Orientation by House et al. (2004, 2007, 2014) were reviewed regarding their suitability to display the conceptual interference of the concept of coping and preventing uncertainties and unknown situations and the concept of future planning. The four societal value items no. V3_3, no. V3_4, no. V3_8, and no. V3_30 were considered to display the conceptual interference between the concept of coping and preventing uncertainties and unknown situations and the concept of future planning, thus by different extents. All four societal value items of the cultural dimension of Future Orientation by House et al. (2004, 2007, 2014) were incorporated into the potential item set of the UDC Uncertainty Avoidance.

The fifth analyzed cultural taxonomy constituted **Inglehart et al. (2014)**, resulting in no evidence for its two cultural dimensions to be related to the concept of uncertainty avoidance. Thus, none of its two cultural dimensions was synthesized into the UDC Uncertainty Avoidance.

Next, the cultural dimensions of **Kluckhohn and Strodtbeck (1961)** were analyzed. The cultural dimensions of the cultural taxonomy indicated no evidence for affiliation to the concept of uncertainty avoidance nor the by A5 projected cultural concept or cultural components for the UDC Uncertainty Avoidance. Thus, none of these cultural dimensions of the cultural taxonomy by Kluckhohn and Strodtbeck (1961) was synthesized into the UDC. The cultural taxonomy by Kluckhohn and Strodtbeck (1961) also encompassed a time-concept-related cultural dimension of Time Orientation, consisting of three dimension sides—past, present, and future. Future-oriented national cultures intend to plan ahead, and decisions are guided by predicted circumstances that could occur in the long run (Kluckhohn & Strodtbeck, 1961). Also, the cultural dimension describes the concept of planning for future perspectives and predictability-guided decision-making. In this dissertation, these concepts were seen as a mechanism for individuals to cope with uncertainties and unknown situations. Conclusively, the cultural dimension of Time Orientation by Kluckhohn and Strodtbeck (1961) was synthesized into the UDC Uncertainty Avoidance.

The seventh analyzed cultural taxonomy constituted **Lewis (2018)**. The two cultural dimensions of Multi-Active and Re-Active by Lewis (2018) did not indicate any conceptual interrelationship to the concept of coping and dealing with uncertainties and unknown situations; thus were rejected for synthesis into the UDC Uncertainty Avoidance. Also, the cultural dimension of Linear-Active by Lewis (2018) was reviewed regarding conceptual evidence for an affiliation between the cultural component of time and the concept of uncertainty avoidance. Lewis (2018) did not explicitly refer to a connection of the cultural dimension of Linear-Active with the concept of uncertainty avoidance, nor did he indicate that Linear-Active national cultures rely on rules and stick to plans in order to prevent or to cope with uncertain situations. It was only mentioned that linear-active cultures tend to stick to plans and rely on strict procedures to prevent uncertainties. The evidence for the conceptual approach was not evaluated as not substantial; even the same approach was applied for the cultural dimensions of Universalism versus Exclusionism by Minkov (2007), Universalism versus Particularism by Parsons and Shils (1951), and Particularism versus Universalism by Trompenaars and Hampden-Turner (2004, 2012) in this dissertation. Conclusively, the cultural dimension of Linear-Active by Lewis (2018) was not synthesized into the UDC.

The cultural taxonomy by **Minkov (2007)** constituted the eight analyzed existing cultural taxonomy. The analysis of the two cultural dimensions of Indulgence versus Restraint and Monumentalism versus Flexhumility by Minkov (2007) revealed no further evidence for their relation to the concept of coping and dealing with uncertainties and unknown situations; thus, both cultural dimensions were rejected for synthesis into the UDC Uncertainty Avoidance.

Also, the cultural dimension of Universalism versus Exclusionism by Minkov (2007) was analyzed regarding the interference of a cultural component of rule and regulation obedience and the concept of uncertainty avoidance. Minkov (2007) elaborated for his cultural dimension of Universalism versus Exclusionism a potential connection to the concept of uncertainty avoidance, displayed in the operationalization of the following five items for the cultural dimension: "one must always love one's parents" (no. A025), "a child needs both a father and a mother" (no. D018), "a woman needs children to be fulfilled" (no. D019), "people from another race are undesirable as neighbors" (no. A125), and "a child should learn tolerance and respect for other people" (no. A03).

Minkov (2007) claimed that the concept of uncertainty avoidance, including the cultural components of orderliness and rule and regulation obedience, are typical concepts and cultural components of Western cultures. Furthermore, Minkov (2007) postulated that the cultural dimension of Uncertainty Avoidance by House et al. (2004, 2007, 2014) constitutes an indicator for Westernization instead of an actual uncertainty avoidance measurement. Minkov (2007) based this assumption on the argument that the Uncertainty Avoidance items by House et al. (2004, 2007, 2014) would only refer to implementing Western orderliness in national culture. In Minkov's (2007) understanding, exclusionism national cultures measure the resistance of cultures towards Western universalistic orders (e.g., rules of laws).

Even though Minkov (2007) did not intend to use the cultural dimension of Universalism versus Exclusionism to distinguish national cultures regarding uncertainty avoidance, he still was aware of the conceptual interference between the two concepts—the concept of universalism versus particularism and the concept of uncertainty avoidance. This acknowledgment of the characteristic feature of rule and regulation obedience as a cultural component of the concept of uncertainty avoidance by Minkov (2007) strengthened its projection in this dissertation.

Conclusively, the cultural dimension of Exclusionism versus Universalism by Minkov (2007) was synthesized into the UDC Uncertainty Avoidance. Although, it was acknowledged that the conceptual connection of the cultural dimension of Universalism versus Exclusionism by Minkov (2007) to the concept of uncertainty avoidance is not as strong as it was for the two title-related cultural dimensions of Uncertainty Avoidance by Hofstede (2001) and House et al. (2004, 2007, 2014). None of the five items (no. A025, no. D018, no. A03, no. A125, and no. D019) was seen as suitable to be incorporated into the potential item set of the UDC Uncertainty Avoidance since none of the five items addressed the concept of dealing and handling of uncertainties and unknown situations nor the concept of rule and regulation obedience under the umbrella of the concept of uncertainty avoidance.

Next, the cultural taxonomy by **Parsons and Shils (1951)** was analyzed. In the four cultural dimensions of Affectivity versus Affective Neutrality, Ascription versus Achievements, Functional Specificity versus Functional Diffuseness, and Self-Interest versus Collectivism Interests, no further evidence was identified that would have justified a synthesis of these cultural dimensions into the UDC Uncertainty Avoidance. The cultural dimension of Universalism versus Particularism by Parsons and Shils (1951) was reviewed regarding the conceptual overlap between the concept of uncertainty avoidance and the cultural component of rule and regulation obedience. Under the same implications for the cultural dimension of Universalism versus Particularism by Trompenaars and Hampden-Turner (2004, 2012), the cultural dimension of Universalism versus Particularism by Parsons and Shils (1951) was synthesized into the UDC Uncertainty Avoidance by assuming that national cultures tend to apply rules and regulations to prevent uncertain situations. It should be acknowledged that the evidence for the synthesis of the cultural dimension of Particularism versus Universalism by Parsons and Shils (1951) into the UDC was not as strong as the evidence for the synthesized cultural dimensions of Uncertainty

Avoidance by Hofstede (2001; Hofstede et al., 2010) and Uncertainty Avoidance by House et al. (2004, 2007, 2014).

The tenth analyzed cultural taxonomy constituted **Schwartz (1992, 1994b)**. Due to the circumstance that the cultural concept of coping and dealing with uncertainties and unknown situations is not connected to the cultural concept of relationship with the environment. None of the cultural dimensions of the cultural taxonomy were suitable to be synthesized.

The last considered cultural taxonomy constituted **Trompenaars and Hampden-Turner (2004, 2012)**. No substantial evidence for synthesis into the UDC Uncertainty Avoidance was found for its cultural dimension of Achievement versus Ascription. The cultural dimension of Universalism versus Particularism by Trompenaars and Hampden-Turner (2004, 2012) pointed to some evidence and was in-depth reviewed.

Trompenaars and Hampden-Turner constructed the following dilemma for the cultural dimensions:

> You are riding in a car driven by a close friend. He hits a pedestrian. You know he was going at least 35 miles per hour in an area of the city where the maximum allowed speed is 20 miles per hour. There are no witnesses. His lawyer says that if you testify under oath that he was only driving 20 miles per hour it may save him from serious consequences. What right has your friend to expect you to protect him? 1a My friend has a definite right as a friend to expect me to testify to the lower figure. 1b He has some right as a friend to expect me to testify to the lower figure. 1c He has no right as a friend to expect me to testify to the lower figure. What do you think you would do in view of the obligations of a sworn witness and the obligation to your friend?1d Testify that he was going 20 miles an hour. 1e Not testify that he was going 20 miles an hour. (Trompenaars & Hampden-Turner, 1997, pp. 33–34)

Trompenaars and Hampden-Turner (2004, 2012) assumed that for universalistic cultures, the seriousness of an event is more prevalent than the value of a relationship to a friend. Universalistic cultures in the above case projection evaluate breaking the law higher than the value of the actual relationship to the friend. The opposite cultural traits account for particularistic cultures. It was assumed from the before elaborated case that universalistic cultures rely on rules (in contrast to particularistic cultures) to prevent uncertain situations, which they would encounter in situations without existing concrete rules. Following these assumptions, the cultural dimension of Universalism versus Particularism by Trompenaars and Hampden-Turner (2004, 2012) was synthesized into UDC Uncertainty Avoidance without the indicated item.

The cultural dimension of Sequential versus Synchronous by Trompenaars and Hampden-Turner (2004, 2012) was reviewed regarding the initially assumed cultural component of time for the UDC Uncertainty Avoidance. By definition, everything has its time and place in sequential national cultures, schedules are tight and followed, and time is measurable.

In contrast, synchronic cultures perceive time as diffuse, and individuals are less likely to follow and stick to arranged appointments. Synchronic national cultures are more likely to factor decisions based on relationships (Trompenaars & Hampden-Turner, 2004, 2012). In summary, the description of the cultural dimension demonstrates that the dimension refers, first, to the concept of stress caused by changed plans. Second, it also refers to the concept of rule and regulation obedience. Conclusively, the cultural dimension of Sequential versus Synchronic by Trompenaars and Hampden-Turner (2004, 2012) was synthesized into the UDC Uncertainty Avoidance.

The cultural dimension of Specific versus Diffuse by Trompenaars and Hampden-Turner (2004, 2012) was reviewed too. Low and Chapman (2003) connected the space component of the cultural dimension (significant versus little private space) to the concept of uncertainty avoidance since keeping an ample private space could indicate a motivation for security. The in-depth review of the cultural dimension of Specific versus Diffuse by Trompenaars and Hampden-Turner (2004, 2012) pointed to no evidence which would have substantiated the approach by Low and Chapman (2003) also for this dissertation. The cultural dimension was not synthesized into the UDC Uncertainty Avoidance

6.4 Delimitation Between the Concepts of Uncertainty Avoidance and Relationship with the (Natural) Environment

Schneider et al. (2014) proposed an interrelationship between the concept of relationship with the (natural) environment and the concept of uncertainty avoidance. In this dissertation, the concept of uncertainty avoidance was operationalized in the UDC Uncertainty Avoidance projected by A5. Neither A2 nor A5 assumed a relationship for the UDCs Uncertainty Avoidance and Relationship with the Natural Environment. In the following, the synthesized cultural dimensions of the UDC Uncertainty Avoidance were analyzed regarding the conceptual interrelationship between the concept of uncertainty avoidance and the concept relationship with the (natural) environment[5].

These are the cultural dimensions of Uncertainty Avoidance by Hofstede (2001; Hofstede et al., 2010), Uncertainty Avoidance by House et al. (2004, 2007, 2014), Time Orientation by Kluckhohn and Strodtbeck (1961), Exclusionism versus Universalism by Minkov (2007), Universalism versus Particularism by Parsons and Shils (1951), Sequential versus Synchronous Time by Trompenaars and Hamden-Turner (2004, 2012), and Universalism versus Particularism by Trompenaars and Hampden-Turner (2004, 2012).

At first, the cultural dimension of Uncertainty Avoidance by Hofstede (2001; Hofstede et al., 2010) was analyzed to demonstrate the delimitation between the concepts of uncertainty avoidance and the relationship with the (natural) environment. Schneider et al. (2014) synthesized the cultural dimension of Uncertainty Avoidance by Hofstede (2001; Hofstede et al., 2010) into their synthesis dimension for the concept of relationship with the (natural) environment. Also, Schneider et al. (2014) subsumed the social environment and natural environment distinct from each other.

The cultural dimension of Uncertainty Avoidance by Hofstede (2001; Hofstede et al., 2010) distinguish national cultures by their "extent to which the members of institutions and organization within a society feel threatened by uncertain, unknown, ambiguous, or unstructured situations" (Hofstede & Minkov, 2013, p. 8). The detailed analysis of the description of the cultural dimension of Uncertainty Avoidance by Hofstede (2001; Hofstede et al., 2010) pointed to no evidence for a relation of the cultural dimension and the concept of relationship with the (natural) environment. Additionally, the items which were applied for the empirical assessment of the cultural dimension of Uncertainty Avoidance by Hofstede and Minkov (2013) were analyzed, revealing no further evidence for a conceptual overlap between the concept of relationship with the (natural) environment and the concept of uncertainty avoidance.

Also, House et al. (2004, 2007, 2014) developed a cultural dimension of Uncertainty Avoidance, defined as the "extent to which society, organization, or group relies on social norms, rules, and procedure to alleviate unpredictability of future events" (House et al., 2004, p. 30). The synthesis methodology by Schneider et al. (2014) demonstrated that the cultural dimension of Uncertainty

[5] The delimitation analysis was done from the angle of the concept of uncertainty avoidance and the UDC Uncertainty Avoidance since Schneider et al. (2014) proposed the concept of relationship with the (natural) environment as a source of coping and dealing mechanism for uncertain and unknown situations.

Avoidance by House et al. (2004, 2007, 2014) could be synthesized into the same synthesis dimension as cultural dimensions addressing the concept of relationship with the (natural) environment.

The analysis of the cultural dimension of Uncertainty Avoidance by House et al. (2004, 2007, 2014) revealed in the description, the definition, and in the items of the cultural dimension no evidence which would point to a conceptual overlap of the cultural dimension with the concept of relationship with the (natural) environment.

The cultural dimension of Time Orientation by Kluckhohn and Strodteck (1961) was also analyzed regarding the delimitation between the concepts of uncertainty avoidance and relationship with the (natural) environment. The analysis of the cultural dimension of Time Orientation by Kluckhohn and Strodtbeck (1961) pointed to no substantial evidence regarding the delimitation of the two concepts.

Next, the cultural dimension of Exclusionism versus Universalism by Minkov (2007) was reviewed, synthesized into the UDC Relationship with the Natural Environment and the UDC Uncertainty Avoidance, only in conceptual terms. Minkov (2007) subsumed the concept of uncertainty avoidance to the idea of Western universalistic cultures and claimed that exclusionism national cultures have the feature of a lower concern for their (natural) environment. Thus, the cultural dimension would substantiate an inevitable overlap between the concepts of uncertainty avoidance and the relationship with the (natural) environment. Likewise, it was concluded for the cultural dimension of Universalism versus Particularism by Parsons and Shils (1951). An analysis of the cultural dimension of Universalism versus Particularism by Parsons and Shils (1951) regarding conceptual overlaps of the concept of uncertainty avoidance and the concept of relationship with the (natural) environment did not lead to any substantial evidence for the overlap. The analysis of the cultural dimension of Universalism versus Particularism by Parsons and Shils (1951) did not confirm the approach by Schneider et al. (2014) for a connection between the cultural concept of uncertainty avoidance and the concept of relationship with the (natural) environment.

Finally, two cultural dimensions of the cultural taxonomy by Trompenaars and Hampden-Turner (2004, 2012) were analyzed for potential a relationship between the concept of uncertainty avoidance and the concept of relationship with the (natural) environment. The two cultural dimensions constitute the cultural dimensions of Sequential versus Synchronous Time and Universalism versus Particularism by Trompenaars and Hampden-Turner (2004, 2012).

The cultural dimension of Sequential versus Synchronous Time by Trompenaars and Hampden-Turner (2004, 2012) distinguishes national cultures by their relative importance on either the past, the present, or the future. Neither the definition nor the description of the cultural dimension of Sequential versus Synchronous Time by Trompenaars and Hampden-Turner (2004, 2012) pointed to evidence for a conceptual overlap of the concept of relationship with the (natural) environment and the concept of uncertainty avoidance.

The cultural dimension of Universalism versus Particularism by Trompenaars and Hampden-Turner (2004, 2012) refers to the judgment of individuals' behavior, distinguishing national cultures in either universalism national cultures or particularism national cultures. Universalistic national cultures focus on rules for the judgment of an encountered event or object. In contrast, particularistic national cultures focus on the exceptional value of any present circumstance by valuing highly the relationship they have with the encountered object or event (Trompenaars & Hampden-Turner, 2004, 2012). The analysis of the cultural dimension of Universalism versus Particularism by Trompenaars and Hampden-Turner (2004, 2012) pointed to no evidence for a relationship between the concept of relationship with the (natural) environment and the concept of uncertainty avoidance.

Schneider et al. (2014) projected in their synthesis dimension of Relationship with the Environment that the cultural dimensions of Uncertainty Avoidance by Hofstede (2001; Hofstede et al., 2010) and by House et al. (2004, 2007, 2014) could be synthesized together with cultural dimensions of Man-Nature Orientation by Kluckhohn and Strodtbeck (1961), Mastery versus Harmony by Schwartz (1992, 1994b), and Internal versus Outer Direction by Trompenaars and Hampden-Turner (2004, 2012) into one synthesis dimension. Schneider et al. (2014) justified their argumentation with that "in many Eastern European countries, for example, the centralized control of the Communist regime served to reduce uncertainty" (Schneider et al., 2014, p. 45). No evidence was identified in the review of the mentioned cultural dimensions that would have justified subsumption of the concepts of relationship with the (natural) environment and uncertainty avoidance.

In conclusion, the analysis of the several previous cultural dimensions did not substantiate the concept of relationship with the (natural) environment as a coping mechanism for uncertain and unknown situations.

6.5 Delimitation Between the Concepts of Perception and Use of Time and Traditionalism versus Secularism

In this dissertation, the two concepts of perception and use of time and traditionalism versus secularism were assumed to constitute two distinct UDCs—by A4 the UDC Perception and Use of Time and by A8 the UDC Traditionalism versus Secularism. More specifically, the cultural concept of traditionalism versus secularism refers to the cultural components of self-stability, feelings of pride, consistency between expressed and felt emotions, religiosity, flexibility, and secular orientation. The critical point lies in the assumption that traditionalism is related to the concept of past orientation as projected by Maleki and de Jong (2014). Maleki and de Jong (2014) incorporated the cultural component of past orientation in their synthesis dimension of Traditionalism versus Secularism. In order to demonstrate the delimitation between the two concepts, the cultural dimensions of Long-Term versus Short-Term Orientation by Hofstede (2001; Hofstede et al., 2010), Traditional Values versus Secular-Rational Values by Inglehart et al. (2014), and the time-concept cultural dimensions of Time Orientation by Trompenaars and Hampden-Turner (2004, 2012), Future Orientation by House et al. (2004, 2007, 2014), Time Orientation by Kluckhohn and Strodtbeck (1961), and Time by Hall (1983).

At first, in the description of the cultural dimension of Time by Hall (1983), no indication was found which would have substantiated a connection to the concept of traditionalism versus secularism. The cultural dimension distinguishes national cultures into monochronic versus polychronic national cultures according to their orientation and perception of time. There was no specific indication for the delimitation of the concepts of traditionalism versus secularism and perception and use of time retrievable from the cultural dimension analysis.

Next, the cultural dimension of Time Orientation by Kluckhohn and Strodtbeck (1961) was reviewed since the cultural dimension was synthesized into the UDC Perception and Use of Time and the UDC Traditionalism versus Secularism in this dissertation. In the description, Kluckhohn and Strodtbeck (1961) mentioned that past-oriented (national) cultures favor traditions and act to maintain traditions. Thus, the cultural dimension analysis would have pointed to the subsumption of the two concepts of traditionalism versus secularism and perception and use of time into one UDC.

The cultural dimension of Long-Term versus Short-Term Orientation by Hofstede (2001; Hofstede et al., 2010) is described as follows:

> Long-term orientation (LTO) stands for the fostering of virtues oriented toward future rewards—in particular, perseverance and thrift. Its opposite pole, short-term orientation, stands for the fostering of virtues related to the past and present—in particular, respect for tradition, preservation of face, and fulfilling social obligations. (Hofstede, 2001, p. 210)

The cultural dimension was synthesized into the UDC Traditionalism versus Secularism. Neither the definition nor one of the four addressed items (relationship, thrift, national pride, and persistency) nor an analysis of further evidence showed any substantial information for a relation of the cultural dimension of Long-Term versus Short-Term Orientation by Hofstede (2001; Hofstede et al., 2010) to the concept of perception and use of time. Although the cultural dimension indicated an assessment of the cultural component of thrift, and therefore, it could have been assumed that the cultural dimension also addresses the concept of time in a broader sense. The review of the cultural dimension of Long-Term versus Short-Term Orientation by Hofstede (2001; Hofstede et al., 2010) substantiated the approach to operationalizing two UDCs for the two concepts—the concept of perception and use of time and the concept of traditionalism versus secularism.

Taken the evidence stated by Kluckhohn and Strodtbeck (1961) that past-time oriented national cultures tend to decide based on traditions, together with evidence in the Hofstede et al. (2010) description of their Long-Term versus Short-Term Orientation cultural dimension into account the proposed cultural component of past-time orientation for the UDC Traditionalism versus Secularism was demonstrated. What remained questionable was the direction of the conception. Either the past-time orientation deduces a focus on traditional traits, or the focus on traditional traits deduces a past-time cultural component of the UDC Traditionalism versus Secularism.

Afterward, the cultural dimension of Time Orientation by Trompenaars and Hampden-Turner (2004, 2012) was reviewed, distinguishing national cultures per their relative importance given to past, present, and future time components. No evidence was found in the cultural dimension, which would have allowed for a delimitation between the two concepts of perception and use of time and traditionalism versus secularism.

An often-studied correlation constituted the correlation between the cultural dimension of Long-Term versus Short-Term Orientation by Hofstede (2001; Hofstede et al., 2010) and the cultural dimension of Future Orientation by House et al. (2004, 2007, 2014). The cultural dimension of Long-Term versus Short-Term Orientation by Hofstede (2001; Hofstede et al., 2010) was synthesized into the UDC Traditionalism versus Secularism. In cross-cultural research, it became common practice to equate these two cultural dimensions with each other. The assumption of an interchangeable application of both cultural dimensions originated mainly because of their title and assumed similarities in their items (Venaik et al., 2013).

Venaik et al. (2013) examined the conceptual and empirical relationship between both cultural dimensions, concluding with no significant correlation between the two cultural dimensions. House et al. (2004) investigated the potential interlink of their Future Orientation cultural dimension with the cultural dimension Long-Term versus Short-Term Orientation by Hofstede et al. (2010). Also, House et al. (2004) did not find any evidence, conceptually nor empirically, for a relationship of the two cultural dimensions. Only Hofstede et al. (2010) revealed that their item thrift relates to the future-oriented behavior of national cultures.

Lastly, the cultural dimension of Traditional Values versus Secular-Rational Values by Inglehart et al. (2014) was reviewed. Overall, neither the definition nor the cultural dimension description pointed to evidence that would have substantiated an interference of the two concepts of traditionalism versus secularism and perception and use of time. Likewise, the applied items for the cultural dimension indicated no affiliation between the two concepts.

In conclusion, the cultural component of past orientation seemed conceptually related to the concept of traditionalism versus secularism. However, none of the synthesized cultural dimensions for the UDC Traditionalism versus Secularism applied a measurement, thus an item, which precisely measured the past-time orientation regarding the concept of traditionalism versus secularism. Therefore, the cultural component of past-time orientation was integrated as a cultural component in the UDC Traditionalism versus Secularism; whereas, it was not operationalized by an item. Also, the delimitation of the two concepts was demonstrated by the previous analysis.

6.6 Results of the Syntheses

Overall, the syntheses of the three UDCs Perception and Use of Time, Traditionalism versus Secularism, and Uncertainty Avoidance substantiated the dominant role of the concept of time among existing cultural taxonomies. It can be stated that the UDC Perception and Use of Time encompassed the solely time-related cultural components of time horizon, perception of time, number of handled tasks at a time, and planning ahead. The concept of planning ahead in terms of future perspective was also operationalized as a cultural component for the UDC

Uncertainty Avoidance as that planning ahead serves as a prevention method for uncertainties since future anxiety is the biggest threat for individuals. The UDC Traditionalism versus Secularism also encompasses a past orientation cultural component. However, as demonstrated, the concept of time plays a crucial role, but each UDC of the three UDCs, Uncertainty Avoidance, Perception and Use of Time, and Traditionalism versus Secularism, referred to a different facet of it.

6.6.1 The Universal Dimension of Culture (UDC) Perception and Use of Time

A4 assumed that the concept of perception and use of time would be applicable as one main factor in classifying and distinguishing national cultures among existing cultural taxonomies. Furthermore, it was projected that the concept of perception and use of time would be represented as a cultural dimension in most existing cultural taxonomies. In more detail, it was projected that the majority of existing cultural taxonomies which classify national cultures by the concept of perception and use of time, refers then to the following five cultural components: perception of time, use of time, number of handled tasks at a time, time horizon, and planning ahead. Additionally, A4 projected a delimitation between the concept of perception and use of time and the concept of traditionalism versus secularism.

The synthesis analysis revealed the following evidence, displayed in summary in Figure 6.4, which partly rejected and partly confirmed the by A4 projected UDC Perception and Use of Time.

Firstly, it was confirmed that the concept of perception and use of time and the concept of traditionalism versus secularism should be treated distinct from each other, as it is applicable in the majority of cultural taxonomies, thus confirming the existence of two separate UDCs in this dissertation.

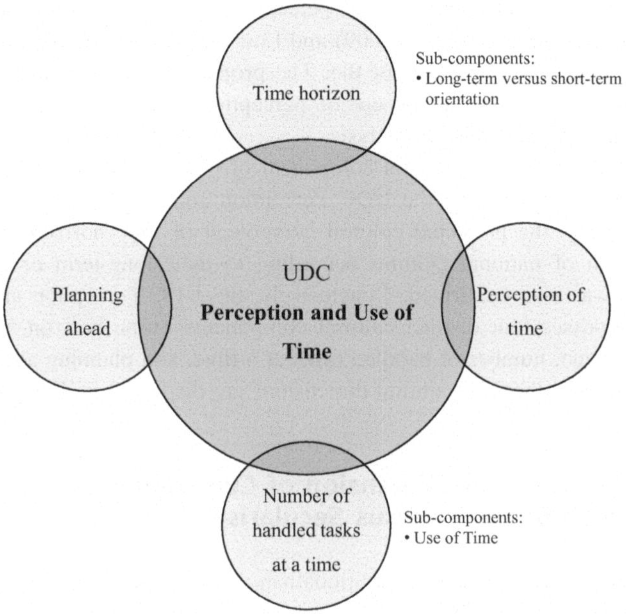

Figure 6.4 The Universal Dimension of Culture (UDC) Perception and Use of Time

Secondly, the cultural component of the use of time, which was proposed by Nardon and Steers (2009) and Low and Chapman (2003) for a synthesis dimension considering the concept of time, was projected by A4 to constitute one distinct cultural component of the UDC Perception and Use of Time in this dissertation. However, during the analysis, this was only partly confirmed. Low and Chapman (2003) and Nardon and Steers (2009) describe the use of time continuously regarding the number of handled tasks at a time in national culture. Each of the analyzed cultural dimensions for the cultural component of the number of handled tasks emphasized the cultural component by a general description of the use of time. Therefore, the initially assumed distinct cultural component of the use of time was merged as a sub-component in the cultural component of the number of handled tasks at a time. This merger does not neglect the existence of the concept of the use of time as a component for the UDC Perception and Use of Time. In this dissertation, its subordination regarding the cultural component of number of handled tasks at a time in the UDC Perception and Use of Time was acknowledged.

Thirdly, the cultural component of perception and view of time, which was projected by Nardon and Steers (2009) and Low and Chapman (2003), was confirmed as a cultural component for the. The projected sub-component company commitment of the cultural concept of perception and view of time was not confirmed during the synthesis analysis.

Fourthly, the projected cultural component of planning ahead was confirmed as a cultural component for the UDC Perception and Use of Time in this dissertation. Fifthly, the projected cultural component of time horizon, addressing the distinction of national cultures according to their long-term or short-term orientation, was also confirmed. Conclusively, the UDC Perception and Use of Time encompasses four distinct cultural components—time horizon, perception and view of time, number of handled tasks at a time, and planning ahead.

The overall synthesized cultural dimensions are displayed in Table 6.1.

6.6.2 The Universal Dimension of Culture (UDC) Traditionalism versus Secularism

A8 assumed that the concept of traditionalism versus secularism is applicable as one main factor in classifying and distinguishing national cultures among existing cultural taxonomies. It should be noted that, in total, only three cultural dimensions were synthesized into the UDC Traditionalism versus Secularism. Also, it was projected that the majority of the cultural taxonomies which classify national cultures by the concept of traditionalism versus secularism refer to the following six cultural components: self-stability, religiosity, secular orientation, feelings of pride, flexibility, and consistency between expressed and felt emotions. A8 also projected a delimitation of the concept of traditionalism versus secularism and the concept of time regarding past-time orientation. The previous analysis revealed the following evidence, which partly rejects and partly confirms A8, displayed in Figure 6.5.

Firstly, the projected cultural components of self-stability, religiosity, secular orientation, and feelings of pride were confirmed as cultural components of the UDC Traditionalism versus Secularism. Additionally, after the analysis, the cultural component of feelings of pride is related and measured by three distinct sub-components—the sub-components of feelings of national pride, self-enhancement, and making your parents proud. Secondly, the projected cultural components of flexibility and consistency between expressed and felt emotions were not confirmed as cultural components since they were not operationalized as

Table 6.1 Synthesized Cultural Dimensions of the Universal Dimension of Culture (UDC) Perception and Use of Time

Fiske (1991, 1992)	Hall (1959, 1966, 1976, 1983; Hall & Hall, 1990)	Hofstede (2001; Hofstede et al., 2010)	House et al. (2004, 2007, 2014)	Inglehart et al. (2014)	Kluckhohn and Strodtbeck (1961)	Lewis (2018)	Minkov (2007)	Parsons and Shils (1951)	Schwartz (1992, 1994b)	Trompenaars and Hampden-Turner (2004, 2012)
~~Authority Ranking~~	~~Context~~	~~Individualism vs. Collectivism~~	~~Assertiveness~~	~~Survival Values vs. Self-Expression Values~~	~~Activity Orientation~~	Linear Active	~~Exclusionism vs. Universalism~~	~~Affectivity vs. Affective Neutrality~~	~~Autonomy vs. Embeddedness~~	~~Achievement vs. Ascription~~
~~Communal Sharing~~	~~Information Flow~~	~~Indulgence vs. Restraint~~	**Future Orientation**	~~Traditional Values vs. Secular-Rational Values~~	~~Human Nature Orientation~~	Multi-Active	~~Indulgence vs. Restraint~~	~~Ascription vs. Achievement~~	~~Hierarchy vs. Egalitarianism~~	~~Communitarianism vs. Individualism~~
~~Equality Matching~~	~~Space~~	~~Long vs. Short-Term Orientation~~	~~Gender Egalitarianism~~	–	~~Man-Nature Orientation~~	Re-Active	~~Monumentalism vs. Flexhumility~~	~~Functional Specificity vs. Functional Diffuseness~~	~~Mastery vs. Harmony~~	**Sequential vs. Synchronous Time**
~~Market Pricing~~	**Time**	~~Masculinity vs. Femininity~~	~~Humane Orientation~~	–	~~Relational Orientation~~	–	–	~~Self-Interest vs. Collectivist Interest~~	–	~~Diffuse vs. Specific~~
–	–	~~Power Distance~~	~~In-Group Collectivism~~	–	**Time Orientation**	–	–	~~Universalism vs. Particularism~~	–	~~Internal vs. Outer Direction~~

(continued)

Table 6.1 (continued)

Fiske (1991, 1992)	Hall (1959, 1966, 1976, 1983; Hall & Hall, 1990)	Hofstede (2001; Hofstede et al., 2010)	House et al. (2004, 2007, 2014)	Inglehart et al. (2014)	Kluckhohn and Strodtbeck (1961)	Lewis (2018)	Minkov (2007)	Parsons and Shils (1951)	Schwartz (1992, 1994b)	Trompenaars and Hampden-Turner (2004, 2012)
–	–	~~Uncertainty Avoidance~~	~~Institutional Collectivism~~		–		–	–	–	~~Neutral vs. Emotional~~
–	–	–	~~Performance Orientation~~	–	–	–	–	–	–	~~Universalism vs. Particularism~~
–	–	–	~~Power Distance~~	–	–	–	–	–	–	–
–	–	–	~~Uncertainty Avoidance~~	–	–	–	–	–	–	–

Note. The in bold written cultural dimensions indicated a stronger affiliation to the concept of perception and use of time; the non-bold cultural dimensions were only partially synthesized into the UDC Perception and Use of Time.

items nor conceptually considered by any of the synthesized cultural dimensions of the UDC.

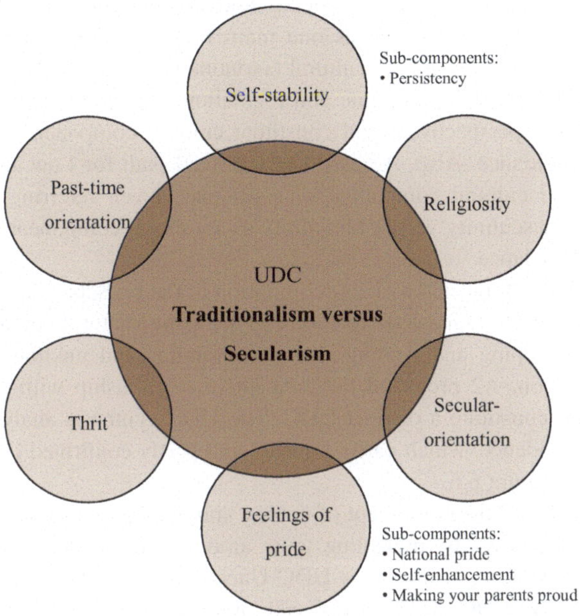

Figure 6.5 The Universal Dimension of Culture (UDC) Traditionalism versus Secularism

Finally, under the UDC Traditionalism versus Secularism assumption by A8, the UDC would have been distinct to the concept time. During the analysis, evidence was identified that substantiated that the concept of traditionalism versus secularism also conceptually includes the cultural component of past-time orientation.

The UDC Traditionalism versus Secularism synthesis analysis results are displayed in Table 6.2.

6.6.3 The Universal Dimension of Culture (UDC) Uncertainty Avoidance and Coping Mechanisms

A5 projected that the concept of coping and dealing with uncertainties and unknown situations is applicable as one main factor in classifying and distinguishing national cultures among cultural taxonomies. Additionally, A5 projected that the cultural components of rule and regulation obedience, innovation orientation, and future perspective could constitute cultural components of the UDC Uncertainty Avoidance. Also, A5 assumed a critical path for Low and Chapman (2003) projected cultural component of confidence level, referring to the sub-component of masculinity versus femininity as a cultural component of the UDC Uncertainty Avoidance.

Finally, H5 also projected a clear delimitation to the by Schneider et al. (2014) proposed cultural component of relationship with the (natural)environment and the concept of coping and dealing with uncertainties and unknown situations. In this dissertation, A2 projected the concept of relationship with the (natural) environment to constitute a distinct UDC. The UDC synthesis analysis revealed the following evidence, which partly rejected and partly confirmed H5, displayed in summary in Figure 6.6.

As projected by A5, the concept of coping and dealing with uncertainties and unknown situations is one prevailing topic among cultural taxonomies, and as such, it was possible to synthesize a UDC Uncertainty Avoidance. It was further confirmed that the UDC classifies national cultures by their way of coping and dealing with uncertainties and unknown situations as well as their coping and prevention mechanisms in case of uncertainty and ambiguity, which is reflected in the cultural component of rule and regulation obedience and the cultural component of future perspective. As Nardon and Steers (2009) proposed, the confidence level of culture was not confirmed in the synthesis analysis. Likewise, the concept of embeddedness of individuals and power distribution as a prevention mechanism for uncertainty was not confirmed. The delimitation of the concept of coping and dealing with uncertainties and unknown situations to the concept of relationship with the (natural) environment was confirmed in the analysis.

Title Revision of the UDC Uncertainty Avoidance

The term *uncertainty avoidance* seemed not to display the range of synthesized cultural components. Six synthesized cultural dimensions—Uncertainty Avoidance by Hofstede (2001; Hofstede et al., 2010), Uncertainty Avoidance by House et al. (2004, 2007, 2014), Universalism versus Particularism by Trompenaars and Hampden-Turner (2004, 2012), Universalism versus Particularism by Parsons and Shils (1951),

Table 6.2 Synthesized Cultural Dimensions of the Universal Dimension of Culture (UDC) Traditionalism versus Secularism

Fiske (1991, 1992)	Hall (1959, 1966, 1976, 1983; Hall & Hall, 1990)	Hofstede (2001; Hofstede et al., 2010)	House et al. (2004, 2007, 2014)	Inglehart et al. (2014)	Kluckhohn and Strodtbeck (1961)	Lewis (2018)	Minkov (2007)	Parsons and Shils (1951)	Schwartz (1992, 1994b)	Trompenaars and Hampden-Turner (2004, 2012)
~~Authority Ranking~~	~~Context~~	~~Individualism vs. Collectivism~~	~~Assertiveness~~	~~Survival Values vs. Self-Expression Values~~	~~Activity Orientation~~	~~Linear Active~~	~~Exclusionism vs. Universalism~~	~~Affectivity vs. Affective Neutrality~~	~~Autonomy vs. Embeddedness~~	~~Achievement vs. Ascription~~
~~Communal Sharing~~	~~Information Flow~~	~~Indulgence vs. Restraint~~	~~Future Orientation~~	**Traditional Values vs. Secular-Rational Values**	~~Human Nature Orientation~~	~~Multi-Active~~	~~Indulgence vs. Restraint~~	~~Ascription vs. Achievement~~	~~Hierarchy vs. Egalitarianism~~	~~Communitarianism vs. Individualism~~
~~Equality Matching~~	~~Space~~	**Long vs. Short-Term Orientation**	~~Gender Egalitarianism~~	–	~~Man-Nature Orientation~~	~~Re-Active~~	**Monumentalism vs. Flexhumility**	~~Functional Specificity vs. Functional Diffuseness~~	~~Mastery vs. Harmony~~	~~Sequential vs. Synchronous Time~~
~~Market Pricing~~	~~Time~~	~~Masculinity vs. Femininity~~	~~Humane Orientation~~	–	~~Relational Orientation~~	–	–	~~Self-Interest vs. Collectivist Interest~~	–	~~Diffuse vs. Specific~~
–	–	~~Power Distance~~	~~In-Group Collectivism~~	–	Time Orientation	–	–	~~Universalism vs. Particularism~~	–	~~Internal vs. Outer Direction~~

(continued)

Table 6.2 (continued)

Fiske (1991, 1992)	Hall (1959, 1966, 1976, 1983; Hall & Hall, 1990)	Hofstede (2001; Hofstede et al., 2010)	House et al. (2004, 2007, 2014)	Inglehart et al. (2014)	Kluckhohn and Strodtbeck (1961)	Lewis (2018)	Minkov (2007)	Parsons and Shils (1951)	Schwartz (1992, 1994b)	Trompenaars and Hampden-Turner (2004, 2012)
–	–	~~Uncertainty Avoidance~~	~~Institutional Collectivism~~		–		–	–	–	~~Neutral vs. Emotional~~
–	–	–	~~Performance Orientation~~	–	–	–	–	–	–	~~Universalism vs. Particularism~~
–	–	–	~~Power Distance~~	–	–	–	–	–	–	–
–	–	–	~~Uncertainty Avoidance~~	–	–	–	–	–	–	–

Note. The in bold written cultural dimensions indicated a stronger affiliation to the concept of traditionalism versus secularism; the non-bold cultural dimensions were only partially synthesized into the UDC Traditionalism versus Secularism.

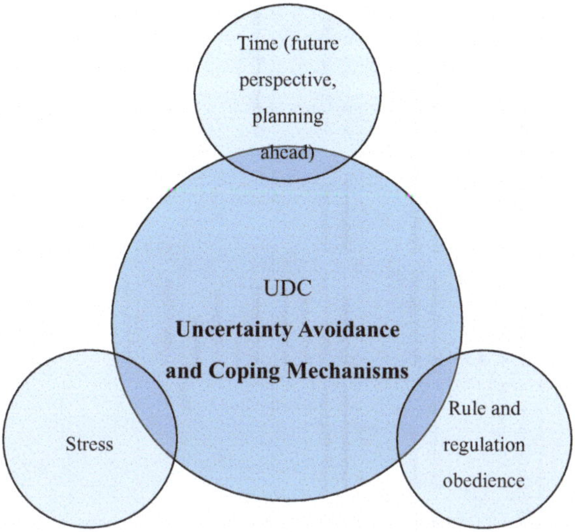

Figure 6.6 The Universal Dimension of Culture (UDC) Uncertainty Avoidance and Coping Mechanisms

Universalism versus Exclusionism by Minkov (2007), and Linear-Active by Lewis (2018)—used the cultural component of rule and regulation obedience.

This indicated a heavy weighting of the cultural component of rules and regulations obedience in the finalized UDC with the original title of *Uncertainty Avoidance.* The extent of the other synthesized cultural component of future perspective (including the sub-component of planning ahead) was not as substantial in the UDC after the synthesis. Therefore, the original title was changed to the heading of *Uncertainty Avoidance and Coping Mechanisms.*

The overall result of the previous synthesis and the synthesized cultural dimensions for the UDC Uncertainty Avoidance and Coping Mechanisms is demonstrated in Table 6.3.

Table 6.3 Synthesized Cultural Dimensions of the Universal Dimension of Culture (UDC) Uncertainty Avoidance and Coping Mechanisms

Fiske (1991, 1992)	Hall (1959, 1966, 1976, 1983; Hall & Hall, 1990)	Hofstede (2001; Hofstede et al., 2010)	House et al. (2004, 2007, 2014)	Inglehart et al. (2014)	Kluckhohn and Strodtbeck (1961)	Lewis (2018)	Minkov (2007)	Parsons and Shils (1951)	Schwartz (1992, 1994b)	Trompenaars and Hampden-Turner (2004, 2012)
~~Authority Ranking~~	~~Context~~	~~Individualism vs. Collectivism~~	~~Assertiveness~~	~~Survival Values vs. Self-Expression Values~~	~~Activity Orientation~~	~~Linear-Active~~	Exclusionism vs. Universalism	~~Affectivity vs. Affective Neutrality~~	~~Autonomy vs. Embeddedness~~	~~Achievement vs. Ascription~~
~~Communal Sharing~~	~~Information Flow~~	~~Indulgence vs. Restraint~~	Future Orientation	~~Traditional Values vs. Secular-Rational Values~~	~~Human Nature Orientation~~	~~Multi-Active~~	~~Indulgence vs. Restraint~~	~~Ascription vs. Achievement~~	~~Hierarchy vs. Egalitarianism~~	~~Communitarianism vs. Individualism~~
~~Equality Matching~~	~~Space~~	~~Long vs. Short-Term Orientation~~	~~Gender Egalitarianism~~	–	~~Man-Nature Orientation~~	~~Re-Active~~	~~Monumentalism vs. Flexhumility~~	~~Functional Specificity vs. Functional Diffuseness~~	~~Mastery vs. Harmony~~	Sequential vs. Synchronous Time
~~Market Pricing~~	~~Time~~	~~Masculinity vs. Femininity~~	~~Humane Orientation~~	–	~~Relational Orientation~~	–	–	~~Self-Interest vs. Collectivist Interest~~	–	~~Diffuse vs. Specific~~
–	–	~~Power Distance~~	~~In-Group Collectivism~~	–	Time Orientation	–	–	Universalism vs. Particularism	–	~~Internal vs. Outer Direction~~

(continued)

Table 6.3 (continued)

Fiske (1991, 1992)	Hall (1959, 1966, 1976, 1983; Hall & Hall, 1990)	Hofstede (2001; Hofstede et al., 2010)	House et al. (2004, 2007, 2014)	Inglehart et al. (2014)	Kluckhohn and Strodtbeck (1961)	Lewis (2018)	Minkov (2007)	Parsons and Shils (1951)	Schwartz (1992, 1994b)	Trompenaars and Hampden-Turner (2004, 2012)
–	–	**Uncertainty Avoidance**	~~Institutional Collectivism~~		–	–	–	–	–	~~Neutral vs. Emotional~~
–	–	–	~~Performance Orientation~~	–	–	–	–	–	–	Universalism vs. Particularism
–	–	–	~~Power Distance~~	–	–	–	–	–	–	–
–	–	–	**Uncertainty Avoidance**	–	–	–	–	–	–	–

Note. The in bold written cultural dimensions indicated a stronger affiliation to the concept of uncertainty avoidance and coping mechanisms; the non-bold cultural dimensions were only partially synthesized into the UDC Uncertainty Avoidance and Coping Mechanism.

Human Behavior—One Connecting Concept?

7

Besides the two themes of environment and time, a third common theme was identified among the eight UDCs, the theme of human behavior. Three of the identified synthesis methodologies—Low and Chapman (2003), Maleki and de Jong (2014), and Nardon and Steers (2009)—proposed several synthesis dimensions commonly addressing the theme of human behavior. In this dissertation, the theme of human behavior was operationalized into the UDC Human Orientation and the UDC Indulgence versus Restraint by A6 and A7. Therefore, the synthesis of the two UDCs is demonstrated in one chapter.

7.1 Synthesis of the Universal Dimension of Culture (UDC) Human Orientation

A6 proposed the UDC Human Orientation, addressing the concept of human orientation and the concept of assertiveness versus tenderness as one concept among existing cultural taxonomies. Only two of the four identified synthesis methodologies developed synthesis dimensions for the concepts of human orientation and assertiveness versus tenderness—the synthesis methodologies by Maleki and de Jong (2014) and Schneider et al. (2014). A critical aspect in the synthesis of the UDC Human Orientation constitutes its delimitation to the concept of masculinity versus femininity. Also, the connection between the concept of human orientation and the concept of human activity was critically assessed during the synthesis of the UDC Human Orientation. Likewise, it accounted for the interference of the concept of human orientation and the concept of assertiveness versus tenderness.

Figure 7.1 displays the projected UDC Human Orientation and its embedded cultural components.

S. Kunert, *The Eight Universal Dimensions of Culture from a Synthesis of Cultural Taxonomies*, Gabler Theses, https://doi.org/10.1007/978-3-658-38765-5_7

Synthesis Analysis Step 1: Title-Related Cultural Dimensions
The following three cultural dimensions were identified to relate by their title to the underlying concept of the UDC Human Orientation: Assertiveness by House et al. (2004, 2007, 2014), Humane Orientation by House et al. (2004, 2007, 2014), and Human Nature Orientation by Kluckhohn and Strodtbeck (1961).

The first title-related analyzed cultural dimension constituted the cultural dimension of **Human Nature Orientation** by **Kluckhohn and Strodtbeck (1961)**, classifying national cultures into evil, evil and good, and good.

Figure 7.1 Assumption 6 (A6): Universal Dimension of Culture (UDC) Human Orientation

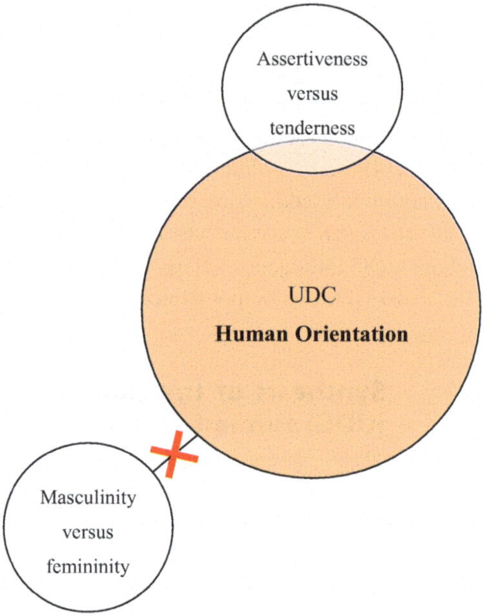

Kluckhohn and Strodtbeck (1961) developed no items to assess their cultural dimensions empirically. Instead, the item by Hills (2002) for the cultural dimension was reviewed, asking respondents as follows: "Most people when they can do something wrong and get away with it will—a) usually do it, b) sometimes do it, c) hardly ever do it" (Hills, 2002, p. 8). Overall, despite the limited information given for the cultural dimension of Human Nature Orientation by Kluckhohn and Strodtbeck (1961), the cultural dimension was considered suitable for synthesis into the UDC Human Orientation. It was concluded that the cultural dimension of Human Nature Orientation by Kluckhohn and Strodtbeck (1961) reflects the concept of human orientation by its core principles to distinct between individuals' evil and good nature. Hills (2002) proposed item was rejected as an item for the potential item set of the UDC Human Orientation in this dissertation since its affiliation to the concept of the UDC was evaluated as not substantial.

The second title-related analyzed cultural dimension constituted the cultural dimension of **Humane Orientation** by **House et al. (2004, 2007, 2014)**, addressing the way individuals treat each other based on their social programs institutionalized. As guiding motivational values for the distinction of national cultures in the cultural dimension served altruism, love, benevolence, kindness, and generosity.

From a conceptual view, the cultural dimension of Humane Orientation by House et al. (2004, 2007, 2014) was interpreted to reflect the concept of human orientation and especially the cultural component of assertiveness versus tenderness as comprehend the UDC Human Orientation. In addition, the by House et al. (n.d.), operationalized items for the cultural dimension of Humane Orientation were in-depth reviewed. In summary, the cultural dimension's four societal value items—items no. V3_9, no. V3_21, no. V3_27, and no. V3_31—assess the values of being concerned for others, sensitive, friendly, and tolerant. Conclusively, the four societal value items of the cultural dimension of Humane Orientation by House et al. (2004, 2007, 2014) were also incorporated into the potential item set of the UDC Human Orientation.

The third analyzed title-related cultural dimension of the assumed UDC Human Orientation constituted the cultural dimension of **Assertiveness** by **House et al. (2004, 2007, 2014)**, defined as "the degree to which individuals are assertive, confrontational, and aggressive in their relationships with others" (House et al., 2004, p. 30). From the description of the cultural dimension, evidence was deductible for its conceptual affiliation to the underlying concepts of the UDC Human Orientation. House et al. (n.d.) operationalized three societal value items for the empirical assessment of his cultural dimension of Assertiveness. The three societal value items no. V3_2, no. V3_10, and no. V3_14 referred to the respondent's values for aggressive, dominant, and tough behavior. These four values are also assumed to be affiliated with the concepts of the UDC Human Orientation.

House et al. (2004) themselves tested the empirical interrelationship of their nine cultural dimensions and identified a significant negative correlation between their cultural dimensions of Humane Orientation and Assertiveness, especially regarding their practices items. In contrast, a significant positive correlation was identified between the value items applied for the two cultural dimensions of Human Orientation and Assertiveness. Conclusively, the cultural dimension of

Assertiveness by House et al. (2004, 2007, 2014) was synthesized into the UDC Human Orientation.

From the analysis of the title-related cultural dimensions for the UDC Human Orientation, it was concluded that the concept of evil or good in terms of the nature of humans also constitutes the basis of the concept of human orientation. In the analysis, it became applicable that the cultural dimension of Human Nature Orientation by Kluckhohn and Strodtbeck (1961) served as the basis for the two cultural dimensions of Assertiveness and Humane Orientation by House et al. (2004, 2007, 2014). As a result, the UDC Human Orientation of this dissertation also displays the extent of the nature of individuals as a distinguishing factor for national cultures.

Synthesis Analysis Step 2: Analysis of the Remaining Cultural Dimensions
Firstly, the four cultural dimensions of Authority Ranking, Communal Sharing, Equality Matching, and Market Pricing of the cultural taxonomy by **Fiske (1991, 1992)** were reviewed. None of the four cultural dimensions pointed to evidence for affiliation to the concepts of the UDC Human Orientation. Therefore, none of the four cultural dimensions was synthesized into the UDC Human Orientation.

Next, the cultural taxonomy by **Hall (1959, 1966, 1976, 1983; Hall & Hall, 1990)** was analyzed. Three of its four cultural dimensions—the cultural dimensions of Context, Information Flow, and Time—revealed no further evidence for interrelationships with the underlying concepts of the UDC Human Orientation. These three cultural dimensions were not synthesized into the UDC Human Orientation. The cultural dimension of Space by Hall (1966) pointed to evidence since conceptually, the cultural dimension addresses the study of proxemics as individual's application of their sensory apparatus to express emotional states. The cultural dimension per se is not unambiguously distinct from the other cultural dimensions of the cultural taxonomy by Hall (1959, 1966, 1976, 1983; Hall & Hall, 1990). The UDC Human Orientation, by its already synthesized cultural dimensions from the first UDC analysis step, encompasses the concept of individuals' emotionality expressed towards each other. Conclusively, under acknowledgment of its less significant influence, the cultural dimension of Space by Hall (1966) was synthesized into the UDC.

The third analyzed cultural taxonomy constituted **Hofstede (2001; Hofstede et al., 2010)**. The five cultural dimensions of Power Distance, Individualism versus Collectivism, Indulgence versus Restraint, Long-Term versus Short-Term Orientation, and Uncertainty Avoidance of the cultural taxonomy pointed to no evidence for affiliations to the concepts of the UDC. Maleki and de Jong (2014) indicated that assertiveness and mastery constitute two different concepts, applied interchangeably, as it was done, among others, by Hofstede (2001; Hofstede et al., 2010) in his cultural dimension of Masculinity versus Femininity. The analysis of the description and definition of the cultural dimension revealed that Hofstede (2001) designed the cultural dimension regarding the dominance of gender role patterns for which he assigned males assertive and females nurturance characteristics. Overall, the cultural dimension of Masculinity versus Femininity seemed to be designed to fit into the corporate world since the masculinity dimension side was described as encompassing national cultures where individuals are assertive, tough, and focussed on material success. On the opposite side, the feminine dimension side was described to encompass national cultures where individuals are characterized by modesty, tenderness, and concerns for the quality-of-life behaviors. The corporate character of the cultural dimension was especially recognizable in the applied items for the cultural dimension, addressing respondents' importance placed on chances for promotion, living in desirable areas, and having pleasant people to work together. In conclusion, the cultural dimension of Masculinity versus Femininity by Hofstede (2001; Hofstede et al., 2010) was synthesized into the UDC Human Orientation due to the solid conceptual evidence. Although none of its items was incorporated into the potential item set of the UDC Human Orientation.

After that, the cultural taxonomy by **House et al. (2004, 2007, 2014)** was analyzed, from which the cultural dimensions of Assertiveness and Humane Orientation were already synthesized into the UDC Human Orientation during the first UDC analysis step. The remaining cultural dimensions of Performance Orientation, Future Orientation, Gender Egalitarianism, Institutional and In-Group Collectivism, Power Distance, and Uncertainty Avoidance were rejected for synthesis into the UDC Human Orientation since their in-depth analysis revealed no further evidence for affiliation to the concepts and cultural components of the UDC.

Thereafter, the two cultural dimensions of **Inglehart et al. (2014)** were reviewed. Both cultural dimensions, Survival Values versus Self- Expression Values and Traditional Values versus Secular-Rational Values, pointed to no further evidence for addressing the concepts and cultural components of the UDC Human Orientation. Thus, both cultural dimensions were not synthesized into the UDC Human Orientation.

Next, the cultural taxonomy by **Kluckhohn and Strodtbeck (1961)** was reviewed. The cultural dimension of Human Nature Orientation by Kluckhohn and Strodtbeck (1961) was already synthesized into the UDC Human Orientation during the first UDC synthesis step. The cultural dimensions of Time Orientation, Relational Orientation, and Man-Nature Orientation indicated no relationship to the concept of the UDC, and therefore, were not synthesized into the UDC Human Orientation. Schneider et al. (2014) synthesized the cultural dimension of Activity Orientation by Kluckhohn and Strodtbeck (1961) into their synthesis dimension of Human Activity. The cultural dimension of Human Activity by Kluckhohn and Strodtbeck (1961) addresses the problem of the nature of "man's mode of self-expression in activities" and divides (national) cultures into the being, being-in-becoming, and doing (national) cultures. The in-depth review of the cultural dimension revealed no substantial evidence for a potential synthesis of the cultural dimension into the UDC Human Orientation.

The seventh analyzed cultural taxonomy constituted the cultural taxonomy by **Lewis (2018)**. Only minor indications were identified in the description of the typical traits for the three cultural dimensions of Linear Active, Multi-Active, and Re-Active for a potential affiliation to the concept and underlying cultural components of the UDC Human Orientation. Each of the three cultural dimensions encompassed information regarding the distinguishing factor of individuals' emotionality extent. Linear active national cultures are considered unemotional, multi-active national cultures are considered emotional, and re-active national cultures are considered introverted. However, the evidence was evaluated as not substantial, and thus, the three cultural dimensions by Lewis (2018) were not synthesized into the UDC Human Orientation.

Likewise was subsumed for the three cultural dimensions of Exclusionism versus Universalism, Indulgence versus Restraint, and Monumentalism versus Flexhumility from the cultural taxonomy of **Minkov (2007)**. None of the three cultural dimensions pointed to evidence for affiliation to the concept of human orientation as understood in the UDC Human Orientation. Thus, none of the three cultural dimensions was synthesized into the UDC Human Orientation.

Also, the cultural dimensions of the cultural taxonomy by **Parsons and Shils (1951)** were in-depth reviewed. None of its five cultural dimensions was suitable for synthesizing the UDC Human Orientation as assumed by A6.

The tenth reviewed cultural taxonomy constituted **Schwartz (1992, 1994b)**. The two cultural dimensions of Autonomy versus Embeddedness and Egalitarianism versus Hierarchy by Schwartz (1992, 1994b) revealed no further evidence for affiliation to the concepts of the UDC Human Orientation.

The cultural dimension of Harmony versus Mastery by Schwartz (1992, 1994b) was assumed to relate to the concept of human orientation, following Maleki and de Jong (2014), which elaborated on the interchangeable application of the concepts of assertiveness and mastery. The in-depth analysis of the cultural dimension pointed to no substantial evidence for the approach. The cultural dimension seemed to relate more to the relationship of individuals with their (natural) environment. Conclusively, none of the three cultural dimensions by Schwartz (1992, 1994b) were synthesized into the UDC Human Orientation.

Last, the cultural taxonomy by **Trompenaars and Hampden-Turner (2004, 2012)** was analyzed. Schneider et al. (2014) synthesized the cultural dimension of Achievement versus Ascription by Trompenaars and Hampden-Turner (2004, 2012) into their synthesis dimension of Nature of Human Activity. Neither this approach nor the synthesis of the other six cultural dimensions of Communitarianism versus Individualism, Sequential versus Synchronous Time, Diffuse versus Specific, Internal versus Outer Direction, Neutral versus Emotional, and Universalism versus Particularism of the cultural taxonomy was substantiated during the in-depth analysis of the cultural taxonomy. As a result, none of the seven cultural dimensions of the cultural taxonomy by Trompenaars and Hampden-Turner (2004, 2012) were synthesized into the UDC Human Orientation.

7.2 Synthesis of the Universal Dimension of Culture (UDC) Gratification and Expression of Emotions, Feelings, and Desires

A7 proposed the UDC Indulgence versus Restraint, illustrating indulgence versus restraint as one concept among existing cultural taxonomies to distinguish national cultures. In this dissertation, A7 projected the UDC Indulgence versus Restraint to distinguish national cultures per the two cultural components of the extent of gratification of desires and feelings and the extent of expression of emotions. Only Maleki and de Jong (2014) synthesized a synthesis dimension for the concept of indulgence versus restraint.

Figure 7.2 displays, in summary, the projected UDC Indulgence versus Restraint (A7).

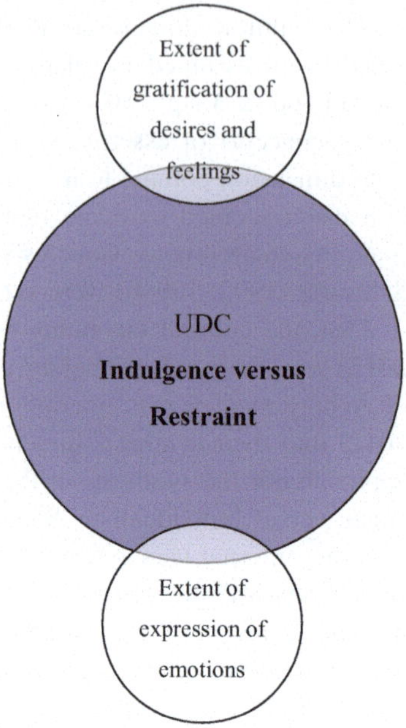

Figure 7.2 Assumption 7 (A7): Universal Dimension of Culture (UDC) Indulgence versus Restraint

Analysis Step 1: Title-Related Cultural Dimensions

For the first analysis step, five cultural dimensions were selected, displaying in their title a relationship to the concept of indulgence versus restraint: Indulgence versus Restraint by Hofstede et al. (2010), Survival Values versus Self-Expression Values by Inglehart et al. (2014), Indulgence versus Restraint by Minkov (2007), Affectivity versus Affective Neutrality by Parsons and Shils (1951), and Neutral versus Emotional by Trompenaars and Hampden-Turner (2004, 2012).

The first analyzed cultural dimension constituted the cultural dimension of **Indulgence versus Restraint** by **Hofstede et al. (2010)**, addressing the concepts of enjoying life and having fun. In summary, the cultural dimension mainly refers to the cultural component of gratification of desires and feelings, which A7 also projected to constitute a cultural component of the UDC Indulgence versus Restraint. According to the framework by Hofstede et al. (2010), the gratification of desires and feelings is either restrained or unrestrained in national cultures, thus distinguishing national cultures in their extent of free or restraint gratification of desires and feelings. Hofstede and Minkov (2013) operationalized the cultural dimension by four items. The four items (items no. 11, no. 12, no. 16, and no. 17 of the

VSM 2013) address the extent of moderation, the importance of leisure, the idea of own life control as a predictor for the level of happiness.

In this dissertation, these four societal value items were considered to be related to the underlying cultural concepts and cultural components of the UDC Indulgence versus Restraint. In summary, the cultural dimension of Indulgence versus Restraint by Hofstede et al. (2010) was synthesized into the UDC Indulgence versus Restraint, including its four items. Furthermore, the identified sub-components of happiness, perception of life control, the importance of leisure time, and moderation were also affiliated as sub-components to the cultural component of extent of gratification of desires and feelings for the UDC Indulgence versus Restraint.

The second analyzed title-related cultural dimension constituted the cultural dimension of **Survival Values versus Self-Expression Values** by **Inglehart et al. (2014)**. The review of the definition of the cultural dimension confirmed, as it was also demonstrated by Hofstede et al. (2010), Inglehart et al. (2014) by intention did not address the concept of happiness. Hofstede et al. (2010) stated further that the cultural dimension of Survival Values versus Self-Expression Values by Inglehart et al. (2014) constitutes a nation's wealth and poverty measurement. The description of the cultural dimension of Self-Expression Values versus Survival Values by Inglehart et al. (2014) revealed no evidence for an affiliation of the cultural dimension to the concept of indulgence versus restraint, nor the cultural components of extent of gratification of desires and feelings and extent of expressions of emotions. The cultural dimension is described by definition as follows:

> Survival values place emphasis on economic and physical security. It is linked with a relatively ethnocentric outlook and low levels of trust and tolerance. Self-expression values give high priority to environmental protection, growing tolerance of foreigners, gays and lesbians and gender equality, and rising demands for participation in decision-making in economic and political life. (World Value Survey Association, 2020, para. 3)

Among the items applied for the empirical measurement of the cultural dimension, only one item (item no. Q46) showed evidence to address the concept of indulgence versus restraint by asking respondents to rate their happiness level. In total, the evidence for a synthesis of the cultural dimension of Self-Expression versus Survival Value of Inglehart et al. (2014) into the UDC Indulgence versus Restraint was rated as not significant. Therefore, neither the items nor the cultural dimension itself was synthesized into the UDC Indulgence versus Restraint, also following Maleki and de Jong (2014).

Thirdly, the cultural dimension of **Indulgence versus Restraint** by **Minkov (2007)** was analyzed. From its description and definition, the cultural dimension pointed to evidence for its affiliation to the concept of indulgence versus restraint since Hofstede et al. (2010) seized explicitly on the work by Minkov (2007). Minkov (2007) retrieved his cultural dimension from the items of the WVS Wave 4 and elaborated that the three items no. A008, no. A173, and no. A003 underpin the intention of the cultural dimension to distinguish national cultures by their individuals' feelings to behave as they please, spend money, and other indulgence-related activities in their leisure time. Maleki and de Jong (2014), which also provided a synthesis dimension for the concept of Indulgence versus Restraint, synthesized the cultural dimension of Indulgence versus Restraint by Minkov (2007) into their synthesis dimension of Indulgence versus Restraint. Conclusively, the cultural dimension Indulgence versus Restraint by Minkov (2007) was synthesized into the UDC Indulgence versus Restraint, and its items no. A008, no. A173, and no. A003 were incorporated into the potential item set of the UDC.

The next analyzed cultural dimension, identified to be related by its title to the concept of indulgence versus restraint, constituted the cultural dimension of **Affectivity versus Affective Neutrality** by **Parsons and Shils (1951)**. From the conceptual evidence given in the definition and description of the cultural dimension, it was concluded that the cultural dimension is suitable to be synthesized into the UDC Indulgence versus Restraint, distinguishing national cultures by their individual's option to evaluate or not a given situation or object as well as if their individuals gratify, inhibit, or postpone impulses (Parson & Shils, 1951). A similar approach was also proposed by Maleki and de Jong (2014). Altogether, the cultural dimension was synthesized into the UDC Indulgence versus Restraint.

The last considered title-related cultural dimension constituted **Neutral versus Emotional** by **Trompenaars and Hampden-Turner (2004, 2012)**. The analysis of the description and definition of the cultural dimension revealed that it relates to the cultural component of the extent of expression of emotions by distinguishing national cultures by their amount of available and visible emotions. The cultural dimension was synthesized into the UDC Indulgence versus Restraint. Empirically, Trompenaars and Hampden-Turner (2004, 2012) pursued a workshop exercise, which was not suitable to be incorporated into the item set of the UDC Indulgence versus Restraint.

Synthesis Analysis Step 2: Analysis of the Remaining Cultural Dimensions
At first, the cultural taxonomy by **Fiske (1991, 1992)** was reviewed. Its four cultural dimensions of Authority Ranking, Communal Sharing, Equality Matching, and Market Pricing displayed no evidence for a relation to the concept of indulgence versus restraint. All four cultural dimensions were not synthesized into the UDC Indulgence versus Restraint.

Likewise, it accounted for the four cultural dimensions of the second analyzed cultural taxonomy by **Hall (1959, 1966, 1976, 1983; Hall & Hall, 1990).** No cultural dimensions were suitable for synthesizing into the UDC Indulgence versus Restraint.

Next, the cultural taxonomy by **Hofstede (2001; Hofstede et al., 2010)** was reviewed, from which the cultural dimension of Indulgence versus Restraint was already synthesized into the UDC Indulgence versus Restraint during the first UDC synthesis analysis step. The two cultural dimensions of Power Distance and Uncertainty Avoidance by Hofstede (2001; Hofstede et al., 2010) were rejected to be synthesized into the UDC Indulgence versus Restraint. Their analysis pointed to no evidence for affiliation to the concept of indulgence versus restraint.

The analysis of the cultural dimension of Individualism versus Collectivism by Hofstede (2001; Hofstede et al., 2010) revealed neither in its description nor definition, but in its items evidence for a conceptual overlap to the concept and cultural components of the UDC Indulgence versus Restraint. Especially one item (item no. 1 from the VSM 2013), addressing the importance of individuals for having sufficient time for personal or home life, was considered to symbolize the cultural component of extent of gratification of desires. Besides this, the other three items (items no. 6, no. 7, and no. 9 from the VSM 2013) did not indicate any further conceptual interferences with the concept of indulgence versus restraint. Overall, the evidence for an affiliation of the cultural dimension of Individualism versus Collectivism by Hofstede et al. (2001; Hofstede et al., 2010) was considered not substantial. As a result, the cultural dimension was not synthesized into the UDC Indulgence versus Restraint.

Regarding the cultural dimension of Long-Term versus Short-Term Orientation by Hofstede (2001; Hofstede et al., 2010), affiliation with the concept of indulgence versus restraint to a broader extent was assumed. By definition, the cultural dimension refers to the concept of preserving traditions that could be subsumed to the overall concept of restraint expression of emotions or restraint gratification of desires and feelings. No further information was identified in the description, items, or other synthesis methodologies that would have substantiated this approach. Therefore, the cultural dimension of Individualism versus Collectivism by Hofstede (2001; Hofstede et al., 2010) was not synthesized into the UDC Indulgence versus Restraint.

In its definition, the cultural dimension of Masculinity versus Femininity by Hofstede (2001; Hofstede et al., 2010) referred to the concept of modesty as a distinguishing factor for national cultures. The cultural component of modesty was also by A7 projected to constitute a sub-component of the cultural concept of the extent of gratification of desires and feelings. The conceptual evidence could not be further substantiated by reviewing the items of the cultural dimension. None of the applied items pointed to interferences with the concept of indulgence versus restraint as operationalized by A7 in this dissertation. Therefore, the cultural dimension of Masculinity versus Femininity by Hofstede (2001; Hofstede et al., 2010) was not synthesized into the UDC Indulgence versus Restraint.

The fourth analyzed cultural taxonomy constituted **House et al. (2004, 2007, 2014)**. The majority of its cultural dimensions—Gender Egalitarianism, In-Group Collectivism, Institutional Collectivism, Power Distance, Uncertainty Avoidance, and Performance Orientation—did not reveal any evidence for synthesis into the UDC Indulgence versus Restraint. The cultural dimension of Assertiveness by House et al. (2004, 2007, 2014), defined as "the degree to which individuals are assertiveness, confrontational, and aggressive in the relationship with others" (House et al., 2004, p. 30), addressed to a certain extent the concept of expression of emotions. To substantiate the synthesis of the cultural dimension of Assertiveness into the UDC Indulgence versus Restraint, the items of the cultural dimension were reviewed. The in-depth analysis of the items did not substantiate the conceptual interference of the cultural dimension with the concept of indulgence versus restraint in terms of a free or restraint expression of emotions, feelings, or desires. Conclusively, the cultural dimension was not synthesized into the UDC Indulgence versus Restraint.

For the cultural dimension of Future Orientation by House et al. (2004, 2007, 2014), also evidence was identified that related the cultural dimension to the concept of indulgence versus restraint. House et al. (2004) elaborated that national cultures with a low extent of future orientation or a high present orientation live for the moment and tend to be spontaneous. Low future-oriented national cultures are free of past worries and future anxiety, seeking hedonistic pleasure. Contrasting cultural traits account for high future-orientated national cultures (House et al., 2004). The in-depth analysis of the cultural dimension of Future Orientation by House et al. (2004, 2007, 2014), including a review of its items, led to no evidence that substantiated the conceptual elaborations by House et al. (2004).

As a result, the cultural dimension was not synthesized into the UDC Indulgence versus Restraint.

Regarding the cultural dimension of Humane Orientation by House et al. (2004, 2007, 2014), evidence was found that the cultural dimension addresses the extent of expression of emotions, since it describes by definition the encouragement and reward of individuals for being fair, altruistic, caring, and generous. To detect further substantial evidence, the items of the cultural dimensions were also reviewed. The review of the items of the cultural dimension of Humane Orientation did not substantiate the projected approach for an affiliation of the cultural dimension to the concept of indulgence versus restraint. Thus, the cultural dimension was not synthesized into the UDC Indulgence versus Restraint. Conclusively, no cultural dimension from the cultural taxonomy by House et al. (2004, 2007, 2014) was synthesized into the UDC Indulgence versus Restraint.

Next, the cultural dimensions of the cultural taxonomy by **Inglehart et al. (2014)** were reviewed. The cultural dimension of Survival Values versus Self-Expression Values was already rejected for synthesis into the UDC Indulgence versus Restraint during the first UDC analysis step. There was also no evidence for an affiliation of the cultural dimension of Traditional Values versus Secular-Rational Values to the concept of indulgence versus restraint detectable. Conclusively, the cultural dimension was not synthesized into the UDC Indulgence versus Restraint.

Afterward, the cultural dimensions of the cultural taxonomy by **Kluckhohn and Strodtbeck (1961)** were reviewed. The four cultural dimensions of Time Orientation, Relational Orientation, Man-Nature Orientation, and Human-Nature Orientation revealed no evidence for a relation to the concept of indulgence versus restraint. Only, for the cultural dimension of Activity Orientation, minimal evidence for affiliation to the concept of indulgence versus restraint was applicable. Kluckhohn and Strodtbeck (1961) indicated that individuals prefer the spontaneous expression of human characteristics for the dimension side of being. Even though the evidence was only conceptually, the cultural dimension was synthesized into the UDC Indulgence versus Restraint, acknowledging its less significant influence in the UDC.

Also, the cultural taxonomy by **Lewis (2018)** and its three cultural dimensions were analyzed. Each of the three cultural dimensions pointed to little conceptual evidence related to the concept of indulgence versus restraint. The evidence was identified in the description of the common traits of national cultures for each cultural dimension. Common traits of linear-active national cultures constitute unemotionality, common traits of multi-active national cultures are extroversion and emotionality, and common traits of re-active national cultures are introversion, demonstrating the extent of expressions of emotions as a distinguishing factor for national cultures. In summary, the three cultural dimensions of Linear-Active, Multi-Active, and Re-Active by Lewis (2018) were synthesized into the UDC Indulgence versus Restraint. Although, the influence of the three cultural dimensions in the UDC Indulgence versus Restraint was considered relatively low.

Next, the cultural taxonomy by **Minkov (2007)** was reviewed, from which the cultural dimension of Indulgence versus Restraint was synthesized into the UDC Indulgence versus Restraint during the first UDC synthesis analysis step. Neither the description nor items of the other cultural dimensions by Minkov (2007) indicated any evidence for affiliation to the concept of indulgence versus restraint. Therefore, the cultural dimensions of Exclusionism versus Universalism and Monumentalism versus Flexhumility were not synthesized into the UDC.

Next, the cultural taxonomy by **Parsons and Shils (1951)** was reviewed. The cultural dimension of Affectivity versus Affective Neutrality by Parsons and Shils (1951) was already synthesized into the UDC Indulgence versus Restraint during the first UDC synthesis analysis step. No further evidence for affiliation to the concept of indulgence versus restraint was identified in the cultural dimensions of Ascription versus Achievement, Self-Interest versus Collectivist Interest, and Universalism versus Particularism. Thus, none of these cultural dimensions was synthesized into the UDC Indulgence versus Restraint.

From a conceptual point of view, the analysis of the cultural dimension of Functional Specificity versus Functional Diffuseness by Parsons and Shils (1951) revealed evidence for a relation of the cultural dimension to the extent of expression of individuals' emotions encountered objects. Parson and Shils (1951) referred to the cultural dimension as the dilemma of an actor to choose from various possible ranges for responding to an object, either taking many aspects or only a limited range of aspects into account. The conceptual evidence was interpreted as substantial enough to synthesize the cultural dimension of Functional Specific versus Functional Diffuseness by Parsons and Shils (1951) into the UDC Indulgence versus Restraint. It was acknowledged that the influence of the cultural dimension of Functional Specific versus Functional Diffuseness by Parsons and Shils (1951) is not as considerable for the UDC as for the other synthesized cultural dimensions of the UDC Indulgence versus Restraint.

One of the last analyzed cultural taxonomies constituted the cultural taxonomy by **Schwartz (1992, 1994b)**. The analysis of the cultural dimensions of Hierarchy versus Egalitarianism and Mastery versus Harmony pointed to no evidence for affiliation to the concept of indulgence versus restraint. The review of the cultural dimension of Autonomy versus Embeddedness by Schwartz (1992, 1994b), addressing the nature of boundaries and relationships of individuals, indicated some evidence for affiliation of the cultural dimension to the UDC Indulgence versus Restraint. Therefore, the items of the cultural dimensions were also in-depth analyzed, substantiating the identified evidence for an affiliation of the cultural dimension to the concept of indulgence versus restraint.

In an overview, item no. 32, assessing the value of moderation, demonstrated the most substantial overlap with the concept of indulgence versus restraints. Item no. 47, assessing the value of obedience, was interpreted as relating to the extent of expression of emotions. Both items were incorporated into the potential item set of the UDC Indulgence versus Restraint. The five cultural items of the dimension side of affective autonomous (items no. 4, no. 9, no. 25, no. 50, and no. 57) were assumed to reflect the gratification of desires and feelings. These items were additionally incorporated into the potential item set of the UDC Indulgence versus Restraint. Furthermore, the dimension side of intellectual autonomy, including its items (items no. 5, no. 16, no. 35, and no. 53), were also assumed to refer to the cultural component of extent of gratification of desires and feelings, but, only on a broader extent.

The evidence of the conceptual interference was considered as not considerable enough. Therefore, the items of the dimension side of intellectual autonomy were not incorporated into the potential item set of UDC Indulgence versus Restraint. Overall, seven items (items no. 32, no. 47, no. 4, no. 9, no. 25, no. 50, and no. 57) were incorporated into the potential item set of the UDC Indulgence versus Restraint, and the cultural dimension of Autonomy versus Embeddedness by Schwartz (1992, 1994b) was synthesized into the UDC Indulgence versus Restraint.

Lastly, the cultural dimensions of the cultural taxonomy by **Trompenaars and Hampden-Turner (2004, 2012)** were reviewed, from which the cultural dimension of Neutral versus Emotional was already synthesized into the UDC Indulgence versus Restraint during the first UDC synthesis analysis step. The five cultural dimensions of Achievement versus Ascription, Communitarianism versus Individualism, Sequential versus Synchronous Time, Internal versus Outer Direction, and Universalism versus Particularism revealed in their analysis no further evidence for a potential synthesis into the UDC Indulgence versus Restraint.

Trompenaars and Hampden-Turner (2004, 2012) developed their cultural dimension of Diffuse versus Specific closely to Functional Specificity versus

Functional Diffuseness by Parsons and Shils (1951), which was already synthesized into the UDC Indulgence versus Restraint. Trompenaars and Hampden-Turner (2004, 2012) elaborated on the considerable interdependence between their cultural dimension of Diffuse versus Specific and their cultural dimension of Neutral versus Emotional. To empirically substantiate the cultural dimension of Diffuse versus Specific, Trompenaars and Hampden-Turner (2004, 2012) applied the model by Lewin (1936), measuring life spaces and personality levels. Taking the evidence in the description of the cultural dimension of Diffuse versus Specific into account, it became applicable that the cultural dimension can be narrowed down to the concept of extent of expression of emotions. In conclusion, even though the Lewin model was not operationalized into the potential UDC Indulgence versus Restraint item set, the cultural dimension of Diffuse versus Specific was evaluated as suitable to be synthesized into the UDC.

7.3 Results of the Syntheses

The previous synthesis analyses of the UDC Human Orientation and the UDC Gratification and Expression of Emotions, Feelings, and Desires demonstrated how the theme of human behavior was interpreted in terms of the underlying concepts for the two UDCs. As the analysis demonstrated, the two UDCs, by their underlying concepts and embedded cultural components, each grasp the theme from different angles, and thus, both UDCs remain distinct from each other. The UDC Human Orientation seizes on the concept in terms of the extent of assertiveness versus tenderness. The UDC Indulgence versus Restraint reached them from the extent of gratification and expression of desires, feelings, and emotions.

7.3.1 The Universal Dimension of Culture (UDC) Human Orientation

A6 assumed the concept of human orientation as one prevalent concept among cultural taxonomies for distinguishing national cultures. Therefore, the concept of human orientation was operationalized into one distinct UDC. A6 projected the UDC Human Orientation with a primary focus on the cultural component of assertiveness versus tenderness, further encompassing a distinction of the UDC to the concept of masculinity versus femininity. In an overview, the UDC

Human Orientation synthesis analysis revealed the following evidence, which partly rejected and partly confirmed A6, as displayed in Figure 7.3.

Figure 7.3 The Universal Dimension of Culture (UDC) Human Orientation

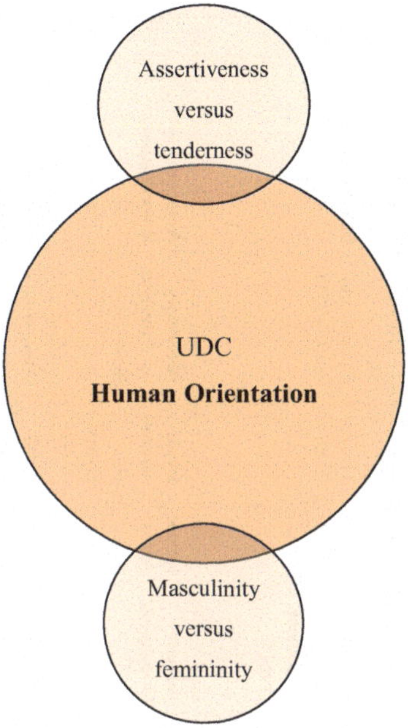

The concept of human orientation and the cultural component of assertiveness versus tenderness was identified among the range of analyzed 11 cultural taxonomies to constitute one general concept for distinguishing national cultures. Thus, the assumed UDC Human Orientation was confirmed for this dissertation. Whereas, only the items of two cultural dimensions from one cultural taxonomy demonstrated suitable items for the empirical measurement of the UDC—the cultural dimensions of Assertiveness and Humane Orientation by House et al. (2004, 2007, 2014). The initially assumed delimitation between the concept of human orientation and the concept of masculinity versus femininity was not confirmed; instead, the analysis revealed that the cultural dimension of Masculinity versus Femininity by Hofstede (2001; Hofstede et al., 2010) encompass enough evidence for an affiliation of both concepts. It should be pointed out that the evidence was only theoretical, and no item was identified that would have been suitable to be incorporated into the item set of the UDC Human Orientation. The other analyzed synthesized cultural dimensions confirmed the underlying cultural

Table 7.1 Synthesized Cultural Dimensions of the Universal Dimension of Culture (UDC) Human Orientation

Fiske (1991, 1992)	Hall (1959, 1966, 1976, 1983; Hall & Hall, 1990)	Hofstede (2001; Hofstede et al., 2010)	House et al. (2004, 2007, 2014)	Inglehart et al. (2014)	Kluckhohn and Strodtbeck (1961)	Lewis (2018)	Minkov (2007)	Parsons and Shils (1951)	Schwartz (1992, 1994b)	Trompenaars and Hampden-Turner (2004, 2012)
~~Authority Ranking~~	~~Context~~	~~Individualism vs. Collectivism~~	**Assertiveness**	~~Survival Values vs. Self Expression Values~~	~~Activity Orientation~~	~~Linear Active~~	~~Exclusionism vs. Universalism~~	~~Affectivity vs. Affective Neutrality~~	~~Autonomy vs. Embeddedness~~	~~Achievement vs. Ascription~~
~~Communal Sharing~~	~~Information Flow~~	~~Indulgence vs. Restraint~~	~~Future Orientation~~	~~Traditional Values vs. Secular-Rational Values~~	**Human Nature Orientation**	~~Multi-Active~~	~~Indulgence vs. Restraint~~	~~Ascription vs. Achievement~~	~~Hierarchy vs. Egalitarianism~~	~~Communitarianism vs. Individualism~~
~~Equality Matching~~	Space	~~Long vs. Short-Term Orientation~~	~~Gender Egalitarianism~~	–	~~Man-Nature Orientation~~	~~Re-Active~~	~~Monumentalism vs. Flex-humility~~	~~Functional Specificity vs. Functional Diffuseness~~	~~Mastery vs. Harmony~~	~~Sequential vs. Synchronous Time~~
~~Market Pricing~~	~~Time~~	**Masculinity vs. Femininity**	**Humane Orientation**	–	~~Relational Orientation~~	–	–	~~Self-Interest vs. Collectivist Interest~~	–	~~Diffuse vs. Specific~~
–	–	~~Power Distance~~	~~In-Group Collectivism~~	–	~~Time Orientation~~	–	–	~~Universalism vs. Particularism~~	–	~~Internal vs. Outer Direction~~
–	–	~~Uncertainty Avoidance~~	~~Institutional Collectivism~~		–		–	–	–	~~Neutral vs. Emotional~~

(continued)

Table 7.1 (continued)

Fiske (1991, 1992)	Hall (1959, 1966, 1976, 1983; Hall & Hall, 1990)	Hofstede (2001; Hofstede et al., 2010)	House et al. (2004, 2007, 2014)	Inglehart et al. (2014)	Kluckhohn and Strodtbeck (1961)	Lewis (2018)	Minkov (2007)	Parsons and Shils (1951)	Schwartz (1992, 1994b)	Trompenaars and Hampden-Turner (2004, 2012)
–	–	–	~~Performance Orientation~~	–	–	–	–	–	–	~~Universalism vs. Particularism~~
–	–	–	~~Power Distance~~	–	–	–	–	–	–	–
–	–	–	~~Uncertainty Avoidance~~	–	–	–	–	–	–	–

Note. The in bold written cultural dimensions indicated a stronger affiliation to the concept of human orientation; the non-bold cultural dimensions were only partially synthesized into the UDC Human Orientation.

component of assertiveness, and the UDC Human Orientation addresses at its core the distinction of (national) cultures regarding their individuals' evil or good nature.

The synthesized cultural dimensions are illustrated for the UDC Human Orientation in an overview in Table 7.1.

7.3.2 The Universal Dimension of Culture (UDC) Gratification and Expression of Emotions, Feelings, and Desires

A7 projected that the concept of indulgence versus restraint is applicable as one main factor in classifying and distinguishing national cultures among cultural taxonomies. The UDC Indulgence versus Restraint was projected to classify national cultures by the concept of indulgence versus restraint, which in more detail refers to the following two cultural components: the extent of gratification of desires and feelings and the extent of expression of emotions. The assumed UDC Indulgence versus Restraint synthesis resulted in the in Figure 7.4 displayed evidence, partially confirming and partially rejecting A7.

Figure 7.4 The Universal Dimension of Culture (UDC) Gratification and Expression of Emotions, Feelings, and Desires

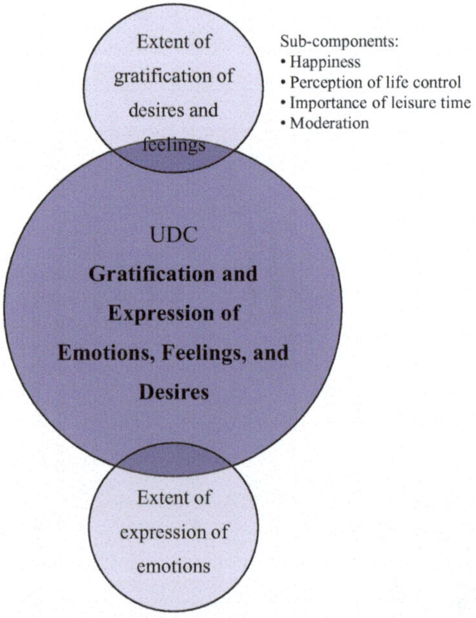

Firstly, the concept of indulgence versus restraint was identified among cultural taxonomies as one prevalent concept to distinguish national cultures. Secondly, the two projected cultural components of extent of gratification of desires and feelings and extent of expression of emotions were also confirmed as cultural components for the UDC Indulgence versus Restraint.

Title Revision of the UDC Indulgence versus Restraint

Based on the previous analysis, the initially projected heading *indulgence versus restraint* for the by A7 projected UDC was not seen as suitable enough since the synthesized cultural dimensions for the UDC mainly address the two cultural components of the extent of gratification of desires and feelings and expression of emotions directly. Therefore, the title was revised to the more specific indication of its two cultural components, and the by A7 projected title for the UDC was reconciled to *Gratification and Expression of Emotions, Feelings, and Desires.*

An overview of the synthesized cultural dimensions of the UDC Gratification and Expression of Emotions, Feelings, and Desires is displayed in Table 7.2.

Table 7.2 Synthesized Cultural Dimensions of the Universal Dimension of Culture (UDC) Gratification and Expression of Emotions, Feelings, and Desires

Fiske (1991, 1992)	Hall (1959, 1966, 1976, 1983; Hall & Hall, 1990)	Hofstede (2001; Hofstede et al., 2010)	House et al. (2004, 2007, 2014)	Inglehart et al. (2014)	Kluckhohn and Strodtbeck (1961)	Lewis (2018)	Minkov (2007)	Parsons and Shils (1951)	Schwartz (1992, 1994b)	Trompenaars and Hampden-Turner (2004, 2012)
~~Authority Ranking~~	~~Context~~	~~Individualism vs. Collectivism~~	~~Assertiveness~~	~~Survival Values vs. Self Expression Values~~	Activity Orientation	Linear Active	~~Exclusionism vs. Universalism~~	**Affectivity vs. Affective Neutrality**	**Autonomy vs. Embeddedness**	Achievement vs. Ascription
~~Communal Sharing~~	~~Information Flow~~	**Indulgence vs. Restraint**	~~Future Orientation~~	~~Traditional Values vs. Secular-Rational Values~~	~~Human Nature Orientation~~	Multi-Active	**Indulgence vs. Restraint**	~~Ascription vs. Achievement~~	~~Hierarchy vs. Egalitarianism~~	~~Communitarianism vs. Individualism~~
~~Equality Matching~~	~~Space~~	~~Long vs. Short-Term Orientation~~	~~Gender Egalitarianism~~	–	~~Man-Nature Orientation~~	Re-Active	~~Monumentalism vs. Flexhumility~~	Functional Specificity vs. Functional Diffuseness	~~Mastery vs. Harmony~~	~~Sequential vs. Synchronous Time~~
~~Market Pricing~~	~~Time~~	~~Masculinity vs. Femininity~~	~~Humane Orientation~~	–	~~Relational Orientation~~	–	–	~~Self-Interest vs. Collectivist Interest~~	–	~~Diffuse vs. Specific~~

(continued)

Table 7.2 (continued)

Fiske (1991, 1992)	Hall (1959, 1966, 1976, 1983; Hall & Hall, 1990)	Hofstede (2001; Hofstede et al., 2010)	House et al. (2004, 2007, 2014)	Inglehart et al. (2014)	Kluckhohn and Strodtbeck (1961)	Lewis (2018)	Minkov (2007)	Parsons and Shils (1951)	Schwartz (1992, 1994b)	Trompenaars and Hampden-Turner (2004, 2012)
–	–	~~Power Distance~~	~~In-Group Collectivism~~	–	~~Time Orientation~~	–	–	~~Universalism vs. Particularism~~	–	~~Internal vs. Outer Direction~~
–	–	~~Uncertainty Avoidance~~	~~Institutional Collectivism~~		–		–	–	–	**Neutral vs. Emotional**
–	–	–	~~Performance Orientation~~	–	–	–	–	–	–	~~Universalism vs. Particularism~~
–	–	–	~~Power Distance~~	–	–	–	–	–	–	–
–	–	–	~~Uncertainty Avoidance~~	–	–	–	–	–	–	–

Note. The in bold written cultural dimensions indicated a stronger affiliation to the concept of indulgence versus restraint; the non-bold cultural dimensions were only partially synthesized into the UDC Gratification and Expression of Emotions, Feelings, and Desires.

8 Questionnaire for the Eight Universal Dimensions of Culture (UDCs)

Another significant advancement of this research constitutes the operationalization of the eight synthesized UDCs into a questionnaire to empirical assess national cultures in terms of the eight UDCs. None of the identified synthesis methodologies (please refer to Chapter 2 Current State of Research) had undertaken a similar step or provided items to operationalize the identified synthesis dimensions. The operationalization of the eight UDCs into a questionnaire was conducted to answer RQ3 of this dissertation. Can the universal dimensions of culture (UDCs) be operationalized, and can a national culture be understood empirically in terms of the eight UDCs?

Figure 8.1 displays the thematical classification of the chapter in this dissertation.

In Social Sciences, exist no unified approach for the conduction of a full-standardized questionnaire yet (Bryman, 2012). In this dissertation, a structured and objective procedure was devised for and applied during the development of the UDC questionnaire, guaranteeing high validity and reliability of the UDC questionnaire.

At first, the 11 selected cultural taxonomies—Fiske (1991, 1992), Hall (1959, 1966, 1976, 1983; Hall & Hall, 1990), Hofstede (2001; Hofstede et al., 2010), House et al. (2004, 2007, 2014), Inglehart et al. (2014), Kluckhohn and Strodtbeck (1961), Lewis (2018), Minkov (2007), Parsons and Shils (1951), Schwartz (1992, 1994a), and Trompenaars and Hampden-Turner (2004, 2012)—were reviewed for information on their item development process. Only eight of the 11

Supplementary Information The online version contains supplementary material available at https://doi.org/10.1007/978-3-658-38765-5_8.

S. Kunert, *The Eight Universal Dimensions of Culture from a Synthesis of Cultural Taxonomies*, Gabler Theses, https://doi.org/10.1007/978-3-658-38765-5_8

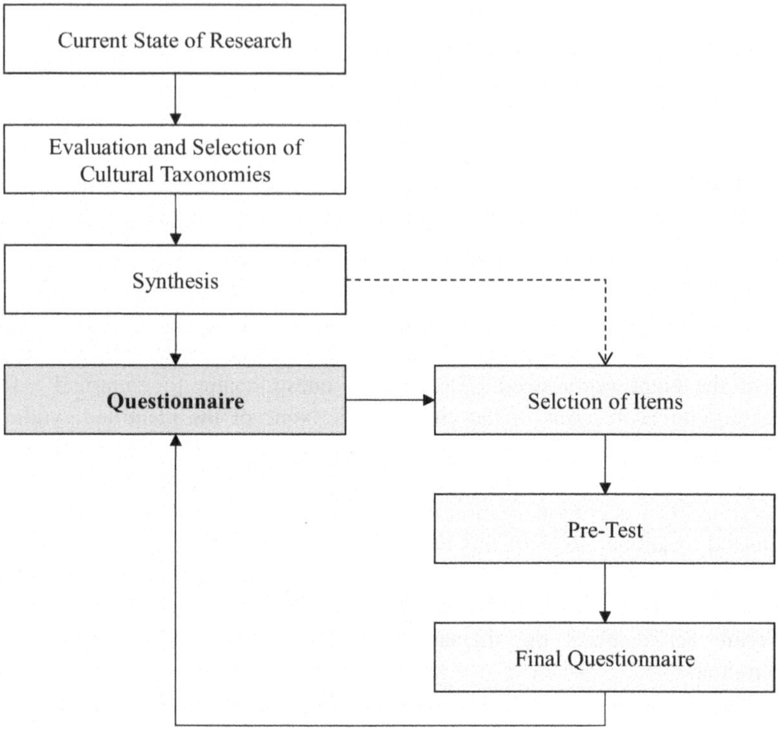

Figure 8.1 Thematic Position of Chapter 8

taxonomies operationalized their cultural dimensions with a standardized questionnaire[1]. As a result of the review of the item development process of the eight cultural taxonomies, only Schwartz (1992, 1994b) and House et al. (2004, 2007, 2014) were identified to provide sufficient and suitable information for the operationalization of items.

Consolidating the information on the item development process by Schwartz (1992, 1994b) and House et al. (2004, 2007, 2014), the following three steps became applicable. First, Schwartz (1992, 1994b) and House et al. (2004, 2007, 2014) reviewed the literature regarding the classification of (national) cultures,

[1] These are Fiske (1991, 1992), Inglehart et al. (2014), Minkov (2007), Trompenaars and Hampden-Turner (2004, 2012), Kluckhohn and Strodtbeck (1961), House et al. (2004, 2007, 2014), Schwartz (1992, 1994b), and Hofstede (2001; Hofstede et al., 2010).

serving as a basis for their hypotheses. Second, they searched for suitable items, displaying their intended cultural dimensions and respective underlying cultural components. Last, they tested their items for validity and reliability. This three-fold approach was followed for the item development for the eight UDCs in this dissertation.

The development process of the UDC questionnaire is displayed in Figure 8.2

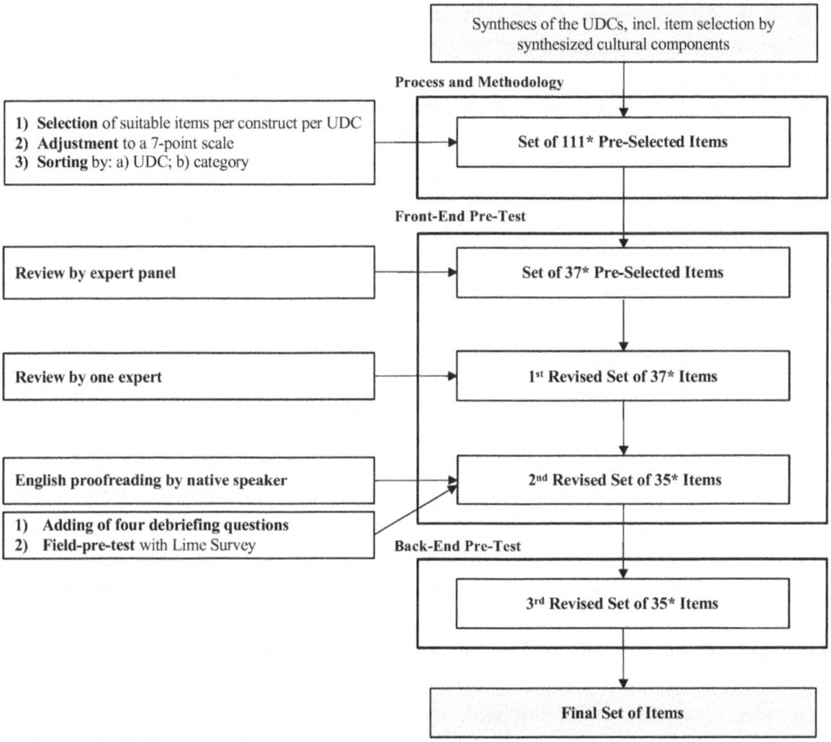

Figure 8.2 Process of Item Selection. (*Note.* *The numbers do not include the numbers of background questions)

8.1 Process and Methodology of Questionnaire Development

In this dissertation, the first step of the item development process constituted the item selection during the syntheses of the eight UDCs. Similiar to House et al. (2004, 2007, 2014) and Schwartz (1992, 1994b), well-proven items from other researchers were utilized for the empirical assessment of the eight UDCs.

During the synthesis of the eight UDCs, 111 potential suitable items were identified. An overview of the 111 items can be reviewed in Appendix B in the Electronic Supplementary Material. Each item of the 111 items mirrors an underlying concept or cultural (sub-) component of one of the eight synthesized UDCs. Likewise, to Schwartz (1992, 1994b) and House et al. (2004, 2007, 2014), the 111 identified items were then screened and evaluated.

Each of the 111 items was reviewed for its suitability to display its cultural components. Appendix B (please refer to Electronic Supplementary Material) also displays the evaluation of each item. As a result, 37 items were selected from the initial 111 items, demonstrating an initial UDC questionnaire.

Each of these 37 items was selected to mirror one underlying concept or cultural component, synthesized into the eight UDCs. Not all synthesized concepts and cultural components were also intended to be operationalized by items for the empirical measurement (please refer to the syntheses descriptions of each UDC in Chapter 5, Chapter 6, and Chapter 7).

At this point of the item development process, critical consideration of the item scales took place. Each of the 37 initially selected items demonstrated another point-scale, ranging from 2-points to 10-points. It can be stated that applying a point-scale greater than 7-points increases the reliability of a questionnaire, but the increase can hardly account for the effort it requires to analyze the resulting data (Croasmun & Ostrom, 2011). However, respondents seem to be more familiar with ratings on a 10-point scale, in comparison to ratings on a 5- or 7-point scale. A 5-point scale is considered simplistic in its application for the respondents, whereas a 7-point scale takes more effort in the respondents' comprehension. A 7-point scale has the advantage of providing more in-depth results than a 5-point scale (Dawes, 2008). In this dissertation, the 37 items were either up- or down-graded to a 7-point scale. Dawes (2008) demonstrates that a transfer of the grading systems can be done by simple re-scaling. 1 constitutes the *minimum* of the scale, and 7 constitutes the *maximum* of the scale in this dissertation. All 37 items were applied as self-reported rating scales; no ranking scales were applied.

After adjusting each scale, the items were first sorted by affiliation to their corresponding UDC—starting from the UDC Distribution of Power and Status (A1) to the UDC Traditionalism versus Secularism (A8). Then, the items were rearranged according to scale categories—general, agreement, importance, and dichotomous with a neutral mean. Finally, five questions asking for the background of the respondents were added to the questionnaire. The resulting UDC questionnaire can be reviewed in Appendix C in the Electronic Supplementary Material to this dissertation.

8.2 Pre-Test of the UDC Questionnaire

Likewise, to the lack of standardized procedures for the development of items, in Social Sciences, no standardized procedure for the conduction of a pre-test of a questionnaire exists yet (Bolton, 1993; Collins, 2003; Hughes, 2004).

In this dissertation, the pre-test of the questionnaire for the eight UDCs was divided into two parts. First, a panel of experts was involved, serving as the front-end method of the pre-test. As Hughes (2004) demonstrated, compared to other pre-test methods (e.g., debriefing questions or coding), experts are able to detect most of the problems in a questionnaire. Second, the expert "polished" version of the UDC questionnaire was tested within a group from the target population. The field pre-test was accompanied by debriefing questions, serving as the back-end method of the pre-test (Bolton, 1993; Hughes, 2004). No (subjective) coding or content analyses took place during the pre-test following other approaches (e.g., Hunt et al. (1982)) due to doubts on the objectivity and suitability of such methods' outcomes (Bolton, 1993).

In Social Sciences, the key predictors of the quality of a questionnaire are validity—e.g., face validity, concurrent validity, predictive validity, construct validity, and convergent validity—and reliability—e.g., stability, internal reliability, and inter-observer consistency (Bryman, 2012; Taherdoost, 2016). In this dissertation, for the UDC questionnaire, the face validity, ensuring that the items measure the concept of (national) cultures, was established by involving a panel of four experts. Furthermore, the involvement of the expert panel also established the content validity of the UDC questionnaire. The construct validity of the questionnaire was not intended to be established with the pre-test, requiring many participants (min. $N > 300$ in case of 35 items). The reliability of the questionnaire was established by the assessment of the pre-test output with various measurements (Bryman, 2012).

8.2.1 Pre-Test with Experts

The involvement of a panel of experts in a pre-test served as a front-end method for the pre-test and followed the Delphi method, ensuring a structured communication with the experts during their interviews (Brady, 2015; Hughes, 2004)[2]. House et al. (2004) also applied the Delphi-method for their pre-tests. Döring and Bortz (2016) suggested six steps for structured and reliable expert interviews. First, the general requirements of the experts should be defined. It was decided that a panel of three experts should be interviewed under identical conditions at first.

Consecutively, a fourth expert was interviewed regarding its evaluation of the results operationalization from the panel of experts and its general evaluation of the design of the UDC questionnaire. Experts from both areas of interest, academia and business, and with robust cross-cultural research expertise in business management or communication research were selected. Also, one expert with profound knowledge in designing and developing questionnaires was chosen.

Table 8.1 illustrates the selected panel of four experts in this dissertation.

Table 8.1 Overview of Panel of Experts

	Expert 1	Expert 2	Expert 3	Expert 4
Age, Gender, Nationality	33, Male, German	38, Female, Equatorian	38, Female, German	39, Female, German
Educational Background	Dr.rer.pol. in the area of Organizational Behavior with a focus on intercultural research	Master's degree in International Relation and Intercultural Communication, additional training in Intercultural Management	Master's degree in Sociology	Master's degree in Business Administration

(continued)

[2] For further information on the Delphi-method, please refer, for example, to Linstone and Turoff (2002) as well as Gordon (1994).

Table 8.1 (continued)

	Expert 1	Expert 2	Expert 3	Expert 4
Professional Experiences with particular regards to Cross-Cultural Research	7 years in the area of Cross-Cultural Research	7 years in the area of Cross-Cultural Management	8 years in research and education in Intercultural Communication	5 years in the area of Organizational Behavior
Current Position	Business development in the start-up sector, coach for junior researchers	Trainer for intercultural management, co-founder of a digital platform for professional personal growth	Research associate at a chair of Intercultural Communication	Research associate at a chair of Management
Other Related Information	Daily professional contacts with colleagues from South America	Studies in Scandinavia	–	–

After defining the expert panel, the availability of the experts was assessed. The interviews were conducted via the web-hosted service GoToMeeting.

Second, the conduction process of the interview was constructed. The interviews of the experts were acquired under the application of a cognitive research method, enhancing the quality of the pre-test (Bolton, 1993). Cognitive interviews allow tracing the interviewees' thoughts by advising them to directly report their internal cognitive process during the interview (Bolton, 1993; Hughes, 2004). This Think-Aloud-Method requires the experts to speak out loud their thoughts while answering the interviewer's questions and reviewing the questionnaire (Bryman, 2012).

Minutes were taken during the interviews, and retro-perspective protocols were written. All four expert interviews were conducted as cognitive interviews under the Think-Aloud-Method. The first three experts—Expert 1, Expert 2, and Expert 3—underwent the same interview procedure. The interviews were conducted partly in German and partly in English because most experts (two of three) were native German speakers, likewise, the interviewer. Bevor the interview, each of the experts was provided, with a presentation including the research questions and motivation of this research, an illustration of the eight UDCs, the process of the item selection, and the interview process. Additionally, each of the three experts was provided with two versions of the questionnaire—one without indication of the corresponding UDC for each item and one displaying the affiliation of the item to a UDC.

Third, the documentation of the interviews was ensured during the interview by the interviewer, the conductor of this dissertation.

The interviews of the first three experts were pursued identically. First, an introduction to the research questions and the eight UDCs was given, focusing on the design of each UDC. Second, the experts were asked to review the UDC questionnaire without knowing the affiliation of the items to the eight UDCs. The experts were informed that each UDC's underlying concept or cultural component was mirrored by one item in the initial UDC questionnaire. Additionally, the experts were asked to consider the following questions while reviewing the questionnaire. Do you understand the meaning of each item? Do you have any doubts about any of the items and their suitability? Do you suggest any additional items? Afterward, following House et al. (2004), the three experts were asked to pursue a Q-sorting of the items regarding their affiliation to the eight UDCs.

The interviews had a duration between 75 to 90 minutes. The interviews took place in February 2021. The information provided by the experts was consolidated (please refer to Appendix D in the Electronic Supplementary Material). After the interviews of the three experts, their recommendations were implemented into the UDC questionnaire (please see Table 8.2). After the first expert interview, some changes were already implemented into the questionnaire, including the implementation of sub-headings. for related question sections.

The same documents sent to Expert 1, Expert 2, and Expert 3 were also sent to Expert 4. Expert 4 was selected due to its strong background in the design and development of questionnaires. The procedure of the interview was adopted accordingly for Expert 4. At first, an introduction to the research questions RQ1 to RQ3 and the eight UDCs was given. Afterward, as applicable in Table 8.2, the revised item set was shown to Expert 4. The following questions were addressed to Expert 4. What is your opinion on the items' sorting/structure? What do you think of the implemented sub-headings? How do you evaluate the application of a 7-point scale instead of a 5-point scale? What do you think about the number of items per UDC?

The interview with Expert 4 had a total duration of 120 minutes. After the fourth interview, all recommendations were reviewed, and the questionnaire was adjusted accordingly. Table 8.3 displays a consolidated overview of general, not item-specific, recommendations of all four experts and the respective implementation into the UDC questionnaire.

Table 8.2 Overview of Development of First Revised Set of the 37 Items

Item No.	Set of 37 Pre-Selected Items	Expert 1–3	Item No.	1st Revised Set of 37 Items
1	Taking all things together, how happy are you? (1 = *completely unhappy* to 7 = *completely happy*)	Too general; in your private life? In your work life? Item is not suitable as the first question.	6	Taking all things together, would you say you are? (1 = *completely unhappy* to 7 = *completely happy*)
2	How often do you feel nervous or tense these days? (1 = *never* to 7 = *every time*)	"These days" seems not suitable during pandemic times.	1	In general, how often do you feel nervous or tense? (1 = *never* to 7 = *every time*)
3	How proud are you to be a citizen of your country? (1 = *not at all proud* to 7 = *extremely proud*)	Respondents could bias the interpretation of "proud".	4	How proud are you to be______________(please specify nationality? (1 = *not at all proud* to 7 = *extremely proud*)
4	Do other people or circumstances ever prevent you from doing what you really want to do? (1 = *never* to 7 = *every time*)	Q-sorting: item too blurry.	2	Do other people or circumstances ever prevent you from doing what you really want to do? (1 = *never* to 7 = *every time*)
5	Please tell me for the action of ABORTION, whether you think it is (1 = *totally unjustifiable* to 7 = *absolutely justifiable*)	Should be asked later in the questionnaire since it could lead to a dismiss of the questionnaire.	37	Please tell me for the action of an abortion, whether you think it is (1 = *totally unjustifiable* to 7 = *absolutely justifiable*)
6	Would you like to have as neighbors PEOPLE OF DIFFERENT RACE? (1 = *totally unacceptable* to 7 = *perfectly acceptable*)	"Race" is a critical term and could lead to a dismiss of the questionnaire.	7	Would you like to have as neighbors people of a different race? (1 = *totally unjustifiable* to 7 = *absolutely acceptable*)

(continued)

Table 8.2 (continued)

Item No.	Set of 37 Pre-Selected Items	Expert 1–3	Item No.	1st Revised Set of 37 Items
7	Consider the relative significance of the past, present, and future. You are asked to indicate your relative time horizons for the past, present, and future by inserting in the lines below the following numbers: 7 = *years*, 6 = *months*, 5 = *weeks*, 4 = *days*, 3 = *hours*, 2 = *minutes*, 1 = *seconds*.	Too much text, not easily understandable, the scale seems not suitable.	5	Please consider the relative significance of the past, present, and future. You are asked to indicate your relative time horizons for the past, present, and future by completing the sentences below with: YEARS, MONTH, WEEKS, DAYS, HOURS, MINUTES, and SECONDS (multiple uses of words is possible.
8	Think of the past, present, and future as being in the shape of circles. Please draw three circles on the space available below, representing past, present, and future. Arrange these circles in any way you want that best shows how you feel the relationship of the past, present, and future. You may use different-sized circles. When you have finished, label each circle to show which one is the past, which one is the present, and which one is the future.	If you ask the question, you will encounter a mix of qualitative and quantitative results, critical for your analysis.	8	Think of the past, present, and future as being in the shape of circles. Please draw three circles on the space available below, representing past, present, and future. Arrange these circles in any way you want that best shows how you feel the relationship of the past, present, and future. You may use different-sized circles. When you have finished, label each circle to show which one is the past, which one is the present, and which one is the future.

(continued)

Table 8.2 (continued)

Item No.	Set of 37 Pre-Selected Items	Expert 1–3	Item No.	1st Revised Set of 37 Items
9	How important is SERVICE TO OTHERS in your life? (1 = *not at all important* to 7 = *extremely important*)	Who is meant by “others”? To what or whom do you refer to with the item?	10	In your private, how important is doing a service to a friend to you? (1 = *not at all important* to 7 = *extremely important*)
10	How important are DETERMINATION and PERSEVERANCE to you? (1 = *not at all important* to 7 = *extremely important*)	Two terms in one question, in your private or in your working life?	15	Persistent efforts are the surest way to results. (1 = *strongly disagree* to 7 = *strongly agree*)
11	How important is RELIGIOUS FAITH to you? (1 = *not at all important* to 7 = *extremely important*)	–	9	How important is religious faith to you? (1 = *not at all important* to 7 = *extremely important*)
12	How important is the value of CHOOSING OWN GOALS (selecting own purposes) as a guiding principle in your life? (1 = *not at all important* to 7 = *extremely important*)	Why do you ask specifically for “guiding principles”?	11	How important is the value of choosing own goals (selecting own purposes) to you? (1 = *not at all important* to 7 = *extremely important*)
13	How important is the value of MODERATE (avoiding extremes of feeling and action) as a guiding principle in your life? (1 = *not at all important* to 7 = *extremely important*)	–	12	How important is the value of moderate (avoiding extremes of feeling an action) to you? (1 = *not at all important* to 7 = *extremely important*)

(continued)

Table 8.2 (continued)

Item No.	Set of 37 Pre-Selected Items	Expert 1–3	Item No.	1st Revised Set of 37 Items
14	How important is the value of PLEASE (gratification of desires) as a guiding principle in your life? (1 = *not at all important* to 7 = *extremely important*)	Why do you ask specifically for "guiding principles"?	13	How important is the value of please (gratification of desires) to you? (1 = *not at all important* to 7 = *extremely important*)
15	How important is the value of OBEDIENT (dutiful, meeting obligations) as a guiding principle in your life? (1 = *not at all important* to 7 = *extremely important*)	–	14	How important is the value of obedient (dutiful, meeting obligations) to you? (1 = *not at all important* to 7 = *extremely important*)
16	I believe that societal requirements and instructions should be spelled out in detail so citizens know what they are expected to do. (1 = *strongly disagree* to 7 = *strongly agree*)	–	16	I believe that societal requirements and instructions should be spelled out in detail so citizens know what they are expected to do. (1 = *strongly disagree* to 7 = *strongly agree*)
17	I believe that, in general, leaders should encourage group loyalty even if individual goals suffer. (1 = *strongly disagree* to 7 = *strongly agree*)	It could be not well understood; too complex.	17	I believe that leaders should encourage group loyalty even if individual goals suffer (1 = *strongly disagree* to 7 = *strongly agree*)

(continued)

Table 8.2 (continued)

Item No.	Set of 37 Pre-Selected Items	Expert 1–3	Item No.	1st Revised Set of 37 Items
18	You feel that you have something unique in common that makes you and other individuals of your group essentially the same. (1 = *strongly disagree* to 7 = *strongly agree*)	Hard to understand "unique" and "same in one question.	18	In your society, people tend to develop very similar attitudes and values. (1 = *strongly disagree* to 7 = *strongly agree*)
19	In your group, in some respect, one of you is entitled to more than the other and should be treated with special respect. (1 = *strongly disagree* to 7 = *strongly agree*)	What is meant by "in your group"? What do you understand by entitled?	19	In your society, in some respect, some individuals are entitled to more than others and should be treated with special respect. (1 = *strongly disagree* to 7 = *strongly agree*)
20	In your group, you make decisions together by consensus. (1 = *strongly disagree* to 7 = *strongly agree*)	What is meant by "in your group"?	20	In your society, people make decisions together by consensus (1 = *strongly disagree* to 7 = *strongly agree*)
21	In your group, one of you makes the decisions and the other generally goes along. (1 = *strongly disagree* to 7 = *strongly agree*)	What is meant by "in your group"?	21	In your society, one individual makes the decisions, and the others generally go along. (1 = *strongly disagree* to 7 = *strongly agree*)
22	How often in your experience are subordinates afraid to contradict their boss (or students their teachers)? (1 = *strongly disagree* to 7 = *strongly agree*)	–	3	How often in your experience are subordinates afraid to contradict their boss (or students their teachers)? (1 = *never* to 7 = *every time*)

(continued)

Table 8.2 (continued)

Item No.	Set of 37 Pre-Selected Items	Expert 1–3	Item No.	1st Revised Set of 37 Items
23	When in disagreement with adults, young people should defer to elders. (1 = *strongly disagree* to 7 = *strongly agree*)	–	22	When in disagreement with adults, young people should defer to elders. (1 = *strongly disagree* to 7 = *strongly agree*)
24	The respect a person gets is highly dependent on the person's family background. (1 = *strongly disagree* to 7 = *strongly agree*)	–	23	The respect a person gets is highly dependent on the person's family background. (1 = *strongly disagree* to 7 = *strongly agree*)
25	Is it worthwhile trying to control important natural forces, such as the weather OR nature should take its course, and we just have to accept it the way it comes and do the best we can? Please use the scale below to rate your choice. (1 = *control over important natural forces* to 7 = *nature should take its course*)	The scale indication is not clear, hard to understand, which could lead to the dismissal of the questionnaire.	24	Is it worthwhile trying to control important natural forces or nature should take its course, and we just have to accept it the way it comes and do the best we can (1 = *control over important natural forces* to 7 = *nature should take its course*)

(continued)

Table 8.2 (continued)

Item No.	Set of 37 Pre-Selected Items	Expert 1–3	Item No.	1st Revised Set of 37 Items
26	Which point on the scale below clearly describes how much weight you place on work (including housework and schoolwork), as compared with leisure or recreation? (1 = *it is leisure that makes life worth living not work* to 7 = *work is what makes life worth living, not leisure*)	–	25	Which point on the scale below clearly describe how much weight you place on work (1 = *it is leisure that makes life worth living not work* to 7 = *work is what makes life worth living, not leisure*)
27	In this society, people should be encouraged to be (1 = *non-aggressive, non-dominant, and tender* to 7 = *aggressive, dominant, and tough*)	In this society or in this group?	26	In your society, people should be encouraged to be (1 = *non-aggressive, non-dominant, and tender* to 7 = *aggressive, dominant, and tough*)
28	Members of this society should take (1 = *take a great deal of pride in being a member of the society* to 7 = *take no pride in being a member of the society*)	What is the difference between this question and the question of how proud you are to be a citizen of your nationality?	27	Members of this society should take (1 = *take a great deal of pride in being a member of the society* to 7 = *take no pride in being a member of the society*)
29	I believe that social gatherings should be (1 = *spontaneous* to 7 = *planned well in advance*)	It could be challenging to ask during pandemic times.	28	I believe that social gatherings should be (1 = *spontaneous* to 7 = *planned well in advance*)

(continued)

Table 8.2 (continued)

Item No.	Set of 37 Pre-Selected Items	Expert 1–3	Item No.	1st Revised Set of 37 Items
30	I believe that this society would be more effectively managed if there were (1 = *many less women in positions of authority than there are now* to 7 = *many more women in positions of authority than there are now*)	–	29	I believe that this society would be more effectively managed if there were (1 = *many less women in positions of authority than there are now* to 7 = *many more women in positions of authority than there are now*)
31	I believe that (1 = *individualism is better than group cohesion* to 7 = *group cohesion is better than individualism*)	Does everyone understand / can understand individualism?	30	I believe that (1 = *individualism is better than group cohesion* to 7 = *group cohesion is better than individualism*)
32	I believe that the accepted norm in this society should be to (1 = *accept the status quo* to 7 = *plan for the future*)	Do the scales contradict? The scales seem not suitable.	31	I believe that the accepted norm in this society should be to (1 = *accept the status quo* to 7 = *plan for the future*)
33	I believe that power should be (1 = *shared throughout the society* to 7 = *concentrated at the top*)	The scale anchor shared throughout society seems not suitable.	32	I believe that power should be (1 = *shared throughout the society* to 7 = *concentrated at the top*)
34	I believe that a person who leads a structured life that has few unexpected events (1 = *is missing a lot of excitement* to 7 = *has a lot to be thankful for*)	The item scale "has a lot to be thankful for" seems not to contradict the scale "is missing a lot of excitement".	33	I believe that a person who leads a structured life that has few unexpected events. (1 = *is missing a lot of excitement* to 7 = *has a lot to be thankful for*)

(continued)

Table 8.2 (continued)

Item No.	Set of 37 Pre-Selected Items	Expert 1–3	Item No.	1st Revised Set of 37 Items
35	I believe that being innovative to improve performance should be (1 = *not rewarded* to 7 = *substantially rewarded*)	–	34	I believe that being innovative to improve performance should be (1 = *not rewarded* to 7 = *substantially rewarded*)
36	I believe that a person's influence in this society should be based primarily on (1 = *one's ability and contribution to the society* to 7 = *to the authority of one's position*)	The item is hard to understand.	35	I believe that a person's influence in this society should be based primarily on (1 = *one's ability and contribution to the society* to 7 = *to the authority of one's position*)
37	In this society, people should be encouraged to be (1 = *not at all concerned about others, sensitive towards others, friendly towards others, and tolerant of mistakes* to 7 = *very concerned, sensitive, friendly towards others, and very tolerant of mistake*)	Too many terms on the scale; respondents cannot understand the scales; hard to understand.	36	In this society, people should be encouraged to be (1 = *not at all concerned about others* to 7 = *very concerned about others*)

Table 8.3 General Recommendations from Experts 1–3

Expert	Description
Expert 1	a) The description of the synthesis of A1 and A3 should elaborate on the delimitation between the UDC Distribution of Power and Status and the UDC Social Organization b) There should be between 3 to 4 items per UDC to guarantee the validity and reliability of the questionnaire. c) You should only indicate the explanation of the minimum, middle, and maximum scale points.
Implementation	a) Yes, the distinction between A1 and A3 was elaborated and demonstrated in an individual chapter. b) Yes, the questionnaire was adapted accordingly. c) Yes, only the three scale anchors are displayed in the revised questionnaire.
Expert 2	a) RQ3 is hard to understand. b) A native English speaker should review the questionnaire. c) During the respondent selection for the field pre-test should be paid attention to the ratio of international respondents in the participant group.
Implementation	a) RQ3 was revised accordingly. b) Yes, the questionnaire was reviewed by a native English speaker. c) Yes, the participant's group of the field pre-test was chosen to involve a maximum of different nationalities.
Expert 3	a) Please review the questionnaire regarding Ethnocentrism. b) A native English speaker should review the questionnaire. c) Please elaborate on the structure of the questionnaire and the application of a 7-point scale in your research.
Implementation	a) Yes, this was done in the semantic analysis of the research b) Yes, the questionnaire was reviewed by a native English speaker. c) Yes, this was done during the development of the questionnaire.
Expert 4	a) You do not need to ask for "I don't know" b) There should be between 3 – 4 items per UDC to guarantee the validity and reliability of the questionnaire. c) Do not use capitalization of single terms in the questionnaire.
Implementation	a) Yes, the scale point "I don't know" was deleted from the questionnaire. b) Yes, after the interview, this approach was operationalized. c) Yes, this was changed for the questionnaire used in the field pre-test.

Mainly, the initially intended mirroring of items with each UDC's underlying concepts and cultural components was assessed as critical in the UDC questionnaire by the experts.

After the fourth interview, the item set was reconciled under the premise to result in four to five items per UDC. The initial item set had the following distribution of items per UDC: UDC Distribution of Power and Status = nine items, UDC Relationship with the Natural Environment = one item, UDC Social Organization = six items, UDC Perception and Use of Time = three items, UDC Uncertainty Avoidance and Coping Mechanisms = four items, UDC Human Orientation = four items, UDC Gratification and Expression of Desires, Feelings, and Emotions = five items, and the UDC Traditionalism versus Secularism = five items. As a result, it was decided to level the number of items per UDC between four to five items.

The resulting expert "polished" item set was checked again by Expert 4, identifying no further need to revise the item set. The suitability of the items to display the respective UDC was ensured by the conductor of this dissertation. The resulting 35 items, constituting the second revised set, were sent for proof to a native English speaker. The resulting item set, including a juxtaposing to the items from the first revision by the expert panel, is demonstrated in Table 8.4. The items were then numbered as they became applicable in the online operationalization for the consecutive field pre-test

Before the field pre-test, the 35 items were evaluated according to the feedback of all four experts, applicable in Table 7.5. Strong indicates that all four experts agreed on the design of the item and its affiliation to the respective UDC. An evaluation with medium indicates that two of three experts from the first panel—Expert 1, 2, and 3—agreed on the item and that the item was later, after its revision, proven by Expert 4. The approval by Expert 4 was a premise that the item could be applied in the UDC questionnaire. The evaluation was conducted to identify potential flaws in the questionnaire, causing problems during the field pre-test.

Finally, questions addressing the respondents' background were added to the questionnaire, as applicable in Table 8.6.

8.2.2 Pre-Test in the Field

The second revised set of 35 items constitutes the basis for the field pre-test, conducted as an online survey via the open-source app LimeSurvey. The field pre-test of the questionnaire within a respective respondent group also encompassed several debriefing questions.

The application of debriefing questions seemed most suitable for the UDC questionnaire, compared to probing methods, since it enables researchers to identify terms, concepts, and words that could be misunderstood and not accurately answered by respondents. Additionally, debriefing questions reveal information on closed-ended response choices and suggestions for the revision of items as well as sensitive items in the questionnaire (Hughes, 2004). The debriefing questions were displayed in the questionnaire in a sixth section, after the background questions.

The following debriefing questions were implemented. Firstly, taken by Campanelli et al. (1991), the respondents of the UDC questionnaire were asked, "For any of the questions, were you unsure about the type of information I wanted you to provide?", providing evidence on potential flaws in the questionnaire. Secondly, following Martin (2006), the respondents were asked: "When I asked you at the beginning "to indicate your relative periods for the past, present, and future" by completing three sentences, did you had any troubles answering the question in the given way?", directly addressing the potential misinterpretation of the question. Also, the sensitivity of the items was assessed by asking respondents, "Were there any questions in this questionnaire that you felt uncomfortable with?" The sensitivity debriefing question was framed following Martin (2006). Likewise, finally, respondents were asked about their general experience with the questionnaire and retrospectively gave general comments on the questionnaire.

The link to the online questionnaire was sent out as personal invitations via email and professional online network platforms (e.g., LinkedIn and Xing), including the request to distribute the questionnaire to other individuals. The pre-test was conducted under the premise to gather as many respondents with a diverse international background since many involved nationalities were considered to guarantee a high validity of the UDC questionnaire, intending to measure cross-cultural differences in international values. Overall, the questionnaire was accessible in LimeSurvey for one week.

Table 8.4 Overview of Development of Second Revised Set of the 35 Items

Item No.	1st Revised Set of Items	Expert 4	Item No.	2nd Revised Set of Items
1	In general, how often do you feel nervous or tense? (1 = *never* to 7 = *every time*)	–	Q11	In general, how often do you feel nervous or tense? (1 = *never* to 7 = *every time*)
2	Do other people or circumstances ever prevent you from doing what you really want to do? (1 = *never* to 7 = *every time*)	None of the experts identified the affiliation of the item with the UDC7; the item was considered challeng-ing to under-stand.	Q12	How much freedom of choice and control do you feel you have over the way your life turns out? (1= *no choice at all* to 7 = *a great deal of choice*)
3	How often in your experience are subordinates afraid to contradict their boss (or students their teachers)? (1 = *never* to 7 = *every time*)	The term "students their teachers" is obsolete	Q13	How often do you think subordinates, in general, are afraid to contradict their boss? (1 = *never* to 7 = *every time*)
4	How proud are you to be________________(please specific nationality)? (1 = *not at all proud* to 7 = *extremely proud*)	–	Q14	How proud are you to be________________(please specific nationality)? (1 = *not at all proud* to 7 = *extremely proud*)
5	Please consider the relative significance of the past, present, and future. You will be asked to indicate your relative time horizons for the past, present, and future by completing the below sentences with the terms, YEARS, MONTH, WEEKS, DAYS, HOURS, MINUTES, and SECONDS.	The prac-ticability of the question seems not to be given.	Q15	Please consider the relative significance of the past, present, and future. You will be asked to indicate your relative time horizons for the past, present, and future by completing the below sentences with the terms, YEARS, MONTH, WEEKS, DAYS, HOURS, MINUTES, and SECONDS.

(continued)

Table 8.4 (continued)

Item No.	1st Revised Set of Items	Expert 4	Item No.	2nd Revised Set of Items
6	Taking all things together, would you say you are (1 = *completely unhappy* to 7 = *completely happy*)	The term "happy" should be applicable already in the item and not only in the scale.	Q16	Are you a happy person? (1 = *never* to 7 = *every time*)
7	Would you like to have individuals of a different race as neighbors (1 = *totally unacceptable* to 7 = *perfectly acceptable*)	The term race should not be used in the questionnaire.	Q17	Would you like to have people of a different society as neighbors? (1 = *totally unacceptable* to 7 = *perfectly acceptable*)
8	Think of the past, present, and future as being in the shape of circles. Please draw three circles on the space available below, representing past, present, and future. Arrange these circles in any way you want that best shows how you feel the relationship of the past, present, and future. You may use different-sized circles. When you have finished, label each circle to show which one is the past, which one is the present, and which one is the future.	The mix of qualitative and quantitative items could lead to a total dismiss of your questionnaire.	Q18	When I donate money to charitable organizations, I think it should be best spent to (1 = *keep the old ways and customs alive* to 4 = *make a better life now* to 7 = *make a better life for the future*)
9	How important is religious faith to you? (1 = *not at all important* to 7 = *extremely important*)	–	Q19	How important is religious faith to you? (1 = *not at all important* to 7 = *extremely important*)

(continued)

Table 8.4 (continued)

Item No.	1st Revised Set of Items	Expert 4	Item No.	2nd Revised Set of Items
10	In your private life, how important is doing a service to a friend to you? (1 = *not at all important* to 7 = *extremely important*)	–	Q111	In your private life, how important is doing a service to a friend to you? (1 = *not at all important* to 7 = *extremely important*)
11	How important is the value of choosing own goals (selecting own purposes) to you? (1 = *not at all important* to 7 = *extremely important*)	Item not suitable.	–	–
12	How important is the value of moderate (avoiding extremes of feeling and action) to you? (1 = *not at all important* to 7 = *extremely important*)	Do not use two terms at once in an item.	Q112	How important is the value of avoiding extreme feelings and actions to you? (1 = *not at all important* to 7 = *extremely important*)
13	How important is the value of please (gratification of desires) to you? (1 = *not at all important* to 7 = *extremely important*)	Not suitable to address UDC 7.	–	–
14	How important is the value of obedient (dutiful, meeting obligations) to you? (1 = *not at all important* to 7 = *extremely important*)	Item not suitable.	–	–
15	Persistent efforts are the surest way to results. (1 = *strongly disagree* to 7 = *strongly agree*)	–	Q115	Persistent efforts are the surest way to successful results. (1 = *strongly disagree* to 7 = *strongly agree*)

(continued)

Table 8.4 (continued)

Item No.	1st Revised Set of Items	Expert 4	Item No.	2nd Revised Set of Items
16	I believe that societal requirements and instructions should be spelled out in detail so citizens know what they are expected to do. (1 = *strongly disagree* to 7 = *strongly agree*)	–	Q118	I believe that societal requirements and instructions should be spelled out in detail so citizens know what they are expected to do. (1 = *strongly disagree* to 7 = *strongly agree*)
17	I believe that leaders should encourage group loyalty even if individual goals suffer. (1 = *strongly disagree* to 7 = *strongly agree*))	–	Q119	I believe that leaders should encourage group loyalty even if individual goals suffer. (1 = *strongly disagree* to 7 = *strongly agree*)
18	In your society, individuals tend to develop very similar attitudes and values. (1 = *strongly disagree* to 7 = *strongly agree*)	–	Q120	In my society, people tend to develop very similar attitudes and values. (1 = *strongly disagree* to 7 = *strongly agree*)
19	In your society, in some respect, some individuals are entitled to more than others and should be treated with special respect. (1 = *strongly disagree* to 7 = *strongly agree*)			
20	In your society, individuals make decisions together by consensus. (1 = *strongly disagree* to 7 = *strongly agree*)	–	Q17	In my society, people make decisions together by consensus. (1 = *strongly disagree* to 7 = *strongly agree*)
21	In your society, one individual makes decisions, and the others generally go along. (1 = *strongly disagree* to 7 = *strongly agree*)	–	–	–

(continued)

Table 8.4 (continued)

Item No.	1st Revised Set of Items	Expert 4	Item No.	2nd Revised Set of Items
22	When in disagreement with adults, young people should defer to elders. (1 = *strongly disagree* to 7 = *strongly agree*)	Not suitable since parent-child ties were not considered in this research.	–	–
23	The respect a person gets is highly dependent on the person's family background. (1 = *strongly disagree* to 7 = *strongly agree*)	–	Q123	The respect a person receives is highly dependent on the person's family background. (1 = *strongly disagree* to 7 = *strongly agree*)
24	Is it worthwhile trying to control important natural forces or nature should take its course, and we just have to accept it the way it comes and do the best we can. (1 = *control over important natural forces* to 7 = *nature should take its course*)	The item seems not suitable, and the content of the item is too widely framed	Q10 Q116 Q121 Q113	How important is preserving nature to you? (1 = *not at all important* to 7 = *extremely important*) It is worthwhile trying to control important natural forces. (1 = *strongly disagree* to 7 = *strongly agree*) Nature should take its course, and we just have to accept it the way it comes and do the best we can. (1 = *strongly disagree* to 7 = *strongly agree*) How important is the value of unity with nature to you? (1 = *not at all important* to 7 = *extremely important*)

(continued)

Table 8.4 (continued)

Item No.	1st Revised Set of Items	Expert 4	Item No.	2nd Revised Set of Items
25	Which point on the scale below clearly describes how much weight you place on work (including housework and schoolwork), as compared with leisure? (1 = *it is leisure that makes life worth living, not work* to 7 = *work is what makes life worth living, not leisure*)	The question should be delaminated for the sake of clear understanding.	Q124	How much significance do you place on work (including housework and schoolwork) as compared to leisure? (1 = *it is leisure that makes life worth living, not work* to 7 = *work is what makes life worth living, not leisure*)
26	In your society, people should be encouraged to be (1 = *non-aggressive, non-dominant, and tender* to 7 = *aggressive, dominant, and tough*)	–	Q125	In a society, people should be encouraged to be (1 = *non-aggressive, non-dominant, and tender* to 7 = *aggressive, dominant, and tough*)
27	Members of society should take (1 = *take a great deal of pride in being a member of the society* to 7 = *take no pride in being a member of the society*)	"takes" needs to be deleted.	Q126	Members of society should take (1 = *a great deal of pride in being a member of the society* to 7 = *no pride in being a member of the society*)
28	In general, I believe that social gatherings should be (1 = *spontaneous* to 7 = *planned well in advance*)	–	Q127	In general, I believe that social gatherings should be (1 = *spontaneous*: to 7 = *planned well in advance*)
29	I believe that society would be more effective management if there were (1 = *many less women in positions of authority than there are now* to 7 = *many more women in position of authority than there are now*)	The connection between management and gender could cause a dismiss of your survey.	Q129	I believe that opportunities for leadership positions should be (1 = *more available for women than for men* to 7 = *more available for men than for women*)

(continued)

Table 8.4 (continued)

Item No.	1st Revised Set of Items	Expert 4	Item No.	2nd Revised Set of Items
30	I believe that (1 = *individualism is better than group cohesion* to 7 = *group cohesion is better than individualism*)	The item seems not suitable.	–	–
31	I believe that the accepted norm in this society should be to (1 = *accept the status quo* to 7 *plan for the future*)	The item is not suitable.	Q130	I believe that people should (1 = *live for the present* to 7 = *live for the future*)
32	I believe that power should be (1 = *shared throughout the society* to 7 = *concentrated at the top*)	–	Q131	I believe that power should be (1 = *shared equally throughout the society* to 7 = *concentrated at the top*)
33	I believe that a person who leads a structured life that has few unexpected events (1 = *is missing a lot of excitement* to 7 = *has as a lot to be thankful for*)	Scale seems not appropri-ate.	Q132	I believe that a person who lives a structured life that has few unexpected events (1 = *is missing a lot of excitement* to 7 = *is living an exciting life*)
34	I believe that being innovative to improve performance should be (1 = *not rewarded* to 7 = *substantially rewarded*)	The item seems not suitable.	Q134	I believe that major rewards should be based on (1= *only factors other than performance effectiveness* to 7 = *only performance effectiveness*)
35	I believe that a person's influence in this society should be based primarily on (1 = *one's ability and contribution to the society* to 7 = *to the authority of one's position*)	Less suitable to address UDC1.	–	–

(continued)

Table 8.4 (continued)

Item No.	1st Revised Set of Items	Expert 4	Item No.	2nd Revised Set of Items
36	In this society, people should be encouraged to be (1 = *not at all concerned about others, sensitive towards others, friendly towards others, and tolerant of mistakes* to 7 = *very concerned, sensitive, friendly towards others, and very tolerant of mistakes*)	The scale points should be clearly defined. It should be opera-tionalized into single items.	Q128 Q 135 Q133	In a society, people should be encouraged to be (1 = *not at all concerned about others* to 7 = *very concerned about others*) In a society, people should be encouraged to be (1 = *very unfriendly* to 7 = *very friendly*) In a society, people should be encouraged to be (1 = *not all sensitive towards others* to 7 = *very sensitive towards others*)
37	Please tell me for the action of abortion whether you think it can (1 = *never be justified* to 7 = *always be justified*)	The item could lead to a complete dismissal of your survey.	Q114	How important is independence to you? (1 = *not at all important* to 7 = *extremely important*)
–	–	–	Q122	I prefer to do two or more activities at the same time. (1 = *strongly disagree* to 7 = *strongly agree*)

Note. The indicated Item No for the 2nd Revised Set of 35 Items is stated as it is indicated in the digitalization of the items for the application in LimeSurvey.

Table 8.5 Expert Evaluation of the Second Revised Set of the 35 Items

Item No.	Item	UDC Affiliation	Origin	Evaluation by Experts
Q11	**In general, how often do you feel nervous or tense?** (1 = *never* to 7 = *every time*)	UDC 5	Hofstede	**Strong**

(continued)

Table 8.5 (continued)

Item No.	Item	UDC Affiliation	Origin	Evaluation by Experts
Q12	**How much freedom of choice and control do you feel you have over the way your life turns out**? (1 = *no choice at all* to 7 = *a great deal of choice*)	UDC 7	Minkov	**Medium** (Expert 4)
Q13	**How often do you think subordinates, in general, are afraid to contradict their boss?** (1 = *never* to 7 = *every time*)	UDC 1	Hofstede	**Strong**
Q14	**How proud are you to be___?** (1 = *not at all proud* to 7 = *extremely proud*)	UDC 8	Minkov	**Strong**
Q15	**Please consider the relative significance of the past, present, and future. You will be asked to indicate your relative time horizons for the past, present, and future by completing the below sentences with the terms, YEARS, MONTH, WEEKS, DAYS, HOURS, MINUTES, and SECONDS.**	UDC 4	Trompenaars	**Medium** (2/3 Experts)

(continued)

Table 8.5 (continued)

Item No.	Item	UDC Affiliation	Origin	Evaluation by Experts
Q16	**Are you a happy person?** (1 = *never* to 7 = *every time*)	UDC 7	Hofstede	**Strong**
Q17	**Would you like to have people of a different society as neighbors?** (1 = *totally unacceptable* to 7 = *perfectly acceptable*)	UDC 3	Minkov	**Medium** (2/3 Experts)
Q18	**When I donate money to charitable organizations, I think it should be best spent to** (1 = *keep the old ways and customs alive* to 4 = *make a better life now* to 7 = *make a better life for the future*)	UDC 4	Kluckhohn and Strodtbeck	**Medium** (Expert 4)
Q19	**How important is religious faith to you?** *(1 = not at all important to 7 = extremely important)*	UDC 8	Inglehart	**Strong**
Q110	**How important is preserving nature to you?** *(1 = not at all important to 7 = extremely important)*	UDC 2	Schwartz	**Medium** (Expert 4)
Q111	**In your private life, how important is doing a service for a friend to you?** *(1 = not at all important to 7 = extremely important 7)*	UDC 8	Hofstede	**Medium** (2/3 Experts)

(continued)

Table 8.5 (continued)

Item No.	Item	UDC Affiliation	Origin	Evaluation by Experts
Q112	**How important is the value of avoiding extreme feelings and actions to you?** (1 = *not at all important* to 7 = *extremely important*)	UDC 7	Schwartz	**Strong**
Q113	**How important is the value of unity with nature to you?** (1 = *not at all important* to 7 = *extremely important*)	UDC 2	Schwartz	**Medium** (Expert 4)
Q114	**How important is independence to you?** (1 = *not at all important* to 7 = *extremely important*)	UDC 8	Inglehart	**Medium** (Expert 4)
Q115	**Persistent efforts are the surest way to successful results.** (1 = *strongly disagree* to 7 = *strongly agree*)	UDC 8	Hofstede	**Medium** (Expert 4)
Q116	**It is worthwhile trying to control important natural forces.** (1 = *strongly disagree* to 7 = *strongly agree*)	UDC 2	Trompenaars	**Medium** (Expert 4)
Q117	**In my society, people make decisions together by consensus.** (1 = *strongly disagree* to 7 = *strongly agree*)	UDC 3	Fiske	**Medium** (2/3 Experts)

(continued)

Table 8.5 (continued)

Item No.	Item	UDC Affiliation	Origin	Evaluation by Experts
Q118	**I believe that societal requirements and instructions should be spelled out in detail so citizens know what they are expected to do.** (1 = *strongly disagree* to 7 = *strongly agree*)	UDC 5	House	**Strong**
Q119	**I believe that leaders should encourage group loyalty even if individual goals suffer.** (1 = *strongly disagree* to 7 = *strongly agree*)	UDC 3	House	**Medium** (2/3 Experts)
Q120	**In my society, people tend to develop very similar attitudes and values.** (1 = *strongly disagree* to 7 = *strongly agree*)	UDC 3	Fiske	**Medium** (2/3 Experts)
Q121	**Nature should take its course, and we just have to accept it the way it comes and do the best we can.** (1 = *strongly disagree* to 7 = *strongly agree*)	UDC 2	Trompenaars	**Medium** (Expert 4)
Q122	**I prefer to do two or more activities at the same time.** (1 = *strongly disagree* to 7 = *strongly agree*)	UDC 4	Lindquist	**Medium** (Expert 4)

(continued)

Table 8.5 (continued)

Item No.	Item	UDC Affiliation	Origin	Evaluation by Experts
Q123	**The respect a person receives is highly dependent on the person's family background.** (1 = *strongly disagree* to 7 = *strongly agree*)	UDC 1	Trompenaars	**Medium** (2/3 Experts)
Q124	**How much significance do you place on work (including housework and schoolwork) as compared with leisure?** (1 = *it is leisure that makes life worth living, not work* to 7 = *work is what makes life worth living, not leisure*)	UDC 7	Hofstede	**Medium** (2/3 Experts)
Q125	**In a society, people should be encouraged to be:** (1 = *non-aggressive, non-dominant, and tender* to 7 = *aggressive, dominant, and tough*)	UDC 6	House	**Medium** (Experts 2/3)
Q126	**Members of a society should take** (1 = *a great deal of pride in being a member of the society* to 7 = *no pride in being a member of the society*)	UDC 3	House	**Strong**

(continued)

Table 8.5 (continued)

Item No.	Item	UDC Affiliation	Origin	Evaluation by Experts
Q127	**In general, I believe that social gatherings should be** (1 = *spontaneous* to 7 = *planned well in advance*)	UDC 4	House	**Strong**
Q 128	**In a society, people should be encouraged to be** (1 = *not at all concerned about others* to 7 = *very concerned about others*)	UDC 6	House	**Strong**
Q129	**I believe that opportunities for leadership positions should be** (1 = *more available for women than for men* to 7 = *more available for men than for women*)	UDC 1	House	**Medium** (2/3 Experts)
Q130	**I believe that people should** (1 = *live for the present* to 7 = *live for the future*)	UDC 5	House	**Medium** (2/3 Experts)
Q131	**I believe that power should be** (1 = *shared equally throughout the society* to 7 = *concentrated at the top*)	UDC 1	House	**Strong**

(continued)

Table 8.5 (continued)

Item No.	Item	UDC Affiliation	Origin	Evaluation by Experts
Q132	**I believe that a person who lives a structured life that has few unexpected events** (1 = *is missing a lot of excitement* to 7 = *is living an exciting life*)	UDC 5	House	**Strong**
Q133	**In a society, people should be encouraged to be** (1 = *not at all sensitive towards others* to 7 = *very sensitive towards others*)	UDC 6	House	**Strong**
Q134	**I believe that major rewards should be based on** (1 = *only factors other than performance effectiveness* to 7 = *only performance effectiveness*)	UDC 1	House	**Medium** (Expert 4)
Q135	**In a society, people should be encouraged to be:** (1 = *very unfriendly* to 7 = *very friendly*)	UDC 6	House	**Strong**

Note. UDC 1 = Distribution of Power and Status, UDC 2 = Relationship with the Natural Environment; UDC 3 = Social Organization; UDC 4 = Perception and Use of Time; UDC 5 = Uncertainty Avoidance and Coping Mechanisms; UDC 6 = Human Orientation; UDC 7 = Gratification and Expression of Emotions, Desires, and Feelings; UDC 8 = Traditionalism versus Secularism.

Table 8.6 Background Questions

No.	Question
1	With what gender do you identify yourself? (Female, Male, Others, Prefer not to disclose)
2	How old are you?
3	With which nationality do you identify (by passport)?
4	What was your nationality at birth?
5	How many years of formal education did you complete, beginning with your primary school education?
6	How many years of professional paid experience do you have?
7	What is your current job position? (If you are a student, please indicate student)

8.2.3 Qualitative Results of Field Pre-Test

In total, 85 respondents participated in the field pre-test. A number of 51 respondents completed the questionnaire. Table 8.7 displays a summary of the background information of the 51 respondents.

Table 8.7 Background Information on Respondents of the Pre-Test

Category	Description
Time of Conduction	Average Time: 22 min. 53 sec. Median: 14 min. 7 sec.
Gender	Female: n = 20 Male: n = 31
Age (in years)	Average: 30.98 Min / Max: 21 / 46
Formal Education (in years)	Average: 18.75 Min / Max: 10 / 26
Professional Work Experience (in years)	Average: 6.39 Min / Max: 0 / 23
Job Position (by category)	Student: n = 9 Professional Worker (e.g., Business Development, Manager, Executive Director, Engineer, Product Owner, Process Engineer): n = 26

(continued)

Table 8.7 (continued)

Category	Description
	Position in (Higher) Education (e.g., Professor, School Teacher, Research Associate): n = 15 Unemployed: n = 1

The remaining 34 responses were analyzed, revealing that the 34 respondents did not answer any questionnaire questions, assumingly because some respondents might only have clicked on their received links to test accessibility. The analysis of the pre-test results was conducted solely for the 51 completely received responses. Next, the nationalities of the 51 respondents were analyzed. Table 8.8 demonstrates the three items, revealing information on the nationality of each respondent (N = 51), juxtaposed and categorized in an overview.

Table 8.8 Overview Respondents Nationality by Category

Category	(n)	National Pride (Q14)	Passport (Q23)	Birth (Q24)
I Identical Indication of Nationality for All Items	9	Canadian	Canadian	Canadian
	11	German	German	German
	1	Spanish	Spanish	Spanish
	6	Brazilian	Brazilian	Brazilian
	1	French	French	French
	1	Jordan	Jordan	Jordan
	2	Iranian	Iranian	Iranian
	1	Polish	Polish	Polish
	1	Croatian	Croatian	Croatian
	1	Chilean	Chilean	Chilean
	1	British	British	British
	1	Danish	Danish	Danish
	1	Algerian	Algerian	Algerian
	1	Singaporean	Singaporean	Singaporean
	1	Mongolian	Mongolian	Mongolian

(continued)

Table 8.8 (continued)

Category	(n)	National Pride (Q14)	Passport (Q23)	Birth (Q24)
II No Indication of Nationality for Item Q14	1	–	German	German
	1	–	Turkish	Turkish
	1	–	Slovakian	Slovakian
III Mixed Indication of Nationality in Items	1	*Independent*	German	Sri Lankan
	1	Bangladeshi/German	German	Bangladeshi
	1	Canadian	Canadian	Romania
	1	–	Canadian	Egyptian
	1	Brazilian	Canadian	Brazilian
	1	Canadian	US	US
	1	Syria/Algeria	Algeria	Stateless
	1	Canadian with Chinese Background	Canadian	Chinese

Note. N = 51. The underlined nationalities in category three demonstrate the nationality which was considered for further analysis.

8.2.4 Results of Debriefing Questions

The first debriefing question was "Were there any questions in this questionnaire that you felt uncomfortable with?" and the respondents were able to choose from "Yes" or "No", and to give comments. Figure 8.3 displays the results of the first debriefing question for the 51 respondents.

The majority of respondents felt comfortable answering the items of the UDC questionnaire. Thirteen of the 15 respondents who felt uncomfortable gave comments, displaying the items they felt uncomfortable answering. A summary of each comment and the corresponding implementation in the UDC questionnaire is displayed in Table 8.9. Not all of the comments were suitable nor possible to implement into the UDC questionnaire.

In the second debriefing question, respondents were asked, "When I asked you at the beginning "to indicate your relative periods for the past, present, and future" by completing three sentences, did you had any troubles answering the question in the given way", allowing the respondents to choose between "Yes", "No", and comment. The second debriefing question was asked in respect of doubts of the four experts on the suitability of the question.

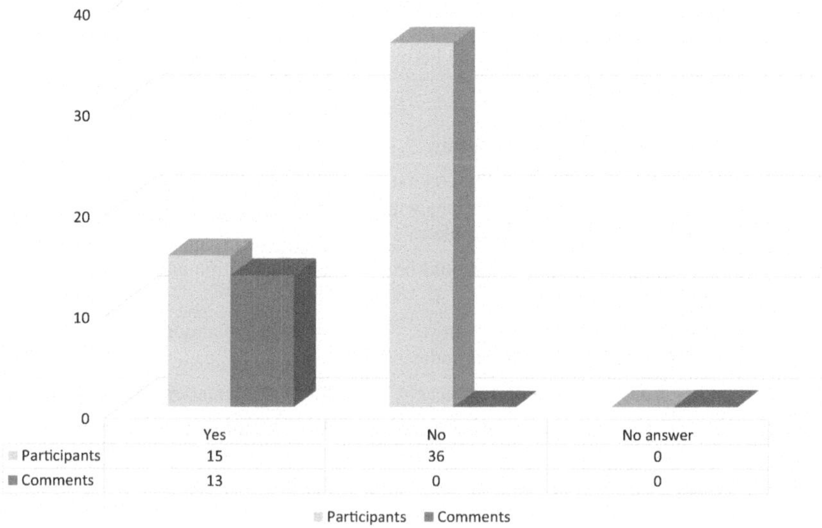

Figure 8.3 Results of the First Debriefing Question. (*Note.* N = 51)

Table 8.9 Comments and Implementation of the First Debriefing Question

(ID)	Summary of Comment	Implementation
1 (4)	Generalization of society in the questions	No implementation in the questionnaire. Please refer to, for example, House et al. (2004).
2 (15)	Equality and Foreign Neighbors	No assessment nor implementation was possible since the comment was not precise.
3 (21)	Q114: The reference option was not clear	No implementation was possible.
	Q115: "Persistent efforts" ambivalent	No implementation was possible.
	Q116: What are the important natural forces?	Implementation in the questionnaire; an example was added to the item.
	Q119: Who are the leaders?	No changes were implemented since the question was intended to address leadership.

(continued)

Table 8.9 (continued)

(ID)	Summary of Comment	Implementation
	Q120: What is the distinction between values and attitudes?	No changes were implemented. The question was adapted from Fiske (1991, 1992).
4 (24)	Q15: The question is confusing.	*Please see debriefing question no. 3.*
5 (27)	General critique on missing context, too many open-ended questions with too many perspectives possible	No implementation was possible.
6 (31)	Q21: The word "gender" should be replaced by sexes.	Implementation was done accordingly.
7 (43)	The section with general ratings (Q124-Q135) is difficult to understand	No implementation was possible.
8 (47)	Q23 & Q24: Indication not clear	No implementation was possible.
	Q21Gender question is missing diverse	Was added to the questionnaire.
9 (51)	Q15: Confusing	*Please see debriefing question no. 3.*
10 (63)	Q15: Confusing	*Please see debriefing question no. 3.*
11 (67)	Q23: Family question too sensitive	No implementation was possible.
12 (71)	Nationality questions are too sensitive	No implementation was possible.

Note. The ID refers to the ID of the respondents given by LimeSurvey.

The results of the second debriefing question are displayed in Figure 8.4.

The majority of respondents (n = 37) indicated that they had trouble answering item Q15. Only a minority of respondents had no trouble answering the question. The 33 comments given for the second debriefing question were reviewed and grouped. Table 8.10 shows the grouped comments.

Conclusively, it was anticipated that by applying item Q15, most respondents would stop pursuing the questionnaire. Therefore, item Q15 was rejected from further application in the UDC questionnaire.

In its origin, item Q15 was intended to measure the respondents' relative time horizon, expressed by either a long-term or a short-term time orientation. The original item was developed by Cottle (1969) in his Duration Inventory and also applied as an item for cross-cultural measurement by Trompenaars and Hampden-Turner (2004, 2012). The item from the initial UDC questionnaire was significantly reconciled and placed at the end of section one. Also, the item was rephrased to the original well-proven version by Cottle (1969). As a result, the item was changed to the following version:

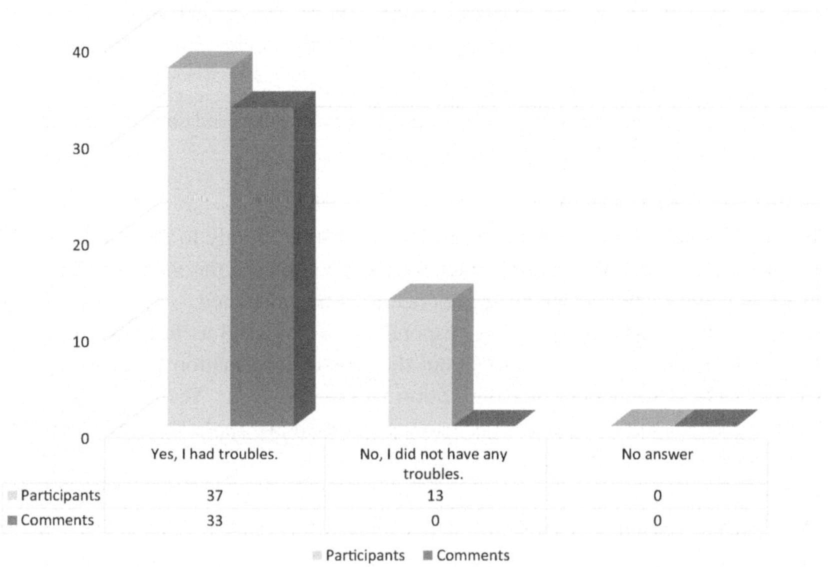

Figure 8.4 Results of the Second Debriefing Question. (*Note.* N = 51)

Table 8.10 Overview of Comments of the Second Debriefing Question

Summary of Comment	(n)
General troubles to answer the item accordingly	26
Missing additional information	2
"now" is no time continuum	2
Time is too relative to be measured	1
Difficulties in distinguishing between "present" and "future"	2

Note. N = 51.

In the following sentences, fill in the blank spaces with one of the words listed below. Indicate your choice by placing the number of the word in the blank space. Select only one word for each blank space. 1 = Seconds, 2 = Minutes, 3 = Hours, 4 = Days, 5 = Weeks, 6 = Month, and 7 = Years.

a) The **present**, as I think of it, extends from ________ ago to_______ from now.

b) As I think of it, the **distant past** includes things and events which occurred_____ago, while the **near past** includes things and events which occurred _______ ago.
c) As I think of it, the **distant future** includes things and events which will occur_____from now, while the **near future** includes things and events which will occur_______ from now. (Cottle, 1969, p. 338)

The slots for indicating the numbers should be restricted only to allow the indication of numbers, not allowing to enter words. To compute the value of the item, the mean score of the six given spaces needs to be calculated.

In the third debriefing question, respondents were asked as follows: "For any of the questions, were you unsure about the type of information I wanted you to provide". The respondents had the option to rate between "Yes" and "No" and comment. The results of the third debriefing question are applicable in Figure 8.5.

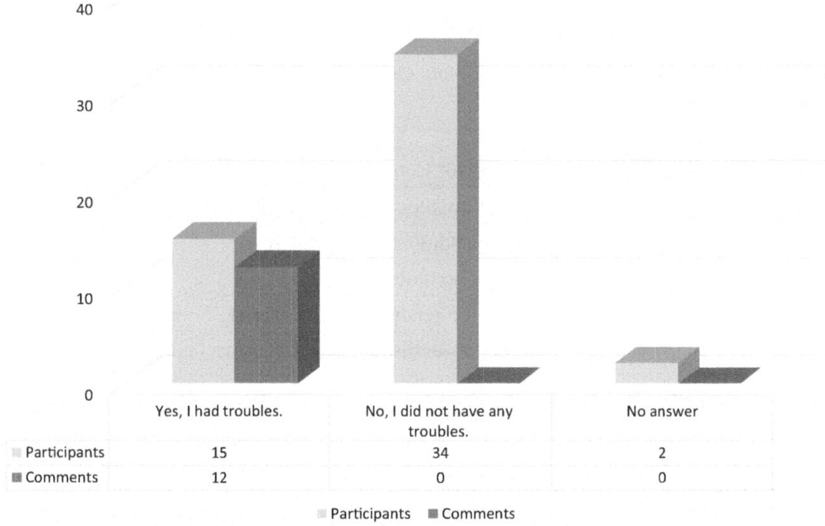

Figure 8.5 Results of the Third Debriefing Question. (*Note.* N = 51)

The majority of respondents (n = 34) did not have any trouble filling out the questionnaire, and 15 respondents were unsure what to indicate for some of the questions they were asked. In total, 12 comments were given by the 51 respondents of the field pre-test. The comments were again, likewise to the comments given for the other debriefing questions, grouped according to their affiliation. An overview of the comments and their respective implementation in the UDC questionnaire is given in Table 8.11.

Table 8.11 Comments and Implementation of the Third Debriefing Question

Item / Comment	(n)	Implementation
Q15: I do not know what and how to indicate my answer/response	8	Reversion of item.
Q112: I did not understand the question.	1	No implementation was possible.
Q 116: I did not know what the important natural forces are.	1	An example was added to the item.
Q17: To what does "different society" refer to?	1	No implementation was possible
General lack of specificity in the questions.	1	–

Note. N = 51. One respondent only copied the comment from the first debriefing question; therefore, only 12 comments are displayed in the table.

At last, respondents were asked to state general comments on the questionnaire. The results of the fourth debriefing question are illustrated in Figure 8.6.

Likewise, to the other three debriefing questions, the 14 comments were analyzed, grouped, and considered for implementation in the questionnaire, as displayed in Table 8.12. In summary, six comments were operationalized, resulting from the qualitative analysis of the debriefing questions. Item Q15 was identified to require a significant revision since most respondents did not know how to answer the question. As a result, item Q15 was revised to the original version by Cottle (1969). For the following qualitative pre-test analysis, item Q15 was not considered further since the reliability of the output seems questionable.

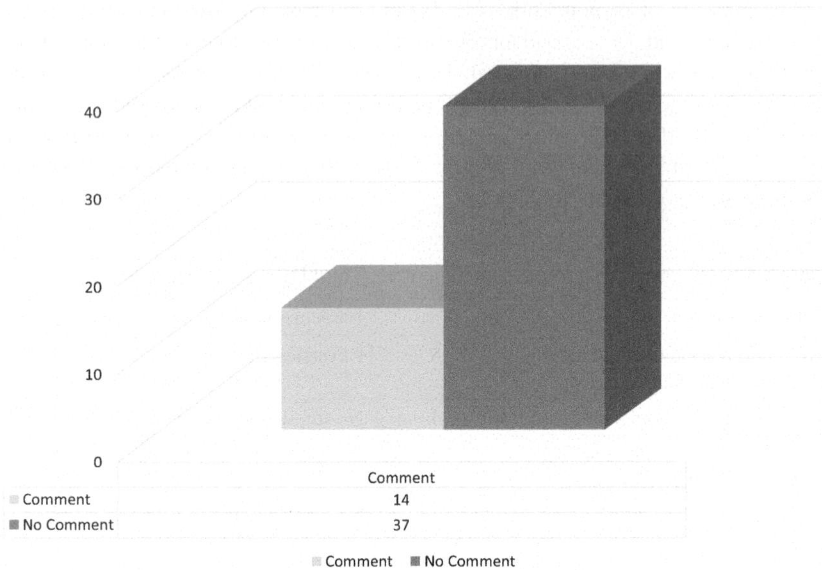

Figure 8.6 Results of the Fourth Debriefing Question. (*Note.* N = 51)

Table 8.12 Comments and Implementation of the Fourth Debriefing Question

Comment	(n)	Implementation
General comment in regards to the topic (e.g., "the topic you brought up is very interesting and I would like to be informed for the future articles/researches and findings")	9	–
Good length/duration of questions	2	–
English needs to be proven	1	After the implementation of the results of all de-briefing questions, the questionnaire was again proven by a native English speaker
Answering choices are too broad	1	The choice of a 7-point scale was evaluated carefully before developing the questionnaire.
Numerous questions are ambiguous	1	–

(continued)

Table 8.12 (continued)

Comment	(n)	Implementation
Lack of question on experiences abroad	1	A question regarding the number of years of experience abroad was added to the background question section.
More details if societal or environmental issues are addressed in the questionnaire.	1	No implementation was possible.
The questionnaire is missing a back-and-forth button	1	As a paper-pencil questionnaire, there would be no need to implement a back-and-forth button, but a back and forth button should be implemented if the questionnaire is conducted with a digital tool.

Note. N = 51. Two comments were split into two separate comments since the comment addressed two different items.

8.2.5 Quantitative Results of Pre-Test

After the qualitative analysis, a quantitative analysis of the results was pursued, ensuring the reliability of the questionnaire. In Social Sciences, the leading indicator for reliability constitutes Cronbach's α[3] (Bryman, 2012).

Before the quantitative analysis, the aggregation of individual responses to country scores was assessed since it cannot easily be assumed that respondents from one country indicate similar response patterns. Sometimes, respondents from the same country and the same national culture indicate complementary and conflicting responses. In general, questionnaires in cross-cultural research are not suitable to test single personalities of individuals (Hofstede, 2001).

The majority of the 22 represented nationalities in the field pre-test were only represented by one respondent (please refer to Table 8.8). Only for Brazil (n = 7), Canada (n = 10), and Germany (n = 12), multiple respondents were present in the field pre-test. Following the approach by Hofstede (2001; Hofstede et al., 2010) and House et al. (2004, 2007, 2014), the quantitative analysis of the results of the field pre-test was conducted with the mean scores for each country (n = 22). Additionally, to the calculation of α with the country mean scores, the α for the average non-mean scores were calculated to assess the differences between the two measurement bases.

[3] In the following, the indication of α refers to Cronbach's alpha.

In Social Sciences, it is advised to involve respondents of 10 x the number of items, which would require for the pre-test of the UDC questionnaire a number of approximately 350 participants (UCLA Institute for Digital Research and Education Statistical Consulting, n.d.). Fifty-one respondents completed the questionnaire. For the statistical analyses, the IBM software SPSS was applied. All items were inserted as ordinal values, once applying country mean scores and once applying no country mean scores. The respective SPSS results can be requested from the author of this dissertation.

UDC Distribution of Power and Status

The first UDC Distribution of Power and Status was represented in the questionnaire by five items as displayed in Table 8.13. All synthesized cultural components and concepts of the UDC were operationalized by items. In total, the UDC Distribution of Power and Status indicated an α of 0.455, using country mean scores (without country mean scores, the α was 0.311). The Item-Total Statistics demonstrated that item Q129 needs to be reversely recoded to fit statistically into the UDC Distribution of Power and Status. The Corrected Item-Total Correlation indicated a value of –0.042 for item Q129. After recoding item Q129 (re-coded item Q129_1), the α increased marginally to 0.481. The Item-Total Statistics showed for the new item set of Q13, Q123, Q129_1, Q131, and Q134 that excluding item Q134 would further increase α to 0.542, and deleting Q129_1 from the UDC questionnaire would lead to an increased α of 0.521. Item Q134 refers to the allocation of status, power, and reward according to individuals' performance. The item was evaluated with a medium by the experts.

The experts stated their disagreement on the affiliation of the cultural component of performance orientation to the concept of distribution of power and status. However, during the UDC Distribution of Power and Status synthesis, the interrelationship between the cultural component of performance orientation and the concept of distribution of power and status became applicable. Conclusively, it was decided to keep item Q134 in the questionnaire. From conceptual terms, the scale of item Q134 should be reversed since 1 describes in the initial version that *performance does not matter* and 7 that *only the factor of performance matters* to allocate and distribute status and power. In contrast, Q123 displays by 1 that *the family background does not matter* and by 7 that *the family background matters.* In order to calculate a total score for the UDC Distribution of Power and Status, the scale ends of Q134 should be reversed. It could be assumed that the revision would increase the fit of the item Q134 into the UDC Distribution of Power and Status item set. Also, for further application of the questionnaire, item Q129 should be reversely recoded.

Table 8.13 The Universal Dimension of Culture (UDC) Distribution of Power and Status by Items and Implications

Acknowledgment and extent of inequalities among individuals, and individual's dependency on higher-ranked individuals					
	Item	Scale	Cultural Component	Scale Implication (Evaluation by Experts)	Original Author
Q13	How often do you think subordinates, in general, are afraid to contradict their boss?	1 = *never* to 7 = *every time*	Employee Fear	1 = *no fear* to 7 = *high fear* (S)	Hofstede & Minkov (2013)
Q123	The respect a person receives is highly dependent on the person's family background.	1 = *strongly disagree* to 7 = *strongly agree*	Allocation of Status by Family Background	1 = *family background does not matter* to 7 = *family background strongly matters* (M)	Trompenaars & Hampden-Turner (2004, 2012)
Q129	I believe that opportunities for a leadership position should be:	1= *more available for women than for men* to 7 = *more available for men than for women*	Gender Egalitarianism	1 = *leadership positions for women* to 7 = *leadership positions for men* (M)	House et al. (n.d.)
Q131	I believe that power should be:	1 = *shared equally throughout the society* to 7 = *concentrated at the top*	Hierarchy versus Egalitarianism	1 = *egalitarianism* to 7 = *hierarchy* (S)	House et al. (n.d.)
Q134	I believe that major rewards should be based on:	1 = *only factors other than performance effectiveness* to 7 = *only performance effectiveness*	Allocation by Performance Orientation	1 = *performance does not matter* to 7 = *only performance matters* (M)	House et al. (n.d.)

Note. "M" = medium, "S" = strong.

When calculated by the average mean score for each item, a low UDC Distribution of Power and Status country score displays a low acknowledgment and extent of inequalities among individuals and a low extent of dependency of individuals on higher-ranked individuals. In more detail, a low UDC Distribution of Power and Status score indicates that the individuals of the national culture are not afraid to contradict superiors, respect is not paid in regards to the family background, leadership positions should be more available for men, power is shared equally throughout the society, and only a person's performance matters for receiving rewards. Vice versa accounts for a high score in the UDC Distribution of Power and Status.

UDC Relationship with the Natural Environment

The UDC Relationship with the Natural Environment was projected to be measured by four items, referring to the in Table 8.14 displayed implications. The UDC Relationship with the Natural Environment encompassed further the conceptual synthesized cultural component of masculinity versus femininity, which was not operationalized by any item for the empirical assessment of the UDC Relationship with the Natural Environment.

Table 8.14 The Universal Dimension of Culture (UDC) Relationship with the Natural Environment by Items and Implications

The extent of relationships of individuals with their natural environment in national cultures is expressed in their desire either to control or to live in harmony with their natural environment

	Item	Scale	Cultural Component	Scale Implication (Evaluation by Experts)	Original Author
Q110	How important is preserving nature to you?	1 = *not at all important* to 7 = *extremely important*	Mastery versus Harmony	1 = *no valuing of nature* to 7 = *valuing of nature* (M)	Schwartz (1992, 1994b)
Q113	How important is the value of unity with nature to you?	1 = *not at all important* to 7 = *extremely important*	Mastery versus Harmony	1 = *no valuing of nature* to 7 = *valuing of nature* (M)	Schwartz (1992, 1994b)

(continued)

Table 8.14 (continued)

The extent of relationships of individuals with their natural environment in national cultures is expressed in their desire either to control or to live in harmony with their natural environment

	Item	Scale	Cultural Component	Scale Implication (Evaluation by Experts)	Original Author
Q116	It is worthwhile trying to control important natural forces.	1 = *strongly disagree* to 7 = *strongly agree*	Relationship with the Nature	1 = *no control* to 7 = *control* (M)	Trompenaars & Hampden-Turner (2004, 2012)
Q121	Nature should take its course, and we just have to accept it the way it comes and to the best, we can.	1 = *strongly disagree* to 7 = *strongly agree*	Relationship with the Nature	1 = *no control* to 7 = *control* (M)	Trompenaars & Hampden-Turner (2004, 2012)

Note. "M" = medium, "S" = strong.

As already applicable in the conceptual analysis of the implications of the four items, either item Q116 or item Q121 should be reversely recoded since their scales refer to opposing measurements. In contrast to the other seven UDCs, the four UDC Relationship with the Natural Environment items measure one cultural component by two items. The two items Q110 and Q113 refer to mastery versus harmony, and the two items (Q116 and Q121) refer to the cultural component of relationship with nature. Each of the two-fold item sets was retrieved from a different cultural taxonomy. The items Q110 and Q113 were retrieved from Schwartz (1992, 1994b), and the items Q116 and Q121 were retrieved from Trompenaars and Hampden-Turner (2004, 2012).

The first SPSS analysis of the UDC Relationship with the Natural Environment data resulted in a negative α of -0.925 using the country mean score, and without the country mean score α resulted in -0.332. The resulting negative α confirmed the conceptual analysis regarding the UDC Relationship with the Natural Environment and its two-fold item set.

Afterward, it was analyzed if the reliability indicator α would increase by applying a rescaled item Q116, identified in the conceptual analysis of the item set (please refer to Table 8.14). Therefore, item Q116 was reversely recoded to Q116_1. The second SPSS analysis of the item set Q110, Q113, Q121, and Q116_1 demonstrated in the Item-Total Statistics that the two items Q110 and Q113 and the two items Q121 and Q116_1 are interrelated. In order to prove the reliability of the four items, the items were split according to their conceptual affiliation, and the Spearman's ρ coefficient, allowing for the assessment of pairs of ordinal variables, was calculated for each set of items (Okada, 2019). The Spearman's ρ coefficient for Q121 and Q116_1 was sufficiently significantly correlated at a 0.05 level by 0.502. The Spearman's ρ coefficient of the items Q110 and Q113 did not indicate a significant correlation with a score of −0.015.

The two items Q110 and Q113 originate from Schwartz (1992, 1994b), and both refer to the concept of mastery versus harmony. No conceptual explanation for the circumstance of the negative Spearman's ρ coefficient for items Q110 and Q113 was applicable. Therefore, it was decided to keep both items in the questionnaire, and the Spearman test should be retaken with a more significant number of involved respondents per national culture in a subsequent field test. In order to keep the flow of the questionnaire by applying the same scale ends in a section, item Q116 should be rephrased to "It is not worthwhile trying to control important natural forces (e.g., such as the weather)" with its scale of 1 (*strongly disagree*) to 7 (*strongly agree*).

After the changes, a low total score in the UDC Relationship with the Natural Environment by calculating the mean scores for each item would indicate that the individuals of the corresponding national culture would hold a low extent of the relationship with their natural environment, expressed by a desire to control the natural environment. In more detail, individuals of national culture with a low score in the UDC Relationship with the Natural Environment would not try to preserve their natural environment, do not value the unity with their nature, try to control critical natural forces, and restrict nature in its course. The opposite cultural traits account for national culture, which scores high in the UDC Relationship with the Natural Environment.

UDC Social Organization

The UDC Social Organization was intended to be measured by five items, referring to the in Table 8.15 displayed implications. Besides the operationalized cultural components, the UDC Social Organization also includes the conceptual synthesized cultural components of context and space, which were not operationalized by any item.

The α indicated a value of 0.235 for the original item set of Q17, Q117, Q119, Q120, and Q126 by calculating using the country mean score. The α without the country mean score resulted in a marginally higher value of 0.275. The Item-Total Statistic of the first SPSS analysis of the UDC Social Organization suggested in the Corrected Item-Total Correlation that item Q120 needs to be recoded, demonstrating a corrected item-total correlation of −0.078. The conceptual analysis of the items of the UDC Social Organization as applicable in Table 8.15 revealed that item Q126 needs to be revelry recoded as well (resulting in Q126_1).

A second SPSS analysis with the item set of Q17, Q117, Q119, Q120, and Q126_1 was conducted, resulting in a minimal decrease of α to 0.233, and the Item-Total Statistic pointed to a need for rescaling of item Q117 (corrected item-total correlation −0.208; Q117_1). Also, the exclusion of item Q117 would increase the UDC's α to 0.451.

Third, the α was calculated, applying a reversely recoded Q117_1 and Q120_1. As a result, α decreased to a negative value of −0.385, and the Corrected Item-Total Correlation demonstrated again to reversely recode both items Q120_1 and Q117_1.

Following the previous three statistical analyses and the conceptual analyses, it was concluded that item Q126 and item Q117 should be reversely recoded to increase their suitability for the item set, resulting in an increased α of 0.477. The Item-Total Statistic of the item set of Q17, Q119, Q120, Q126_1, and Q117_1 indicated that a deletion of item Q119 would further increase α to 0.521.

Table 8.15 The Universal Dimension of Culture (UDC) Social Organization by Items and Implications

The structure of social relationships by the concept of individualism versus collectivism in national cultures					
	Item	Scale	Cultural Component	Scale Implication (Evaluation by Experts)	Original Author
Q17	Would you like to have people of a different society as neighbors?	1 = *totally unacceptable* to 7 = *perfectly acceptable*	Universalism versus Particularism	1 = *individualism* to 7 = *collectivism* (M)	Minkov (2007)

(continued)

Table 8.15 (continued)

The structure of social relationships by the concept of individualism versus collectivism in national cultures

	Item	Scale	Cultural Component	Scale Implication (Evaluation by Experts)	Original Author
Q117	In my society, people make decisions together by consensus.	1 = *strongly disagree* to 7 = *strongly agree*	Group Decision Making	1 = *individualism* to 7 = *collectivism* (M)	Fiske (1991, 1992)
Q119	I believe that leaders should encourage group loyalty even if individual goals suffer	1 = *strongly disagree* to 7 = *strongly agree*	Loyalty	1 = *individualism* to 7 = *collectivism* (M)	House et al. (n.d.)
Q120	In my society, people tend to develop very similar attitudes and values	1 = *strongly disagree* to 7 = *strongly agree*	Group Affiliation	1 = *individualism* to 7 = *collectivism* (M)	Fiske (1991, 1992)
Q126	Members of a society should take	1 = *a great deal of pride in being a member of the society* to 7 = *no pride in being a member of the society*	Pride	1 = *collectivism* to 7 = *individualism* (M)	House et al. (n.d.)

Note. "M" = medium, "S" = strong.

In conceptual terms, item Q119 refers to the underlying cultural component of loyalty, which was synthesized into the UDC Social Organization. During the UDC Social Organization synthesis, the conceptual affiliation of the cultural component of loyalty to the concept of social organization regarding individualism versus collectivism was demonstrated accordingly.

As a result of the analysis of the item set of the UDC Social Organization, the scale of item Q126 should be reversely recoded, which should also be pursued in the actual UDC questionnaire. Item Q117 did not point to reverse rescaling in the questionnaire, but the statistical analysis of the UDC Social Organization item set indicated that the scale of the item could be recoded for statistical purposes. No conceptual evidence was identified for a reverse re-coding of item Q117.

Conclusively and in a summary of the changes, a low total score in the UDC Social Organization indicates that the corresponding national culture is considered individualistic. In more detail, a low score displays that a corresponding national culture does not accept people from a different society as neighbors, decisions should not be made by consensus, group loyalty should not be encouraged if individual goals suffer, people do not develop similar attitudes and values, and members of a society should not take a great deal of pride in being a member of the society. Vice versa accounts for a high score.

UDC Perception and Use of Time

The UDC Perception and Use of Time was operationalized in the UDC questionnaire by four items. As the qualitative analysis of the field pre-test revealed, the output of item Q15 from the pre-test is not suitable for further analyses. Therefore, the following SPSS analyses of the item set of the UDC Perception and Use of Time was conducted without the data of item Q15. Furthermore, item Q18 was only indicated with a 3-point scale in the online questionnaire in LimeSurvey, whereas the other items Q122 and Q127 were measured by a 7-point scale. Hence, item Q18 was up-scaled to a 7-point scale. Table 8.16 illustrates the three items and their UDC implications. The synthesized UDC Perception and Use of Time encompass no other conceptual synthesized cultural concepts.

The UDC Perception and Use of Time statistical analysis resulted in an α of 0.452 under the country mean score (without the country mean score α constituted 0.079). The Item-Total Statistics indicated a minor increase of α to 0.464 if item Q127 was deleted from the UDC Perception and Use of Time item set. Item Q127 refers to the cultural component of planning ahead. The conceptual affiliation of the cultural component of planning ahead to the concept of perception and use of time was demonstrated in the synthesis of the UDC Perception and Use of Time.

No further SPSS analyses were conducted for the UDC Perception and Use of Time since the item set of four items could not be entirely assessed due to the lack of data for item Q15. In summary, a total low UDC in the UDC Perception and Use of Time would display that the individuals of the corresponding national culture tend to stick to the past or present, but not to the future, and have monochronic handling of tasks. Vice versa accounts for national cultures which score high in the UDC Perception and Use of Time score.

Table 8.16 The Universal Dimension of Culture (UDC) Perception and Use of Time by Items and Implications

The extent of perception (incl., view of) and use of time in national cultures					
	Item	Scale	Cultural Component	Scale Implication (Evaluation by Experts)	Original Author
Q18	When I donate money to charitable organizations, I think it should be best spent to	1 = *keep the old ways and customs alive* to 2 = *make a better life now* to 3 = *make a better life for the future*	Perception of Time	1 = *past* to 2 = *present* to 3 = *future* (M)	Kluckhohn & Strodtbeck (1961)
Q122	I prefer to do more activities at the same time	1 = *strongly disagree* to 7 = *strongly agree*	Number of Handled Tasks at a Time	1 = *monochronic* to 7 = *polychronic* (M)	Lindquist & Kaufman-Scarborough (2007)
Q127	In general, I believe that social gatherings should be:	1 = *spontaneous* to 7 = *planned well in advance*	Planning Ahead	1 = *present* to 7 = *future* (S)	House et al. (n.d.)

Note. "M" = medium, "S" = strong.

UDC Uncertainty Avoidance and Coping Mechanisms

The UDC Uncertainty Avoidance and Coping Mechanisms was measured by four items, referring to in Table 8.17 displayed implications. The UDC Uncertainty Avoidance and Coping Mechanisms does not encompass conceptual synthesized cultural components.

The α of the original item set of the UDC Uncertainty Avoidance and Coping Mechanisms accounted for a value of 0.367 when calculated with the country mean scores. Without the country mean score, the α resulted in 0.033. The analysis of the Item-Total Statistic indicated that item Q130 should be reversely recoded to increase its suitability for the item set of the UDC Uncertainty Avoidance and Coping Mechanisms. The Item-Total Statistic indicated a Corrected Item-Total Correlation for Q130 of −0.082 and an α of 0. 574 when item Q130 would be removed.

Table 8.17 The Universal Dimension of Culture (UDC) Uncertainty Avoidance and Coping Mechanisms by Items and Implications

The extent of uncertainty avoidance and mechanisms for coping and dealing with uncertain and unknown situations in national cultures					
	Item	Scale	Cultural Component	Scale Implication (Evaluation by Experts)	Original Author
Q11	In general, how often do you feel nervous or tense?	1 = *never* to 7 = *every time*	Stress	1 = *never feeling nervous or tense* to 7 = *every time feeling nervous or tense* (S)	Hofstede & Minkov (2013)
Q118	I believe that societal requirements and instructions should be spelled out in detail so citizens know what they are expected to do:	1 = *strongly disagree* to 7 = *strongly agree*	Rule and Regulation Obedience	1 = *preference for uncertainty* to 7 = *preference for certainty* (S)	House et al. (n.d.)
Q130	I believe that people should:	1 = *live for the present* to 7 = *live for the future*	Future Orientation as a Coping Mechanism	1 = *preference for uncertainty* to 7 = *preference for certainty* (M)	House et al. (n.d.)
Q132	I believe that a person who leads a structured life that as few unexpected events:	1 = *is missing a lot of excitement* to 7 = *is living an exciting life*	Coping and Dealing with Uncertainty	1 = *preference for uncertainty* to 7 = *preference for certainty* (M)	House et al. (n.d.)

Note. "M" = medium, "S" = strong.

The conceptual analysis of the scales of the item set (please see Table 8.17) did not demonstrate a necessity of rescaling item Q130. Albeit, a second SPSS analysis of the UDC Uncertainty Avoidance and Coping Mechanisms was conducted, under the application of a reversely recoded Q130_1. The α increased to 0.478. Furthermore, the Item-Total Statistic advised that a deletion of item Q130_1 would further increase α to 0.574. Item Q130 was added to the UDC questionnaire after following the four experts' advice—Expert 1, Expert 2, Expert 3, and Expert 4. In the first version of the questionnaire, the item was stated as follows "I believe that the accepted norm in this society should be to (1 (*plan for the future*) to 7 (*accept the status quo*))". The first three experts—Expert 1, Expert 2, and Expert 3—evaluated the item as unsuitable since the scale indicated "to plan for the future" and "to accept the status quo" seemed contractionary. Therefore, item Q130 was rewritten to the current version of "I believe that people should (1 (*live for the present*) to 7 (*live for the future*))".

From a conceptual point of view, no indication was applicable to reversely rescale item Q130 (please refer to Table 8.17). The statistical implied deletion of item Q130 from the item set of the UDC Uncertainty Avoidance and Coping Mechanisms could also result from the low number of 51 participants of the pre-test. The affiliation of the concept of uncertainty avoidance to the coping mechanism of planning ahead was considerably demonstrated in the synthesis of the UDC Uncertainty Avoidance and Coping Mechanisms in conceptual terms. The evidence for the deletion or reversely recoding of item Q130 was evaluated as weak by the author of this dissertation. Therefore, item Q130 was kept in the UDC questionnaire in its current version.

Overall, a low total country score in the UDC Uncertainty Avoidance and Coping Mechanisms, when calculated with the mean scores from each item, displays a low extent of uncertainty avoidance in the corresponding national culture, expressed in a low level of stress, societal requirements, and instructions do not need to be spelled out in detail, individuals should live for the present, and a life with few unexpected circumstances misses on excitement. Vice versa would account for a high score in the UDC Uncertainty Avoidance and Coping Mechanisms.

UDC Human Orientation

Four items measured the UDC Human Orientation, referring to the in Table 8.18 displayed implications.

The UDC Human Orientation encompassed the conceptual synthesized cultural component of masculinity versus femininity; no item was operationalized for the cultural component of masculinity versus femininity in the UDC Human Orientation.

Table 8.18 The Universal Dimension of Culture (UDC) Human Orientation by Items and Implications

The extent of assertiveness versus tenderness in national cultures					
	Item	Scale	Cultural Component	Scale Implication (Evaluation by Experts)	Original Author
Q125	In a society, people should be encouraged to be:	1 = *non-aggressive, non-dominant, and tender* to 7 = *aggressive, dominant, tough*	Human Nature	1 = *soft* to 7 = *hard* (M)	House et al. (n.d.)
Q128	In a society, people should be encouraged to be:	1 = *not at all concerned about others* to 7 = *very concerned about others*	Assertiveness versus Tenderness	1 = *hard* to 7 = *soft* (S)	House et al. (n.d.)
Q133	In a society, people should be encouraged to be:	1 = *not at sensitive towards others* to 7 = *very sensitive towards others*	Assertiveness versus Tenderness	1 = *hard* to 7 = *soft* (S)	House et al. (n.d.)
Q135	In a society, people should be encouraged to be:	1 = *very unfriendly* to 7 = *very friendly*	Assertiveness versus Tenderness	1 = *hard* to 7 = *soft* (S)	House et al. (n.d.)

Note. "M" = medium, "S" = strong.

The first SPSS analysis of the UDC Human Orientation item set resulted in an α of 0.323 using the country mean score, without the country mean score α accounting for 0.175. As indicated in the Item-Total Statistics of the first SPSS analysis of the UDC Human Orientation, item Q125 should be recoded to increase the correlation of the UDC Human Orientation item set (corrected item-total correlation of −0.072). Likewise, a similar indication was identified in the conceptual analysis of the UDC Human Orientation item set (please see Table 8.18).

The scale ends of item Q125 should be reversely re-coded, and the item should be rephrased in the questionnaire accordingly. With a reversely recoded item Q125 (indicated as Q125_1), the α of the UDC Human Orientation increased to 0.453. Furthermore, it should be pointed out that the exclusion of item Q125_1 would result in an increased α of 0.682. Item Q125 was evaluated with "medium" by the four experts—Expert 1, Expert 2, Expert 3, and Expert 4. Expert 2 critically appraised the affiliation of the item to the UDC Human Orientation since the item could also refer to the UDC Social Organization. The other three experts—Expert 1, Expert 3, and Expert 4—did not mention any issues with the item. Therefore, it was advised to keep item Q125 in the questionnaire but with reversely recoded scale points.

Overall, a low country score in the UDC Human Orientation indicates a low extent of tenderness in the national culture, thus, a great extent of assertiveness. In more detail, individuals of national culture with a low country score in the UDC Human Orientation tend to aggressive, dominant, though, and unfriendly behavior, are not concerned about and not sensitive towards others. Vice versa accounts for individuals of the national cultures with a high score in the UDC Human Orientation.

UDC Gratification and Expression of Emotions, Feelings, and Desires

Four items were operationalized to measure the UDC Gratification and Expression of Emotions, Feelings, and Desires, addressing the in Table 8.19 displayed implications. The UDC Gratification and Expression of Emotions, Feelings, and Desires does not encompass only conceptually synthesized cultural components.

The conceptual analysis (please refer to Table 8.19) demonstrated that items Q12 and Q16 or Q112 and Q124 should be rescaled to match the item set's scale points. The α of the first SPSS analysis of the item set Q12, Q16, Q112, and Q124 of the UDC Gratification and Expression of Emotions, Feelings, and Desires resulted in a negative value of −0.148 under application of the country mean score and without the country mean score α resulted in −0.732. The Item-Total Statistic demonstrated that item Q112 and item Q124 should be reversely recoded by a corrected item-total correlation for Q112 of −0.271 and Q124 of −0.141. A second SPSS analysis was conducted under the application of the reversely recoded items Q112_1 and Q124_1.

Under the application of Q112_1 and Q124_1 and the country mean scores, α decreased to −0.462. Likewise, the Item-Total Statistics indicated negative values for the Corrected Item-Total Correlation for Q112_1 (−0.271) and for Q124_1 (−0.431).

The first SPSS analysis of the item set of the UDC Gratification and Expression of Emotions, Feelings, and Desires indicated that the α of the item set would increase if item Q122 were deleted from the item set. The α for the item set Q12, Q16, and Q124 accounted for 0.394 under application of country mean score. Furthermore, the results of the SPSS analysis indicated that item Q112 does not, from a statistical point of view, fit into the intended initial item set of the UDC.

Table 8.19 The Universal Dimension of Culture (UDC) Gratification and Expression of Emotions, Desires, and Feelings by Items and Implications

The extent of gratification and expression of desires, feelings, and emotions in national cultures					
	Item	Scale	Cultural Component	Scale Implication (Evaluation by Experts)	Original Author
Q12	How much freedom of choice and control do you feel you have over the way your life turns out?	1 = *no choice at all* to 7 = *a great deal of choices*	Life Control	1 = *restraint* to 7 = *free* (M)	Minkov (2007)
Q16	Are you a happy person?	1 = *never* to 7 = *every time*	Happiness	1 = *restraint* to 7 = *free* (S)	Hofstede & Minkov (2013)
Q112	How important is the value of avoiding extreme feelings and actions to you?	1 = *not at all important* to 7 = *extremely important*	Moderation	1 = *free* to 7 = *restraint* (S)	Schwartz (1992, 1994b)
Q124	How much significance do you place on work (including housework and schoolwork) as compared with leisure?	1 = *it's leisure that make life worth living, not work* to 7 = *work is what makes life worth living, not leisure*	Importance of Leisure	1 = *free* to 7 = *restraint* (M)	Hofstede & Minkov (2013)

Note. "M" = medium, "S" = strong.

Item Q112 was the only item from the original four items—Q12, Q16, Q112, and Q124—of the UDC Gratification and Expression of Emotions, Desires, and Feelings, which was retrieved from Schwartz (1992, 1994b). The other three items Q12, Q16, and Q124, were adapted from Hofstede (2001; Hofstede et al., 2010) and

Minkov (2007). The expert panel evaluated the item with strong suitability to measure the intended concept of moderation, and thus the affiliated UDC Gratification and Expression of Emotions, Feelings, and Desires.

Under the evidence of the previous analyses of the UDC Gratification and Expression of Emotions, Feelings, and Desires, item Q112 was revised. In the original set of 111 collected items during the synthesis of the UDCs (please refer to Appendix B in the Electronic Supplementary Material), two items for assessing the concept of moderation were identified. Hofstede et al. (2010) ask respondents as follows "In your private life, how important is each of the following to you: moderation (having few desires)"—on a 5-point scale with 1 (*of utmost importance*) to 5 (*very little or no importance*). In contrast, Schwartz (1992, 1994b) asked his respondents as follows "As a guiding principle in my life, this value is moderate (avoiding extremes of feelings)"—on a 9-point scale with −1 (*opposed to my values*) to 7 (*of supreme importance*). As a result of the analysis, item Q112 was revised to "In your private life, how important is moderation to you", measured on a 7-point scale with 1 (*not at all important*) to 7 (*extremely important*). Besides the changes in Q112, also items Q12 and Q16 were reversely recoded due to conceptual purposes.

A low country score in the UDC Gratification and Expression of Emotions, Desires, and Feelings indicates a free gratification and expression of desires, feelings, and emotions in the corresponding national culture. Individuals of low UDC Gratification and Expression of Emotions, Desires, and Feelings countries feel to have a great deal of choice over the way their life turns out, tend to be happy, do not avoid extreme feelings and actions, and place more significance on leisure instead of work in their life. Vice versa accounts for individuals from national cultures with a high total score in the UDC Gratification and Expression of Emotions, Desires, and Feelings.

UDC Traditionalism versus Secularism

Five items measured the UDC Traditionalism versus Secularism, referring to the in Table 8.20 displayed implications, encompassing the conceptual component of past-time orientation.

The α of the five original projected items for the UDC Traditionalism versus Secularism account for an α 0.356 by applying the country mean score. Without the application of the country mean score, α accounted for 0.242. The Item-Total Statistic demonstrated that item Q111 should be reversely recoded by a corrected item-total correlation of −0.162.

Table 8.20 The Universal Dimension of Culture (UDC) Traditionalism versus Secularism by Items and Implications

The extent of feelings of pride, flexibility, consistency between expressed and felt emotions, secular orientation, religiosity, and self-stability in national cultures					
	Item	Scale	Cultural Component	Scale Implication (Evaluation by Experts)	Original Author
Q14	How proud are you to be (please specific nationality)?	1 = *not at all proud* to 7 = *extremely proud*	National Pride	1 = *secularism* to 7 = *traditionalism* (S)	Minkov (2007)
Q19	How important is religious faith to you?	1 = *not at all important to* 7 = *extremely important*	Religiosity	1 = *secularism* to 7 = *traditionalism* (S)	Inglehart et al. (2014)
Q111	In your private life, how important is doing a service for a friend to you?	1 = *not at all important to* 7 = *extremely important* 7	Self-enhancement	1 = *secularism* to 7 = *traditionalism* (M)	Hofstede & Minkov (2013)
Q114	How important is independence to you?	1 = *not at all important to* 7 = *extremely important*	Secular Orientation	1 = *traditionalism* to 7 = *secularism* (M)	Inglehart et al. (2014)
Q115	Persistent efforts are the surest way to successful results	1 = *strongly disagree* to 7 = *strongly agree*	Self-stability	1 = *traditionalism* to 7 = *secularism* (M)	Hofstede & Minkov (2013)

Note. "M" = medium, "S" = strong.

Item Q111 was reversely recoded, and a second SPSS analysis was conducted under the application of Q111_1. The α of the item set of Q14, Q114, Q115, Q19, and Q111_1 increased to 0.454, pointing to an even further increase of α to 0.480 if item Q19 would be deleted from the item set. There was no conceptual indication applicable, which would have justified an elimination of item Q19 from the item set of the UDC Traditionalism versus Secularism. However, the conceptual analysis of the item set of the UDC Traditionalism versus Secularism (please refer to Table 8.20) revealed that item Q19 should be reversely recoded to match the item's scale point. The α of the item set Q14, Q114, Q115, Q111_1, and Q19_1 marginal decreased to 0.443, compared to the original item set of the UDC Traditionalism versus Secularism. The expert panel evaluated item Q19 with strong in its suitability. Although the statistical analysis pointed to a deletion of item Q19 from the item set of the UDC Traditionalism versus Secularism, no conceptual implication was applicable.

Another explanation for the weak correlation of item Q19 with the other items from the item set of the UDC Traditionalism versus Secularism was assumed in the underlying concept of the item; item Q19 refers to the concept of religiosity. To answer a question related to someone's religiosity could be high sensitivity for some respondents, leading to somewhat dishonest or rejected responses. In conclusion of the quantitative analysis, the items Q4, Q19, and Q111 should be reversely rescaled when calculating the country mean score for the UDC Traditionalism versus Secularism. This would then result in the following implications for a low country mean score in the UDC Traditionalism versus Secularism: the corresponding national culture displays a low extent of secularism, thus, a relatively high extent of traditionalism. The national culture would be characterized by high feelings for national pride, religion, and service to a friend and low feelings of independence and persistency.

Critical Appraisal of the Quantitative Results of the Pre-Test

The pre-test's qualitative analysis was conducted to meet the standards of a full-standardized questionnaire, establishing the internal reliability of the developed UDC questionnaire (Döring & Bortz, 2016). As pointed out by Hofstede (2001; Hofstede et al., 2010), solid statistical factors do not automatically also indicate high suitability of the items to measure the intended cultural components and concepts. In other words, a solid statistical correlation does not automatically imply a solid conceptual correlation between the items (Hofstede, 2001).

House et al. (2004, 2007, 2014), Hofstede (2001; Hofstede et al., 2010), and Schwartz (1992, 1994b) computed cross-national factor analyses—Confirmatory and Explanatory Analysis, and Pearson Correlations—for their data. An Explanatory Factor Analysis was conducted for the pre-test data of the developed UDC questionnaire too. But, the sample size of 51 full-responses does not hold the minimum sample size requirements for conducting a factor analysis (Pearson & Mundform, 2010; Sakaluk & Short, 2017). For example, the researchers Sakaluk and Short

(2017) advised a sample size between 50 to 1000, with an overall adequate output for a sample size of 200–250. However, as most researchers agree on—e.g., Pearson and Mundform (2010) as well as Sakaluk and Short (2017)—the adequate sample size depends on the number of intended components to measure. The UCLA Institute for Digital Research and Education (n.d.) points to a minimum rule of 10 observations per variable, which would imply, in the UDC questionnaire, a total required sample size of 350.

Also, the methodology of Cronbach's α has flaws in its implication, even though it is widely applied to measure reliability and internal consistency. In general, an α of 0.7 is widely advised as statistically desirable (Taber, 2018). None of the item sets for the eight UDCs scored or scored greater than 0.7. Almost all items of each UDC (one exemption constitutes the UDC Relationship with the Natural Environment) refer to different underlying cultural components. The statistical significance of α decreases if the items in an item set refer to different cultural components (Taber, 2018). Overall, it should be pointed out that the statistical analyses for the UDCs were conducted based on 51 responses. A consecutive study with the revised and polished UDC questionnaire is highly recommendable, also under the premise to include as many as possible various national cultures. Additionally, in the pre-test, some of the national cultures were only represented by one respondent. Table 8.21 displays the changes pursued in the item set of the UDC questionnaire. As it should be used for further application, the final UDC questionnaire is displayed in Appendix E in the Electronic Supplementary Material to this dissertation.

Table 8.21 Overview of Item Adaptation after Field Pre-Test

	Question (incl. original scale)	**Change**	Further Advice
Q12	**How much freedom of choice and control do you feel you have over the way your life turns out?** (1 = *no choice at all* to 7 = *a great deal of choice*)	The scale ends need to be reversed to 1 (*a great deal of choice*) to 7 (*no choice at all*)	–
Q16	**Are you a happy person?** (1 = *never* to 7 =*every time*)	Change of item to: "**Are you an unhappy person?**" (1 = *never* to 7 = *every time*)	

(continued)

Table 8.21 (continued)

	Question (incl. original scale)	Change	Further Advice
Q18	**When I donate money to charitable organizations, I think it should be best spent to** (1 = *keep the old ways and customs alive* to 7 = *make a better life now* to 4 = *make a better life for the future*)	–	The online version of the questionnaire should indicate a 7-point scale for the item.
Q14	**How proud are you to be_______?** (1 = *not at all proud* to 7 = *extremely proud*)		The analysis suggested that the item needs to be reversely recoded.
Q19	**How important is religious faith to you?** (1 = *not at all important* to 7 = *extremely important*)	–	The analysis suggested that the item needs to be reversely recoded.
Q111	**In your private life, how important is doing a service for a friend to you?** (1 = *not at all important* to 7 = *extremely important*)	–	The SPSS analysis suggested that the item should be reversely recoded.
Q112	**How important is the value of avoiding extreme feelings and actions to you?** (1 = *not at all important* to 7 = *extremely important*)	A new item resulted from the analysis: **How important is moderation to you in your private life?** (1 = *not at all important* to 7= *extremely important*)	The SPSS analysis suggested that the item should be reversely recoded for statistical purposes to increase α
Q116	**It is worthwhile trying to control important natural forces (e.g., such as the wind).** (1 = *strongly disagree* to 7 = *strongly agree*)	It is not worthwhile trying to control important natural forces (e.g., such as the wind). (1 = *strongly disagree* to 7 = *strongly agree*)	–
Q117	**In my society, people make decisions together by consensus.** (1 = *strongly disagree* to 7 = *strongly agree*)	–	The SPSS analysis suggested that the scale should be reversely recoded for statistical purposes to increase α.

(continued)

Table 8.21 (continued)

	Question (incl. original scale)	Change	Further Advice
Q125	**In a society, people should be encouraged to be** (1 = *non-aggressive, non-dominant, and tender* to 7 = *aggressive, dominant, and tough*)	The scale ends need to be reversed to 1 (*aggressive, dominant, and tough*) to 7 (*non-aggressive, non-dominant, and tender*)	–
Q126	**Members of a society should take** (1 = *a great deal of pride in being a member of the society* to 7 = *no pride in being a member of the society*)	The scale ends need to be reversed to 1 (*no pride in being a member of the society*) to 7 (*a great deal of pride in being a member of the society*)	–
Q129	**I believe that opportunities for a leadership position should be** (1 = *more available for women than for men* to 7 = *more available for men than for women*)	The scale ends need to be reversed to 1 (*more available for men than for women*) to 7 (*more available for women than for men*)	–
Q130	**I believe that people should** (1 = *live for the present* to 7 = *live for the future*)	–	The SPSS analysis suggested that the scale should be reversely recoded for statistical purposes to increase α.
Q134	**I believe that major rewards should be based on** (1 = *only factors other than performance effectiveness* to 7 = *only performance effectiveness*)	The scale ends need to be reversed to 1 (*only performance effectiveness*) to 7 (*only factors other than performance effectiveness*)	–

8.3 A Country Study for Brazil, Canada, and Germany

Three countries (national cultures) with multiple respondents were identified in the pre-test data—Brazil, Canada, and Germany. The upcoming chapter demonstrates a country study for Brazil, Canada, and Germany regarding the extent of each UDC. The following numbers of respondents by each country participated and fully completed the UDC questionnaire in the pre-test: Brazil n = 7, Canada n = 10, and Germany n = 12. It is acknowledged that a number of 7, 10, or 12 is not representative to display the complete national culture profile. However, the upcoming country study should give insights into the design of the UDCs measured by the developed UDC questionnaire.

The mean scores of each of the 34 items (without item Q15) from the UDC questionnaire were calculated. For the comparison of the UDC scores with the national culture scores of existing cultural taxonomies, the scores of the corresponding cultural dimension were considered; thus, no item-specific scores were retrieved from the existing cultural taxonomies since these were not applicable in most cases.

Table 8.22 demonstrates the respondents' background information from the pre-test for Brazil, Canada, and Germany.

Table 8.22 Overview of Pre-Test Respondents for Brazil, Canada, and Germany

Information	**Brazil**	**Canada**	**Germany**
Gender	Female n = 2, Male n = 5	Female n = 4, Male n = 6	Female n = 5, Male n = 7
Age (Ø years)	31.42	29.9	30.58
Formal Education (Ø years)	20.71	18.8	17.75
Professional Work (Ø years)	7.86	8.7	3.92
Current Job	Professional Worker n = 3, Position in Higher Education n = 3	Professional Worker n = 6, Position in Higher Education n = 4	Professional Worker n = 3, Position in Higher Education n = 8, Unemployed n = 1

Each researcher of the 11 selected cultural taxonomies calculated their national culture scores differently. Therefore, the country score calculations and their adjustment to a 7-point scale were reviewed as applied in the UDC questionnaire of the respective cultural taxonomy. The calculation for the eight cultural taxonomies is demonstrated in Table 8.23. For each item, a pre-check of the scale ends affiliation was conducted, causing in case if needed a reversely rescaling. The rescaling was done by subtracting eight from the calculated item score. Furthermore, it should be taken into consideration that some of the cultural taxonomies (e.g., Minkov (2007) and Schwartz (1992, 1994b)) distinguished between French and English Canadian respondents as well as between east and west German respondents. In the pre-test of the UDC questionnaire, no distinguishing between French and English Canadians or between east and west Germany was considered.

UDC Distribution of Power and Status

The UDC Distribution of Power and Status refers to the acknowledgment and extent of inequalities among individuals, and the extent of dependency of individuals on higher-ranked individuals in national culture, encompassing three cultural components—the components of structure of power relationships (hierarchy versus egalitarianism), allocation of power and status (by family background, gender egalitarianism, and performance orientation), and employee fee. The UDC Distribution of Power and Status was represented in the questionnaire by the five items Q13, Q123, Q129, Q131, and Q134.

The country profiles for Brazil, Canada, and Germany for the UDC Distribution of Power and Status are displayed in Table 8.24.

In total, the Brazilian respondents (n = 7) from the pre-test sample revealed a total UDC Distribution of Power and Status score of 3.924, indicating in more detail that Brazilian subordinates tend to be most likely afraid to contradict their boss, respect could depend on the family background of an individual, leadership positions should be slightly more available for women than for men, power should be equally shared throughout the society, and major rewards should be based slightly more on only performance effectiveness.

The Brazilian sample scored the highest total UDC Distribution of Power and Status score compared to Canadians and Germans. Comparing the Brazilian UDC scores with the scores from the original cultural dimensions, two peculiarities became applicable regarding the items Q129 and Q134. In the original cultural dimension of Gender Egalitarianism by House et al. (2004, 2007, 2014), item Q129 was retrieved. It was indicated that Brazilians tend to have a relatively high degree of gender egalitarianism, pointing to a relatively high interest in minimizing gender inequalities. The scale indication in the original item V3_39 from House et al. (2004, 2007, 2014) demonstrated for the maximum scale end of 7 that leadership positions should be more available for women than for men. Thus, a score of 4.99 would then indicate that Brazilians tend to favor a higher availability of leadership positions for women than for men. Regarding item Q134, Brazilians cultural score of the cultural dimension of Performance Orientation by House et al. (2004, 2007, 2014) indicated that Brazilians tend to a high degree of encouragement and reward of group members for constant performance improvement and excellence by a score of 6.13.

Table 8.23 Implications Country Score Calculation per Cultural Taxonomy

Cultural Taxonomy	Implications
Fiske (1991, 1992)	*No specific country scores were applicable.*
Hofstede (2001; Hofstede et al., 2010)	The following formula was operationalized for the calculation of the country score suitable to a scale from 1 to 7: $\left(\frac{\text{Indicated Country Score}}{100}\right) \times 7 = \text{Revised Country Score}$ The latest applicable country scores for the Hofstede cultural taxonomy were retrieved, as applicable on his website[4].
House et al. (2004, 2007, 2014)	The latest scores, as applicable on the website,[5] were taken into consideration, in some cases requiring a reverse rescaling.
Inglehart et al. (2014)	For the two selected items—item Q19 and Q114—from the cultural taxonomy by Inglehart et al. (2014), the respondents in the original questionnaire could choose between the value of religious faith/interdependency is important or is not important. In order to rescale the item score to the 7-point scale of the UDC questionnaire, the following formula was applied: $\frac{7 \times \text{No. of Respondents Important} + 1 \times \text{No. of Respondents Not Important}}{\text{Total No. of Country Respondents}} = \text{Revised Country Score}$ The numbers of WVS wave 5[6] were retrieved since, in wave 6 and wave 7, not all three countries were applicable.
Kluckhohn and Strodtbeck (1961)	*No concrete country scores were applicable.*
Minkov (2007)	The following formula was developed and applied; based on the country score indication in Minkov (2007): $\left(\frac{\text{Indicated Country Score} \times 7}{\text{Max. of Indicated Country Score}}\right) = \text{Revised Country Score}$

(continued)

[4] https://www.hofstede-insights.com/country-comparison/brazil,canada,germany/; retrieval date March 2021.

[5] https://globeproject.com/results/countries/BRA?menu=list#list; https://globeproject.com/results/countries/CAN?menu=list# list; https://globeproject.com/results/countries/DEU?menu=list#list; retrieval date March 2021.

[6] https://www.worldvaluessurvey.org/WVSOnline.jsp, retrieval date April, 2021.

Table 8.23 (continued)

Cultural Taxonomy	Implications
Schwartz (1992, 1994b)	First, the item affiliation to the indicated cultural dimension side was checked. Schwartz (1992, 1994) used for his country score calculation a 9-point scale. A scale shift by 2 needed to be conducted. As a result, the following formula was developed in order to calculate the revised country scores: $\left(\frac{(\text{Indicated Country Score}+2)\times 7}{9}\right) = \text{Revised Country Score}$
Trompenaars and Hampden-Turner (2004, 2012)	The calculation of the revised country scores required mixed methods since each of the items was measured on a different scale. Mainly, the following formula was applied: $\left(\frac{\text{Indicated Country Score}\times 7}{100}\right) = \text{Revised Country Score}$

Compared to Brazilians, the Canadian respondents (n = 10) from the pre-test scored the lowest in the UDC Distribution of Power and Status by a total score of 3.42. The respondents from the pre-test sample indicated that Canadian subordinates tend to be afraid to contradict their bosses, respect does somewhat not dependent on an individual's family background, leadership positions should be slightly more available for women than for men, power should be equally shared throughout the society, and major rewards should be eventually based on only performance effectiveness.

Compared to the original scores, three main discrepancies in the items Q13, Q129, and Q134 became applicable. For item Q13, the Canadian respondents from the pre-test indicated that subordinates are afraid to contradict their boss; Hofstede (2001; Hofstede et al., 2010) original cultural dimension score pointed to the opposite circumstance. The discrepancy could stem from applying the total score of the cultural dimension of Power Distance by Hofstede (2001; Hofstede et al., 2010), consisting of four items and calculated based on a specific weighted formula.

Likewise, to the discrepancy in the Brazilian item score for Q129, also the Canadian pre-test respondents indicated that leadership positions should be more available for women than for men; in contrast to the applicable score of 5.11 for the cultural dimension of Gender Egalitarianism by House et al. (2004, 2007, 2014). The cultural dimension of Gender Egalitarianism by House et al. (2004, 2007, 2014) displays the degree to which a collective tends to minimize gender inequality. When reviewing the item V3_39 from House et al. (2004, 2007, 2014), the indicated score of 5.11 would imply that respondents also tend to favor that leadership positions

Table 8.24 Country Study Results for the Universal Dimension of Culture (UDC) Distribution of Power and Status

Item (Origin)	**Brazil** (Extent UDC Brazil; Extent Original Dimension)	**Canada** (Extent UDC Canada; Extent Original Dimension)	**Germany** (Extent UDC Germany; Extent Original Dimension)
Q13 (Hofstede / Power Distance)	Subordinates are never afraid to contradict their boss — 4.83, 5.3 — Subordinates are every time afraid to contradict their boss	Subordinates are never afraid to contradict their boss — 2.73, 4.8 — Subordinates are every time afraid to contradict their boss	Subordinates are never afraid to contradict their boss — 2.45, 4.6 — Subordinates are every time afraid to contradict their boss
Q123 (Trompenaars / Ascription vs. Achievement)	Respect depends not on the family background — 3.1, 4.0 — Respect depends highly on the family background	Respect depends not on the family background — 1.91, 2.7 — Respect depends highly on the family background	Respect depends not on the family background — 2.82, 2.8 — Respect depends highly on the family background
Q129 (House et al. / Gender Egalitarianism)	Leadership positions should be more available for women than for men — 3.6, 4.99 — Leadership positions should be more available for men than for women	Leadership positions should be more available for women than for men — 3.4, 5.11 — Leadership positions should be more available for men than for women	Leadership positions should be more available for women than for men — 3.6, 4.9 — Leadership positions should be more available for men than for women
Q131 (House et al. / Power Distance)	Power should be shared equally throughout the society — 2.35, 2.3 — Power should be concentrated at the top	Power should be shared equally throughout the society — 1.8, 2.7 — Power should be concentrated at the top	Power should be shared equally throughout the society — 2.69, 3.5 — Power should be concentrated at the top
Q134 (House / Performance Orientation	Major rewards should be based on only factors other than performance effectiveness — 4.1, 6.13 — Major rewards should be based on only performance effectiveness	Major rewards should be based on only factors other than performance effectiveness — 4.4, 6.15 — Major rewards should be based on only performance effectiveness	Major rewards should be based on only factors other than performance effectiveness — 4.0, 6.15 — Major rewards should be based on only performance effectiveness
Total Score	3.925	3.42	3.7

Note. The cultural taxonomies, as indicated for the origin of the items, are only displayed in an abbreviated way.

should be more available for women than for men; which would be in line with the findings of the UDC and the pre-test sample. Finally, the discrepancy for item Q124 between the House et al. (2004, 2007, 2014) score and the UDC score could also be explained by the lack of respondents in the pre-test sample. Thus, both scores indicate that Canadians value reward by performance effectiveness, the score by House et al. (2004, 2007, 2014) indicates higher volatility for that circumstance.

In the overall UDC Distribution of Power and Status score, the German participants (n = 12) of the pre-test scored between the Canadian and Brazilian respondents with a total score of 3.7. In detail, the respondents indicated that German subordinates tend to be afraid to contradict their bosses, respect does rather not depend on the family background, leadership positions should be slightly more available for women than for men, power should also be slightly shared equally throughout the society, and major rewards could be or could not be based on performance effectiveness. Likewise, to the Canadian respondence sample, the German respondents from the pre-test revealed three significant discrepancies in the original cultural dimensions scores regarding Q13, Q129, and Q134.

Likewise, to Brazil and Canada, the discrepancy in the German pre-test sample for the items Q129 and Q134 could be explained by the same evidence. Q13 indicated a substantial discrepancy between 2.45 and 4.6. According to Hofstede (2001; Hofstede et al., 2010), Germans tend not to be afraid to contradict their bosses; in the UDC pre-test sample, the German respondents indicated the opposite. A possible explanation for the discrepancy could lie in the multi-fold cultural components of the cultural dimension of Power Distance by Hofstede (2001; Hofstede et al., 2010), whereas the score of 4.6 of the UDC sample only refers to the concept of employee fear.

UDC Relationship with the Natural Environment

The UDC Relationship with the Natural Environment displays the extent of relationships of individuals with their natural environment, expressed in their desire either to control or to live in harmony with their natural environment. The UDC Relationship with the Natural Environment encompasses two cultural components—the cultural component of mastery versus harmony and the cultural component of relationship with nature. The UDC was operationalized by the four items Q110, Q113, Q116, and Q121 in the UDC questionnaire.

The overall country profile for Brazil, Canada, and Germany of the pre-test sample compared to the original item scores for the UDC Relationship with the Natural Environment is displayed in Table 8.25.

The calculation of the rescaled scores for the cultural dimension of Internal versus Outer Direction by Trompenaars and Hampden-Turner (2004, 2012) required

Table 8.25 Country Study Results for the Universal Dimension of Culture (UDC) Relationship with the Natural Environment

Item (Origin)	Brazil (Extent UDC Brazil; Extent Original Dimension)	Canada (Extent UDC Canada; Extent Original Dimension)	Germany (Extent UDC Germany; Extent Original Dimension)
Q110 (Schwartz / Harmony)	Natural preservation is not at all important — 4.69 — 6.6 — Natural preservation is extremely important	Natural preservation is not at all important — 4.66 — 6.2 — Natural preservation is extremely important	Natural preservation is not at all important — 5.09 — 6.0 — Natural preservation is extremely important
Q113 (Schwartz / Harmony)	Unity with nature is not at all important — 4.69 — 5.9 — Unity with nature is extremely important	Unity with nature is not at all important — 4.66 — 5.5 — Unity with nature is extremely important	Unity with nature is not at all important — 5.09 — 5.5 — Unity with nature is extremely important
Q116* (Trompenaars / Internal vs. Outer Direction)	It is not worthwhile to control important natural forces — 2.73 — 4.0 — It is worthwhile to control important natural forces	It is not worthwhile to control important natural forces — 2.94 — 4.4 — It is worthwhile to control important natural forces	It is not worthwhile to control important natural forces — 2.1 — 4.7 — It is worthwhile to control important natural forces
Q121 (Trompenaars / Internal vs. Outer Direction)	Nature should not take its course, and we should not accept it — 4.0 — 4.27 — Nature should take ist course, and we have to accept it	Nature should not take its course, and we should not accept it — 3.8 — 4.06 — Nature should take ist course, and we have to accept it	Nature should not take its course, and we should not accept it — 3.6 — 4.9 — Nature should take ist course, and we have to accept it
Total Score	5.125	4.77	4.6

Note. * For the total UDC score, the indicated UDC score was reversely re-coded to display the correct extent of the scale ends (for further explanation, please refer to Table 8.14). The cultural taxonomies, as indicated for the origin of the items, are only displayed in an abbreviated way.

special treatment, since in the original version, the separated items Q116 and Q121, constituted one item, allowing respondents to choose between the one extreme *trying to control important natural forces* and the other extreme *nature should take its course*. Trompenaars and Hampden-Turner (2004, 2012) only indicated the percentage of respondents who believe it is worth trying to control natural forces.

In total, the Brazilian respondents achieved the highest total score for the UDC Relationship with the Natural Environment by 5.125, indicating a relatively high degree for the relationship with the natural environment.

In total, Brazil achieved the highest total score for the UDC Relationship with the Natural Environment by 5.125, indicating a relatively high degree of the concept of relationship with the natural environment. More precisely, the Brazilian respondents of the pre-test indicated that they tend to place high importance on preserving their natural environment, high importance on the unity with nature, rather a medium position in if it is worthwhile controlling important natural forces or not, as well as a medium position between to accept nature's course or not. Besides minor discrepancies in the scores of the items Q113 and Q116, a more significant discrepancy between the UDC pre-test score and the score of the original cultural dimension became applicable for item Q110. In the UDC score, the Brazilian respondents indicated that natural preservation is of extreme importance; in contrast, in the original cultural dimension score of Harmony versus Mastery by Schwartz (1992, 1994b), the respondents indicated that they only slightly tend to place importance on natural preservation. Possible explanations for the differences could be either the not representative number or Brazilian pre-test respondents, and the applied rescaling calculation for the cultural dimension scores by Schwartz (1992, 1994b), please refer to Table 8.23, or the rising urgency to take on actions in regards to environmental issues.

A lower total score was reached by the Canadian respondents of the pre-test for the UDC Relationship with the Natural Environment with a score of 4.775, indicating a relatively high degree for the relationship of individuals with their natural environment. The in-depth review of the single item scores revealed the following extent of each underlying cultural component for the Canadian respondents in the pre-test: high importance is placed on the preservation of nature and the unity with nature, a minor tendency to the worthwhileness to control important natural forces, and slight tendency to let nature take its course.

For the Canadian sample, minor discrepancies between the UDC score and the original cultural dimension score were applicable for Q110, Q113, and Q121. A more significant discrepancy between the original score of the cultural dimension of Internal versus Outer Direction by Trompenaars and Hampden-Turner (2004, 2012) and the UDC score became applicable for item Q116. The UDC score of the

Canadian respondents of the pre-test sample reached 4.4, indicating that they found it worthwhile trying to control natural forces.

In contrast, the original score by Trompenaars and Hampden-Turner (2004, 2012) would indicate a tendency to it is not worthwhile trying to control natural forces. It could be assumed that either the sample of the UDC pre-test was too small (Canada n = 10) or flaws in the rescaling of the original cultural dimension score took place.

The German respondents reached a total UDC Relationship with the Natural Environment score of 4.6, indicating a relatively high score of the extent of the relationship of individuals with their natural environment. In more detail, the following became applicable in the scores of the German respondents from the pre-test sample: high importance is placed on the preservation of the natural environment, and relatively high importance on the unity with nature; the German respondents instead try to control important natural forces than to let nature take its course. The most significant discrepancy between the UDC score and the original cultural dimension score for the German respondents was identified for item Q116. Likewise, to the other two respondents' groups of Canadians and Brazilians, possible explanations for the significant discrepancy of the score could either lie in the rescaling calculation of the score of the cultural dimension of Internal versus Outer Direction by Trompenaars and Hampden-Turner (2004, 2012) or the not representative sample score of n = 12 German respondents in the pre-test.

UDC Social Organization

The third UDC refers to the structures of social relationships regarding the concept of individualism versus collectivism in national culture, represented by the following five underlying cultural components: universalism versus particularism, group decision making, loyalty, group affiliation, and pride. The UDC Social Organization was operationalized by five items Q17, Q117, Q119, Q120, and Q126.

Table 8.26 displays the country profiles for Brazil, Canada, and Germany for the UDC Social Organization.

For the items Q117 and Q120, retrieved from the cultural taxonomy by Fiske (1991, 1992), no country scores in the original cultural dimension of Communal Sharing by Fiske (1991, 1992) were retrievable. Thus, no comparison between the UDC score and the original cultural dimensions score was conceivable for items Q117 and Q120.

Germany's highest total UDC score was reached with a value of 5.12, indicating a relatively high degree in the structure of social relationships regarding the concept of individualism versus collectivism. In more detail, the German respondents of the pre-test sample indicated that people of a different society are perfectly acceptable as neighbors, decisions tend to be made by consensus, leaders should highly encourage

Table 8.26 Country Study Results for the Universal Dimension of Culture (UDC) Social Organization

Item (Origin)	**Brazil** (Extent UDC Brazil / Extent Original Dimension)	**Canada** (Extent UDC Canada / Extent Original Dimension)	**Germany** (Extent UDC Germany / Extent Original Dimension)
Q17 (Minkov / Exclusionism vs. Universalism)	People of a different society are totally unacceptable as neighbors (1) — 3.57 (Original); 6.3 (UDC) — People of a different society are totally acceptable as neighbors (7)	People of a different society are totally unacceptable as neighbors (1) — 5.57 (Original); 6.1 (UDC) — People of a different society are totally acceptable as neighbors (7)	People of a different society are totally unacceptable as neighbors (1) — 5.36 (Original); 6.3 (UDC) — People of a different society are totally acceptable as neighbors (7)
Q117 *(Fiske / Communal Sharing)*	Decisions are not made by consensus (1) — 3.3 (UDC) — Decisions are made by consensus (7)	Decisions are not made by consensus (1) — 4.2 (UDC) — Decisions are made by consensus (7)	Decisions are not made by consensus (1) — 4.9 (UDC) — Decisions are made by consensus (7)
Q119 (House / Institutional Collectivism)	Leaders should not encourage group loyalty even if individual goals suffer (1) — 4.4 (UDC); 5.62 (Original) — Leaders should encourage group loyalty even if individual goals suffer (7)	Leaders should not encourage group loyalty even if individual goals suffer (1) — 3.1 (UDC); 4.17 (Original) — Leaders should encourage group loyalty even if individual goals suffer (7)	Leaders should not encourage group loyalty even if individual goals suffer (1) — 4.68 (Original); 5.6 (UDC) — Leaders should encourage group loyalty even if individual goals suffer (7)
Q120 *(Fiske / Communal Sharing)*	People of the society develop no similar attitudes and values (1) — 4.4 (UDC) — People of the society develop very similar attitudes and values (7)	People of the society develop no similar attitudes and values (1) — 3.6 (UDC) — People of the society develop very similar attitudes and values (7)	People of the society develop no similar attitudes and values (1) — 4.5 (UDC) — People of the society develop very similar attitudes and values (7)
Q126* (House / In-Group Collectivism)	Members of a society should take a great deal of pride in being a member of the society (1) — 2.85 (Original); 3.1 (UDC) — Members of a society should take no pride in being a member of the society (7)	Members of a society should take a great deal of pride in being a member of the society (1) — 2.03 (Original); 2.8 (UDC) — Members of a society should take no pride in being a member of the society (7)	Members of a society should take a great deal of pride in being a member of the society (1) — 2.78 (Original); 3.7 (UDC) — Members of a society should take no pride in being a member of the society (7)
Total Score	4.66	4.44	5.12

Note. The scores for item Q126 were reversely recoded to adjust the scale ends to calculate the total country score. The cultural taxonomies, as indicated for the origin of the items, are only displayed in an abbreviated way.

group loyalty even if individual goals suffer, people develop to a slight extent similar attitudes and values, and members should take some pride in being a member of the German society. The comparison of the UDC scores and the original scores for the sample of German respondents revealed no peculiarities, and the UDC measured scores tend to mirror the indications of the original cultural dimension scores.

The Brazilian respondents in the pre-test sample scored lower than the German respondents, with a total score of 4.66 in the UDC Social Organization. The Brazilian respondents of the pre-test displayed the following information: people of a different society are perfectly acceptable as neighbors, decision tent not to be made by consensus in Brazilian, leaders should slightly encourage group loyalty even if individual goals suffer, people slightly tend to develop similar attitudes and values, and members should take a deal of pride in being a member of the Brazilian society. A significant discrepancy in the sample was applicable for item Q17. The Brazilian respondents of the pre-test indicated that people of a different society are perfectly acceptable as neighbors, whereas, in the original cultural dimension by Minkov (2007), Brazilian respondents indicated that individuals of a different society are unacceptable as neighbors. An explanation could be again the low sample size ($n = 7$) of the Brazilian respondents in the UDC pre-test; or that Minkov (2007) analyzed the WVS wave 4, conducted between 1999–2004, whereas the pre-test was conducted in 2021. A potential cultural change could have taken place.

The Canadian respondents reached the lowest total score for the UDC Social Organization with a score of 4.44, indicating a slightly higher degree of structures of social relationships regarding the concept of individualism versus collectivism. The Canadian respondents of the pre-test indicated in more detail that people of a different society are almost perfectly acceptable as neighbors, decisions tend to be made by consensus in Canada, leaders should instead slightly tend not to encourage group loyalty if individual goals suffer, people have a slight tendency not to develop similar attitudes and values, and members should take pride in being a member of the society. The UDC item scores and the original scores indicated no peculiarities.

UDC Perception and Use of Time

The fourth UDC Perception and Use of Time refer to the extent of perception, including the view of and use of time, displayed by the following four underlying cultural components: perception of time (for past, present, and future), number of handled tasks at a time, planning ahead, and time horizon (long-term versus short-term orientation). In total, the UDC Perception and Use of Time was operationalized by the five items Q14, Q18, Q122, and Q127.

As identified in the qualitative analysis of the pre-test, item Q14 seems unsuitable to measure the time horizon and was not chosen to be integrated into the analysis of this case study. Furthermore, item Q122, addressing the number of handled tasks at a time, was retrieved from Lindquist and Kaufman-Scarborough (2007), from which no country scores could be retrieved. Likewise, it accounts for item Q18, retrieved from Hills (1977, 1998) and Lane (1976), which developed a questionnaire for the cultural taxonomy by Kluckhohn and Strodtbeck (1961). Since the three indicated items—item Q18, Q122, and Q127—have no identical scale end for the underlying components pointing to one similar conceptual extent, no total UDC Perception and Use of Time scores were calculated.

Table 8.27 displays the country profile for Brazil, Canada, and Germany for the UDC Perception and Use of Time, without item Q15.

In total, the Brazilian respondents of the pre-test revealed the following picture for the UDC Perception and Use of Time: in case of donating money, Brazilians think it should be best spent to make a better life for the future, they slightly tend to polychronism, and social gatherings should be planned. The UDC score and the original score for item Q127 by House et al. (2004, 2007, 2014) did not indicate any significant discrepancy. The Canadian respondents indicated a slightly different picture for donating money, indicating that it would best spend to make a better life now; they slightly tend to monochronism, and only slightly to plan social gatherings well in advance. Likewise, to the Brazilian sample, the UDC score for item Q127 only indicates a minor discrepancy to the original cultural dimension item score by House et al. (2004, 2007, 2014). The German respondents indicate a strong tendency to spend donated money to make a better life in the future, with a minor extent Germans tend to polychronism, and social gatherings should be rather spontaneous than planned.

A minor discrepancy between the UDC score and the score for the original cultural dimension of Future Orientation by House et al. (2004, 2007, 2014) was applicable for item Q127, which could be explained by the non-representative number of German respondents ($n = 12$) of the UDC pre-test.

UDC Uncertainty Avoidance and Coping Mechanisms

The UDC Uncertainty Avoidance and Coping Mechanisms refers to the extent of uncertainty avoidance and the mechanisms for coping and dealing with uncertain and unknown situations in national cultures, including the four operationalized cultural components of stress, rule and regulation obedience, future orientation, and coping and dealing with uncertainty. The UDC questionnaire's items Q11, Q118, Q130, and Q132 operationalized these four underlying cultural components.

The country profiles of Brazil, Canada, and Germany are displayed for the UDC Uncertainty Avoidance and Coping Mechanisms in Table 8.28.

Table 8.27 Country Study Results for the Universal Dimension of Culture (UDC) Perception and Use of Time

Item (Origin)	**Brazil** (Extent UDC Brazil; Extent Original Dimension)	**Canada** (Extent UDC Canada; Extent Original Dimension)	**Germany** (Extent UDC Germany; Extent Original Dimension)
Q18 (Kluckhohn / Time Orientation)	Donated money should be best spend to keep the old ways and customs alive — 5.7 — Donated money should be best spend to make a better life for the future	Donated money should be best spend to keep the old ways and customs alive — 4.9 — Donated money should be best spend to make a better life for the future	Donated money should be best spend to keep the old ways and customs alive — 6.8 — Donated money should be best spend to make a better life for the future
Q122 (Lindquist & Scarboroguh)	Preferences to do only one activity at the same time (monochronism) — 4.3 — Preferences to do more activities at the same time (polychronism)	Preferences to do only one activity at the same time (monochronism) — 3.8 — Preferences to do more activities at the same time (polychronism)	Preferences to do only one activity at the same time (monochronism) — 4.6 — Preferences to do more activities at the same time (polychronism)
Q127 (House / Future Orientation)	Social gatherings should be spontaneous — 4.9 — 5.69 — Social gatherings should be planned well in advance	Social gatherings should be spontaneous — 4.4 — 5.35 — Social gatherings should be planned well in advance	Social gatherings should be spontaneous — 3.9 — 5.23 — Social gatherings should be planned well in advance
Total Score	*4.97*	*4.37*	*5.1*

Note. The cultural taxonomies, as indicated for the origin of the items, are only displayed in an abbreviated way.

Comparing the country profiles, it became applicable that the German and Brazilian respondents from the pre-sample reached almost the same total score value of the UDC total score for the UDC Uncertainty Avoidance and Coping Mechanisms—Brazil indicated a total UDC score of 4.075 and Germany 4.025. In contrast, the Canadian respondents yield a marginal lower total UDC score of 3.7.

In more detail, the Brazilian respondents displayed the following country profile: Brazilians tend to feel less likely nervous or tense, societal instructions and requirements should be spelled out in detail, people should rather live for the present, and people living a structured life with few unexpected events are seen to miss a lot of excitement. One peculiarity in comparing the UDC scores and the country scores became applicable for item Q11 which in the original version stemmed from Hofstede and Minkov (2013), referring to the cultural dimension of Uncertainty Avoidance. The following several explanations are possible: the pre-test of the UDC sample was conducted during COVID-19 pandemic times in 2021, which would instead assume an overall higher level of nervousness. This was not the case for the Brazilian respondents of the UDC pre-test, displaying a score of 3.3 for item Q11.

In the original version by Hofstede and Minkov (2013), the items for stress were encompassed into a set of four items, and the Uncertainty Avoidance score by Hofstede and Minkov (2013) was calculated by that the stress item was subtracted from the item "how would you describe your state of health these days". This circumstance could lead to a discrepancy between the score of the UDC for item Q11 and Hofstede and Minkovs' (2013) cultural dimension score. Additionally, in the original version of the items by Hofstede and Minkov (2013) of the cultural dimension of Uncertainty Avoidance, the scale ends are displayed reversely, 1 (*always*) to 5 (*never*). In contrast, item Q11 was displayed in the UDC questionnaire with 1 (*never*) to 7 (*always*).

The German country displayed a similar profile than the Brazilian, as Germans tend slightly never to feel nervous or tense, societal requirements and instructions should be spelled out in detail, people should live for the future, and people living a structured life with few unexpected events are seen to miss the excitement. Likewise, to the Brazilian sample, a discrepancy for item Q11 was applicable between the UDC score and the original cultural dimension item score by Hofstede and Minkov (2013). Similar explanations as for the Brazilian sample (please refer to the previous paragraph) could be assumed.

The Canadian respondents displayed a slightly different picture for the UDC Uncertainty Avoidance and Coping Mechanisms, indicating that Canadians tend never to feel nervous or tense, societal requirements and instructions should be

Table 8.28 Country Study Results for the Universal Dimension of Culture (UDC) Uncertainty Avoidance and Coping Mechanisms

Item (Origin)	**Brazil** (Extent UDC Brazil / Extent Original Dimension)	**Canada** (Extent UDC Canada / Extent Original Dimension)	**Germany** (Extent UDC Germany / Extent Original Dimension)
Q11 (Hofstede / Uncertainty Avoidance)	I never feel nervous or tense — 3.3 — 5.32 — I feel ever time nervous or tense 1 2 3 4 5 6 7	I never feel nervous or tense — 3.2 — 3.36 — I feel ever time nervous or tense 1 2 3 4 5 6 7	I never feel nervous or tense — 3.3 — 4.55 — I feel ever time nervous or tense 1 2 3 4 5 6 7
Q118 (House / Uncertainty Avoidance)	Societal requirements and instructions should not be spelled out in detail — 4.99 — 5.0 — Societal requirements and instructions should be spelled out in detail 1 2 3 4 5 6 7	Societal requirements and instructions should not be spelled out in detail — 3.75 — 5.0 — Societal requirements and instructions should be spelled out in detail 1 2 3 4 5 6 7	Societal requirements and instructions should not be spelled out in detail — 3.94 — 5.2 — Societal requirements and instructions should be spelled out in detail 1 2 3 4 5 6 7
Q130 (House / Future Orientation)	People should live for the present — 4.3 — 5.69 — People should live for the future 1 2 3 4 5 6 7	People should live for the present — 3.0 — 5.35 — People should live for the future 1 2 3 4 5 6 7	People should live for the present — 4.5 — 5.23 — People should live for the future 1 2 3 4 5 6 7
Q132 (House / Uncertainty Avoidance)	A structured life with few unexpected events is missing a lot of excitement — 3.7 — 4.99 — A structured life with few unexpected events is an exciting life 1 2 3 4 5 6 7	A structured life with few unexpected events is missing a lot of excitement — 3.6 — 3.75 — A structured life with few unexpected events is an exciting life 1 2 3 4 5 6 7	A structured life with few unexpected events is missing a lot of excitement — 3.1 — 3.94 — A structured life with few unexpected events is an exciting life 1 2 3 4 5 6 7
Total Score	4.075	3.7	4.025

Note. The cultural taxonomies, as indicated for the origin of the items, are only displayed in an abbreviated way.

spelled out in detail, people should rather live for the present, and people living a structured life are seen to miss out on excitements.

A discrepancy in the UDC score and the original cultural dimension score in the Canadian country profile was applicable for item Q130. House et al. (2004, 2007, 2014) indicated in their cultural dimension of Future Orientation that Canadians would tend to live for the future, whereas the UDC score indicated that Canadians tend to favor living for the present. The item analysis did not reveal any plausible explanation for the discrepancy, only the sample size of the pre-test, which was not represented with only 10 participants and not equally the respondents from the GLOBE study by House et al. (2004, 2007, 2014), could be again an explanation for the discrepancy.

UDC Human Orientation

The UDC Human Orientation displays the extent of assertiveness versus tenderness in national culture, addressing two the cultural components of human orientation and assertiveness versus tenderness. The UDC Human Orientation was operationalized by the items Q125, Q128, Q133, and Q135 in the UDC questionnaire. The country profiles for Brazil, Canada, and Germany for the UDC Orientation are displayed in Table 8.29.

The set of items—Q125, Q128, Q133, and Q135—was retrieved from two different cultural dimensions of one cultural taxonomy. The items Q128, Q133, and Q135, are retrieved from the cultural dimension of Humane Orientation by House et al. (2004, 2007, 2014); thus, the UDC scores should demonstrate similar values for the items and extent of the cultural dimension. All three total country scores for the UDC Human Orientation range between relatively high (Germany with a total UDC score of 5.175) and high (Brazil with a total UDC score of 5.825 and Canada with 5.525). As subsumed before, ideally, the scores of the UDC should equal the scores from the two cultural dimensions of Assertiveness versus Tenderness and Humane Orientation by House et al. (2004, 2007, 2014). In the analysis, this circumstance was confirmed since no significant discrepancy between the UDC scores and the scores from the original dimensions was applicable for Brazil, Canada, and Germany in the pre-test sample.

The Brazilian respondents from the pre-test indicated a high score in the UDC Human Orientation. Likewise, to the original scores, the Brazilians tend to have non-aggressive, non-dominant, and tender behavior, as well as people should be encouraged to be very concerned, very sensitive, and very friendly towards others.

The Canadian respondents from the pre-test yield a score between relatively high and high in the UDC Human Orientation. Again, likewise to the original cultural dimension scores, the Canadian respondents indicated a relative tendency to

Table 8.29 Country Study Results for the Universal Dimension of Culture (UDC) Human Orientation

Item (Origin)	**Brazil** (Extent UDC Brazil; Extent Original Dimension)	**Canada** (Extent UDC Canada; Extent Original Dimension)	**Germany** (Extent UDC Germany; Extent Original Dimension)
Q125* (House / Assertiveness)	Non-agressive, non-dominant, and tender — 2.7; 2.9 — Agressive, dominant, and tough	Non-agressive, non-dominant, and tender — 3.3; 4.15 — Agressive, dominant, and tough	Non-agressive, non-dominant, and tender — 2.9; 3.23 — Agressive, dominant, and tough
Q128 (House / Humane Orientation)	People should be encouraged to be not at all concerned about others — 6.0; 5.68 — People should be encouraged to be very concerned about others	People should be encouraged to be not at all concerned about others — 5.7; 5.64 — People should be encouraged to be very concerned about others	People should be encouraged to be not at all concerned about others — 5.1; 5.44 — People should be encouraged to be very concerned about others
Q133 (House / Humane Orientation)	People should be encouraged to be not at all sensitive towards others — 5.9; 5.68 — People should be encouraged to be very sensitive towards others	People should be encouraged to be not at all sensitive towards others — 5.5; 5.64 — People should be encouraged to be very sensitive towards others	People should be encouraged to be not at all sensitive towards others — 5.1; 5.44 — People should be encouraged to be very sensitive towards others
Q135 (House / Humane Orientation)	People should be encouraged to be very unfriendly — 6.1; 5.68 — People should be encouraged to be very friendly	People should be encouraged to be very unfriendly — 6.2; 5.64 — People should be encouraged to be very friendly	People should be encouraged to be very unfriendly — 5.1; 5.44 — People should be encouraged to be very friendly
Total Score	5.825	5.525	5.175

Note. * The scores needed to be reversely recoded to calculate the total score (for further explanation, please refer to Table 8.18). The cultural taxonomies, as indicated for the origin of the items, are only displayed in an abbreviated way.

non-aggressive, non-dominant, and tender behavior, whereas individuals should be encouraged to be very concerned, sensitive, and friendly towards others. The German respondents displayed the lowest UDC score and a tendency to non-aggressive, non-dominant, and tender behavior and a relatively great extent to encourage people to be concerned, sensitive, and friendly towards others.

UDC Gratification and Expression of Emotions, Feelings, and Desires
The UDC Gratification and Expression of Emotions, Feelings, and Desires refers to the extent of gratification and expression of desires, feelings, and emotions. The UDC encompasses the two cultural components of the extent of gratification of desires and feelings and expression of emotions. In contrast, only the cultural component of the extent of gratification of desires and feelings and its sub-components of the importance of leisure, moderation, level of happiness, and perception of life control were empirically operationalized. As a result, four items were operationalized for the UDC Gratification and Expression of Emotions, Feelings, and Desires in the UDC questionnaire—the items Q12, Q16, Q112, and Q124.

The country profiles for Brazil, Canada, and Germany are displayed Table 8.30 in an overview for the UDC Gratification and Expression of Emotions, Desires, and Feelings.

The Canadian respondents from the pre-test sample scored the highest total score for the UDC Gratification and Expression of Emotions, Desires, and Feelings by 4.8, indicating a relatively high extent of gratification and expression of desires, feelings, and emotions in the Canadian culture. In more detail, the Canadian respondents indicated that they feel to a relatively high degree to have a great deal of choice/control over the way their life turns out, almost highly tend to be happy every time, whereas they instead tend to place no importance on the avoidance of extreme feelings and actions, and instead tend to that leisure makes their life worth living not to work. Only for item Q12, a discrepancy between the UDC score and the original cultural dimension score of the cultural dimension of Indulgence versus Restraint by Minkov (2007) was applicable.

In the original cultural dimension of Indulgence versus Restraint by Minkov (2007), the Canadian respondents indicated to tend to have rather no choice or control over how their lives turn out. It could be assumed that the discrepancy stemmed from the insufficient and not representative number of respondents of the UDC pre-test; as well as Minkov (2007) differentiated between French and English Canadians (the total mean score was taken for the calculation), which was not done for the pre-test sample of the UDC questionnaire. Likewise, the same discrepancy was applicable for item Q12 in the sample of Brazilian respondents, which scored the lowest value in the total UDC score by 4.35.

Table 8.30 Country Study Results for the Universal Dimension of Culture (UDC) Gratification and Expression of Emotions, Desires, and Feelings

Item (Origin)	**Brazil** (Extent UDC Brazil; Extent Original Dimension)	**Canada** (Extent UDC Canada; Extent Original Dimension)	**Germany** (Extent UDC Germany; Extent Original Dimension)
Q12 (Minkov / Indulgence vs. Restraint)	No choice/control at all over the way your life turns out — 3.62 — 4.7 — A great deal of choice/control over the way your life turns out (scale 1–7)	No choice/control at all over the way your life turns out — 3.25 — 5.1 — A great deal of choice/control over the way your life turns out (scale 1–7)	No choice/control at all over the way your life turns out — 4.7 — 5.83 — A great deal of choice/control over the way your life turns out (scale 1–7)
Q16 (Hofstede / Indulgence vs. Restraint)	Never happy — 4.13 — 5.4 — Every time happy (scale 1–7)	Never happy — 4.76 — 5.7 — Every time happy (scale 1–7)	Never happy — 2.8 — 5.08 — Every time happy (scale 1–7)
Q112* (Schwartz / Autonomy vs. Restraint)	Not at all important to avoide extreme feelings and actions — 4.37 — 4.4 — Extreme important to avoide extreme feelings and actions (scale 1–7)	Not at all important to avoide extreme feelings and actions — 3.8 — 4.1 — Extreme important to avoide extreme feelings and actions (scale 1–7)	Not at all important to avoide extreme feelings and actions — 3.9 — 4.04 — Extreme important to avoide extreme feelings and actions (scale 1–7)
Q124* (Minkov / Indulgence vs. Restraint)	It's leisure that makes life worth living, not work — 3.62 — 4.3 — Work is what makes life worth living, not leisure (scale 1–7)	It's leisure that makes life worth living, not work — 3.25 — 3.8 — Work is what makes life worth living, not leisure (scale 1–7)	It's leisure that makes life worth living, not work — 4.2 — 5.83 — Work is what makes life worth living, not leisure (scale 1–7)
Total Score	4.35	4.8	4.42

Note. *The scores for the items Q112 and Q124 were reversely re-coded to calculate the total UDC score (for further information, please refer to Table 8.19). The cultural taxonomies, as indicated for the origin of the items, are only displayed in an abbreviated way

Overall, the Brazilian respondents indicated in more detail that they relatively tend to feel they have a great deal of choice and control over the way their lives turn out, they also tend to be happy every time, as well as place slight importance on the avoidance of extreme feelings and action, and work is what makes their life worth living, not leisure. No other than the explanation for the Canadian sample for the discrepancy in the item scores Q12 became applicable.

The German respondents scored in total in between the Brazilian and Canadian respondents by 4.42, indicating the following specifics: the German respondents felt that they have to a slight degree the choice and control over the way their life turns out, they are relatively highly happy every time, they place to a slight degree no importance on the avoidance of extreme feelings and actions, and also slightly tend to that work is what makes their life worth living, not leisure. A significant discrepancy between the pre-test score and the original cultural dimension score was applicable in item Q16, displaying the original cultural dimension of Indulgence versus Restraint by Hofstede and Minkov (2013). Germans tend to be never happy. In the original cultural dimension score calculation, the item was embedded into a four-item set, and item Q12 was subtracted from the item "Do other people or circumstances ever prevent you from doing what you really want to do"? This circumstance could explain the significant discrepancy in the item score between Q12 and the original cultural dimension of Indulgence versus Restraint by Hofstede and Minkov (2013).

UDC Traditionalism versus Secularism

The UDC Traditionalism versus Secularism refers to the extent of feelings of pride, flexibility, consistency between expressed and felt emotions, secular orientation, religiosity, and self-stability in national culture.

The UDC Traditionalism versus Secularism was operationalized by the following five items, referring to five different underlying cultural components: Q14 (national pride), Q19 (religiosity), Q111 (self-enhancement), Q114 secular-orientation, and Q115 (self-stability). The country profiles for Brazil, Canada, and Germany for the UDC Traditionalism versus Secularism are applicable in Table 8.31.

The German respondents from the pre-test sample scored the lowest total score in the UDC Traditionalism versus Secularism by 3.28, indicating that the German respondents instead tend to traditionalism.

In more detail, the German respondents indicated to have a slight tendency to be not at all proud of their German nationality, and religious faith seems almost not important, but doing a service to a friend is of great importance, similar to the value of independence, and persistency is seen as the surest way to successful results.

Table 8.31 Country Study Results for the Universal Dimension of Culture (UDC) Traditionalism versus Secularism

Item (Origin)	**Brazil** (Extent UDC Brazil; Extent Original Dimension)	**Canada** (Extent UDC Canada; Extent Original Dimension)	**Germany** (Extent UDC Germany; Extent Original Dimension)
Q14** (Minkov / Monumentalism vs. Flexhumility)	Not at all proud of own nationality; 5.0; 5.51; Extremely proud of own nationality	Not at all proud of own nationality; 3.44; 5.3; Extremely proud of own nationality	Not at all proud of own nationality; 3.5; Extremely proud of own nationality
Q19 (Inglehart / Traditionalism vs. Secularism)	Religious faith is not at all important; 4.3; 4.1; Religious faith is extremely important	Religious faith is not at all important; 2.82; 2.6; Religious faith is extremely important	Religious faith is not at all important; 1.56; 2.2; Religious faith is extremely important
Q111 (Hofstede / Long-Term vs. Short-Term Orientation)	Doing a service to a friend is not at all important; 4.92; 6.3; Doing a service to a friend is extremely important	Doing a service to a friend is not at all important; 5.48; 6.4; Doing a service to a friend is extremely important	Doing a service to a friend is not at all important; 2.19; 5.9; Doing a service to a friend is extremely important
Q114* (Inglehart / Traditionalism vs. Secularism)	Independency is not at all important; 2.71; 6.3; Independency is extremely important	Independency is not at all important; 4.49; 5.4; Independency is extremely important	Independency is not at all important; 5.65; 6.0; Independency is extremely important
Q115* (Hofstede / Long-Term vs. Short-Term Orientation)	Persistant efforts are not the surest way to successful results; 4.92; 4.9; Persistant efforts are the surest way to successful results	Persistant efforts are not the surest way to successful results; 5.48; 5.4; Persistant efforts are the surest way to successful results	Persistant efforts are not the surest way to successful results; 2.19; 5.2; Persistant efforts are the surest way to successful results
Total Score	4.04	3.9	3.28

Note. *The UDCs scores were reversely recoded for the calculation of the total UDC score. **No score for Germany was applicable in the cultural dimension of Monumentalism versus Flexhumility by Minkov (2007). The cultural taxonomies, as indicated for the origin of the items, are only displayed in an abbreviated way.

Two major discrepancies became applicable between the UDC scores and the original cultural dimensions scores for the German sample. The scores for the items Q111 and Q115 displayed contrasting results—both original scores were retrieved from the cultural dimension of Long-Term versus Short-Term Orientation by Hofstede (2001; Hofstede et al., 2010). Several explanations for the discrepancy are possible: Firstly, reviewing the score calculation by Hofstede (2001; Hofstede et al., 2010), it became applicable that Hofstede and Minkov (2013) applied four different cultural components in order to compile his score for the cultural dimension of Long-Term versus Short-Term Orientation. Hofstede (2001; Hofstede et al., 2010) combined the cultural components of doing a service to a friend and persistence with the cultural components of thrift and national pride. Furthermore, the score of the cultural component of the importance of doing a service to a friend was subtracted by the score of the cultural component of thrift; as well as the score for the cultural component of persistency was subtracted from the score of the cultural component of national pride. The in Table 8.31 applicable scores display the scores corresponding to each item. The UDCs, in general, do not encompass any specific weighting of an item; all items are equal. Secondly, another course for the discrepancy could be the low sample size of the UDC pre-test and/or other not detectable flaws in the calculation of the cultural dimension scores

A second place was scored for the total UDC score by the Canadian respondents from the UDC pre-test sample, with a total score of 3.9, demonstrating a slight tendency to traditionalism. The Canadian respondents from the pre-test indicated that they tend to be extremely proud of their nationality, religious faith does not seem to be of high importance, whereas doing a service to a friend is rather extremely important, almost similar important than independence, as well as persistent efforts seem to be evaluated as the surest way to successful results. Only one significant discrepancy between the scores for the UDC and the original cultural dimension scores became applicable in item Q14, initially developed by Minkov (2007) for his cultural dimension of Monumentalism versus Flexhumility.

The discrepancy could stem from either the low sample size of the pre-test of the UDCs and/or different calculation procedures, as well as the UDC score for item Q14 of 5.3 for the Canadian respondents only symbolize the score for the item, not any overall cultural dimension as it was applied in comparison to the Minkov (2007) score for the cultural dimension of Monumentalism versus Flexhumility. It could be assumed that some cultural change occurred since Minkov (2007) developed his cultural dimension based on an analysis of wave 4 from the WVS, conducted between 1999–2004. The UDC pre-test sample was conducted in February 2021.

The Brazilian respondents of the pre-test sample scored a total UDC score of 4.04, demonstrating a medium position in between traditionalism and secularism.

In detail, the Brazilian respondents indicated that they are somewhat proud of their nationality, they tend somewhere between religious faith is essential and is not essential, whereas doing a service to a friend and independence is extremely important, and persistent efforts are seen as they could be the surest way to successful results. One discrepancy between the UDC score and the original cultural dimension score became applicable for item Q114. It should be pointed out that the original score addressed the value of independence as child quality, which could be a possible explanation for the discrepancy. Furthermore, the sample size and calculation of the original cultural dimension score could also cause flaws in the data, since, in the Inglehart et al. (2014) sample, the respondents had to choose only between essential or not as well as had to choose only up to five values which they rate as important. Taking this evidence into account, discrepancies in the scores could occur.

Summary of Country Study for Brazil, Canada, and Germany

In the **UDC Distribution of Power and Status**, the respondents from Germany and Brazil demonstrated to a certain extent a similar country profile by displaying an approximately middle extent in the total UDC score (Germany 3.7, Brazil 3.9). The Canadian respondents indicated an even fewer extent for the UDC Distribution of Power and Status than the German and Brazilian respondents, with an overall UDC score of 3.42. Besides the total score, the countries displayed specific swings for certain items that contradict the total scores (please refer to Table 8.24). Generally, the UDC Distribution of Power and Status displays the acknowledgment and extent of inequalities among individuals and individuals' dependency on higher-ranked individuals in national culture.

In detail, as mentioned previously with specific outliers, the pre-test respondents for Brazil, Germany, and Canada tend to be as subordinates not afraid to contradict their bosses, respect depends on the family background, leadership positions should be more available for women than for men, power should be shared equally throughout the society, and reward can be gained by only factors other than performance effectiveness.

Also, for the **UDC Relationship with the Natural Environment**, the pre-test respondents of Brazil, Canada, and Germany, displayed a similar, although not identical, amplitude in the UDC. The maximum differences were applicable between Brazil, with a total UDC score of 5.124, and Germany, with a total UDC score of 4.6. The Canadian respondents scored a total UDC score of 4.77. Likewise, to the UDC Distribution of Power and Status country scores, specific swings were applicable for single items (mainly in the country profiles of Canada and Germany; please refer to Table 8.25). Overall, the pre-test respondents from Germany, Brazil, and Canada prefer that nature take its course, and individuals accept it. In addition, respondents find it worthwhile to control important natural forces, the unity with nature is essential, and natural preservation is considered highly important.

Regarding the **UDC Social Organization**, the pre-test's Canadian, Brazilian, and German respondents displayed a similar amplitude, but not an identical one, in the extent of the structure of social relationships regarding the concept of individualism versus collectivism. The maximum differences were seen between Canada with a UDC total score of 4.44 and Brazil with a total UDC score of 5.21. Germany scored a total UDC score of 4.66. The total UDC score of the three respondent groups indicates that the three tend to collectivism, with Germany having the most significant tendency compared to the Brazilian and Canada. In detail, the Brazilian, German, and Canadian respondents tend to see people from a different society as neighbors as acceptable; decisions are more likely to be made by consensus, leaders should encourage group loyalty even if then individual goals suffer, and similar attitudes and values are developed.

No final UDC scores were calculated for the **UDC Perception and Use of Time** (please refer to Table 8.27) since one item (item Q15) was excluded from the pre-test analyses due to its unreliable results. By calculated the total UDC scores based on the three items Q18, Q122, and Q127, the following was applicable:

Brazil 4.97, Canada 4.37, and Germany 5.1. In general, the UDC Perception and Use of Time display the extent of perception, including the view and use of time. In regards to the Brazilian, German, and Canadian UDC scores from the pre-test, the following can be concluded, that the respondents tend to think that donated money should be best spend to make a better life for the future, tent to polychronism and social gatherings should be planned well in advance.

The **UDC Uncertainty Avoidance and Coping Mechanisms** refers to the extent of uncertainty avoidance and mechanisms for coping and dealing with uncertain and unknown situations in national cultures. The Brazilian and German pre-test respondents displayed similar total UDC scores, with Brazil scoring 4.075 and Germany 4.025. The Canadian respondents from the pre-test indicated a lower total UDC score of 3.7. Thus, it can be stated for Brazil and Germany that their individuals tend not to feel nervous or tense, societal requirements and instructions should be spelled out, tend to live for the future, and a structured life with few unexpected events is seen as exciting. For Canada, it can be concluded that the individuals tend to feel less often nervous, societal requirements and instructions should not be spelled out, tend to live for the present, and a structured life with few unexpected events is seen as less exciting. However, each country profile (please refer to Table 8.28) displayed outliers for some items.

Regarding the **UDC Human Orientation**, displaying the extent of assertiveness versus tenderness, the Brazilian respondents from the pre-test scored the highest total UDC score with 5.825, and the German pre-test respondents scored the lowest total UDC score by 5.175. The Canadian respondents scored in the middle with a total UDC score of 5.525. In the country profiles (please see Table 8.29), no outliers in opposing dimension sides were applicable. All three respondents' groups tend to tenderness, including the tendency towards non-aggressive, non-dominant, and tender behavior. Individuals in these national cultures tend to encourage individuals to be concerned about others, sensitive towards others, as well as friendly.

The Canadian pre-test respondents scored the highest total UDC score in the **UDC Gratification and Expression of Emotions, Feelings, and Desires**, displaying the extent of gratification and expression of desires, feelings, and emotions in national culture 4.8. The German and Brazilian pre-test respondents scored close to each other, with Germany 4.42 and Brazil 4.35.

Outliers occurred in the country profiles (please refer to Table 8.30). All three countries indicated, thus, not a strong tendency towards free expression and gratification of desires, feelings, and emotions. In more detail, the individuals of the three respondents' groups from the pre-test indicated that they feel a to a certain extent that they have the choice and/or control how their lives turn out, they are relatively happy, it is not so crucial to avoid extreme feelings and actions, and leisure is seen to make life worth living, not work.

The last **UDC Traditionalism versus Secularism** displays the extent of feelings of pride, flexibility, consistency between expressed and felt emotions, secular orientation, religiosity, and self-stability. The pre-test respondents from Germany scored the lowest with a total score of 3.28, indicating a tendency towards secularism. In contrast, the Brazilian and Canadian pre-test respondents scored between the two extreme dimension sides with a 4.04 for Brazil and a 3.9 for Canada. Therefore, it is hard to make any conclusions for the specific cultural components of the UDC Traditionalism versus Secularism for Brazil, Canada, and Germany since also outliers were applicable in the country profiles (please refer to Table 8.31).

Table 8.32 summarizes the total UDC scores for the pre-test respondents from Brazil, Canada, and Germany.

Table 8.32 Summary on Country Study per Country and Universal Dimension of Culture (UDC)

Universal Dimension of Culture (UDC)	Brazil	Canada	Germany
Distribution of Power and Status Acknowledgment of the extent of inequalities among individuals and individuals' dependency on higher-ranked individuals (1 = *low* to 7 = *high*)	**3.925**	**3.42**	**3.7**
Relationship with the Natural Environment Extent of relationships with the natural environment expressed in their desire to control or to live in harmony (1 = *control* to 7 = *harmony*)	**5.125**	**4.77**	**4.6**
Social Organization Structure of social relationships regarding the concept of individualism versus collectivism (1 = *individualism* to 7 = *collectivism*)	**4.66**	**4.44**	**5.12**
Perception and Use of Time Extent of perception (including the view of) and use of time (1 = *past and monochronism* to 7 = *future and polychronsim*)	4.97	4.37	5.1
Uncertainty Avoidance and Coping Mechanisms Extent of uncertainty avoidance and mechanisms for coping and dealing with uncertain and unknown situations (1 = *low* to 7 = *high*)	**4.075**	**3.7**	**4.025**
Human Orientation Extent of assertiveness versus tenderness (1 = *assertiveness* to 7 = *tenderness*)	**5.825**	**5.525**	**5.175**
Gratification and Expression of Emotions, Desires, and Feelings Extent of gratification and expression of desires, feelings, and emotions (1 = *restraint* to 7 = *free*)	**4.35**	**4.8**	**4.42**
Traditionalism versus Secularism Extent of feelings of pride, flexibility, consistency between expressed and felt emotions, secular-orientation, religiosity, and self-stability (1 = *secularism* to 7 = *traditionalism*)	**4.04**	**3.9**	**3.28**

Conclusion 9

9.1 Implications

As introduced in the beginning, this dissertation aims to shed light on the theory jungle of cultural taxonomies including their cultural dimensions with a subsequent operationalization of results. RQ1, RQ2, and RQ3 guided this dissertation's research, including theoretical and practical implications.

First, an SLR was conducted to identify the research gap and to answer RQ1. The extensive and structured SLR revealed four synthesis methodologies—Low and Chapman (2003), Nardon and Steers (2009), Maleki and de Jong (2014), and Schneider et al. (2014)—which demonstrate syntheses of cultural dimensions from cultural taxonomies. The review of the four methodologies demonstrated their failure to provide a synthesis based on a carefully selected research base, included an in-depth analysis of the concepts and cultural components of the considered cultural dimensions, delineated the identified synthesis dimensions by their encompassed cultural components to other synthesis dimensions, and proposed a subsequent operationalization of results validated by a questionnaire.

Second, the analysis of the four synthesis methodologies resulted in the development of eight assumptions, displaying the eight UDCs of this dissertation. As stated in RQ2, the subsequent research addressed the design of the UDCs resulting from a synthesis of cultural dimensions under the application of a structured and rigid procedure. Before conducting the synthesis, a solid research base of 11 cultural taxonomies was selected from a range of 34 cultural taxonomies. These were evaluated and assessed by a developed assessment and evaluation framework. Due to their scientific significance, validity, and reliability, the 11 identified cultural taxonomies were assumed to constitute a solid and objective research base for synthesizing the eight UDCs.

S. Kunert, *The Eight Universal Dimensions of Culture from a Synthesis of Cultural Taxonomies*, Gabler Theses, https://doi.org/10.1007/978-3-658-38765-5_9

Third, as it was omitted by all identified synthesis methodologies, the operationalization and empirical understanding of national culture in terms of the eight synthesized UDCs, was demonstrated. A standardized questionnaire was developed to comprehend the eight UDCs as the core of cultural dimensions in any setting of interest. In addition, the questionnaire was extensively pre-tested. The final UDC questionnaire can be reviewed in Appendix E in the Electronic Supplementary Material.

9.1.1 Theoretical Implications

In Social Sciences, and more specifically in cross-cultural research, many researchers apply cultural taxonomies for their purposes, as it was demonstrated, for example, extensively by Søndergaard (1994) for the cultural taxonomy of Hofstede (1980). The cultural taxonomy by Hofstede (1980) takes on a unique role among existing cultural taxonomies as many researchers use this cultural taxonomy as a paradigm with taken-for-granted assumptions (Søndergaard, 1994). Moreover, many researchers apply cultural taxonomies to underline or substantiate their intentions. For example, Kim and Kim (2010) applied the cultural dimensions by Hofstede (2001; Hofstede et al., 2010) on Korean public relation practitioners. Another common way of comprehending cultural dimensions is their replication, as also pursued by Søndergaard (1994). For example, Waldman et al. (2006) replicated the GLOBE study by House et al. (2004, 2007, 2014) in 15 countries to demonstrate cultural and leadership predictors of corporate social responsibility values. Merritt (2000) investigated the replication of Hofstede's (1980) cultural dimensions in the cockpit. For example, other researchers such as Trompenaars and Hampden-Turner (2020) use their developed cultural dimensions to explain business-related circumstances as they did, for example, in their book *Riding the Wave of Culture: Understanding Diversity in Global Business*.

In this dissertation, 34 cultural taxonomies were reviewed to identify 11 cultural taxonomies for synthesizing the eight UDCs. In the review, as presented in Table 3.1, many of the cultural taxonomies seized on other cultural taxonomies, applying them as a foundation for their cultural dimensions. This dissertation's research demonstrated the synthesis of the universal concepts of cultural taxonomies and the importance of a critical assessment of cultural taxonomies for each corresponding purpose.

Based on this dissertation's research, it can be assumed that it is not sufficient to apply only one cultural taxonomy, utilizing it until the desired implication becomes obvious. Instead, a careful and solid evaluation before applying or replicating a cultural taxonomy should be undertaken. This dissertation can serve as a basis, illustrating the filtered and synthesized universal concepts, including sub-cultural components, of existing cultural dimensions.

The eight UDCs were synthesized following three themes. First, the UDCs Distribution of Power and Status, Relationship with the Natural Environment, and Social Organization were synthesized to address the extent of an individuals' handling their social environment, natural environment, or hierarchical order of the environment. Second, the three UDCs Perception and Use of Time, Traditionalism versus Secularism, and Uncertainty Avoidance and Coping Mechanisms were described together under the overall theme of time. Finally, the two UDCs, Human Orientation and Gratification and Expression of Emotions, Feelings, and Desires, were subsumed to the theme of human behavior.

The final synthesized versions of the eight UDCs are demonstrated in Table 9.1. The indicated evaluation of the eight UDCs is based on the number of synthesized cultural dimensions, expressing the extent of the notional value of the corresponding concept of each UDC. The UDCs were either evaluated as strong or medium.

For example, the following characteristics describe the as strong evaluated UDC Distribution of Power and Status. Seven cultural dimensions were synthesized and operationalized for the UDC Distribution of Power and Status. Additionally, three cultural dimensions were partly synthesized into the UDC Distribution of Power and Status (please refer to Table 5.1). Only two cultural dimensions were synthesized into the UDC Uncertainty Avoidance and Coping Mechanisms, but several other cultural dimensions were partly synthesized as well (please refer to Table 6.2). The UDC Uncertainty Avoidance and Coping Mechanisms was also evaluated as strong. In contrast, the UDC Traditionalism versus Secularism was evaluated with a medium since only three cultural dimensions were synthesized, and an additional dimension was synthesized in conceptual terms.

Summarizing the theoretical implications of this dissertations' research, the eight UDCs enable future research to seize on a set of eight dimensions, displaying the core of cultural taxonomies. As such, the benefits of multiple cultural taxonomies are comprehendible. This is seen in the UDC questionnaire, which empirically measures each UDC's extent in a representative group.

Table 9.1 Overview of the Eight Universal Dimensions of Culture (UDCs)

UDC	Definition	Evaluation
Distribution of Power and Status	The acknowledgment and extent of inequalities among individuals and individuals' dependency on higher-ranked individuals in national cultures.	Strong
Relationship with the Natural Environment	The extent of relationships of individuals with their natural environment in national cultures is expressed in their desire either to control or to live in harmony with their natural environment.	Medium
Social Organization	The structure of social relationships by the concept of individualism versus collectivism in national cultures.	Strong
Perception and Use of Time	The extent of perception (incl., view of) and use of time in national cultures.	Strong
Uncertainty Avoidance and Coping Mechanisms	The extent of uncertainty avoidance and mechanisms for coping and dealing with uncertain and unknown situations in national cultures.	Strong
Human Orientation	The extent of assertiveness versus tenderness in national cultures.	Medium
Gratification and Expression of Emotions, Feelings, and Desires	The extent of gratification and expression of desires, feelings, and emotions in national cultures.	Strong
Traditionalism versus Secularism	The extent of feelings of pride, flexibility, consistency between expressed and felt emotions, secular orientation, religiosity, and self-stability in national cultures.	Medium

Note. The layout and idea for the table were adapted with changes from *Culture, Leadership, and Organizations: The GLOBE study of 62 Societies* (p. 30), by R. J. House, P. J. Hanges, M. Javidan, P. W. Dorfman, and V. Gupta, 2004, Sage Publications, Inc. Copyright 2004 by Sage Publications, Inc.

9.1.2 Practical Implications

The practical implications for this dissertations' research and its eight UDCs mainly originate from understanding national cultures. The concept of national culture allows individuals to understand who they are and which behaviors are appropriate in a society (Bright et al., 2019).

Aside from the applied definition for national culture, written by Kluckhohn and Strodtbeck (1961), Hofstede (2001) developed a short-hand definition, defining national cultures as "the collective programming of the mind that distinguishes the members of one group or category of people from another" (p. 9). The concept of national cultures, and thus, the synthesized UDCs of this dissertation, are prevalent in many aspects of human lives. Understanding the influence of national culture in the eight UDCs can beneficially contribute to decreasing misunderstandings or tensions in the *interdependent global society* (Bright et al., 2019). Furthermore, understanding national culture in the eight UDCs is essential to deal with increasingly diverse workforces due to immigration and the increasing extent of expatriate workers. For example, the eight UDCs can help understand organizational structures, entrepreneurial acclivities, managerial authorities, the relationship of employees with their supervisors and companies, and human resource activities (Bright et al., 2019).

In the business context, understanding national culture in terms of the eight UDCs can enhance the understanding of marketing mechanisms, including product branding in different national cultures and the development of marketing strategies according to respective national cultures. Similar conclusions can be drawn for the areas of finance and accounting. Considering the eight UDCs for the provision of information for investors or the consideration of market circumstances. Another area benefiting from this UDC research could be corporate culture, especially regarding M&A transactions (Trompenaars & Woolliams, 2004).

The business area gives the potential for practical implications for applying the eight UDCs, but also other areas benefit from the research as well. For example, as Nagy and Molnárné (2018) demonstrated, understanding national culture also inhibits the potential for shaping environmentally conscious behaviors of humans. In a broader sense, the concept of national culture and this dissertation's research can predict the importance of religion, the family, civic activism, or the extent of national pride per se in a society. For example, these factors could be considered to design national culture-specific political programs (Inglehart & Welzel, 2005).

The previous examples illustrate only a starting point of applying the eight UDCs of this dissertation in practice. Several more examples could be stated.

The research of this dissertation, the eight UDCs, and their operationalization into a questionnaire are of great value for comprehending national cultures, seizing on well-proven cultural taxonomies by providing the core and universal concepts of their cultural dimensions.

9.2 Limitations of Research

The conducted research of this dissertation sufficiently provides a comprehensive and all-inclusive study of the core concepts and cultural components of cultural taxonomies by synthesizing them and subsequently operationalizing the findings. Nevertheless, the conducted research of this dissertation encompasses limits as well.

First, it should be noted that the SLR from which the research gaps and the eight assumptions in terms of the UDCs were retrieved was only conducted between May and June 2019. The conducted SLR focused on articles published in German and English due to the language capabilities of the author of this dissertation. During the SLR, articles that provided a comparison of specific cultural dimensions and existing cultural taxonomies became applicable (e.g., Basabe and Ros (2005), Venaik et al. (2013), Yeganeh (2013)). This research could have given additional evidence for conceptual overlaps among cultural dimensions from existing cultural taxonomies. Just recently, before the end of this dissertation, it became evident that also other researchers are currently working on synthesizing cultural dimensions from cultural taxonomies (please refer, for example, to Kaasa (2021)).

Second, the selection and evaluation of the cultural taxonomies were not free of limitations. The review of the cultural taxonomies was only conducted by one reviewer—the author of this dissertation. This is typical for dissertations but could cause flaws and misjudgment of potential studies (Kitchenham, 2004).

Third, the synthesis of the eight UDCs was conducted in a structured way, following implications and a rigid research procedure. Nevertheless, the synthesis of the eight UDCs based on cultural taxonomies was also pursued by only one reviewer, the author of this dissertation. This circumstance could induce a certain level of subjectivity, even though objective and stringent standards were followed during the synthesis.

Conclusively, one main limitation of this dissertation is its dependency and influence on the author's cultural view. Likewise, to the critiques mentioned for Hofstede (2001; Hofstede et al., 2010), House et al. (2004, 2007, 2014), and Trompenaars and Hampden-Turner (2004, 2012) by, for example, Ailon (2008),

McCrae et al. (2008), and McSweeney (2002), the author of this dissertation and thus the developer of the eight UDCs descended from a Western society and received training in a Western educational system. This dissertation cannot be seen as detached from its original cultural background.

The eight UDCs demonstrated and developed in this dissertation display a synthesis of cultural concepts and components of cultural dimensions from existing cultural taxonomies. Any subsequent research applying similar standards and premises should detect the same eight cultural concepts representing the eight UDCs this dissertation pursues. The limitations regarding the subjectivity of this dissertation's research could cause different configurations of the concept for each UDC. The assignment of the specific cultural components to each UDC leaves room for discussion.

Fourth, the eight cultural taxonomies of the 11 selected taxonomies that operationalized items for their cultural dimensions critically appraised the subjective nature of operationalizing them into items. It also remains debatable if questionnaires constitute a suitable tool to measure cultural differences overall due to their generalization of results (Hofstede, 2001; House et al., 2004). Respondents of questionnaires are influenced by their unique cultural heritage, not necessarily mirroring the national culture's cultural heritage (Aneas & Sandín, 2009). Such circumstances could raise cultural response biases inducing cultural bonded response patterns. In some cases, the flaws of the respondents could then lead to deviations of the results from the original concept of interest. A particular subjectivity induced by the synthesis and the measurement of the concepts and cultural components in terms of value and practice items could cause research subjectivity (Hofstede, 2001; House et al., 2004). Also, as Hofstede (2001) identified, the language and resulting translations of items can cause biases, and culturally loaded idioms should be handled carefully. These mentioned flaws and limitations regarding the operationalizations of items also apply to the developed questionnaire of the UDCs in this dissertation.

Fifth, the pre-test of the UDC questionnaire and its low number of respondents did not allow for the conduction of a Confirmatory or Explanatory Factor Analysis. The calculation of Cronbach's α was pursued despite its low significance.

A statistically reliable calculation of α would have required a more significant number of respondents (UCLA Institute for Digital Research and Education Statistical Consulting, n.d.). The provided country study, illustrating the country profile of Brazil, Canada, and Germany for the eight UDCs, should also be handled with care since the number of respondents for the three countries was relatively low and not considered as representative (Brazil $n = 7$, Canada $n =$

10, and Germany n = 12). The country study results displayed the great potential of applying the eight UDCs to retrieve country profiles.

9.3 Outlook

The limitations of this dissertation serve as a starting point for prospective and consecutive research—the outlook of this dissertation. The proposed subsequent research potentials should be seen as expansions of this dissertation's research and not necessarily as limitations of the results of this dissertation (Kaasa, 2021).

First, it could be of great benefit to include studies in the area of cross-cultural research that investigate single cultural taxonomies and identify improvements on cultural dimensions. The inclusion of extended studies on existing cultural taxonomies could enhance, substantiate, and confirm the synthesized cultural concepts of each of the eight UDCs. Examples for such potential further research are Beugelsijk and Welzel (2018) and Smith (2006).

This dissertation demonstrated an in-depth and structured conceptual synthesis of cultural dimensions' concepts and cultural components from cultural taxonomies. Maleki and de Jong (2014) reviewed statistical interrelationships between their analyzed cultural taxonomies based on the provided country scores of each cultural taxonomy. Subsequent research to this dissertation could also explore the eight UDCs in terms of underlying country score correlations of the considered 11 cultural taxonomies. The country score correlations of the 11 cultural taxonomies could be investigated and juxtaposed to the findings of the conceptual analysis of this dissertation's research. At the same time, not all of the 11 cultural taxonomies provided country scores (e.g., Hall (1959, 1966, 1976, 1983; Hall & Hall, 1990), Lewis (2018)).

It should also be carefully considered that the concept of (national) culture cannot precisely be defined and depends considerably on the cultural understanding of research, inducing a bijective selection of items for its operationalization.

Further advancement of this dissertation's research could constitute a representative study with the pre-tested, valid, and reliable UDC questionnaire presented in this dissertation. For a consecutive representative study, the following should be taken into account: The study object, thus, the boundaries of national cultures should be carefully defined for the study. The UDCs of this dissertation were developed in regards to the passport approach for national cultures. To interpret the results, it should be kept in mind that the results display extents of underlying cultural concepts, as illustrated for the definition of the UDCs (please refer to Table 9.1). Since the pre-test did not include a sufficient number of respondents, it is advisable to pursue a Confirmatory Factor Analysis for the developed questionnaire and thus to substantiate the concept affiliation to the eight synthesized UDCs. Subsequent empirical research using the, in this dissertation developed, questionnaire for the eight UDCs could reveal further insights into the potentials for applying a mathematical formula to calculate country scores for each UDC.

So far, the country score for each UDC would be calculated as the sum of each item's mean score. Such mathematical formulas were developed and demon strated in the cultural taxonomy by Hofstede (2001; Hofstede et al., 2010). In comparison, House et al. (2004, 2007, 2014) calculated their numerical values for countries as the sum of the mean scores of the items of each of their cultural dimensions. As introduced at the beginning of this dissertation, Kaasa (2021) recently published an article on a synthesis of cultural taxonomies—Hofstede (1980), Schwartz (1994b), and Inglehart (1997)—and their cultural dimensions. Kaasa (2021) only analyzed three cultural taxonomies, grouping their cultural dimensions into a single system without further operationalization. Subsequent research could juxtapose Kaasa's (2021) findings and the eight UDCs developed in this dissertation and identify similarities and contrasts. The eight UDCs developed and demonstrated in this dissertation provide valuable insights into the core concepts and cultural components. The eight UDCs shed light on the theory jungle of cultural taxonomies and explain an understanding of international cooperation, effective intercultural communication, and collaboration.

Overall, the eight UDCs, as the synthesized core concepts of cultural components of cultural taxonomies, allow individuals to understand other than the personal cultural settings and give insights into coping and understanding models for them. In conclusion, as the introduction quotation by one of the pioneers of cross-cultural analysis, Edward T. Hall, stated, "culture hides much more than it reveals, and strangely enough, what it hides most effectively from its own participants" (Hall, 1959, p. 39) the developed eight UDCs, including the questionnaire to measure and test them, serve as a valuable starting point clarify the jungle of cultural taxonomies. This dissertation demonstrates an enhancement for the areas of international cooperation, improving co-country relationships, and making intercultural communication and collaborations more effective.

References

Adler, N. J. (1981). Re-entry: Managing cross-cultural transitions. *Group & Organization Studies*, *6*(3), 341–356. https://doi.org/10.1177/105960118100600310

Adler, N. J. (1991). *International dimensions of organizational behavior* (2nd ed.). PWS-KENT Publishing Company. https://doi.org/10.5465/amp.2008.31217520

Adler, N. J., & Gundersen, A. (2008). *International dimensions of organizational behavior* (5th ed.). Thomson South-Western.

Ailon, G. (2008). Mirror, mirror on the wall: "Culture's consequences" in a value test of its own design. *Academy of Management Review*, *33*(4), 885–904. https://doi.org/10.5465/amr.2008.34421995

Allport, G. W. (1961). *Pattern and growth in personality*. Holt, Rinehart and Winston.

Aneas, A. M., & Sandín, M. P. (2009). Intercultural and cross-cultural communication research : Some reflections about culture and qualitative methods. *Forum: Qualitative Social Research*, *10*(1), 1–19. https://doi.org/10.17169/FQS-10.1.1251

Basabe, N., & Ros, M. (2005). Cultural dimensions and social behavior correlates: Individualism-Collectivism and Power Distance. *Revue Internationale de Psychologie Sociale*, *18*(1), 189–225. https://citeseerx.ist.psu.edu/viewdoc/download?doi=10.1.1.535.5185&rep=rep1&type=pdf

Beugelsdijk, S., & Welzel, C. (2018). Dimensions and dynamics of national culture: Synthesizing Hofstede with Inglehart. *Journal of Cross-Cultural Psychology*, *49*(10), 1469–1505. https://doi.org/10.1177/0022022118798505

Bhagat, R. S., & Steers, R. M. (2009). *Cambridge handbook of culture, organizations, and work*. Cambridge University Press. https://doi.org/10.1017/CBO9780511581151

Bolton, R. N. (1993). Pretesting questionnaires: Content analyses of respondents' concurrent verbal protocols. *Marketing Science*, *12*(3), 280–303. https://doi.org/10.1287/mksc.12.3.280

Brady, S. R. (2015). Utilizing and adapting the delphi method for use in qualitative research. *International Journal of Qualitative Methods*, *14*(5), 1–6. https://doi.org/10.1177/1609406915621381

Bright, D. S., Cortes, A. H., Hartmann, E., Parboteeah, K. P., Pierce, J. L., Reece, M., Shah, A., Terjesen, S., Weiss, J., White, M. A., Gardner, D. G., Lambert, J., Leduc, L. M., Leopold, J., Muldoon, J., & O'Rourke, J. S. (2019). *Principles of management* (12th ed.). OpenStax Rice University.

S. Kunert, *The Eight Universal Dimensions of Culture from a Synthesis of Cultural Taxonomies*, Gabler Theses, https://doi.org/10.1007/978-3-658-38765-5

Brown, J. D. (2003). The self-enhancement motive in collectivistic cultures: The rumors of my death have been greatly exaggerated. *Journal of Cross-Cultural Psychology*, *34*(5), 603–605. https://doi.org/10.1177/0022022103256482

Bryman, A. (2012). *Social research methods* (4th ed.). Oxford University Press. https://www.academia.edu/38228560/Alan_Bryman_Social_Research_Methods_4th_Edition_Oxford_University_Press_2012_pdf

Campanelli, P. C., Martin, E. A., & Rothgeb, J. M. (1991). The use of respondent and interviewer debriefing studies as a way to study response error in survey data. *Journal of the Royal Statistical Society. Series D (The Statistician)*, *40*(3), 253–264. https://doi.org/10.2307/2348278

Catalin, P., & Micu, A. (2013). The quantification of culture—A critical evaluation of the theory of national cultural dimensions. *Metalurgia International*, *18*(7), 321–323. https://www.proquest.com/docview/1346657436/fulltext/C8BA56DFC7EC4575PQ/1?accountid=17183

Centre for Reviews and Dissemination. (2009). *Systematic reviews. CRD's guidance for undertaking reviews in health care* (3rd ed.). CRD, University of York.

Chanchani, S., & Theivananthampillai, P. (2009). Typologies of culture. *SSRN Electronic Journal*, 1–28. https://doi.org/10.2139/ssrn.1441609

Chapman, M. (1996). Preface: Social anthropology, business studies, and cultural issues. *International Studies of Management & Organization*, *26*(4), 3–29. https://doi.org/10.1080/00208825.1996.11656692

Chinese Culture Connection. (1987). Chinese values and the search for culture-free dimensions of culture. *Journal of Cross-Cultural Psychology*, *18*(2), 143–164. https://doi.org/10.1177/0022002187018002002

Collins, D. (2003). Pretesting survey instruments: An overview of cognitive methods. *Quality of Life Research*, *12*(3), 229–238. https://doi.org/10.1023/A:1023254226592

Cottle, T. J. (1967). The circles test: An investigation of perceptions of temporal relatedness and dominance. *Journal of Projective Techniques and Personality Assessment*, *31*(5), 58–71. https://doi.org/10.1080/0091651X.1967.10120417

Cottle, T. J. (1969). The duration inventory: Subjective extensions of temporal zones. *Acta Psychologica*, *1969*, 333–352. https://doi.org/10.1016/0001-6918(69)90026-2

Croasmun, J. T., & Ostrom, L. (2011). Using likert-type scales in the social sciences. *Journal of Adult Education*, *40*, 19–22. https://files.eric.ed.gov/fulltext/EJ961998.pdf

Dawes, J. (2008). Do data characteristics change according to the number of scale points used? An experiment using 5-point, 7-point and 10-point scales. *International Journal of Market Research*, *51*(1), 61–104. https://doi.org/10.1177/147078530805000106

de Mooij, M. (1998a). *Global marketing and advertising: Understanding cultural paradox.* SAGE Publications, Inc.

de Mooij, M. (1998b). Masculinity/femininity and consumer behavior. In G. Hofstede & Associates (Eds.), *Masculinity and femininity: The taboo dimension of national cultures* (pp. 55–73). SAGE Publications, Inc.

de Mooij, M. (2001). *Convergence-divergence.* Unpublished doctoral dissertation. Universidad de Navarra.

de Mooij, M. (2013). On the misuse and misinterpretation of dimensions of national culture. *International Marketing Review*, *30*(3), 253–261. https://doi.org/10.1108/02651331311321990

DiStefano, J. J., & Maznevski, M. L. (2000a). Creating value with diverse teams in global management. *Organizational Dynamics, 29*(1), 45–63. https://doi.org/10.1016/S0090-2616(00)00012-7

DiStefano, J. J., & Maznevski, M. L. (2000b). Global leaders are team players: Developing global leaders through membership on global teams. *Human Resource Management, 39*(2–3), 195–208. https://doi.org/10.1002/1099-050x(200022/23)39:2/3<195::aid-hrm9>3.3.co;2-9

DiStefano, J. J., & Maznevski, M. L. (2003). Developing global managers: Integrating theory, behavior, data and performance. *Advances in Global Leadership, 3*, 341–371. https://doi.org/10.1016/S1535-1203(02)03016-2

Döring, N., & Bortz, J. (2016). *Forschungsmethoden und evaluation* (5th ed.). Springer-Verlag. https://doi.org/10.1007/978-3-642-41089-5

Douglas, M. (1973). *Natural symbols: Explorations in cosmology*. Penguin.

EBSCO Information Services. (2014). *CINAHL user guide*. http://www.lib.ui.ac.id/manualod/kesehatan/CINAHL.pdf

Feather, N. T. (1995). Values, valences, and choice: The influences of values on the perceived attractiveness and choice of alternatives. *Journal of Personality and Social Psychology, 68*(6), 1135–1151. https://doi.org/10.1037/0022-3514.68.6.1135

Featherstone, M. (1990). Global culture: An introdcution. *Theory, Culture & Society, 7*(2–3), 1–14. https://doi.org/10.1177/026327690007002001

Fiske, A. P. (1991). *Structures of social life: The four elementary forms of human relations: Communal sharing, authority ranking, equality matching, market pricing*. Free Press.

Fiske, A. P. (1992). The four elementary forms of sociality: Framework for a unified theory of social relations. *Psychological Review, 99*(4), 689–723. https://doi.org/10.1037/0033-295X.99.4.689

Ford, G., Kotzè, P., & Marcus, A. (2005). Cultural dimensions: Who is stereotyping whom? *Internationalization, Online Communities and Social Computing: Design and Evaluation, 10*, 1–10. https://www.researchgate.net/profile/Gabrielle-Ford-3/publication/228516559_Cultural_dimensions_Who_is_stereotyping_whom/links/0fcfd50a27309507e0000000/Cultural-dimensions-Who-is-stereotyping-whom.pdf

Fukuyama, F. (1995a). Social capital and the global economy. *Foreign Affairs, 74*(5), 89–103. https://doi.org/10.2307/20047302

Fukuyama, F. (1995b). *Trust: The social virtues and the creation of prosperity*. The Free Press.

Fukuyama, F. (1999). *The great disruption: Human nature and the reconstitution of social order*. The Free Press.

Gordon, T. J. (1994). The delphi method. *Future Research Methodology, 2*(3), 1–30. https://www.researchgate.net/profile/Gholamreza-Gholampour/post/In_Delphi_model_for_the_responds_in_second_round_which_are_less_than_70_but_more_than_50_third_round_should_be_done/attachment/59d633b379197b80779915d0/AS%3A375824315371524%401466614907277/do

Green, E. G. T., Deschamps, J. C., & Páez, D. (2005). Variation of individualism and collectivism within and between 20 countries: A typological analysis. *Journal of Cross-Cultural Psychology, 36*(3), 321–339. https://doi.org/10.1177/0022022104273654

Groseschl, S., & Doherty, L. (2000). Conceptualising culture. *Cross Cultural Management: An International Journal, 7*(4), 12–17. https://doi.org/10.1108/13527600010797138

Gross, C., & Seebaß, K. (2014). *The standard stress scale (SSS): Measuring stress in life course.* (NEPS Working Paper No. 45). Leibniz Institut for Educational Trajectories, National Educational Panel Study. https://www.neps-data.de/Portals/0/Working Papers/WP_XLV.pdf

Gudykunst, W. B., Ting-Toomey, S., & Chua, E. (1988). *Culture and interpersonal communication.* SAGE Publications, Inc.

Haddaway, N. R., Woodcock, P., Macura, B., & Collins, A. (2015). Making literature reviews more reliable through application of lessons from systematic reviews. *Conservation Biology, 29*(6), 1596–1605. https://doi.org/10.1111/cobi.12541

Haerpfer, C., Inglehart, R., Moreno, A., Welzel, C., Kizilova, K., Diez-Medrano, J., Lagos, M., Norris, P., Ponarin, E., & Puranen, B. (2020). *World values survey: Round seven—country-pooled datafile.* JD Systems Institute & WVSA Secretariat. https://doi.org/10.14281/18241.13

Hall, E. T. (1959). *The silent language.* Anchor Press/Doubleday.

Hall, E. T. (1966). *The hidden dimension.* Anchor Press/Doubleday.

Hall, E. T. (1976). *Beyond culture.* Anchor Press.

Hall, E. T. (1983). *The dance of life: The other dimension of time.* Anchor Press/Doubleday.

Hall, E. T., & Hall, M. R. (1990). *Understanding cultural differences.* Intercultural Press Inc.

Hamel, R. E. (2007). The dominance of English in the international scientific periodical literature and the future of language use in science. *AILA Review, 20*(1), 53–71. https://doi.org/10.1075/aila.20.06ham

Haslam, N., & Fiske, A. P. (1999). Relational models theory: A confirmatory factor analysis. *Personal Relationships, 6*(2), 241–250. https://doi.org/10.1111/j.1475-6811.1999.tb00190.x

Heine, S. J. (2003). An exploration of cultural variation in self-enhancing and self-improving motivations. In V. Murphy-Berman & J. J. Berman (Eds.), *Cross-cultural differences in perspectives on the self* (pp. 118–145). University of Nebraska Press.

Hills, M. D. (1977). Values in the South Pacific. *Values in the South Pacific. Paper Presented at the Annual Conference of the New Zealand Psychological Society in Auckland, New Zealand.*

Hills, M. D. (1998). Devloping the Kluckhohn-Strodtbeck values orientation instrument in New Zealand. *Paper Presented at the Biennial Conference of the International Association for Cross-Cultural Psychology.*

Hills, M. D. (2002). Kluckhohn and Strodtbeck ' s values orientation theory. *Online Readings in Psychology and Culture, 4*(4), 1–14. https://doi.org/10.9707/2307-0919.1040

Hofstede, G. (1980). *Culture's consequences: International differences in work-related values.* SAGE Publications, Inc.

Hofstede, G. (1991). *Cultures and organizations: Software of the mind.* McGraw-Hill.

Hofstede, G. (1994). Management scientists are human. *Management Science, 40*(1), 4–13. https://doi.org/10.1287/mnsc.40.1.4

Hofstede, G. (2001). *Culture's consequences : Comparing values, behaviors, institutions, and organizations across nations* (2nd ed.). SAGE Publications, Inc.

Hofstede, G. (2006). What did GLOBE really measure? Researchers' minds versus respondents' minds. *Journal of International Business Studies, 37*(6), 882–896. https://doi.org/10.1057/palgrave.jibs.8400233

Hofstede, G. (2010). *Dimension data matrix*. https://geerthofstede.com/research-and-vsm/dimension-data-matrix/

Hofstede, G., & Hofstede, G. J. (2005). *Cultures and organizations: Software of the mind* (2nd ed.). McGraw-Hill.

Hofstede, G., Hofstede, G. J., & Minkov, M. (2010). *Cultures and organizations: Software of the mind* (3rd ed.). McGraw-Hill.

Hofstede, G., & Minkov, M. (2013). VSM 2013. *Values Survey Module*. https://geerthofstede.com/wp-content/uploads/2016/07/VSM-2013-English-2013-08-25.pdf

Hogan, R. T., & Emler, N. P. (1978). The biases in contemporary social psychology. *Social Research: An International Quarterly, 45*(3), 478–534. https://www.jstor.org/stable/40970345

Hoggart, R. (1957). *The uses of literacy*. Transaction publishers.

House, R. J., Chhokar, J. S., & Brodbeck, F. C. (2007). *Culture and leadership across the world: The GLOBE book of in-depth studies of 25 societies*. Lawrence Erlbaum Associates Publishers.

House, R. J., Dorfman, P. W., Javidan, M., Hanges, P. J., & de Luque, M. F. S. (2014). *Strategic leadership across cultures: The GLOBE study of CEO leadership behavior and effectiveness in 24 countries*. Sage Publications, Inc. https://doi.org/10.4135/9781506374581

House, R. J., Hanges, P. J., Javidan, M., Dorfman, P., & Gupta, V. (n.d.). *GLOBE culture dimensions, definitions, and scale items*. https://globeproject.com/data/GLOBE-Dimensions-Definitions-and-Scale-Items.pdf

House, R. J., Hanges, P. J., Javidan, M., Dorfman, P., & Gupta, V. (2004). *Culture, leadership and organizations: The GLOBE study of 62 societies*. Sage Publications, Inc.

House, R. J., Javidan, M., Hanges, P. J., & Dorfman, P. (2002). Understanding cultures and implicit leadership theories across the globe: An introduction to project GLOBE. *Journal of World Business, 37*(1), 3–10. https://doi.org/10.1016/s1090-9516(01)00069-4

Hughes, K. (2004). Comparing pretesting methods: Cognitive interviews, respondent debriefing, and behavior coding. *Survey Methodology, 2*, 1–20. https://www.census.gov/srd/papers/pdf/rsm2004-02.pdf

Hunt, S. D., Sparkman, R. D., & Wilcox, J. B. (1982). The pretest in survey research: Issues and preliminary findings. *Journal of Marketing Research, 19*(2), 269–273. https://doi.org/10.2307/3151627

Inglehart, R. (1997). *Modernization and postmodernization: Cultural, economic and political change in 43 societies*. Princeton University Press.

Inglehart, R. (2006). Mapping global values. *Comparative Sociology, 5*(2–3), 115–136. https://doi.org/10.1163/156913306778667401

Inglehart, R., & Baker, W. E. (2000). Modernization, cultural change, and the persistence of traditional values. *American Sociological Review, 65*(1), 19–51. https://doi.org/10.2307/2657288

Inglehart, R., Haerpfer, C., Moreno, A., Welzel, C., Kizilova, K., Diez-Medrano, J., Lagos, M., Norris, P., Ponarin, E., & Puranen, B. (2014). *World values survey: All rounds*. http://www.worldvaluessurvey.org/WVSDocumentationWVL.jsp

Inglehart, R., & Welzel, C. (2005). *Modernization, cultural change, and democracy: The human development sequence*. Cambridge University Press.

Kaasa, A. (2021). Merging Hofstede, Schwartz, and Inglehart into a single system. *Journal of Cross-Cultural Psychology, 52*(4), 339–353. https://doi.org/10.1177/00220221211011244

Keesing, R. M. (1974). Theories of culture. *Annual Review of Anthropology, 3*(2), 73–97. https://doi.org/10.1080/03149099009508482

Kim, Y., & Kim, S.-Y. (2010). The influence of cultural values on perceptions of corporate social responsibility: Application of Hofstede's dimensions to Korean public relations practitioners. *Journal of Business Ethics, 91*, 485–500. https://doi.org/10.1007/s10551-009-0095-z

Kirkman, B. L., Lowe, K. B., & Gibson, C. B. (2006). A quarter century of culture's consequences: A review of empirical research incorporating Hofstede's cultural values framework. *Journal of International Business Studies, 37*(3), 285–320. https://doi.org/10.1057/palgrave.jibs.8400202

Kitchenham, B. (2004). Procedures for performing systematic reviews. In *NICTA Technical Report*. https://www.inf.ufsc.br/~aldo.vw/kitchenham.pdf

Kluckhohn, C. (1949). *Mirror for man: The relation of anthropology to modern life*. Whittlesey House.

Kluckhohn, C. (1951). 2. Values and value-orientations in the theory of action: An exploration in definition and classification. In T. Parsons & E. A. Shils (Eds.), *Toward a general theory of action* (pp. 389–433). Harvard University Press. https://doi.org/10.4159/harvard.9780674863507.c8

Kluckhohn, F. R., & Strodtbeck, F. L. (1961). *Variations in value orientations*. Row, Peterson.

Kroeber, A. L., & Kluckhohn, C. (1952). *Culture: A critical review of concepts and definitions*. Peabody Museum of Archaeology & Ethnology, Harvard University.

Kuppens, P., Ceulemans, E., Timmerman, M. E., Diener, E., & Kim-Prieto, C. (2006). Universal intracultural and intercultural dimensions of the recalled frequency of emotional experience. *Journal of Cross-Cultural Psychology, 37*(5), 491–515. https://doi.org/10.1177/0022022106290474

Lane, R. H. (1976). *Polynesia and Europe meet: A new heritage*. University of Waikatore, Hamilton, New Zealand.

Lessem, R., & Neubauer, F.-F. (1994). *European management systems : Towards unity out of cultural diversity*. McGraw-Hill.

Levine, R. V., & Norenzayan, A. (1999). The pace of life in 31 countries. *Journal of Cross-Cultural Psychology, 30*(2), 178–205. https://doi.org/10.1177/0022022199030002003

Levine, R. V., Norenzayan, A., & Philbrick, K. (2001). Cross-cultural differences in helping strangers. *Journal of Cross-Cultural Psychology, 32*(5), 543–560. https://doi.org/10.1177/0022022101032005002

Lewin, K. (1936). *Principles of topological psychology*. McGraw-Hill. https://doi.org/10.1037/10019-000

Lewis, R. (2018). *When cultures collide: Leading across cultures* (4th ed.). Nicholas Brealey International.

Lewis, R., & Finland, D. (1992). *Cultural lone wolf: Consequences in international business*. Richard Lewis Communications.

Libraries, A. (2013). *What is a boolean operator?* https://library.alliant.edu/screens/boolean.pdf

Lindquist, J. D., & Kaufman-Scarborough, C. (2007). The polychronic-monochronic tendency model: Pmts scale development and validation. *Time & Society*, *16*(2–3), 253–285. https://doi.org/10.1177/0961463X07080270

Linstone, H. A., & Turoff, M. (2002). *The delphi method: Techniques and applications*. Addison-Wesley. https://web.njit.edu/~turoff/pubs/delphibook/delphibook.pdf

Low, D., & Chapman, R. (2003). Organisational and national culture : A study of overlap and interaction in the literature. *International Journal of Employment Studies*, *11*(1), 55–75. https://web.a.ebscohost.com/ehost/pdfviewer/pdfviewer?vid=0&sid=4075d83b-03fd-4e0a-8ff6-b518cef0760c%40sdc-v-sessmgr02

Major, L., Kyriacou, T., & Brereton, O. P. (2011). Systematic literature review: Teaching novices programming using robots. *IET Software*, *6*(6), 502–513. https://doi.org/10.1049/iet-sen.2011.0125

Maleki, A., & de Jong, M. (2014). A proposal for clustering the dimensions of national culture. *Cross-Cultural Research*, *48*(2), 107–143. https://doi.org/10.1177/1069397113510268

Mangas-Vega, A., Dantas, T., Sánchez-Jara, J. M., & Gómez-Díaz, R. (2018). Systematic literature reviews in social sciences and humanities. *Journal of Information Technology Research*, *11*(1), 1–17. https://doi.org/10.4018/jitr.2018010101

Martin, E. (2006). Vignettes and respondent debriefing for questionnaire design and evaluation. *Research Resport Series (Survey Methodology)*, *8*, 1–22. http://citeseerx.ist.psu.edu/viewdoc/download?doi=10.1.1.80.711&rep=rep1&type=pdf

Maseland, R., & Van Hoorn, A. (2009). Explaining the negative correlation between values and practices: A note on the Hofstede-GLOBE debate. *Journal of International Business Studies*, *40*(3), 527–532. https://doi.org/10.1057/jibs.2008.68

Massaro, M., Dumay, J., & Guthrie, J. (2016). On the shoulders of giants: Undertaking a structured literature review in accounting. *Accounting, Auditing and Accountability Journal*, *29*(5), 767–801. https://doi.org/10.1108/AAAJ-01-2015-1939

McCrae, R. R. (2002). Cross-cultural research on the five-factor model of personality. *Online Readings in Psychology and Culture*, *4*(4). https://doi.org/10.9707/2307-0919.1038

McCrae, R. R., & Terracciano, A. (2005). Personality profiles of cultures: Aggregate personality traits. *Journal of Personality and Social Psychology*, *89*(3), 407–425. https://doi.org/10.1037/0022-3514.89.3.407

McCrae, R. R., Terracciano, A., Realo, A., & Allik, J. (2008). Interpreting GLOBE societal practice scales. *Journal of Cross-Cultural Psychology*, *39*(6), 805–810. https://doi.org/10.1177/0022022108323806

McSweeney, B. (2002). Hofstede's model of national cultural differences and their consequences: A triumph of faith—A failure of analysis. *Human Relations*, *55*(1), 89–118. https://doi.org/10.1177/0018726702551004

Merritt, A. (2000). Culture in the cockpit: Do Hofstede's dimensions replicate? *Journal of Cross-Cultural Psychology*, *31*(3), 283–301. https://doi.org/10.1177/0022022100031003001

Minkov, M. (2007). *What makes us different and similar: A new interpretation of the world values survey and other cross-cultural data*. Klasika i Stil Publishing House.

Minkov, M. (2008). Self-enhancement and self-stability predict school achievement at the national level. *Cross-Cultural Research*, *42*(2), 172–196. https://doi.org/10.1177/1069397107312956

Minkov, M. (2013). *Cross-cultural analysis: The science and art of comparing the world's modern societies and their cultures*. SAGE Publications, Inc. https://doi.org/10.4135/9781483384719

Minkov, M., & Hofstede, G. (2011). The evolution of Hofstede's doctrine. *Cross Cultural Management: An International Journal, 18*(1), 10–20. https://doi.org/10.1108/13527601111104269

Mulder, M. (1976). Reduction of power differences in practice: The power distance reduction theory and its applications. In G. Hofstede & M. S. Kassem (Eds.), *European contribution to organization theory* (pp. 79–94). Van Gorcum.

Mulder, M. (1977). *The daily power game*. Springer US. https://doi.org/10.1007/978-1-4684-6951-6

Nagy, S., & Molnárné, C. K. (2018). The effects of Hofstede's cultural dimensions on pro-environmental behaviour: How culture influences environmentally conscious behaviour. *"Club of Economics in Miskolc" Theory, Methodology, Practice, 14*(1), 27–36. https://doi.org/10.18096/TMP.2018.01.03

Nardon, L., & Steers, R. M. (2006). Navigating the culture theory jungle: Divergence and convergence in models of national culture. *Vlerick Leuven Gent Working Paper Series, 38*, 3–22. https://www.researchgate.net/publication/23646752_Navigating_the_culture_theory_jungle_divergence_and_convergence_in_models_of_national_culture

Nardon, L., & Steers, R. M. (2009). The culture theory jungle: Divergence and convergence in models of national culture. In R. S. Bhagat & R. M. Steers (Eds.), *Cambridge handbook of culture, organizations, and work* (pp. 3–22). Cambridge University Press. https://doi.org/10.1017/CBO9780511581151.002

Needleman, I. G. (2002). A guide to systematic reviews. *Journal of Clinical Periodontology, 29*(3), 6–9. https://doi.org/10.1034/j.1600-051x.29.s3.15.x

Oehlrich, M. (2019). *Wissenschafliches arbeiten und schreiben. Schritt für schritt zur bachelor- und master-thesis in den wirtschaftswissenschaften.* (2nd ed.). Springer Gabler.

Okada, S. (2019). *Spearman's rank correlation coefficient using ordinal data. Discover the strength of monotonic relation.* https://towardsdatascience.com/discover-the-strength-of-monotonic-relation-850d11f72046

Parsons, T., & Shils, E. A. (1951). *Toward a general theory of action.* Harvard University Press. https://doi.org/10.4159/harvard.9780674863507

Paulhus, D. L. (1991). Measurement and control of response bias. In *Measures of Personality and Social Psychological Attitudes* (Issue December 1991, pp. 17–59). Elsevier. https://doi.org/10.1016/B978-0-12-590241-0.50006-X

Pearson, R. H., & Mundform, D. J. (2010). Recommended sample size for conducting exploratory factor analysis on dichotomous data. *Journal of Modern Applied Statistical Methods, 9*(2), 359–368. https://doi.org/10.22237/jmasm/1288584240

Peterson, M. F., & Smith, P. B. (2008). Chapter 3: Social structures and processes in cross-cultural management. In *The Handbook of Cross-Cultural Management Research* (pp. 35–58). SAGE Publications, Inc. https://doi.org/10.4135/9781412982764.n3

Pianos, T., & Krüger, N. (2014). *Erfolgreich recherchieren—Wirtschaftswissenschaften.* De Gruyter Saur. https://doi.org/10.1515/9783110301007

Poortinga, Y. (2015). Is "culture" a workable concept for (cross-)cultural psychology? *Online Readings in Psychology and Culture, 2*(1), 1–21. https://doi.org/10.9707/2307-0919.1139

Read, R. (1993). *Politics and policies of national economic growth.* Stanford University.

RMIT University. (n.d.). *Database Elsevier ScienceDirect*. Retrieved September 3, 2021, from https://rmit.primo.exlibrisgroup.com/discovery/dbfulldisplay?context=L&vid=61RMIT_INST:RMITU&docid=alma9921495412001341

Rokeach, M. (1973). *The nature of human values*. The Free Press.

Rother, E. T. (2007). Systematic literature review X narrative review. *Acta Paulista de Enfermagem, 20*(2), vi–vi. https://acta-ape.org/wp-content/uploads/articles_xml/1982-0194-ape-S0103-21002007000200001/1982-0194-ape-S0103-21002007000200001-en.pdf

Sakaluk, J. K., & Short, S. D. (2017). A methodological review of exploratory factor analysis in sexuality research: Used practices, best practices, and data analysis resources. *The Journal of Sex Research, 54*(1), 1–9. https://doi.org/10.1080/00224499.2015.1137538

Samovar, L., Porter, R., McDaniel, E. R., & Roy, C. S. (2016). *Communication between cultures* (9th ed.). Cengage Learning.

Sarangi, S. (1995). Culture. In J. Verschueren, J.-O. Östman, & C. Bulcaen (Eds.), *Handbook of Pragmatics* (pp. 1–30). John Benjamins Publishing Company.

Schaffer, B. S., & Riordan, C. M. (2003). A review of cross-cultural methodologies for organizational research: A best- practices approach. *Organizational Research Methods, 6*(2), 169–215. https://doi.org/10.1177/1094428103251542

Schein, E. H. (1985). *Organizational culture and leadership*. Jossey-Bass Publishers.

Schein, E. H. (1987). *The clinical perspective in fieldwork*. Sage Publications, Inc.

Schein, E. H., & Schein, P. A. (2016). *Organizational culture and leadership* (5th ed.). Wiley-Liss, Inc.

Schimmack, U., Oishi, S., & Diener, E. (2002). Cultural influences on the relation between pleasant emotions and unpleasant emotions: Asian dialectic philosophies or individualism-collectivism? *Cognition and Emotion, 16*(6), 705–719. https://doi.org/10.1080/02699930143000590

Schmitt, D. P. (2005). Sociosexuality from Argentina to Zimbabwe: A 48-nation study of sex, culture, and strategies of human mating. *Behavioral and Brain Sciences, 28*(2), 247–275. https://doi.org/10.1017/s0140525x05000051

Schmitt, D. P., Allik, J., McCrae, R. R., & Benet-Martínez, V. (2007). The geographic distribution of big five personality traits: Patterns and profiles of human self-description across 56 nations. *Journal of Cross-Cultural Psychology, 38*(2), 173–212. https://doi.org/10.1177/0022022106297299

Schneider, S. C., & Barsoux, J.-L. (1997). *Managing across cultures*. Prentice Hall.

Schneider, S. C., & Barsoux, J.-L. (2003). *Managing across cultures* (2nd ed.). Pearson Education Limited.

Schneider, S. C., Barsoux, J.-L., & Stahl, G. K. (2014). *Managing across cultures* (3rd ed.). Pearson Education Limited.

Schwartz, S. H. (1992). Universals in the content and structure of values: Theoretical advances and empirical tests in 20 countries. *Advances in Experimental Social Psychology, 25*, 1–65. https://doi.org/10.1016/s0065-2601(08)60281-6

Schwartz, S. H. (1994a). Are there universal aspects in the structure and contents of human values? *Journal of Social Issues, 50*(4), 19–45. https://doi.org/10.1111/j.1540-4560.1994.tb01196.x

Schwartz, S. H. (1994b). Beyond individualism-collectivism: New cultural dimensions of values. In U. Kim, H. C. Triandis, C. Kagitcibasi, S.-C. Choi, & G. Yoon (Eds.), *Cross-cultural research and methodology series* (Volume 18, pp. 85–119). Sage Publications, Inc.

Schwartz, S. H. (1999). A theory of cultural values and some implications for work. *Applied Psychology: An International Review*, *48*(1), 23–47. https://doi.org/10.1111/j.1464-0597.1999.tb00047.x

Schwartz, S. H. (2004). Mapping and interpreting cultural differences around the world. In H. Vinken, J. Soeters, & P. Ester (Eds.), *Comapring cultures, dimensions of culture in a comparative perspective* (pp. 43–47). Brill.

Schwartz, S. H. (2006). A theory of cultural values orientations: Explications and applications. *Comparative Sociology*, *5*(2/3), 137–182. https://doi.org/10.1163/ej.9789004170346.i-466.55

Schwartz, S. H. (2012). An overview of the Schwartz theory of basic values. *Online Readings in Psychology and Culture*, *2*(1), 1–20. https://doi.org/10.9707/2307-0919.1116

Schwartz, S. H., & Bilsky, W. (1987). Toward a universal psychological structure of human values. *Journal of Personality and Social Psychology*, *53*(3), 550–562. https://doi.org/10.1037/0022-3514.53.3.550

Schwartz, S. H., & Bilsky, W. (1990). Toward a theory of the universal content and structure of values: Extensions and cross-cultural replications. *Journal of Personality and Social Psychology*, *58*(5), 878–891. https://doi.org/10.1037/0022-3514.58.5.878

Shweder, R. A., & Levine, R. V. (1984). *Culture theory. Essay on mind, self, and emotions.* Cambridge University Press.

Smith, P. B. (2004). Nations, cultures, and individuals: New perspectives and old dilemmas. *Journal of Cross-Cultural Psychology*, *35*(1), 6–12. https://doi.org/10.1177/0022022103260460

Smith, P. B. (2006). When elephants fight, the grass gets trampled: The GLOBE and Hofstede projects. *Journal of International Business Studies*, *37*(6), 915–921. https://doi.org/10.1057/palgrave.jibs.8400235

Smith, P. B., Peterson, M. F., & Schwartz, S. H. (2002). Cultural values, sources of guidance, and their relevance to managerial behavior: A 47-nation study. *Journal of Cross-Cultural Psychology*, *33*(2), 188–208. https://doi.org/10.1177/0022022102033002005

Smith, P. B., Trompenaars, F., & Dugan, S. (1995). The rotter locus of control scale in 43 countries: A test of cultural relativity. *International Journal of Psychology*, *30*(3), 377–400. https://doi.org/10.1080/00207599508246576

Søndergaard, M. (1994). Research note: Hofstede's consequences: A study of reviews, citations and replications. *Organization Studies*, *15*(3), 447–456. https://doi.org/10.1177/017084069401500307

Street, B. V. (2019). *Sir Edward Burnett Tylor*. Encyclopaedia Britannica. https://www.britannica.com/biography/Edward-Burnett-Tylor

Taber, K. S. (2018). The use of Cronbach's alpha when developing and reporting research instruments in science education. *Research in Science Education*, *48*(6), 1273–1296. https://doi.org/10.1007/s11165-016-9602-2

Taherdoost, H. (2016). Validity and reliability of the research instrument; How to test the validation of a questionnaire/survey in a research. *International Journal of Academic Research in Management*, *5*, 28–36. https://doi.org/10.2139/ssrn.3205040

Taras, V., Rowney, J. I. A., & Steel, P. D. G. (2009). Half a century of measuring culture: Review of approaches, challenges, and limitations based on the analysis of 121 instruments for quantifying culture. *Journal of International Management*, *15*(4), 357–373. https://doi.org/10.1016/j.intman.2008.08.005

Taras, V., Steel, P., & Kirkman, B. (2016). Does country equate with culture? Beyond geography in the search for cultural boundaries. *Management International Review*, *56*(4), 455–487. https://doi.org/10.1007/s11575-016-0283-x

Tayeb, M. H. (1994). Organizations and national culture: Methodology considered. *Organization Studies*, *15*(3), 429–445. https://doi.org/10.1177/017084069401500306

Thompson, E. P. (1963). *The making of the English working class*. Vintage Books.

Tranfield, D., Denyer, D., & Smart, P. (2003). Towards a methodology for developing evidence-informed management knowledge by means of systematic review. *British Journal of Management*, *14*(3), 207–222. https://doi.org/10.1111/1467-8551.00375

Triandis, H. C. (1989). Cross-cultural studies of invidiualism-collectivism. In J. Berman (Ed.), *Nebraska symposium on motivation: Cross-cultural perspectives* (pp. 41–133). University of Nebraska Press.

Triandis, H. C. (1995). *Individualism & collectivism*. Westview Press.

Triandis, H. C. (1996). The psychological measurement of cultural syndromes. *American Psychologist*, *51*(4), 407–415. https://doi.org/10.1037/0003-066X.51.4.407

Triandis, H. C. (2000). Culture and conflict. *International Journal of Psychology*, *35*(2), 145–152. https://doi.org/10.1080/002075900399448

Triandis, H. C. (2001). The study of corss-cultural management and organization: The future. *International Journal of Cross Cultural Management*, *1*(1), 17–20. https://doi.org/10.1177/147059580111003

Triandis, H. C. (2002). Generic individualism and collectivism. In K. L. Newmann & M. J. Gannon (Eds.), *Handbook of corss-cultural management* (pp. 16–35). Blackwell.

Triandis, H. C. (2004). The many dimensions of culture. *Academy of Management Perspectives*, *18*(1), 88–93. https://doi.org/10.5465/ame.2004.12689599

Trompenaars, F., & Hampden-Turner, C. (1993). *Riding the waves of culture: Understanding cultural diversity in business* (2nd ed.). Nicholas Brealey Publishing.

Trompenaars, F., & Hampden-Turner, C. (1997). *Riding the waves of culture: Understanding cultural diversity in business*. Nicholas Brealey Publishing.

Trompenaars, F., & Hampden-Turner, C. (2004). *Managing people across cultures*. Capstone Publishing Ltd.

Trompenaars, F., & Hampden-Turner, C. (2012). *Riding the waves of culture: Understanding diversity in global business* (3rd ed.). Nicholas Brealey Publishing.

Trompenaars, F., & Hampden-Turner, C. (2020). *Riding the waves of culture: Understanding diversity in global businss* (4th ed.). Nicholas Brealey Publishing.

Trompenaars, F., & Woolliams, P. (2004). *Business across Cultures*. Capstone Publishing Ltd (Original work published 2003). https://doi.org/10.1108/ijppm.2004.07953gae.001

Tylor, E. B. (1871). *Primitive culture: Researches into the development of mythology, philosophy, religion, art, and custom*. John Murray. https://doi.org/10.1017/CBO9780511705960

UCLA Institute for Digital Research and Education Statistical Consulting. (n.d.). *Factor analysis: SPSS annotated output*. Retrieved May 11, 2021, from https://stats.idre.ucla.edu/spss/output/factor-analysis/

United Nations Department of Economic and Social Affairs. (2017). *New globalization report: Three mega-trends expected to impact our future*. https://www.un.org/development/desa/en/news/intergovernmental-coordination/new-globalization-report.html

van de Vliert, E., & Janssen, O. (2002). "Better than" performance motives as roots of satisfaction across more and less developed countries. *Journal of Cross-Cultural Psychology, 33*(4), 380–397. https://doi.org/10.1177/0022102033004002

Venaik, S., & Brewer, P. (2010). Avoiding uncertainty in Hofstede and GLOBE. *Journal of International Business Studies, 41*(8), 1294–1315. https://doi.org/10.1057/jibs.2009.96

Venaik, S., Zhu, Y., & Brewer, P. A. (2013). Looking into the future: Hofstede long term orientation versus GLOBE future orientation. *Cross Cultural Management: An International Journal, 20*(3), 361–385. https://doi.org/10.1108/CCM-02-2012-0014

Vijver, F. J. R. van de, & Hutschemaekers, G. J. M. (1990). *The investigation of culture: Current issues in cultural psychology*. Tilburg University Press.

Voss, R. (2018). *Wissenschaftliches arbeiten:...leicht verständlich!* (6th ed.). utb GmbH.

Waldman, D. A., de Luque, M. F. S., Washburn, N., House, R. J., Adetoun, B., Barrasa, A., Bobina, M., Bodur, M., Chen, Y.-J., Debbarma, S., Dorfman, P., Dzuvichu, R. R., Evicmen, I., Fu, P., Grachev, M., Duarte, R. G., Gupta, V., Den Hartog, D. N., de Hoogh, A. H. B., … Wilderom, C. P. M. (2006). Cultural and leadership predictors of corporate social responsibility values of top management: A GLOBE study of 15 countries. *Journal of International Business Studies, 37*(6), 823–837. https://doi.org/10.1057/palgrave.jibs.8400230

Welzel, C. (2010). How selfish are self-expression values? A civicness test. *Journal of Cross-Cultural Psychology, 41*(2), 152–174. https://doi.org/10.1177/0022022109354378

Williams, R. (1958). *Culture and society, 1780–1950*. Chatto & Windus.

Williams, R. (1976). *Keywords: A vocabulary of culture and society*. Oxford University Press. https://doi.org/https://doi.org/10.1093/english/25.122.186

World Value Survey Association. (2020). *Findings and insights*. https://www.worldvaluessurvey.org/WVSContents.jsp

Yeganeh, H. (2013). A compound index of cultural dimensions: Implications and applications. *International Journal of Organizational Analysis, 21*(1), 53–65. https://doi.org/10.1108/19348831311322533

Yeganeh, H., Su, Z., & Sauers, D. (2009). The applicability of widely employed frameworks in cross-cultural management research. *Journal of Academic Research in Economics, 1*(1), 1–24. https://www.researchgate.net/publication/46542980_THE_APPLICABILITY_OF_WIDELY_EMPLOYED_FRAMEWORKS_IN_CROSS-CULTURAL_MANAGEMENT_RESEARCH

The manufacturer's authorised representative in the EU is Springer Nature Customer Service Centre GmbH, Europaplatz 3, 69115 Heidelberg, Germany. If you have any concerns regarding our products, please contact ProductSafety@springernature.com

Printed and bound by CPI Group (UK) Ltd, Croydon, CR0 4YY
30/09/2026
02225434-0008